尾田栄一郎とある一味

Eiichiro Oda and friends

A dragon lives in Enoshima.
The living being closest to the gods-that is the dragon.

I wonder if you can eat dragons?

-Eiichiro Oda, 2000

Eiichiro Oda began his manga career at the age of 17, when his one-shot cowboy manga **Wanted!** won second place in the coveted Tezuka manga awards. Oda went on to work as an assistant to some of the biggest manga artists in the industry, including Nobuhiro Watsuki, before winning the Hop Step Award for new artists. His pirate adventure **One Piece**, which debuted in **Weekly Shonen Jump** in 1997, quickly became one of the most popular manga in Japan.

ONE PIECE VOL. 13
BAROQUE WORKS PART 2

SHONEN JUMP Manga Edition

This graphic novel contains material that was originally
published in English in **SHONEN JUMP** #45–47.

STORY AND ART BY EIICHIRO ODA

English Adaptation/Lance Caselman
Translation/JN Productions
Touch-up Art & Lettering/Vanessa Satone
Additional Touch-up/Josh Simpson
Design/Sean Lee
Editor/Urian Brown

Published by VIZ Media, LLC
P.O. Box 77010
San Francisco, CA 94107

10 9
First printing, January 2007
Ninth printing, December 2017

SHONEN JUMP MANGA

ONE PIECE

Vol. 13
IT'S ALL RIGHT!

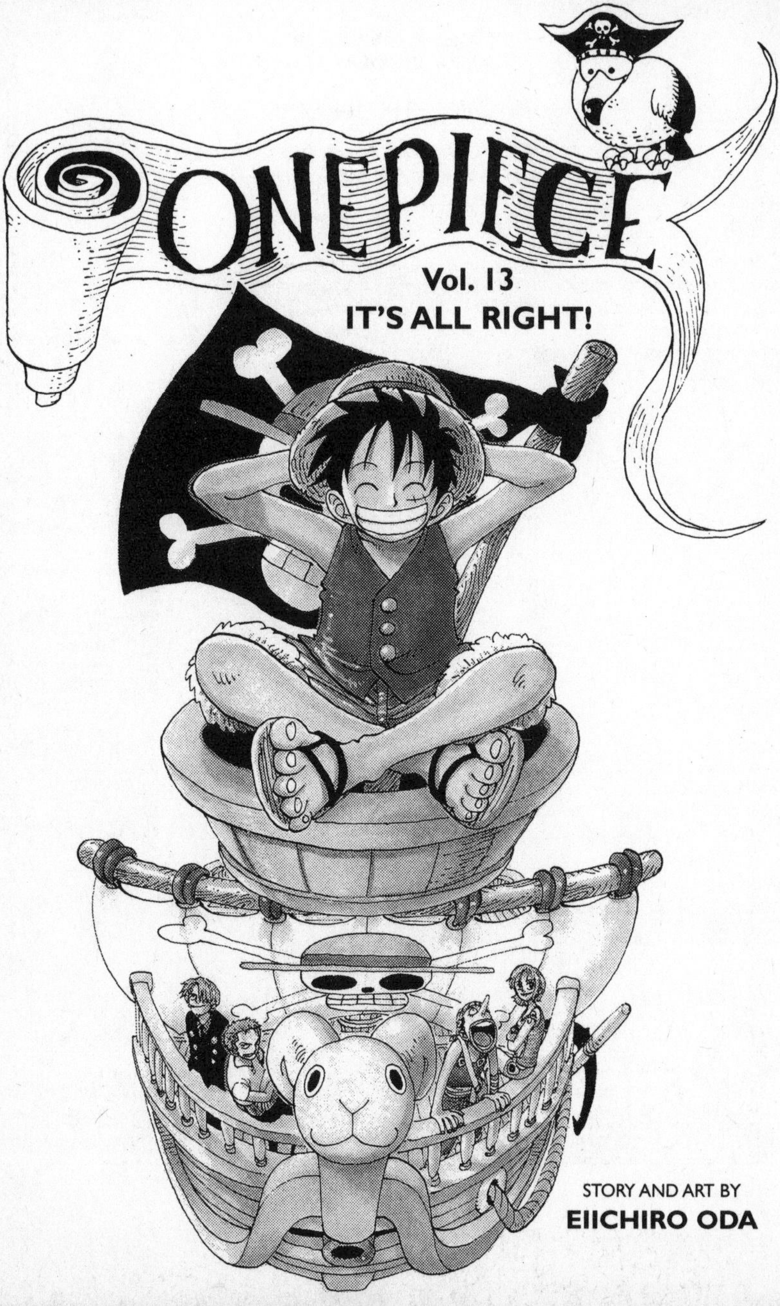

STORY AND ART BY
EIICHIRO ODA

THE STORY OF ONE PIECE

Volume 13

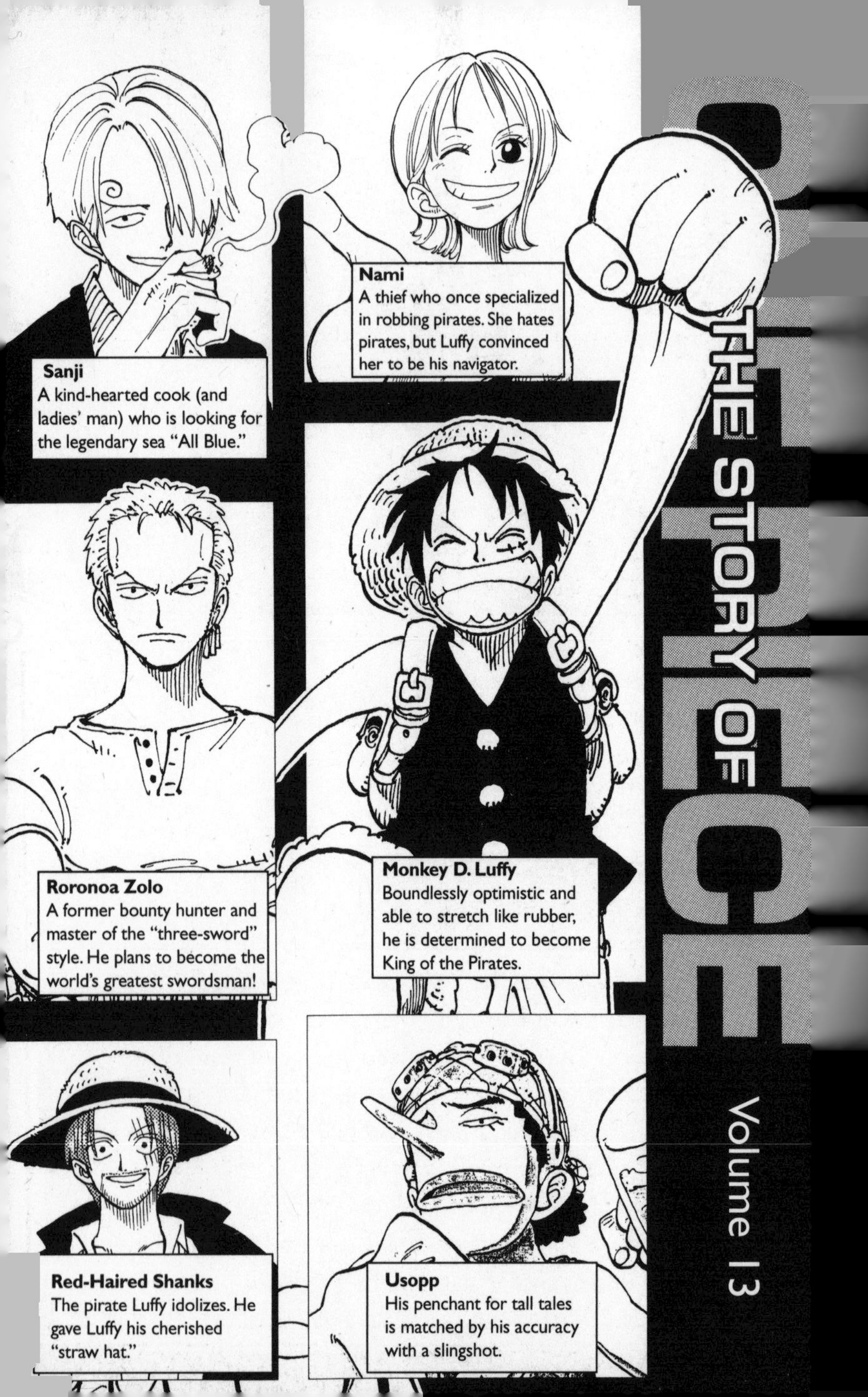

Nami
A thief who once specialized in robbing pirates. She hates pirates, but Luffy convinced her to be his navigator.

Sanji
A kind-hearted cook (and ladies' man) who is looking for the legendary sea "All Blue."

Monkey D. Luffy
Boundlessly optimistic and able to stretch like rubber, he is determined to become King of the Pirates.

Roronoa Zolo
A former bounty hunter and master of the "three-sword" style. He plans to become the world's greatest swordsman!

Usopp
His penchant for tall tales is matched by his accuracy with a slingshot.

Red-Haired Shanks
The pirate Luffy idolizes. He gave Luffy his cherished "straw hat."

BAROQUE WORKS

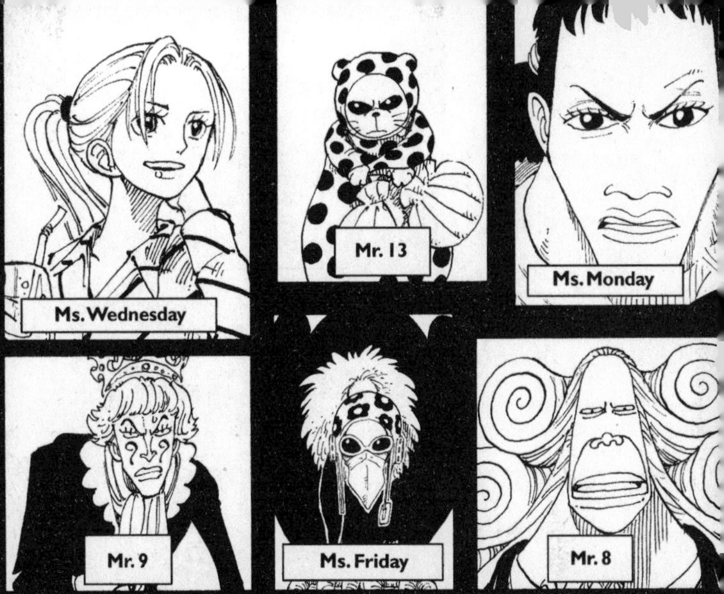
Ms. Wednesday
Mr. 13
Ms. Monday
Mr. 9
Ms. Friday
Mr. 8

Luffy and his friends sail up a river—to the top of a mountain!—to enter the Grand Line. A huge whale appears before them, and swallows them whole. After making a quick escape, they learn of the whale's sad story, and how it has been waiting for many years for a ship of sailors that will never return. Impressed by the whale's undying loyalty, Luffy challenges it to a duel, in order to give it a new goal. As he leaves, he tells the whale to wait for his return to finish the fight. Next stop on the crew's voyage is Whisky Peak, where they are welcomed heartily and end up in a drunken stupor. But as night sets in, the ominous air thickens... Yes, this town is a den of bounty hunters belonging to a criminal organization known as Baroque Works!! Zolo is the only one who has discovered the truth, and he must fight the cadre of villains by himself...

BAROQUE WORKS

Vol. 13
IT'S ALL RIGHT!

CONTENTS

Chapter 109: A Question of Duty		7
Chapter 110: The Night Isn't Over		27
Chapter 111: The Secret Criminal Organization		46
Chapter 112: Luffy vs. Zolo		65
Chapter 113: It's All Right		85
Chapter 114: The Course		105
Chapter 115: Little Garden of Adventure		124
Chapter 116: Big		143
Chapter 117: Dorry and Broggy		162

Chapter 109:
A QUESTION OF DUTY

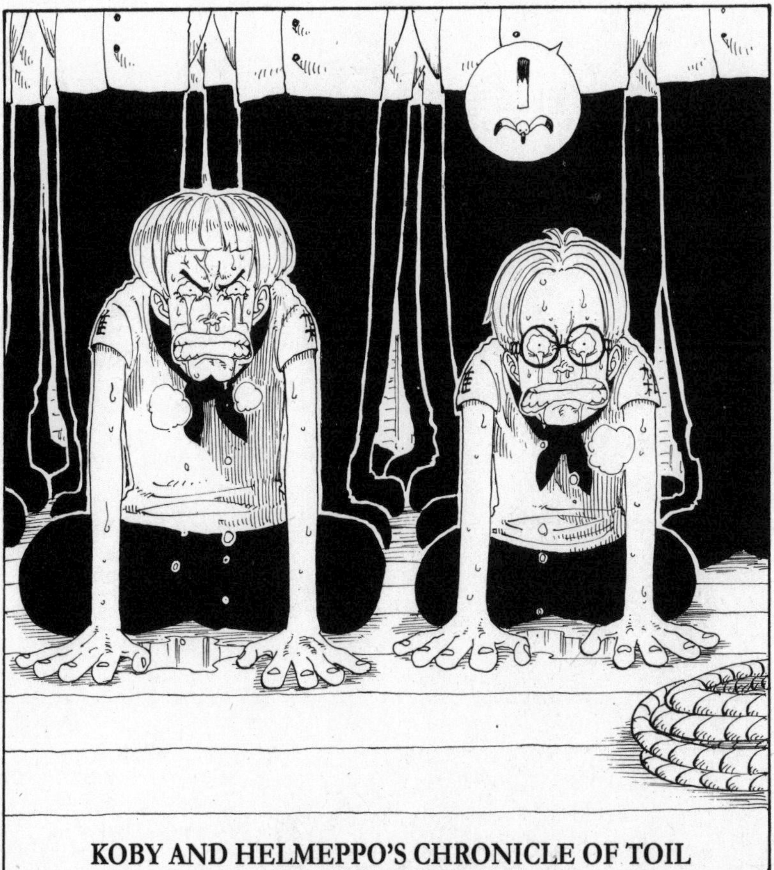
!
KOBY AND HELMEPPO'S CHRONICLE OF TOIL
VOL. 22: "WE'RE SO USELESS"

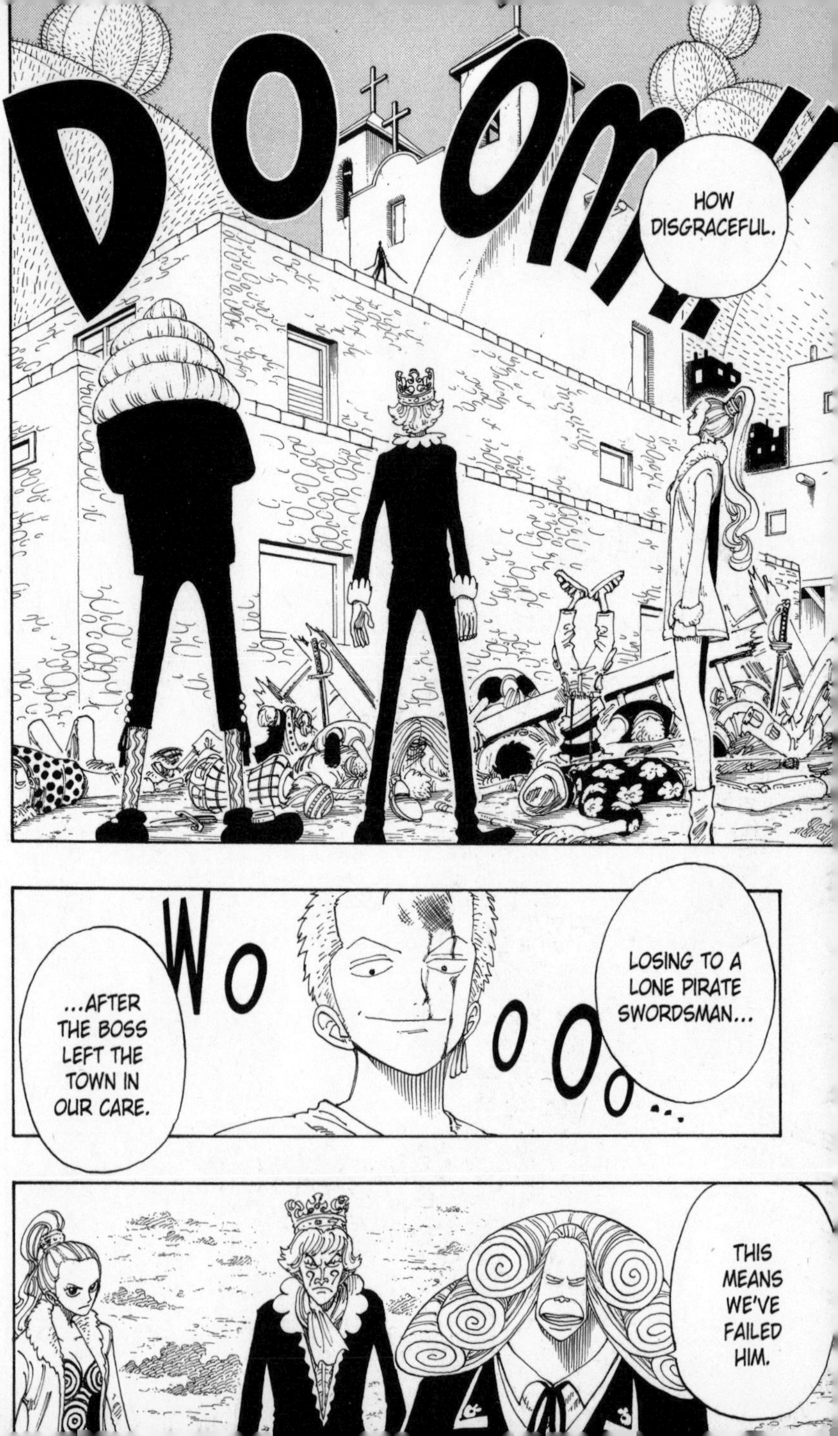
DOOM!!
HOW DISGRACEFUL.
LOSING TO A LONE PIRATE SWORDSMAN...
WOOOO...
...AFTER THE BOSS LEFT THE TOWN IN OUR CARE.
THIS MEANS WE'VE FAILED HIM.

READ THIS WAY

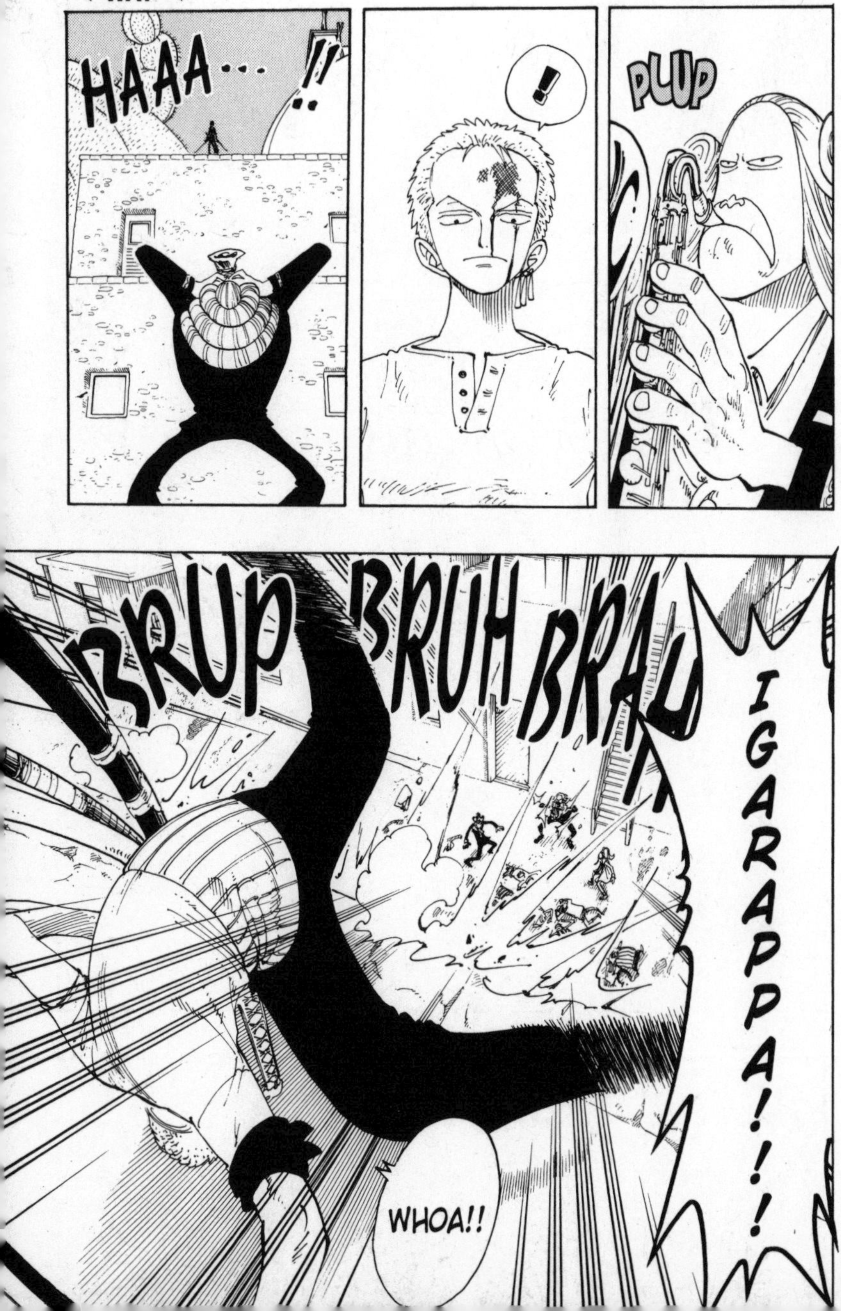
PLUP
!
HAAA...!!
IGARAPPA!!!!
BRUP BRUH BRAU
WHOA!!

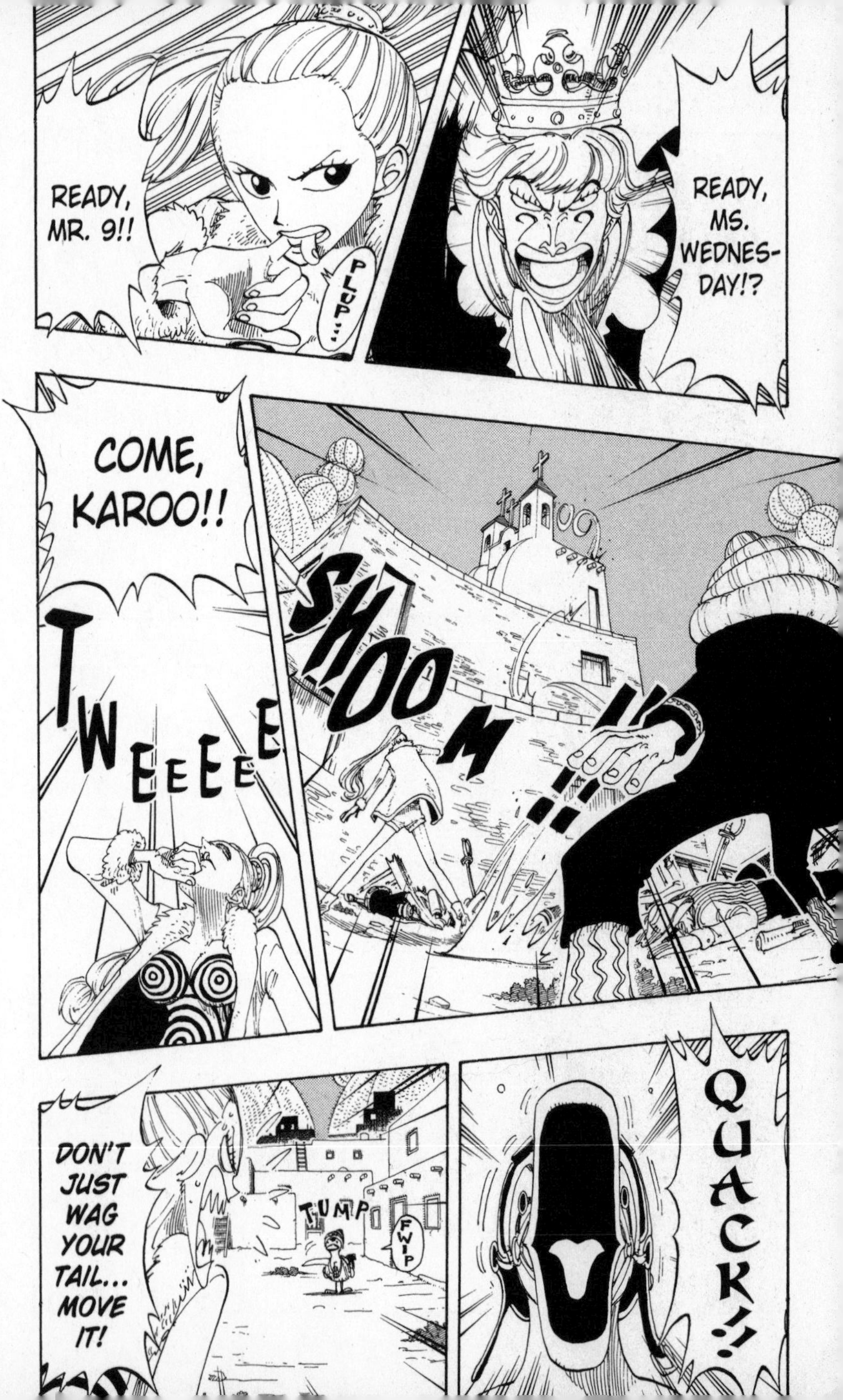
READY, MS. WEDNES-DAY!?
READY, MR. 9!!
PLUP...
SHOOM!!
COME, KAROO!!
TWEEEEE
QUACK!?
FWIP
TUMP
DON'T JUST WAG YOUR TAIL... MOVE IT!

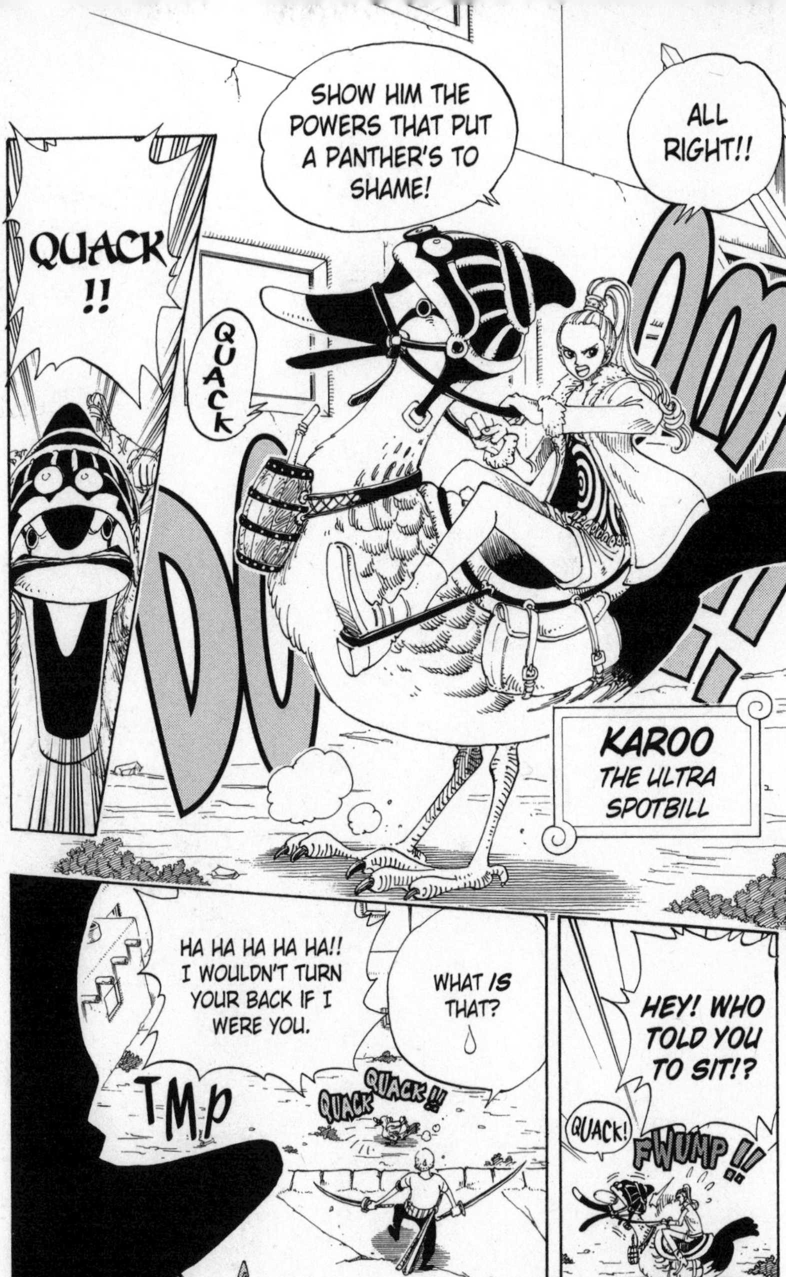
SHOW HIM THE POWERS THAT PUT A PANTHER'S TO SHAME!
ALL RIGHT!!
QUACK
KAROO THE ULTRA SPOTBILL
QUACK !!
HEY! WHO TOLD YOU TO SIT!?
QUACK!
FWUMP !!
TA-DOOM!
WHAT *IS* THAT?
HA HA HA HA HA!! I WOULDN'T TURN YOUR BACK IF I WERE YOU.
QUACK QUACK !!
TMP

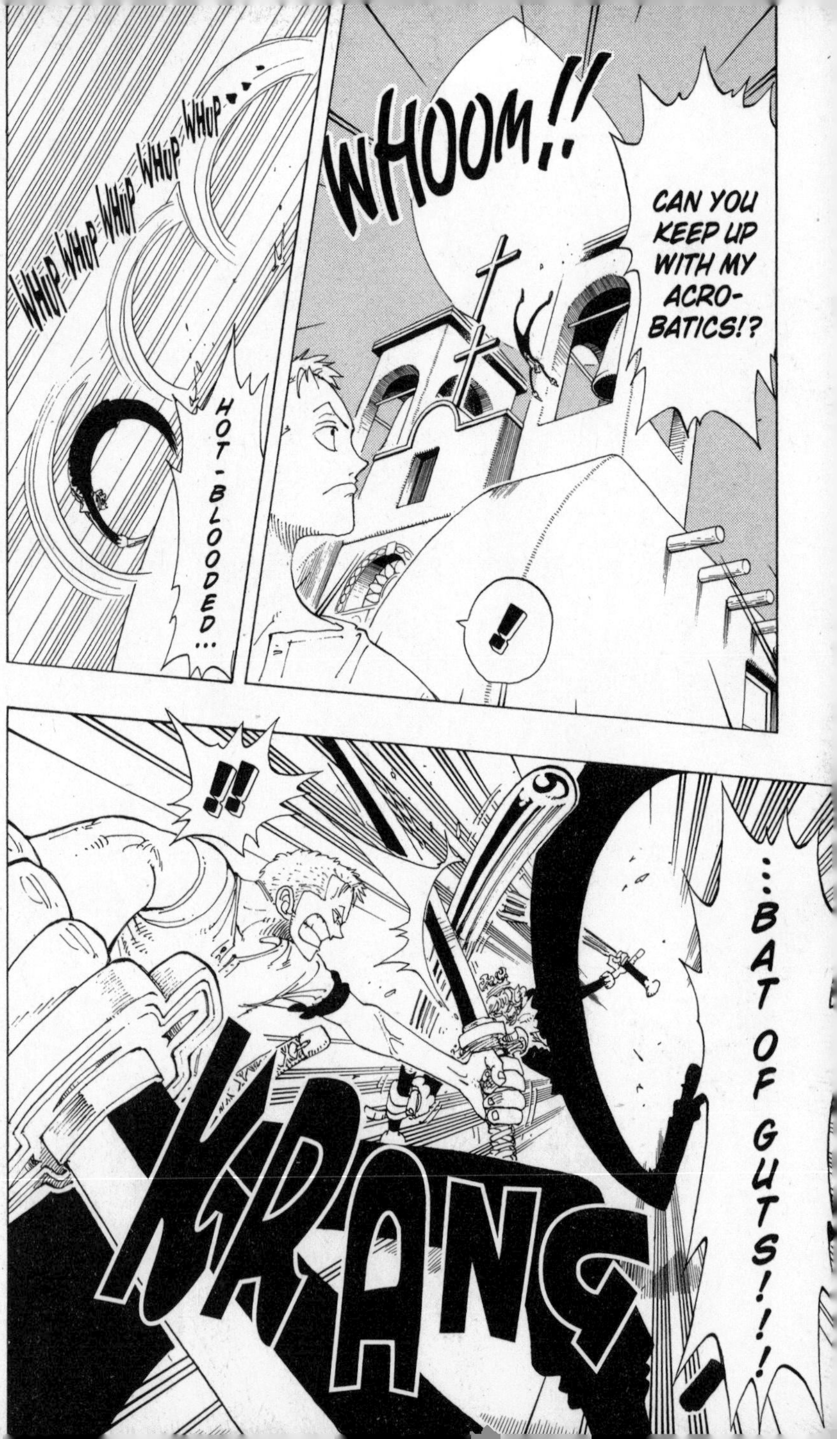
CAN YOU KEEP UP WITH MY ACRO-BATICS!?
WHOOM!!
WHIP WHIP WHIP WHIP WHIP WHIP...
HOT-BLOODED...
!
!!
...BAT OF GUTS!!!
KRANG

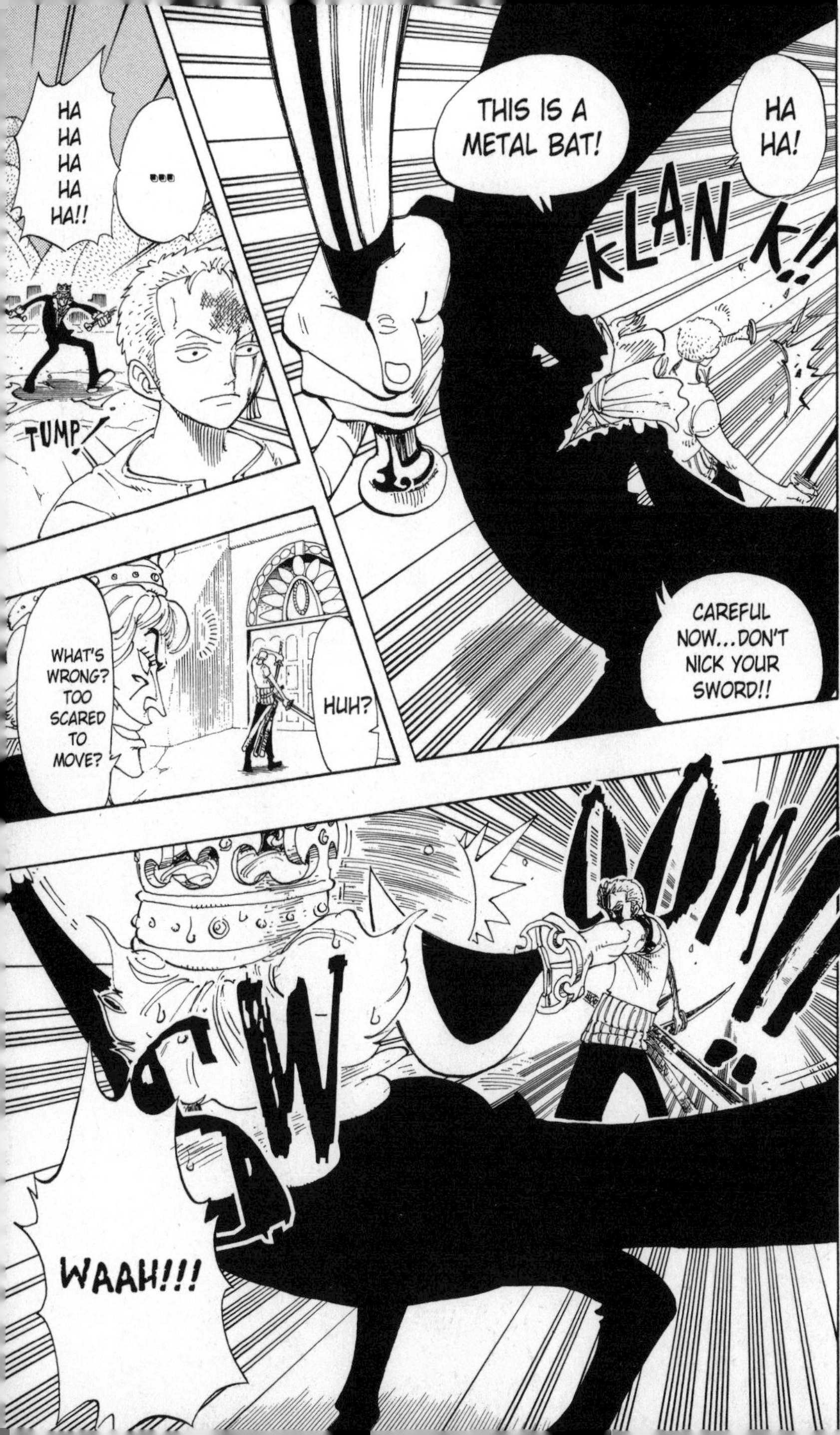
HA HA!
THIS IS A METAL BAT!
KLANK!!
CAREFUL NOW...DON'T NICK YOUR SWORD!!
HA HA HA HA HA!!
...
TUMP!
HUH?
WHAT'S WRONG? TOO SCARED TO MOVE?
DOM!!
WAAH!!!

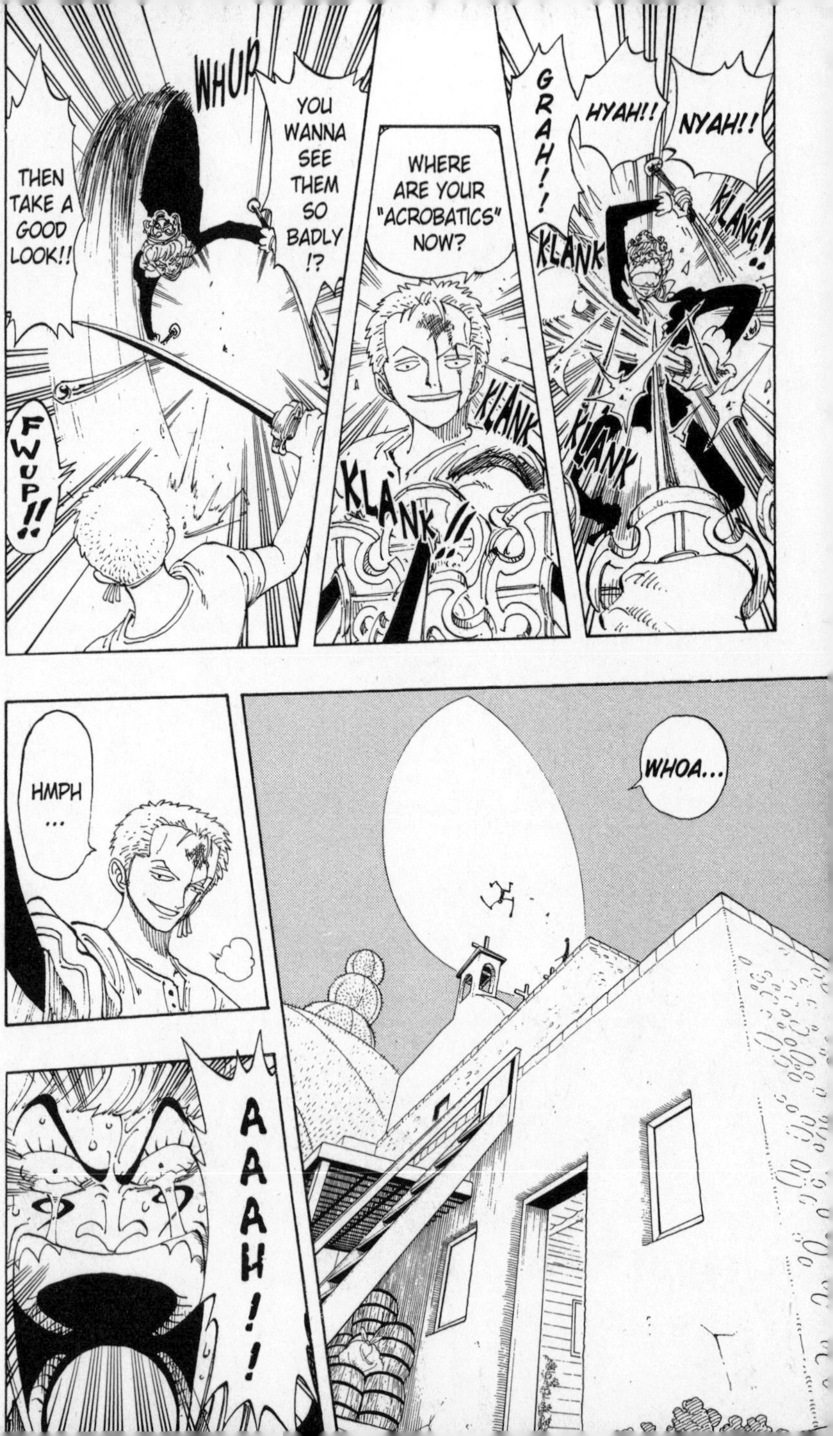
NYAH!!
HYAH!!
GRAH!!
KLANG!!
KLANK
KLANK
KLANK
WHERE ARE YOUR "ACROBATICS" NOW?
KLANK
KLANK!!
YOU WANNA SEE THEM SO BADLY!?
WHUP
THEN TAKE A GOOD LOOK!!
FWUP!!
WHOA...
HMPH ...
AAAAH!!!

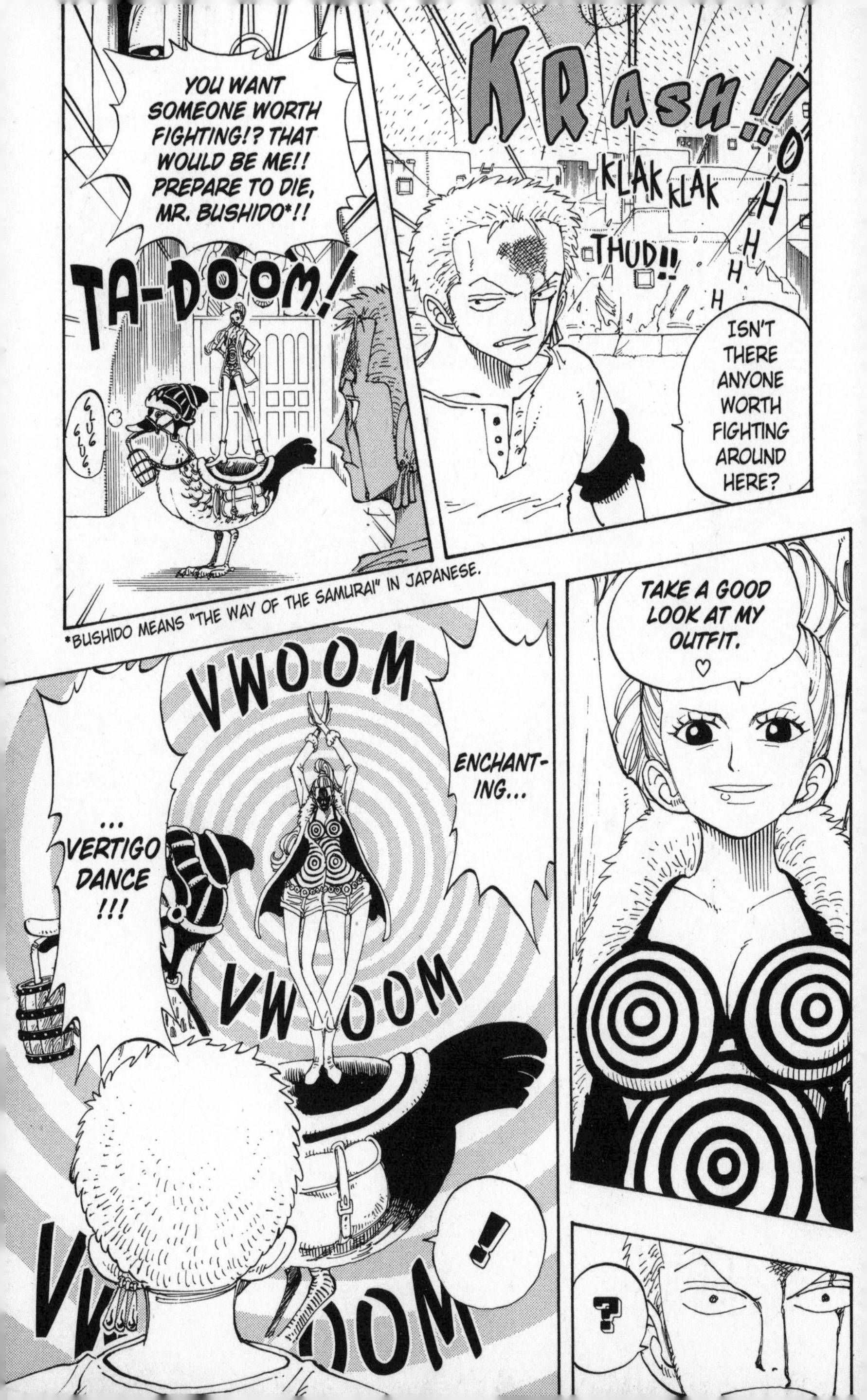
KRASH!!
KLAK KLAK
THUD!!
OHHHHH
ISN'T THERE ANYONE WORTH FIGHTING AROUND HERE?
YOU WANT SOMEONE WORTH FIGHTING!? THAT WOULD BE ME!! PREPARE TO DIE, MR. BUSHIDO*!!
TA-DOOM!
GLUG GLUG...
TAKE A GOOD LOOK AT MY OUTFIT. ♡
VWOOM
ENCHANT-ING...
... VERTIGO DANCE !!!
VWOOM
VWOOM
!
?

*BUSHIDO MEANS "THE WAY OF THE SAMURAI" IN JAPANESE.

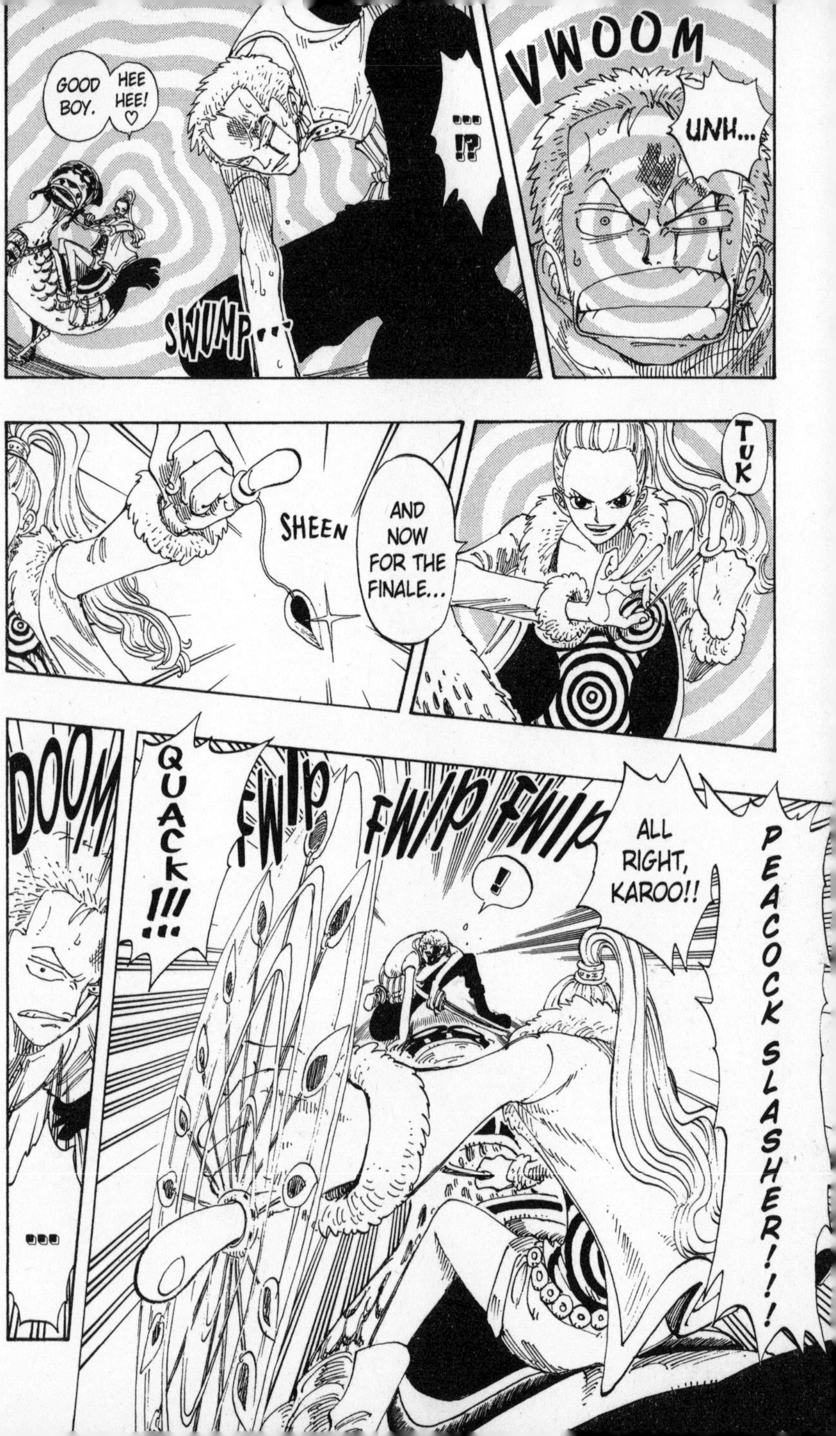
VWOOM
UNH...
...!?
HEE HEE! ♡
GOOD BOY.
SWUMP...
TUK
AND NOW FOR THE FINALE...
SHEEN
PEACOCK SLASHER!!!
ALL RIGHT, KAROO!!
!
FWIP FWIP
FWIP
QUACK!!!
DOOM
...

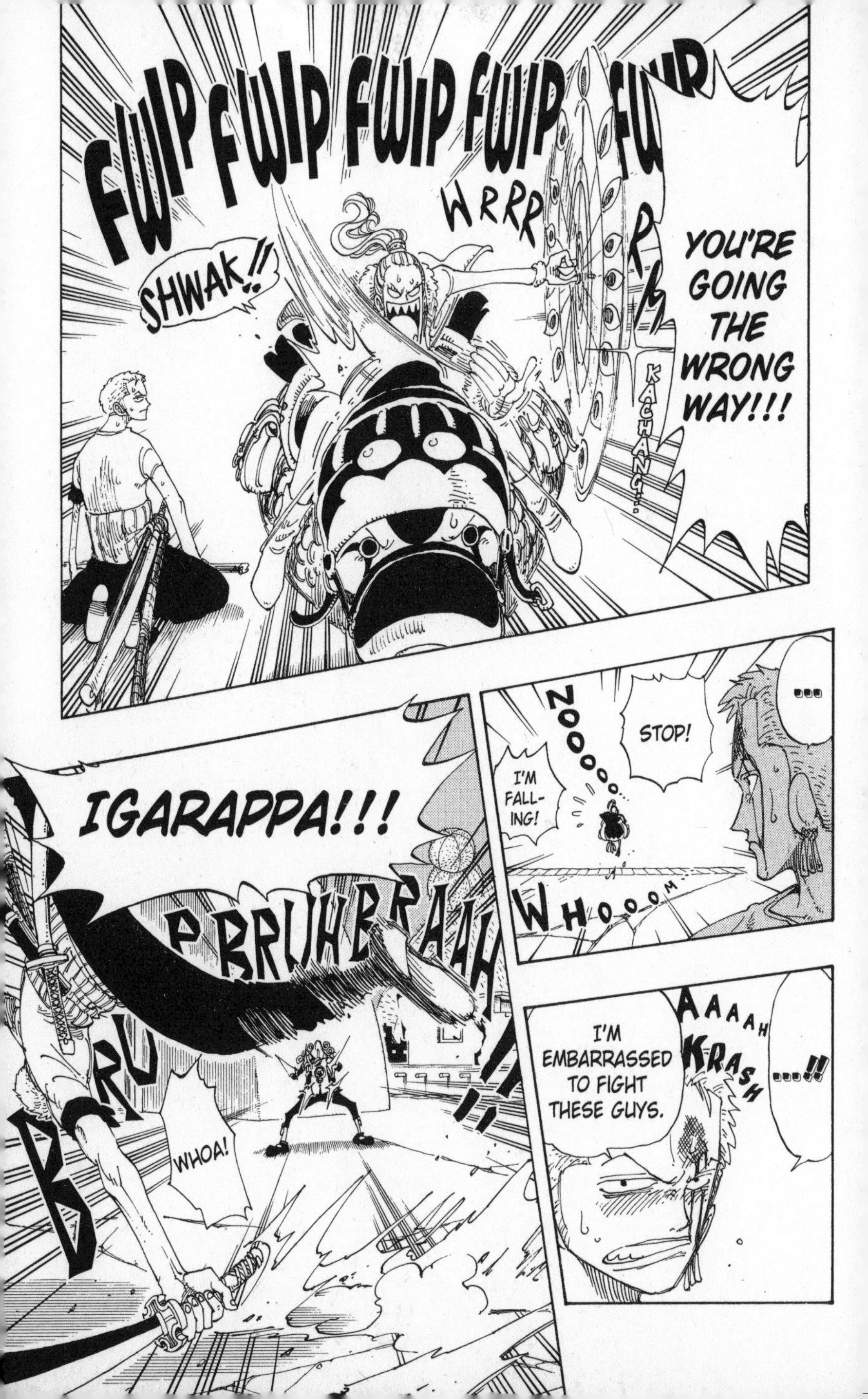
FWIP FWIP FWIP FWIP FWIP
YOU'RE GOING THE WRONG WAY!!!
KACHANG!!
WRRR
SHWAK!!
...
STOP!
NOOOOOO...
I'M FALLING!
WHOOOM
...!!
I'M EMBARRASSED TO FIGHT THESE GUYS.
AAAAH
KRASH
IGARAPPA!!!
BRUHBRAAH
BRU
WHOA!

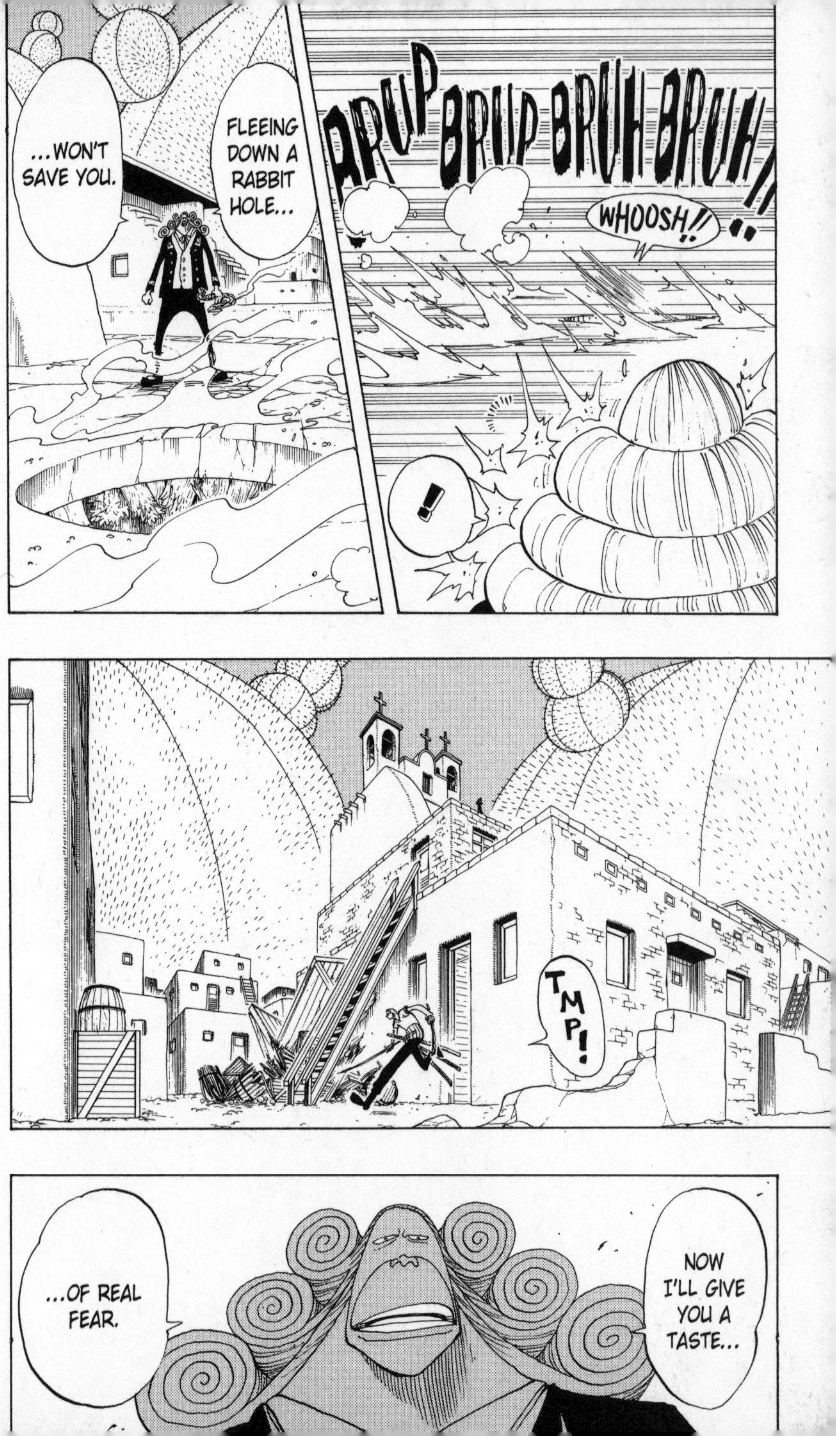
BRUP BRUP BRUH BRUH!!
WHOOSH!!
!
FLEEING DOWN A RABBIT HOLE...
...WON'T SAVE YOU.
TMP!
NOW I'LL GIVE YOU A TASTE...
...OF REAL FEAR.

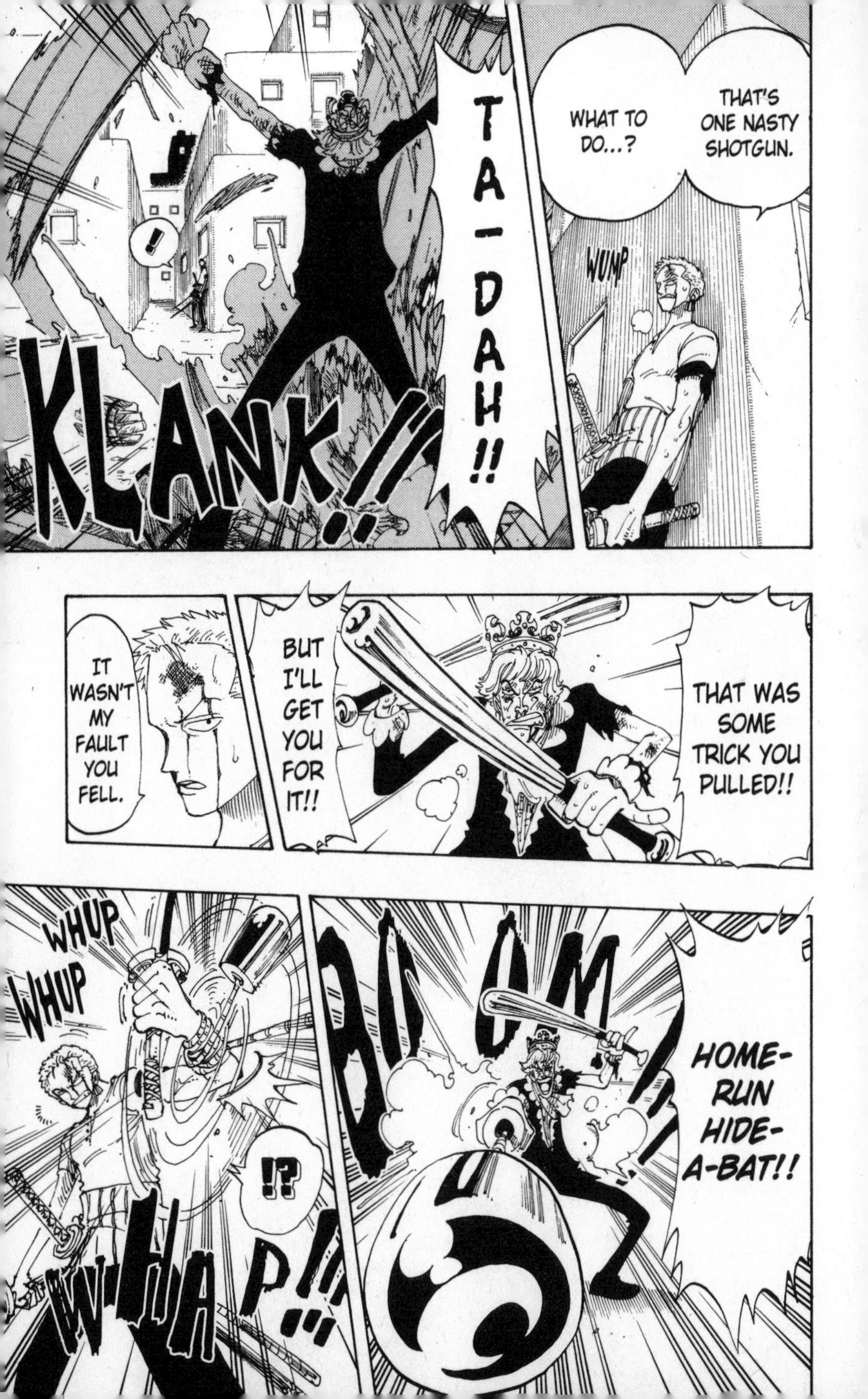

THAT'S ONE NASTY SHOTGUN.
WHAT TO DO...?
WUMP
TA-DAH!!
!
KLANK!!
THAT WAS SOME TRICK YOU PULLED!!
BUT I'LL GET YOU FOR IT!!
IT WASN'T MY FAULT YOU FELL.
HOME-RUN HIDE-A-BAT!!
BOOM
WHUP
WHUP
!?
WHAP!!

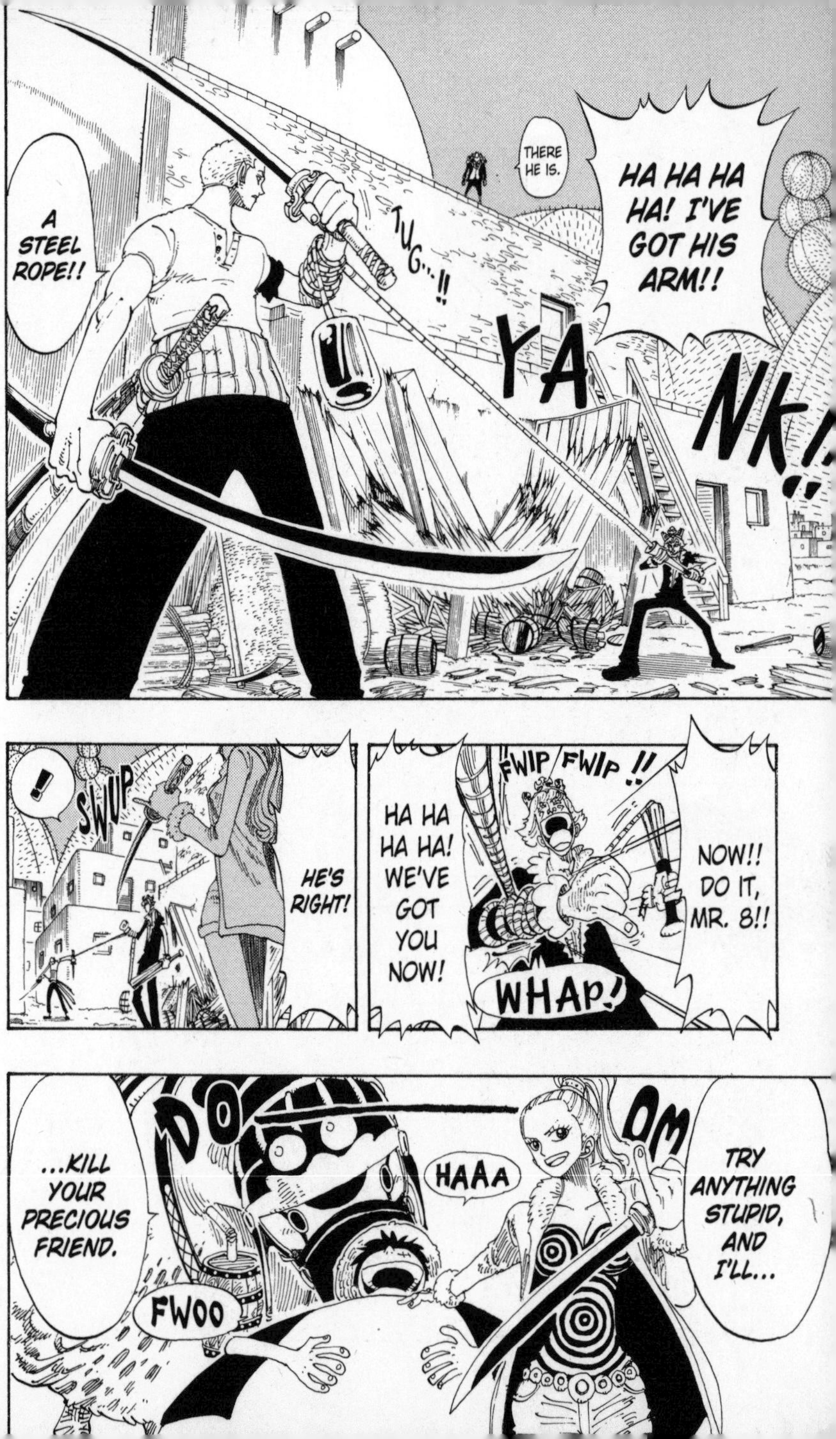
HA HA HA HA! I'VE GOT HIS ARM!!
THERE HE IS.
YANK!!
TUG...!!
A STEEL ROPE!!
NOW!! DO IT, MR. 8!!
FWIP FWIP!!
HA HA HA HA! WE'VE GOT YOU NOW!
WHAP!
HE'S RIGHT!
SWUP
!
TRY ANYTHING STUPID, AND I'LL...
DOOM
HAAA
...KILL YOUR PRECIOUS FRIEND.
FWOO

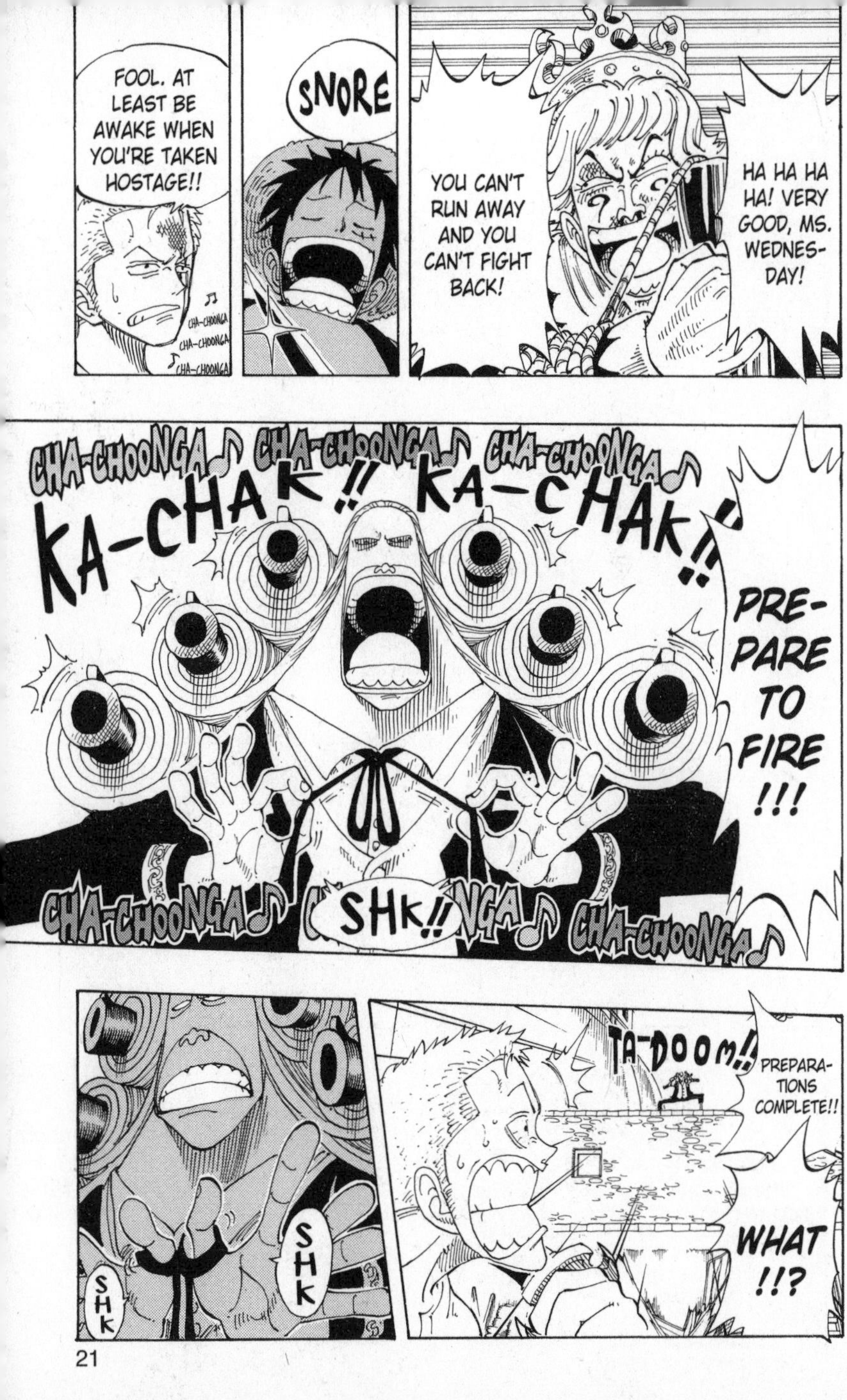

HA HA HA HA! VERY GOOD, MS. WEDNESDAY!
YOU CAN'T RUN AWAY AND YOU CAN'T FIGHT BACK!
SNORE
FOOL. AT LEAST BE AWAKE WHEN YOU'RE TAKEN HOSTAGE!!
CHA-CHOONGA
CHA-CHOONGA
CHA-CHOONGA
PREPARE TO FIRE!!!
CHA-CHOONGA♪ CHA-CHOONGA♪ CHA-CHOONGA♪
KA-CHAK!! KA-CHAK!!
CHA-CHOONGA♪
SHK!!
NGA♪
CHA-CHOONGA♪
TA-DOOM!!
PREPARATIONS COMPLETE!!
WHAT!!?
SHK
SHK

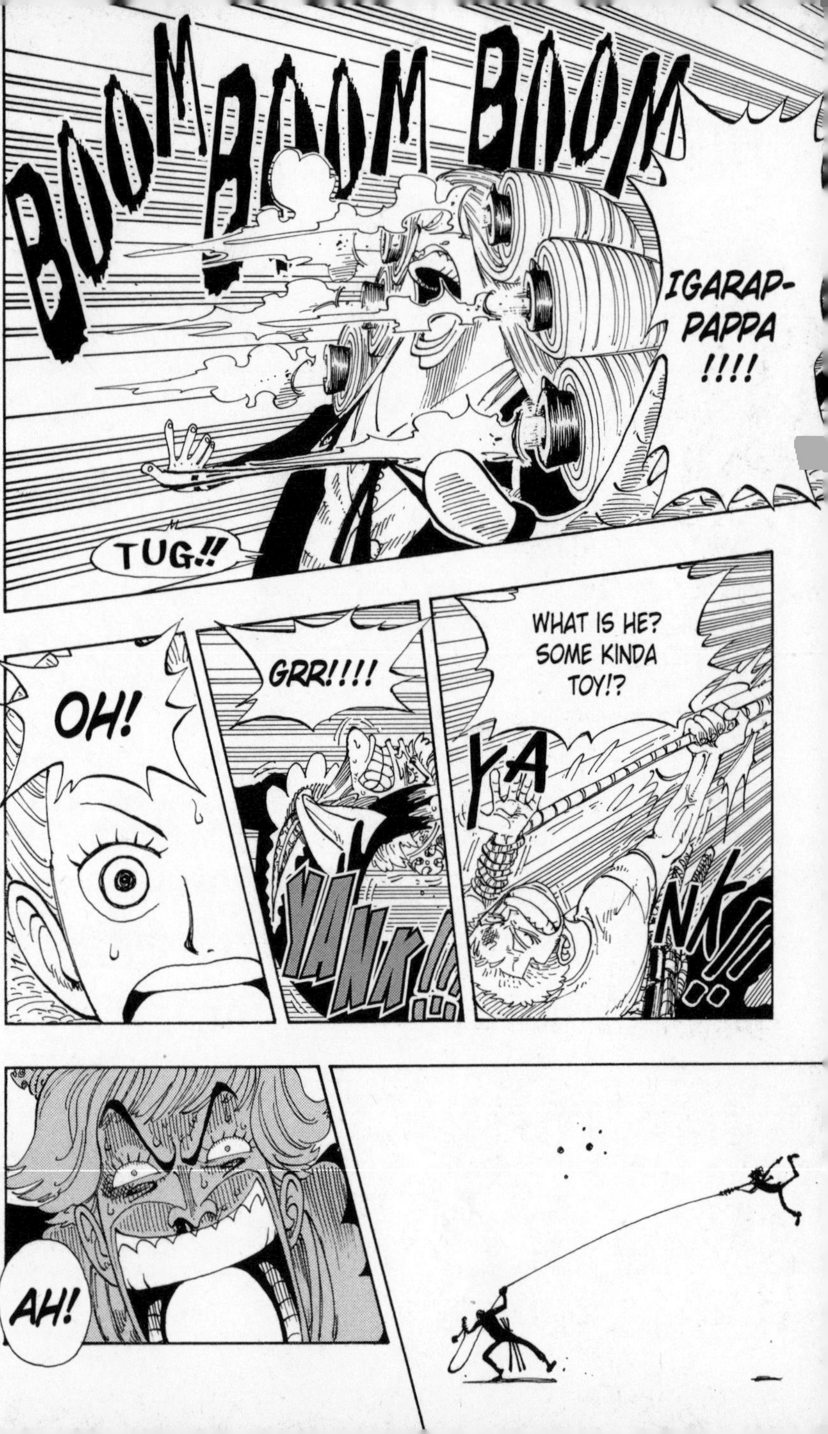
BOOM BOOM BOOM
IGARAP-PAPPA!!!!
TUG!!
WHAT IS HE? SOME KINDA TOY!?
YANK!!
GRR!!!!
YANK!!!
OH!
AH!

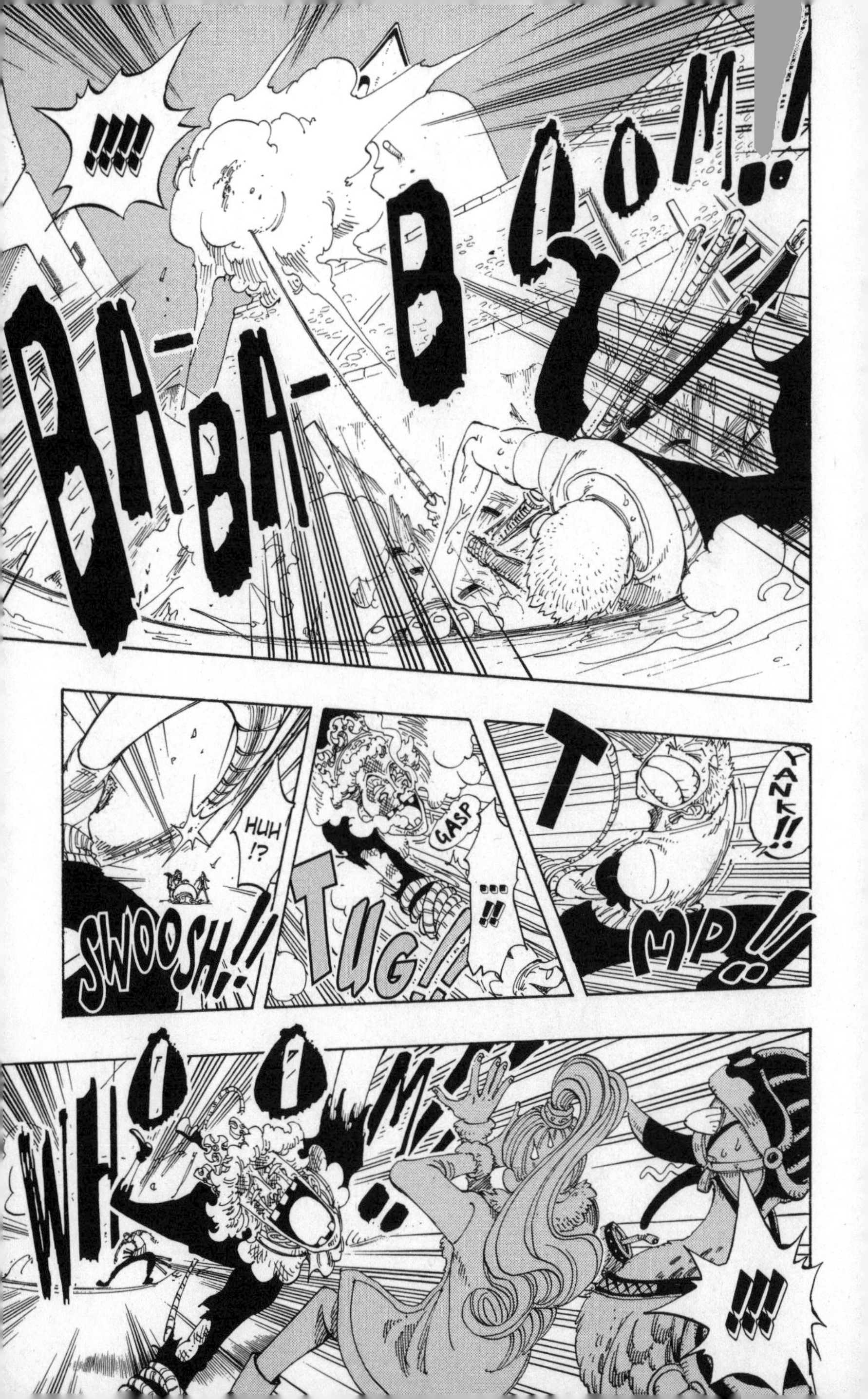
BA-BA-BOOM!!
!!!!
YANK!!
T
MP!!
GASP
...!!
TUG!!
HUH!?
SWOOSH!!
WHOOM!!
!!!

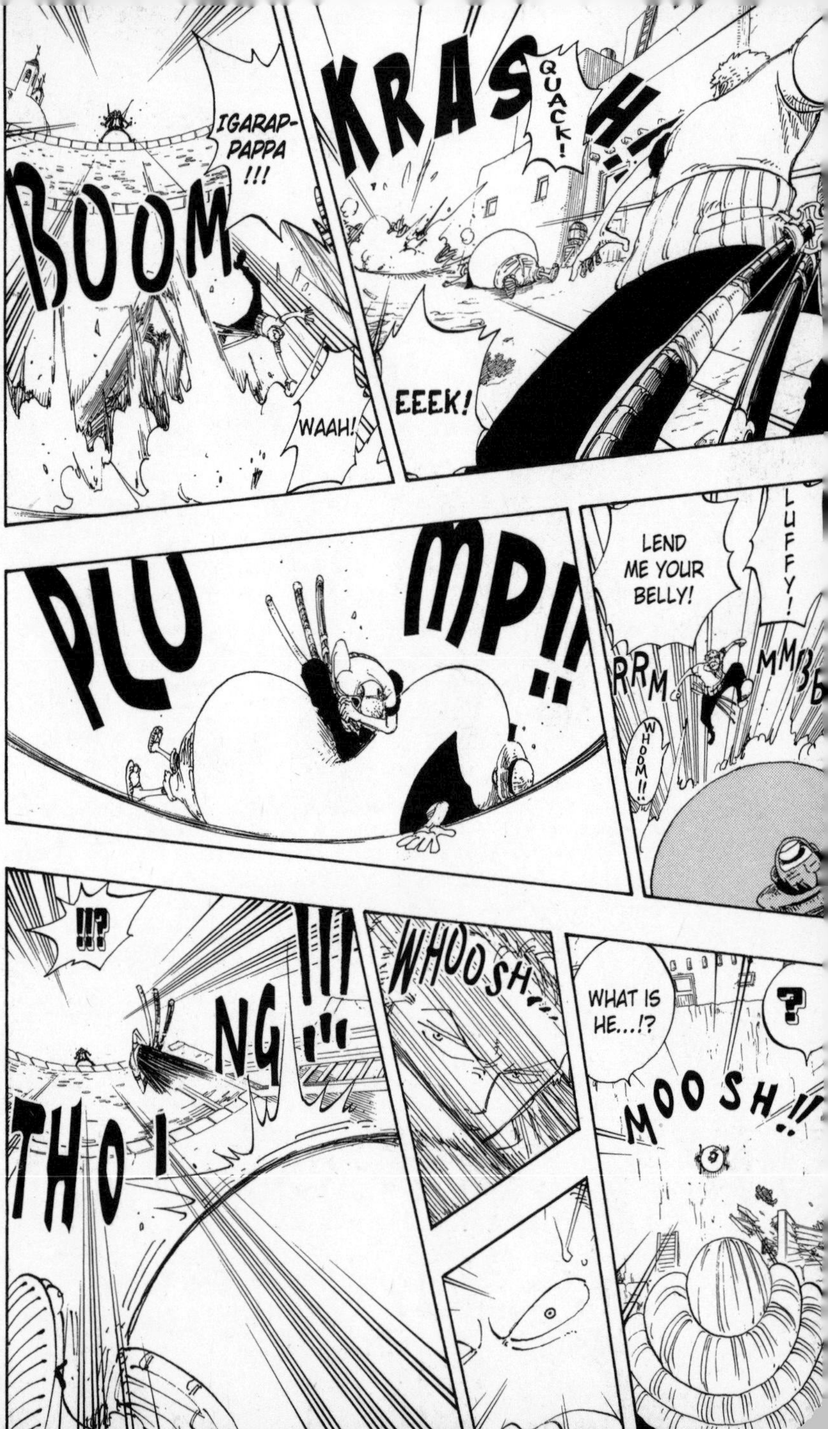
KRASH!!
QUACK!
EEEK!
IGARAP-PAPPA!!!
BOOM
WAAH!
LUFFY!
LEND ME YOUR BELLY!
RRM MMB
WHOOM!!
PLUMP!!
?
WHAT IS HE...!?
MOOSH!!
WHOOSH
!!?
THOING!!!

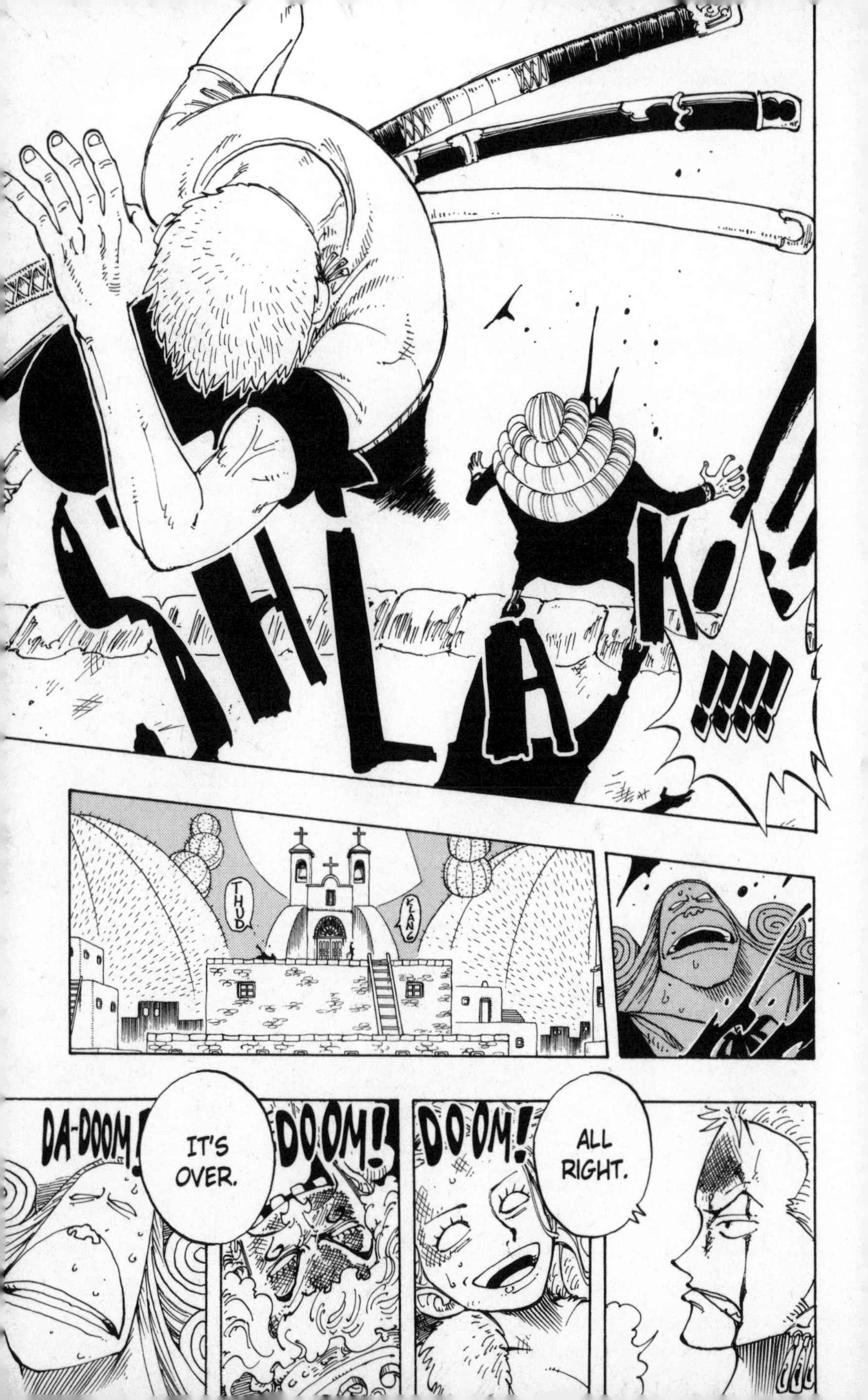
SHLAK!!!!
THUD
KLANG
DOOM!
ALL RIGHT.
DOOM!
IT'S OVER.
DA-DOOM!

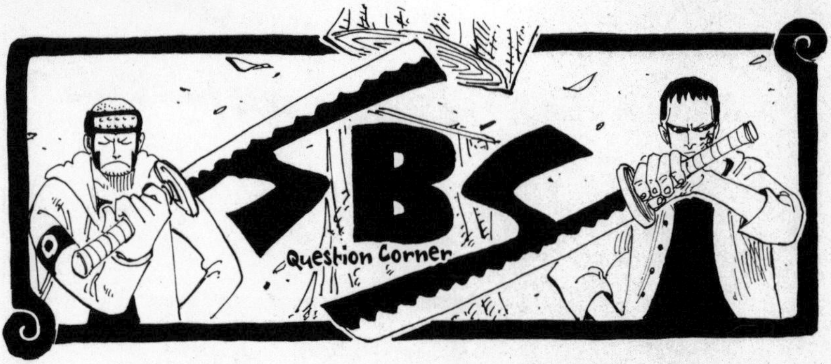
SBS
Question Corner

Oda: Before I begin the Question Corner, I want you all to see a letter that I received from a reader who hopes to save this column from a certain group that's been disrupting things. It pleased me very much.

Letter: Hello! I have some good news for you, Oda Sensei. Since the SBS Takeover Gang has been bugging you lately, I'm here to protect you! I'm Richard, leader of the "Facilitators of the Destruction of the SBS Takeover Gang"! We begin our mission on this auspicious day! Yay! Yay! Hurray!!

Oda: Let's start the Question Corner!

Hey, are you starting it!?

Q: I've been pondering a serious matter for the last five years: Why is it that in manga no one's trousers ever get ripped during the action scenes!? (Bam!)

A: If the characters fought naked, wouldn't that be distracting?

Q: I have a question about Ms. Tashigi, who appears in volume 11. On page 119, she seems really nearsighted, but on page 132, when she looks at the sword, she lifts her glasses. Then on page 161, when she's running, she's not even wearing glasses. So are they just for show, or what?

A: No, they're not just for show. She's a little nearsighted. She can see things up close, but not as well from a distance. That's all...I think.

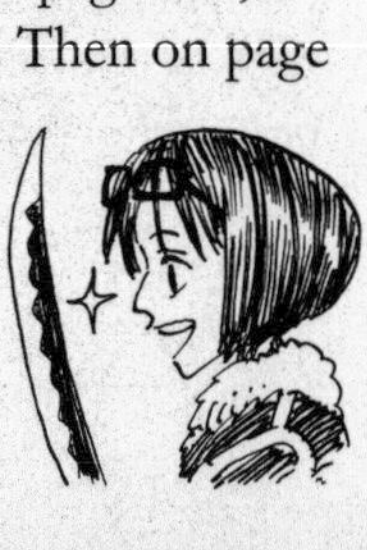

Chapter 110:
THE NIGHT ISN'T OVER

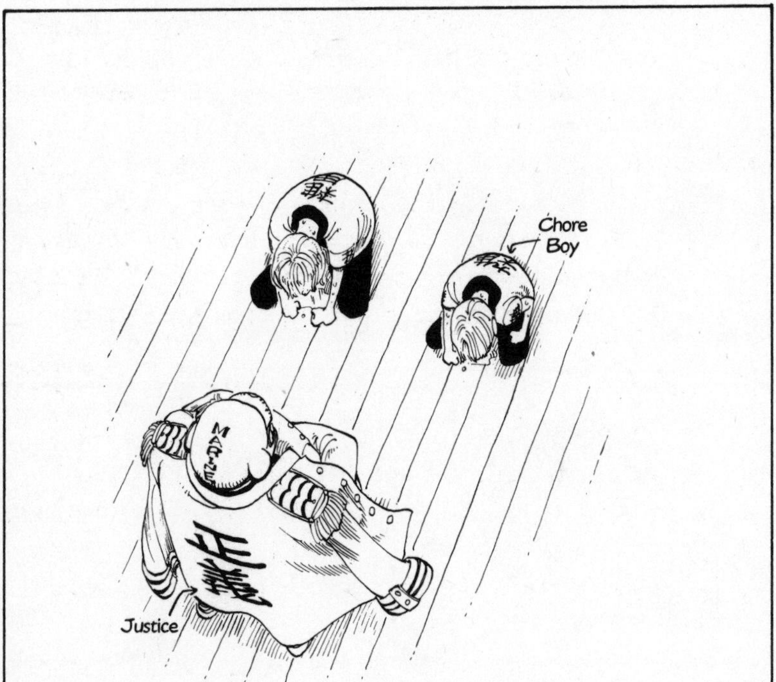
Chore Boy
MARINE
Justice

KOBY AND HELMEPPO'S CHRONICLE OF TOIL, VOL. 20:
"FIVE SECONDS BEFORE GARP'S ANNOUNCEMENT"

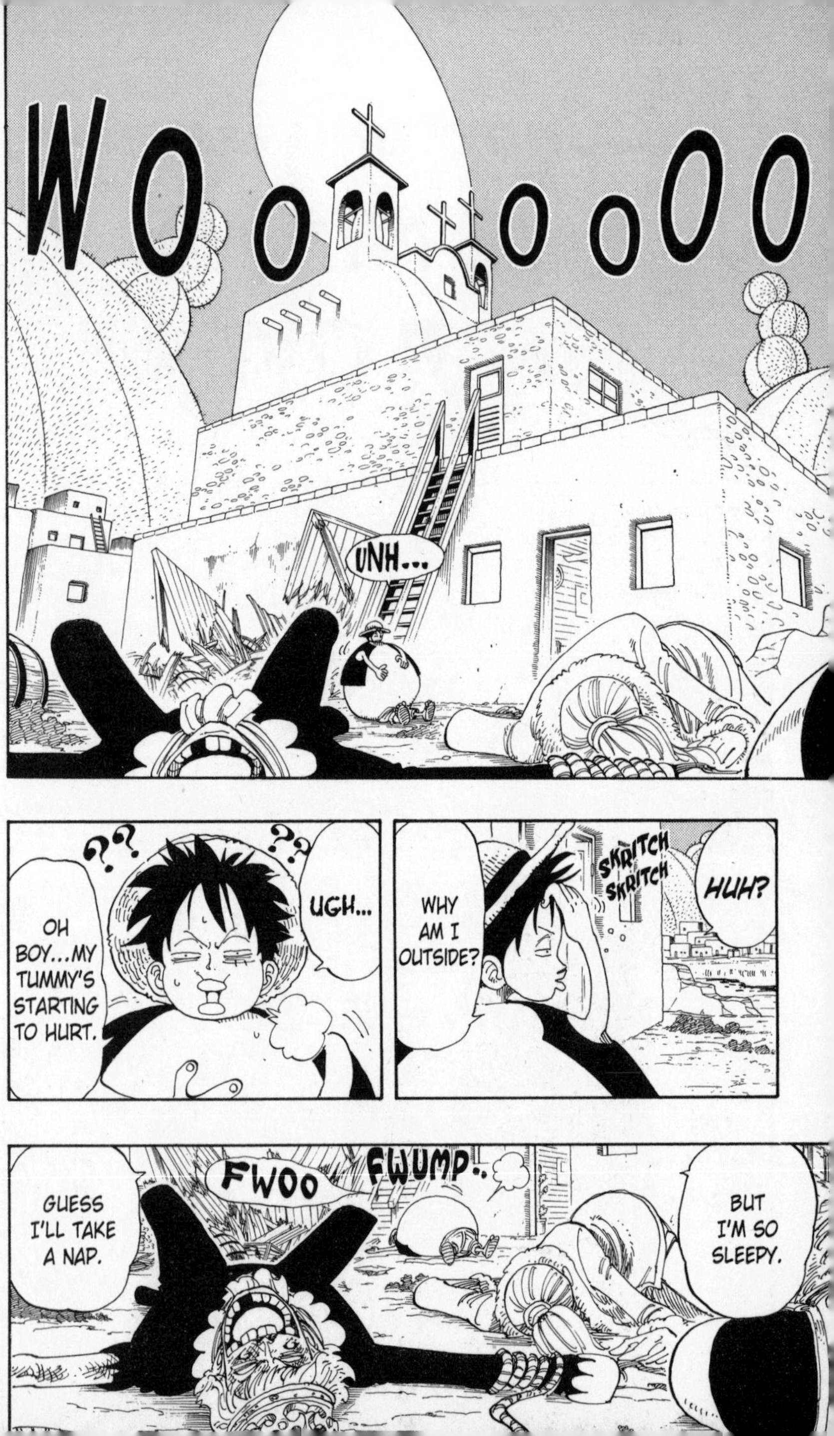
WOOoooOO
UNH...
HUH?
SKRITCH SKRITCH
WHY AM I OUTSIDE?
UGH...
OH BOY...MY TUMMY'S STARTING TO HURT.
BUT I'M SO SLEEPY.
FWUMP..
FWOO
GUESS I'LL TAKE A NAP.

READ THIS WAY

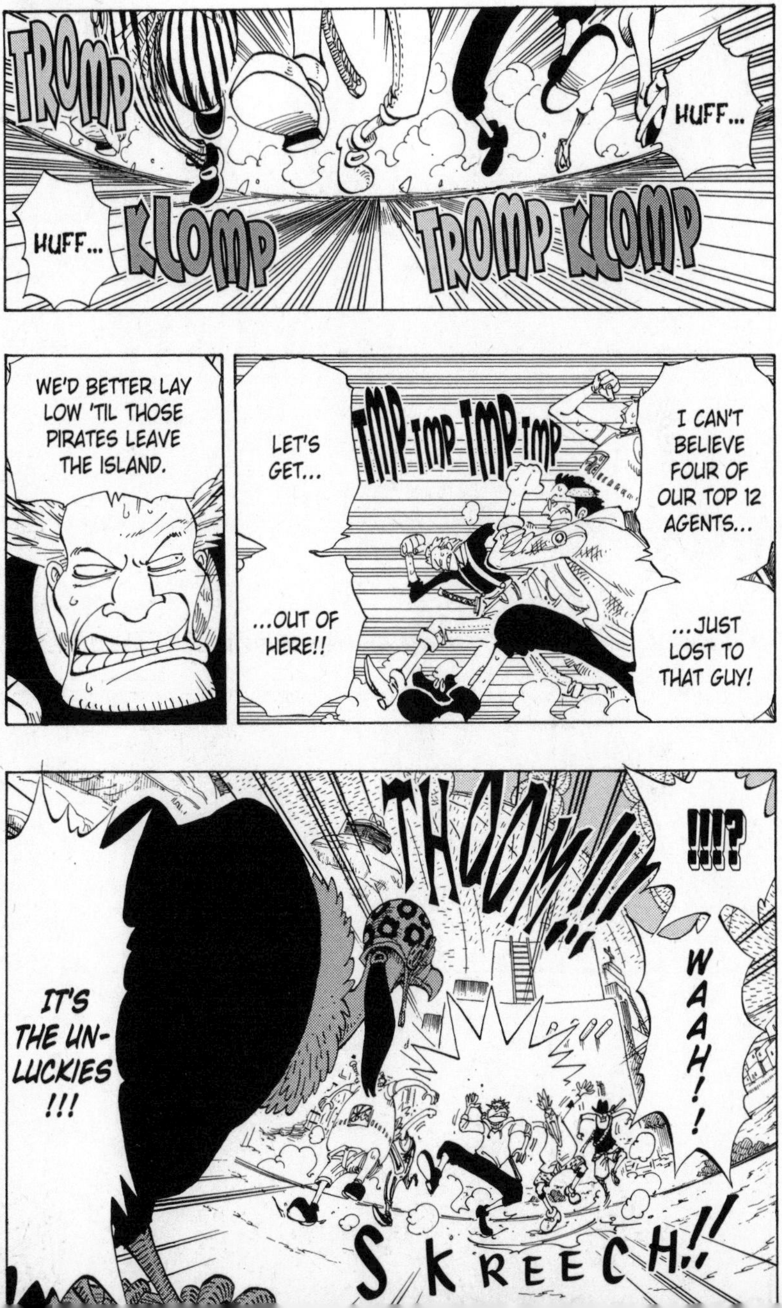
TROMP
HUFF...
TROMP KLOMP
KLOMP
HUFF...
I CAN'T BELIEVE FOUR OF OUR TOP 12 AGENTS...
...JUST LOST TO THAT GUY!
TMP tmp TMP tmp
LET'S GET...
...OUT OF HERE!!
WE'D BETTER LAY LOW 'TIL THOSE PIRATES LEAVE THE ISLAND.
!!!?
THOOM!!
WAAH!!
IT'S THE UN-LUCKIES !!!
SKREECH!!

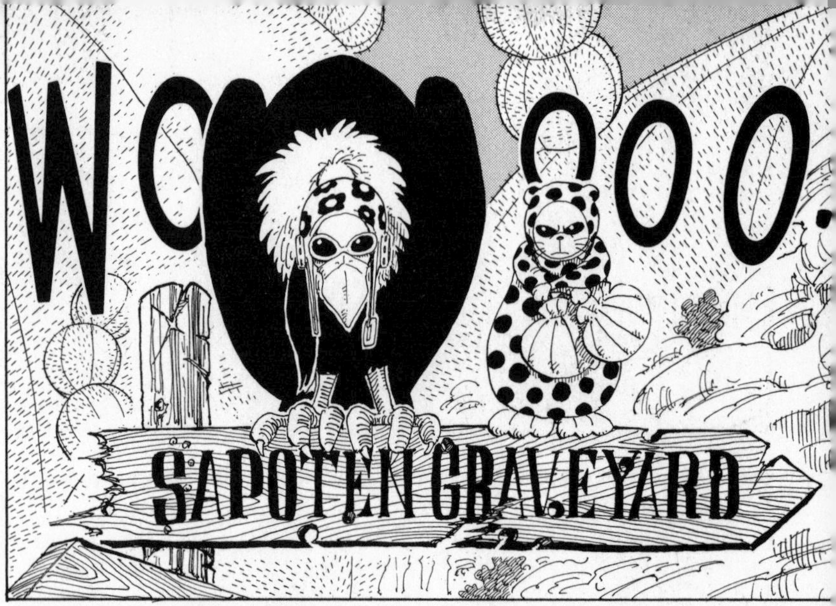
WO OOO.
SAPOTEN GRAVEYARD

SAPOTEN MEANS "CACTUS" IN JAPANESE.

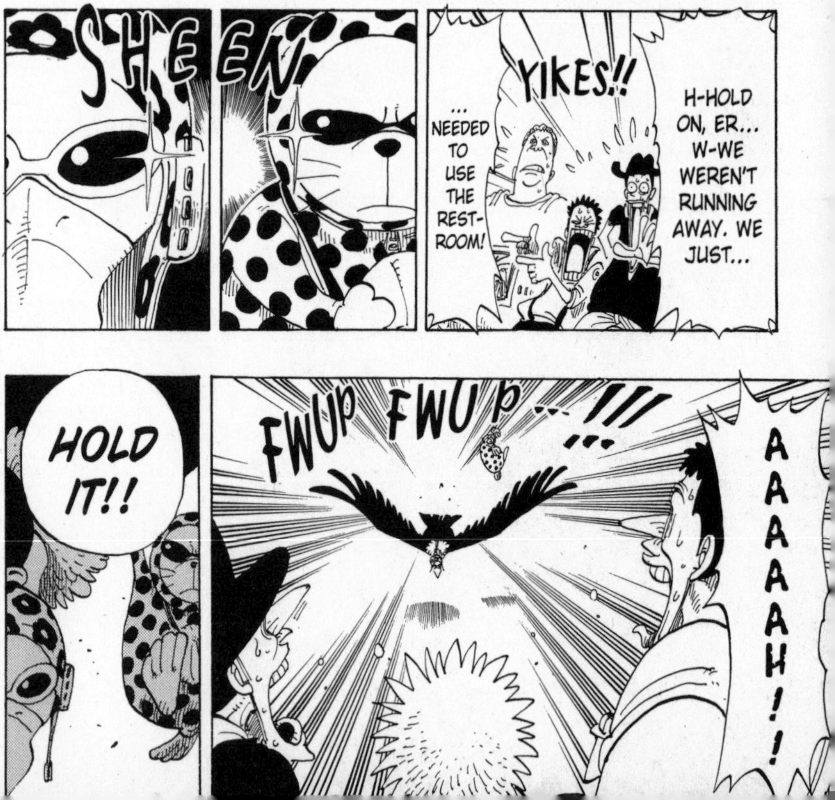
H-HOLD ON, ER... W-WE WEREN'T RUNNING AWAY. WE JUST...
YIKES!!
...NEEDED TO USE THE REST-ROOM!
SHEEN
AAAAAAH!!!
FWUP FWUP...!!!
HOLD IT!!

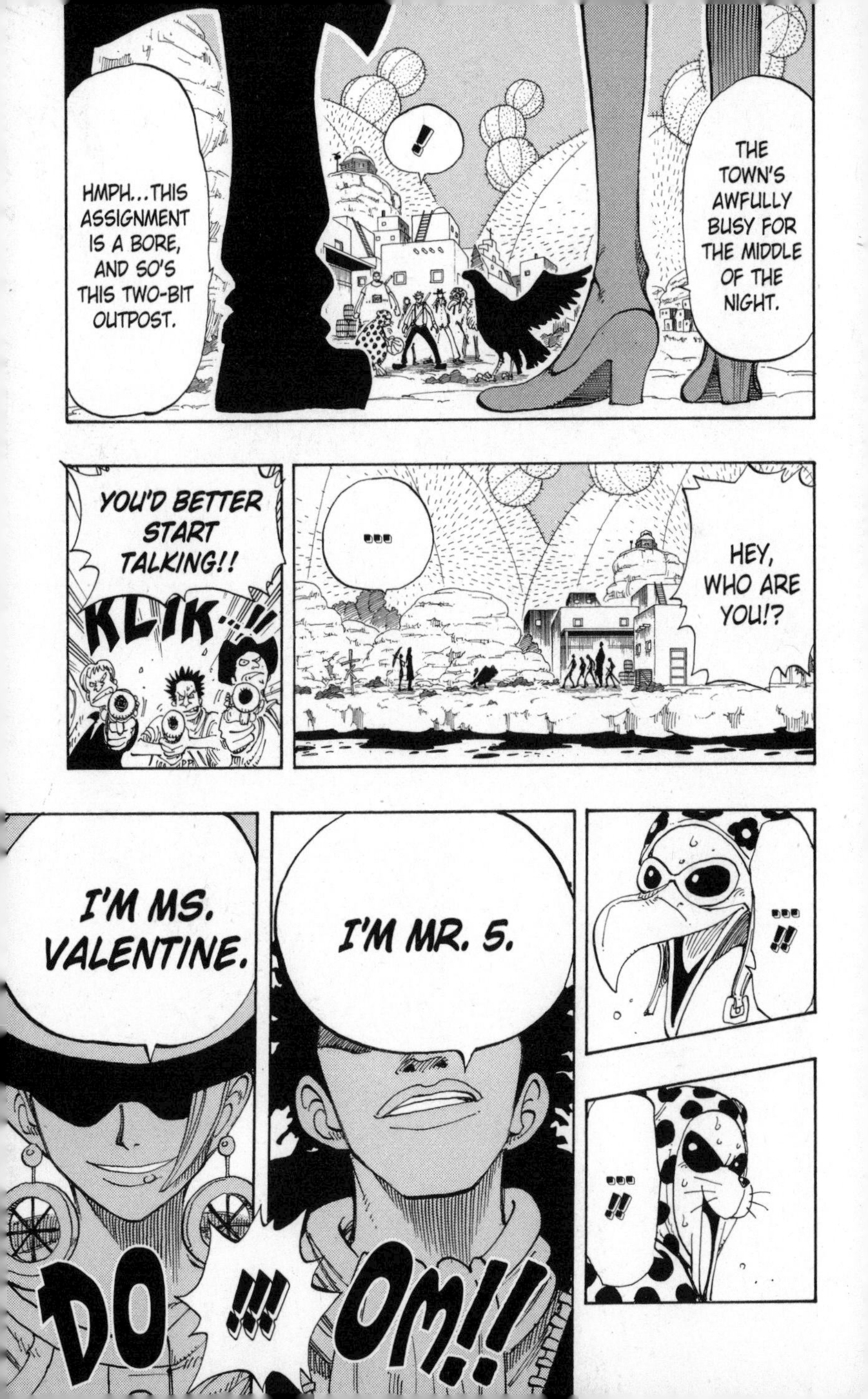
THE TOWN'S AWFULLY BUSY FOR THE MIDDLE OF THE NIGHT.
!
HMPH...THIS ASSIGNMENT IS A BORE, AND SO'S THIS TWO-BIT OUTPOST.
HEY, WHO ARE YOU!?
...
YOU'D BETTER START TALKING!!
KLIK...!!
...!!
...!!
I'M MR. 5.
I'M MS. VALENTINE.
DO...!!! OM!!

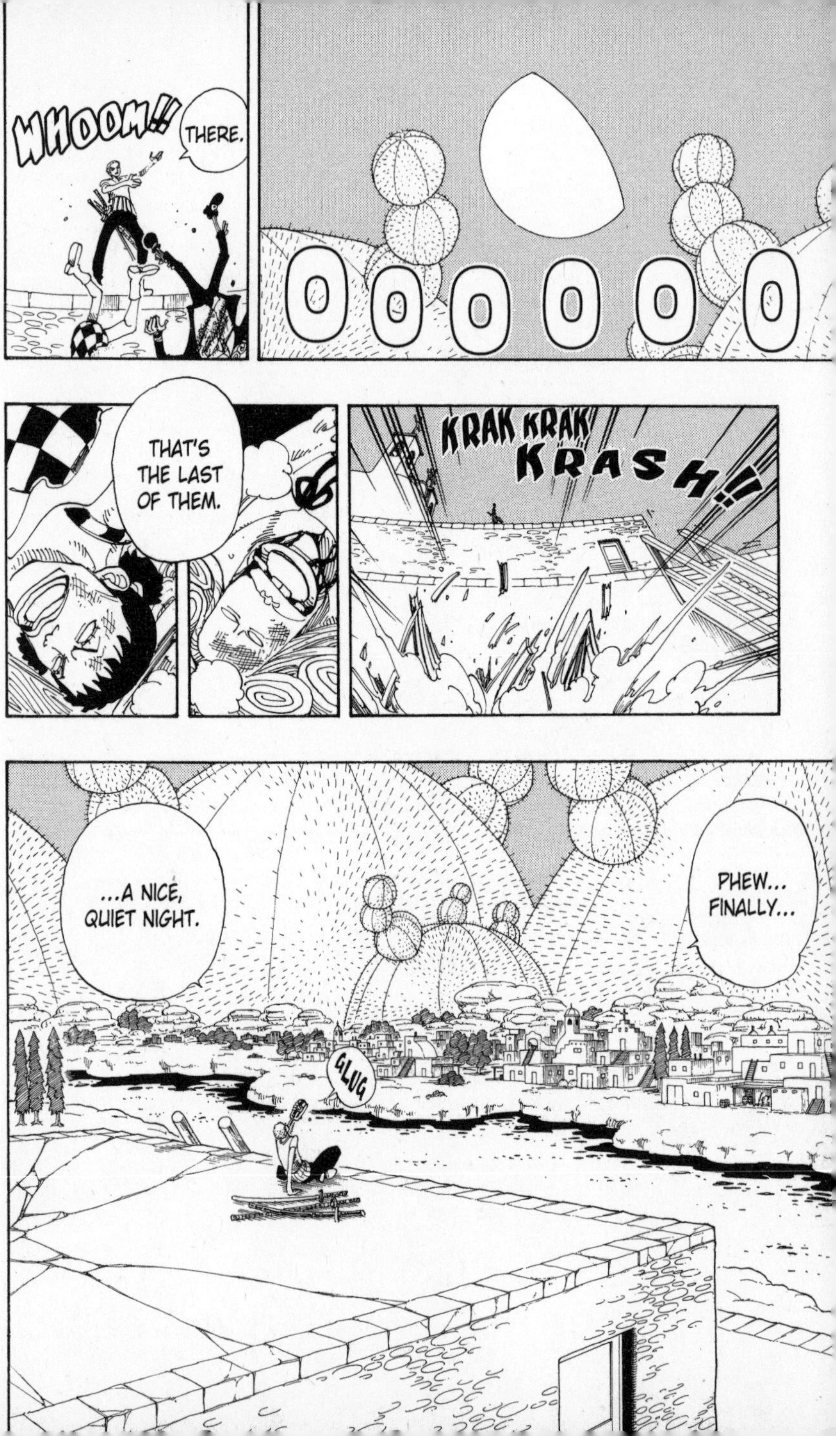
OOOOOO
WHOOM!!
THERE.
KRAK KRAK
KRASH!!
THAT'S THE LAST OF THEM.
PHEW... FINALLY...
...A NICE, QUIET NIGHT.
GLUG

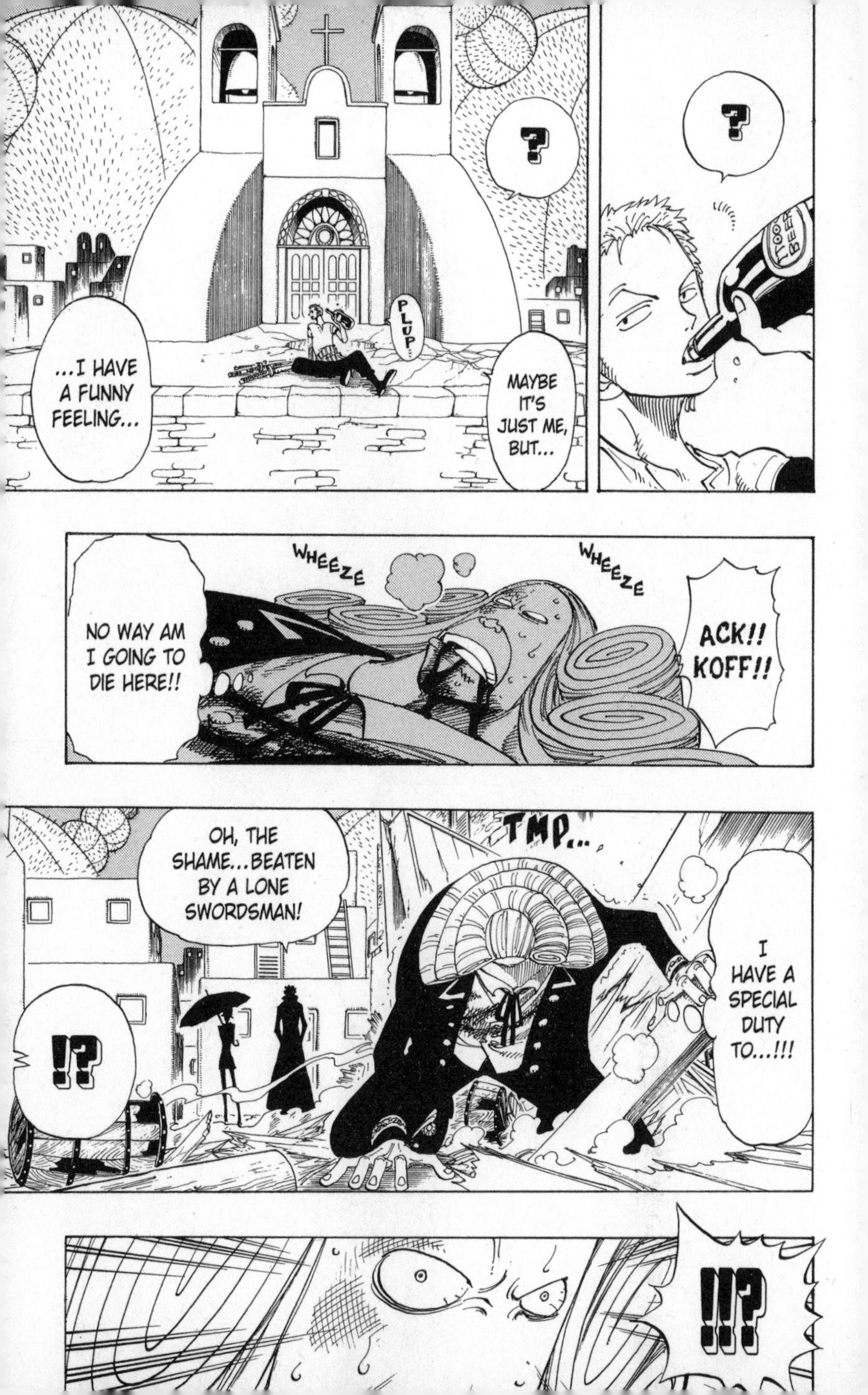
?
?
MAYBE IT'S JUST ME, BUT...
PLUP...
...I HAVE A FUNNY FEELING...
WHEEZE
ACK!! KOFF!!
WHEEZE
NO WAY AM I GOING TO DIE HERE!!
TMP...
I HAVE A SPECIAL DUTY TO...!!!
OH, THE SHAME...BEATEN BY A LONE SWORDSMAN!
!?
!!?

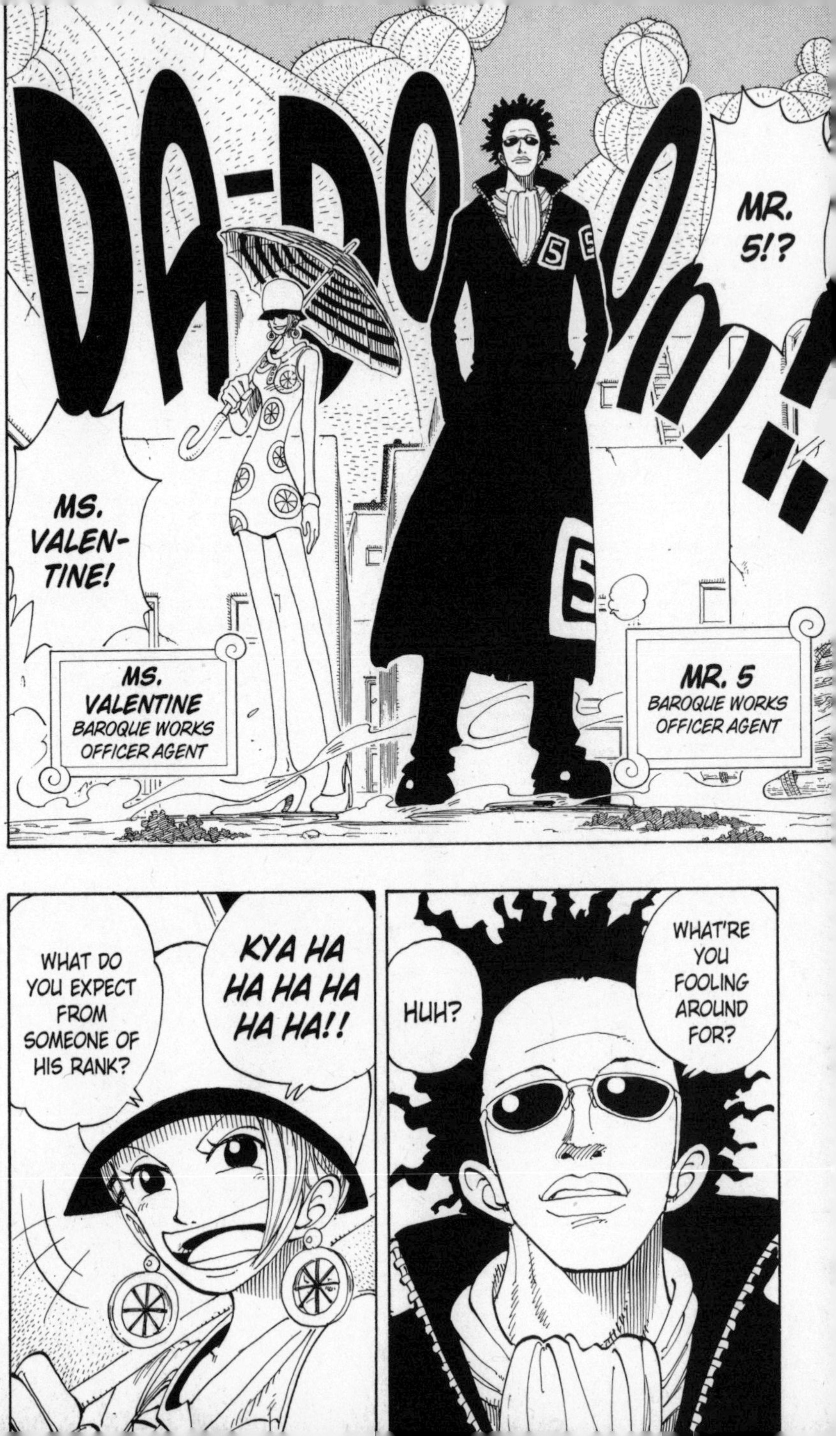
MR. 5!?
DA-DOOM!!
MR. 5
BAROQUE WORKS OFFICER AGENT
MS. VALENTINE!
MS. VALENTINE
BAROQUE WORKS OFFICER AGENT
WHAT'RE YOU FOOLING AROUND FOR?
HUH?
KYA HA HA HA HA HA HA!!
WHAT DO YOU EXPECT FROM SOMEONE OF HIS RANK?

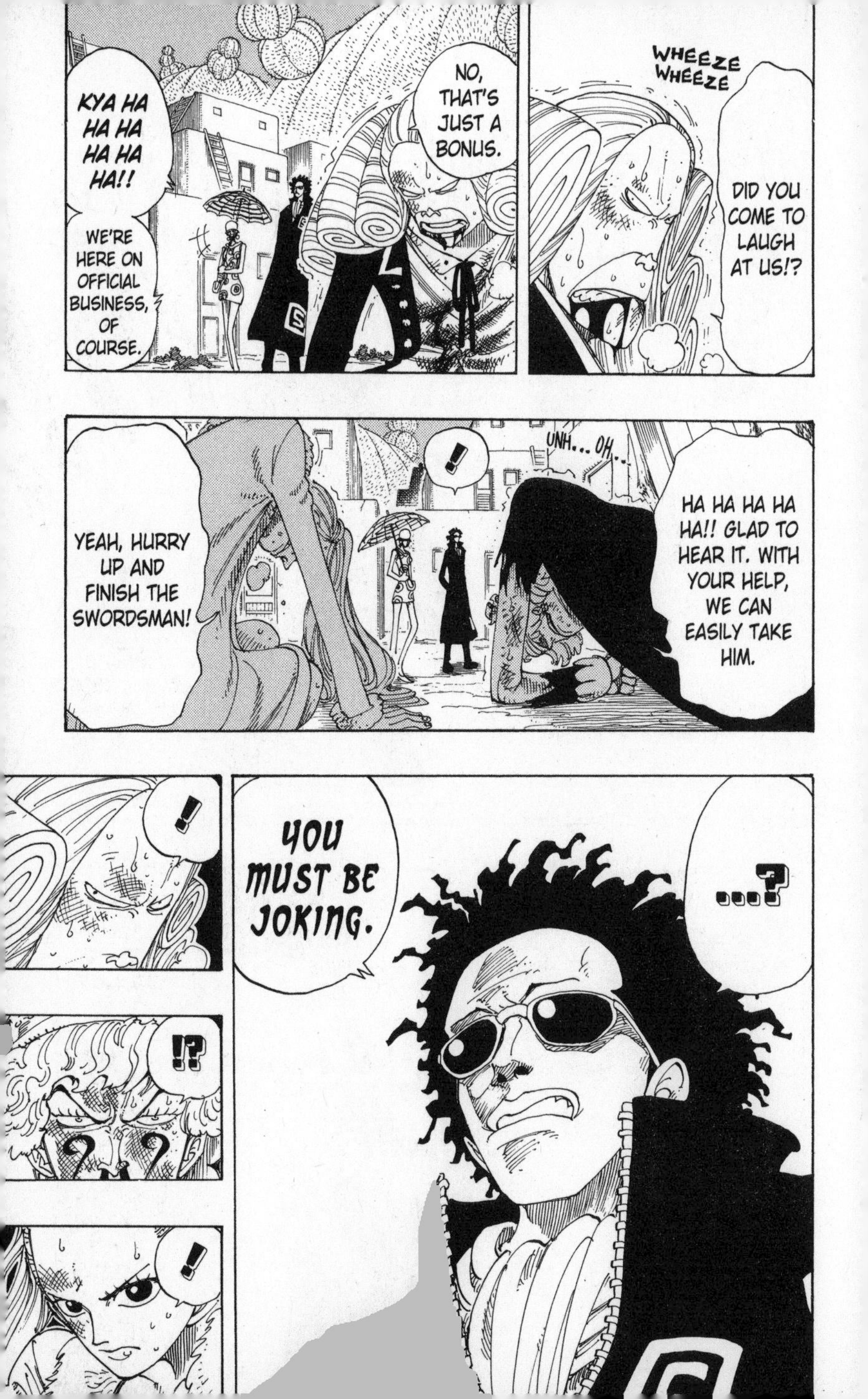
WHEEZE WHEEZE
DID YOU COME TO LAUGH AT US!?
NO, THAT'S JUST A BONUS.
KYA HA HA HA HA HA HA!!
WE'RE HERE ON OFFICIAL BUSINESS, OF COURSE.
HA HA HA HA HA!! GLAD TO HEAR IT. WITH YOUR HELP, WE CAN EASILY TAKE HIM.
UNH... OH...
!
YEAH, HURRY UP AND FINISH THE SWORDSMAN!
...?
YOU MUST BE JOKING.
!
!?
!

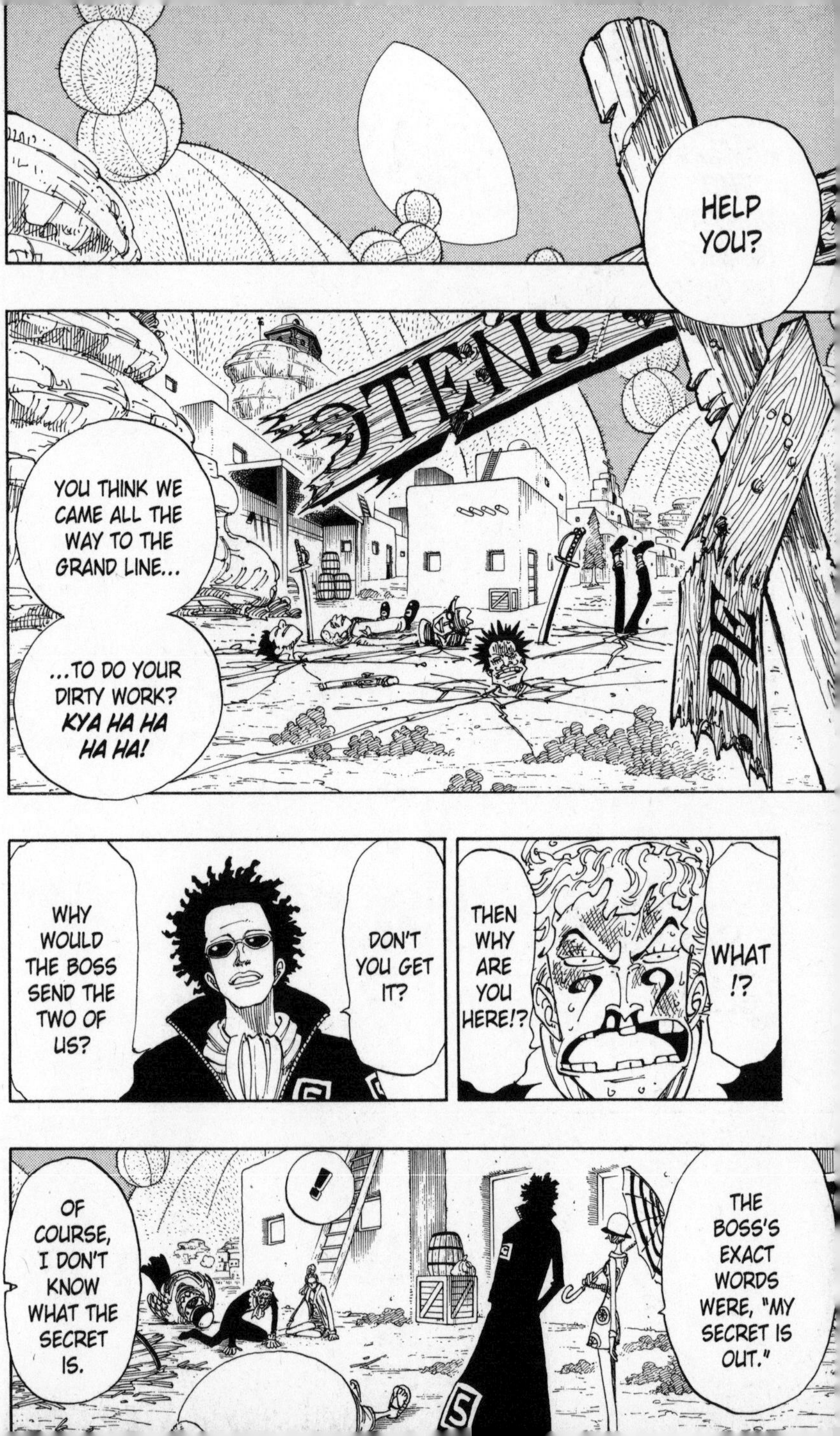
HELP YOU?
YOU THINK WE CAME ALL THE WAY TO THE GRAND LINE...
...TO DO YOUR DIRTY WORK? KYA HA HA HA HA!
PE
TENS
WHAT !?
THEN WHY ARE YOU HERE!?
DON'T YOU GET IT?
WHY WOULD THE BOSS SEND THE TWO OF US?
THE BOSS'S EXACT WORDS WERE, "MY SECRET IS OUT."
!
OF COURSE, I DON'T KNOW WHAT THE SECRET IS.

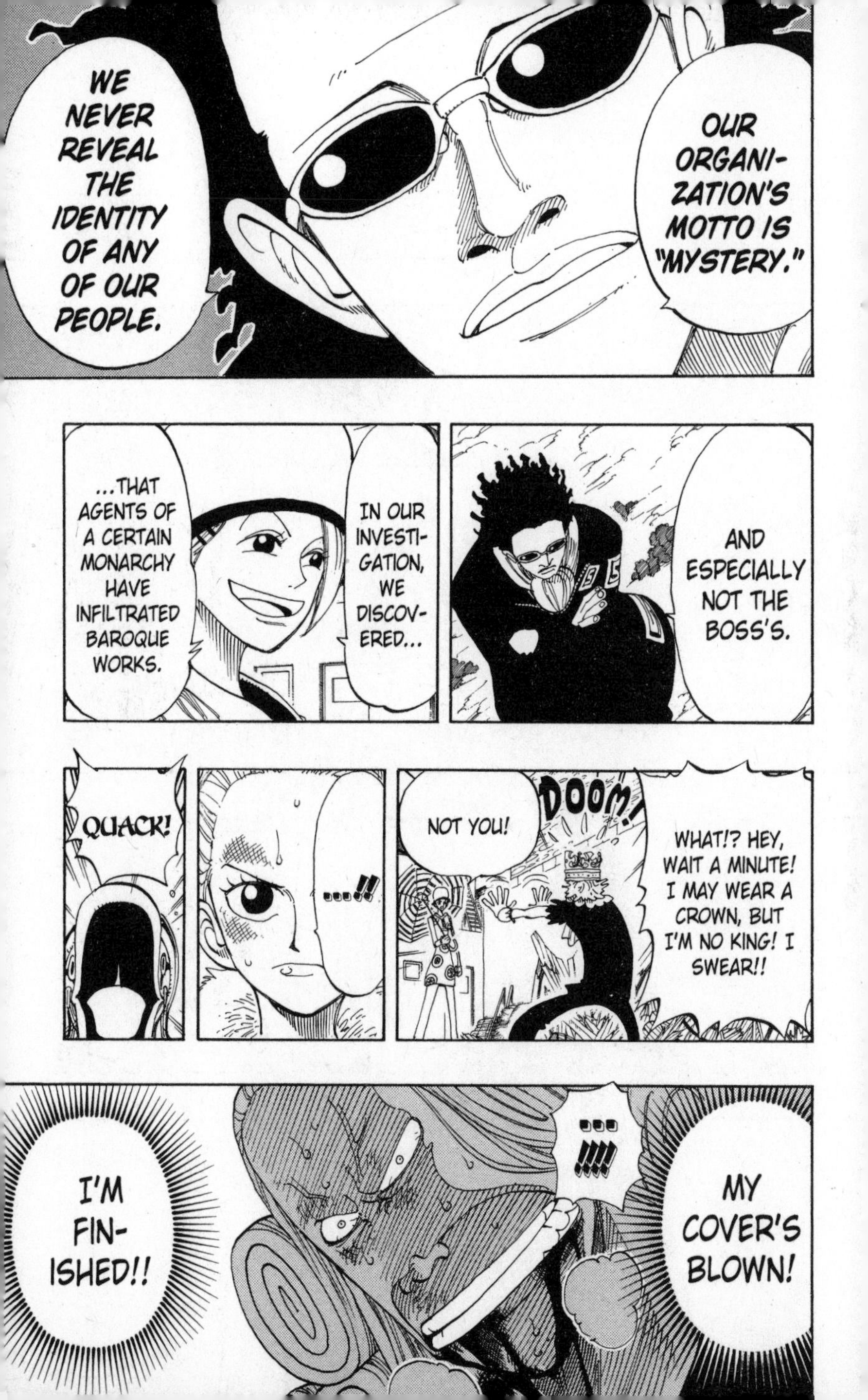
OUR ORGANIZATION'S MOTTO IS "MYSTERY."
WE NEVER REVEAL THE IDENTITY OF ANY OF OUR PEOPLE.
AND ESPECIALLY NOT THE BOSS'S.
IN OUR INVESTIGATION, WE DISCOVERED...
...THAT AGENTS OF A CERTAIN MONARCHY HAVE INFILTRATED BAROQUE WORKS.
WHAT!? HEY, WAIT A MINUTE! I MAY WEAR A CROWN, BUT I'M NO KING! I SWEAR!!
DOOM!
NOT YOU!
...!!
QUACK!
MY COVER'S BLOWN!
...!!!!
I'M FINISHED!!

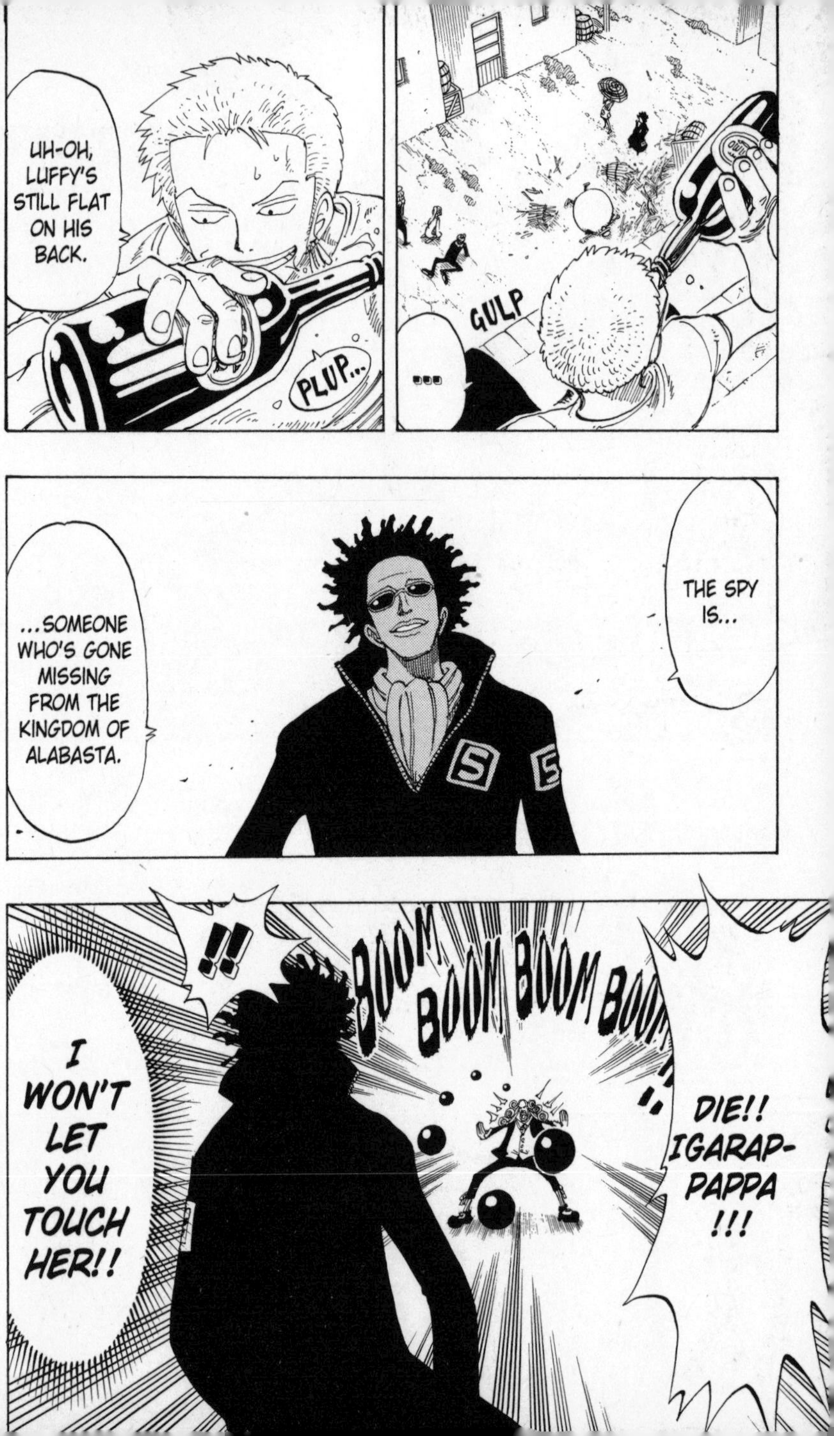
GULP
...
UH-OH, LUFFY'S STILL FLAT ON HIS BACK.
PLUP...
THE SPY IS...
...SOMEONE WHO'S GONE MISSING FROM THE KINGDOM OF ALABASTA.
DIE!! IGARAP-PAPPA!!!
BOOM BOOM BOOM BOO
!!
I WON'T LET YOU TOUCH HER!!

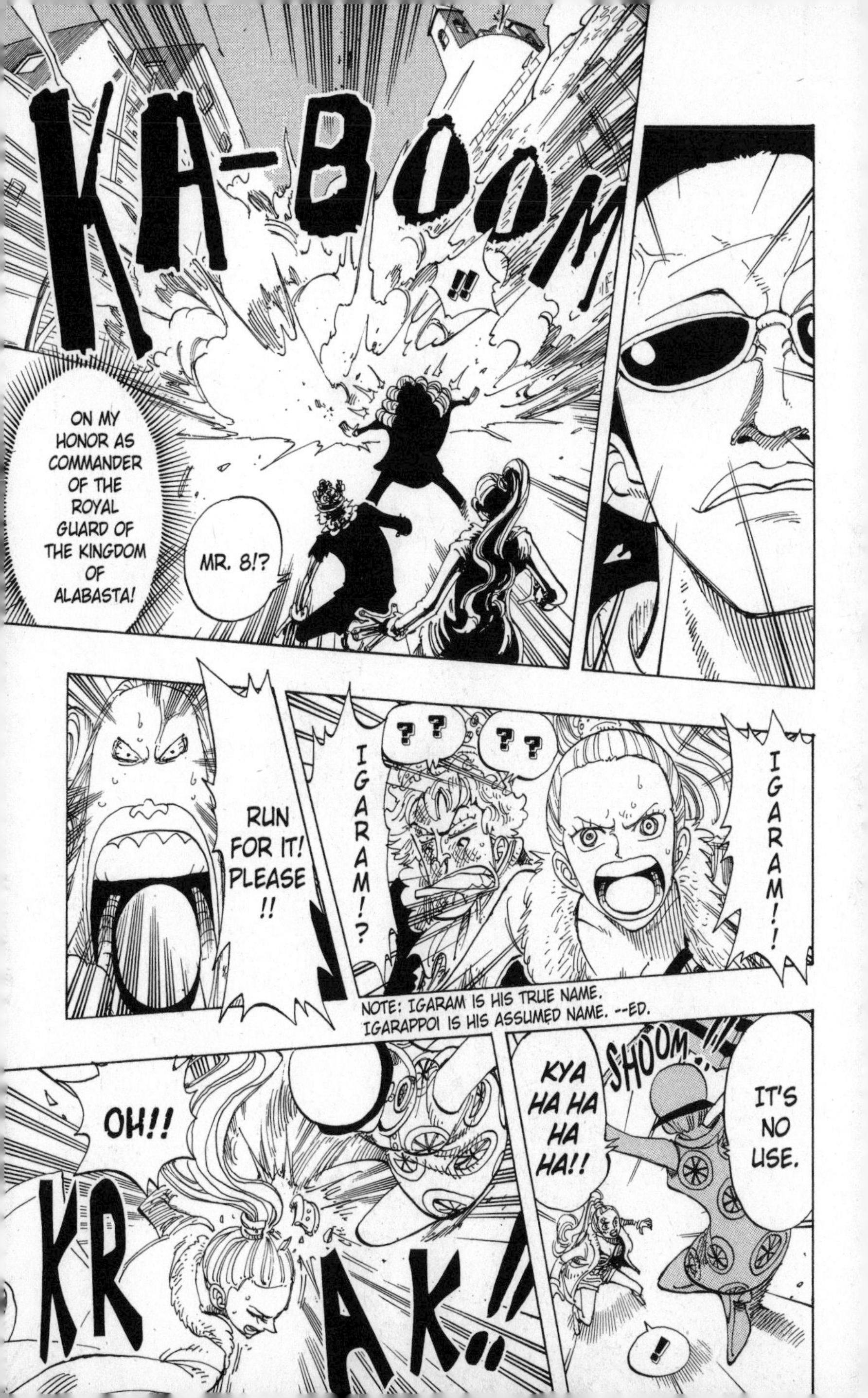
KA-BOOM!!
MR. 8!?
ON MY HONOR AS COMMANDER OF THE ROYAL GUARD OF THE KINGDOM OF ALABASTA!
IGARAM!!
??
??
IGARAM!?
RUN FOR IT! PLEASE!!
NOTE: IGARAM IS HIS TRUE NAME. IGARAPPOI IS HIS ASSUMED NAME. --ED.
IT'S NO USE.
SHOOM..!!
KYA HA HA HA HA!!
!
OH!!
KRAK..!!

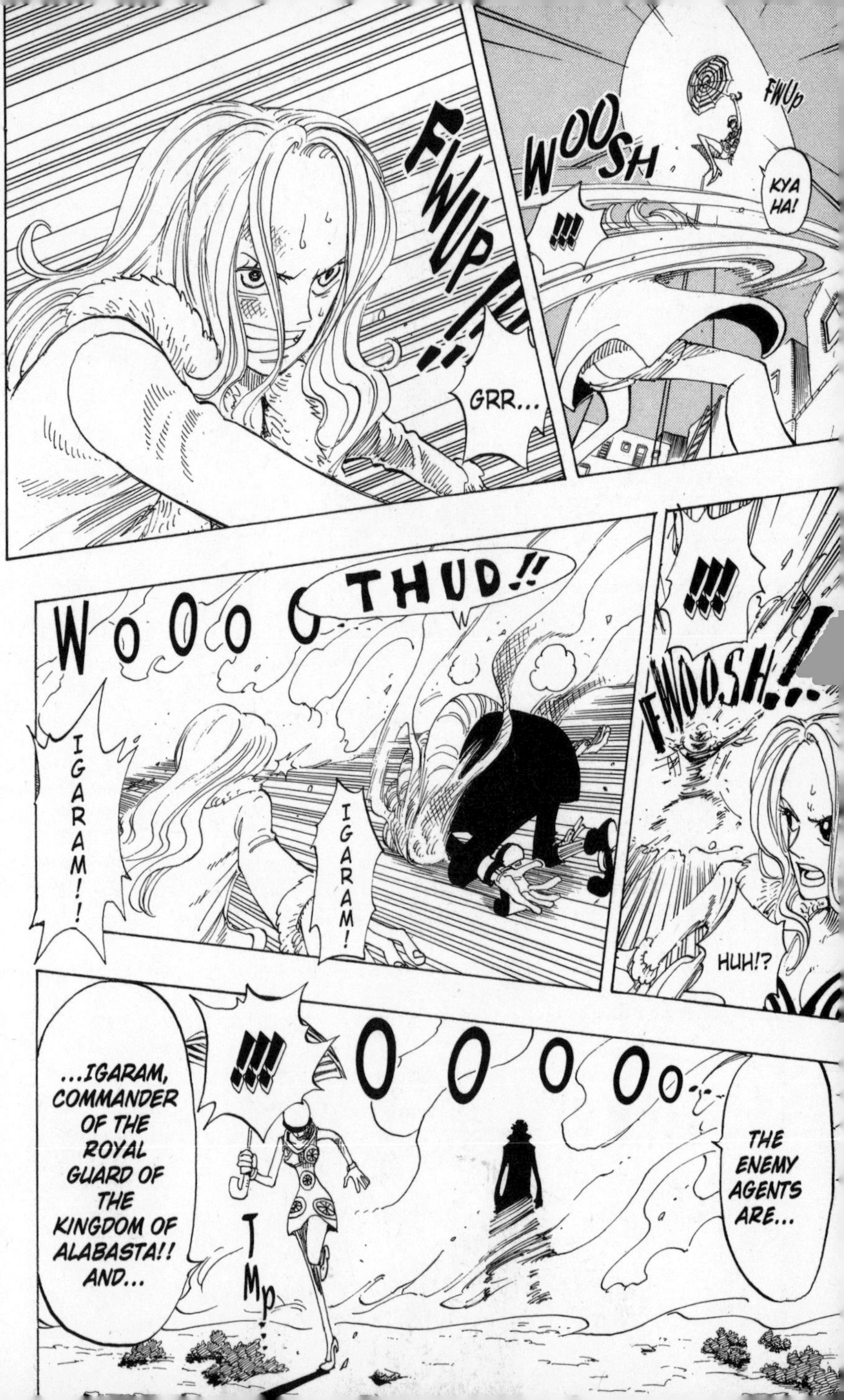
FWUp
KYA HA!
WOOSH
!!!
FWUP!!
GRR...
!!!
FWOOSH!!
HUH!?
THUD!!
WOOOO
IGARAM!
IGARAM!!
THE ENEMY AGENTS ARE...
OOOOO
!!!
...IGARAM, COMMANDER OF THE ROYAL GUARD OF THE KINGDOM OF ALABASTA!! AND...
TMp

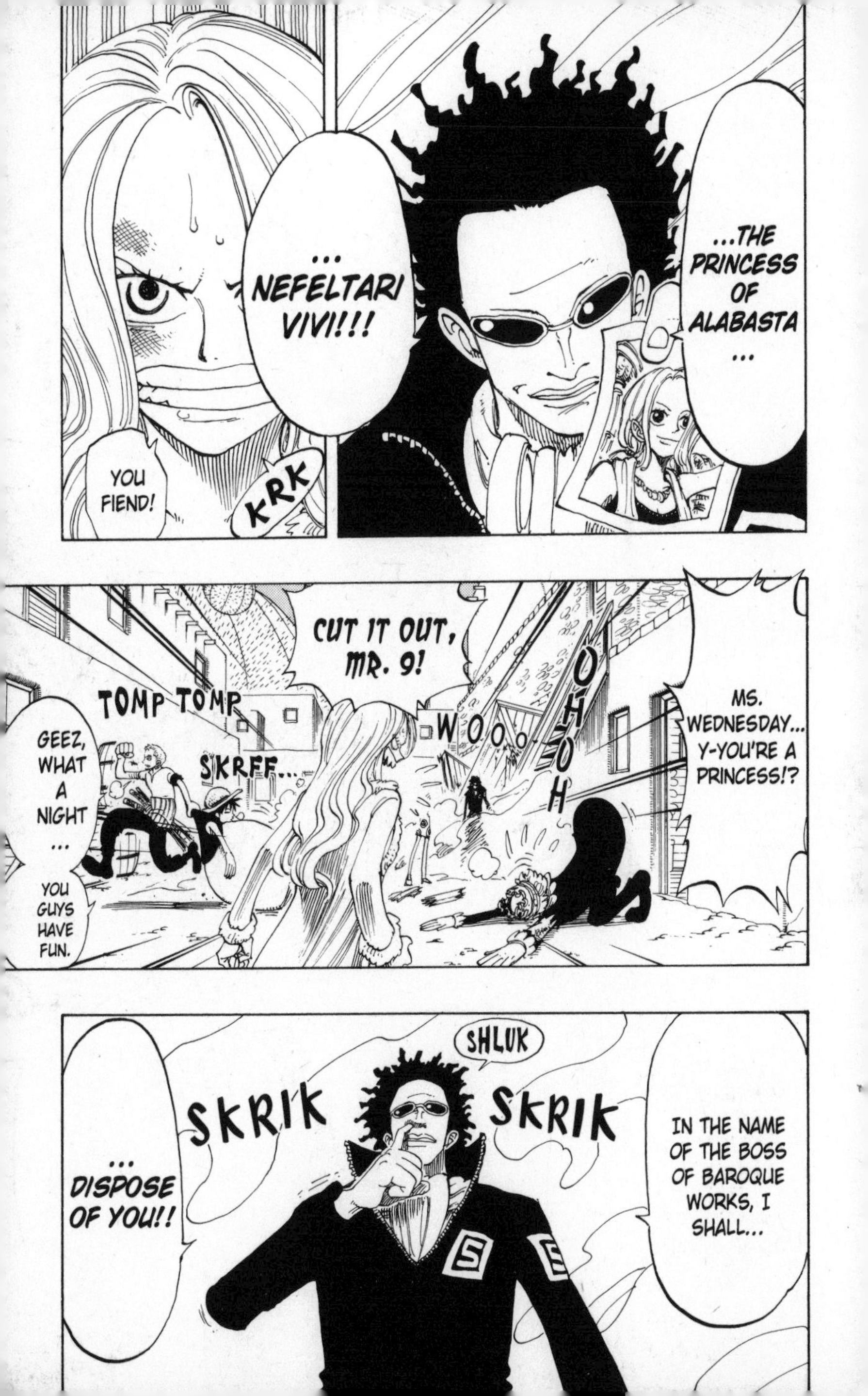
...THE PRINCESS OF ALABASTA ...
... NEFELTARI VIVI!!!
YOU FIEND!
KRK
MS. WEDNESDAY... Y-YOU'RE A PRINCESS!?
WOOO OHOH
CUT IT OUT, MR. 9!
SKRFF...
TOMP TOMP
GEEZ, WHAT A NIGHT ...
YOU GUYS HAVE FUN.
IN THE NAME OF THE BOSS OF BAROQUE WORKS, I SHALL...
SHLUK
SKRIK SKRIK
... DISPOSE OF YOU!!

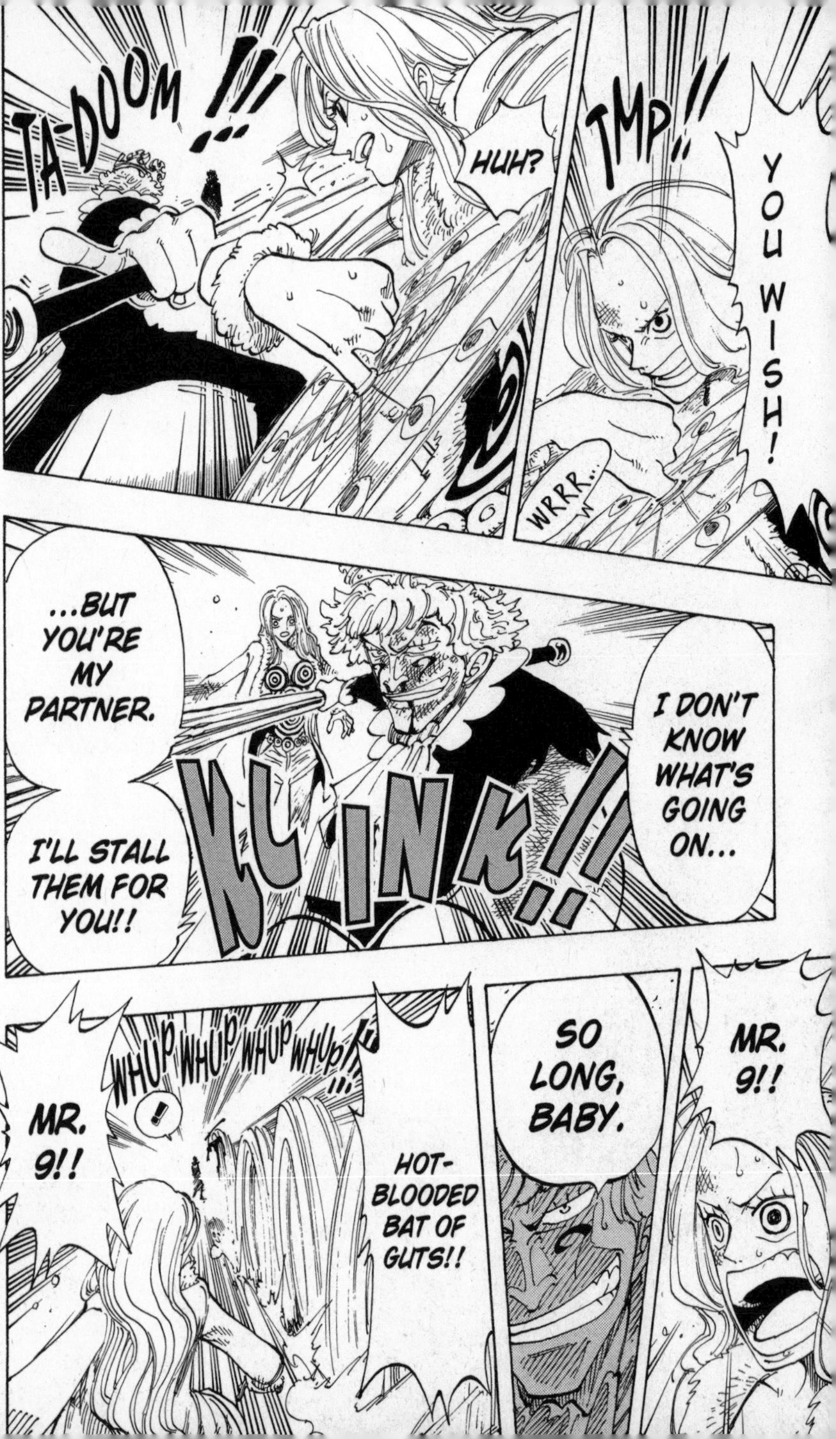
TMP!!
YOU WISH!
WRRR...
TA-DOOM!!!
HUH?
I DON'T KNOW WHAT'S GOING ON...
...BUT YOU'RE MY PARTNER.
KLINK!!
I'LL STALL THEM FOR YOU!!
MR. 9!!
SO LONG, BABY.
WHUP WHUP WHUP WHUP!!
!
MR. 9!!
HOT-BLOODED BAT OF GUTS!!

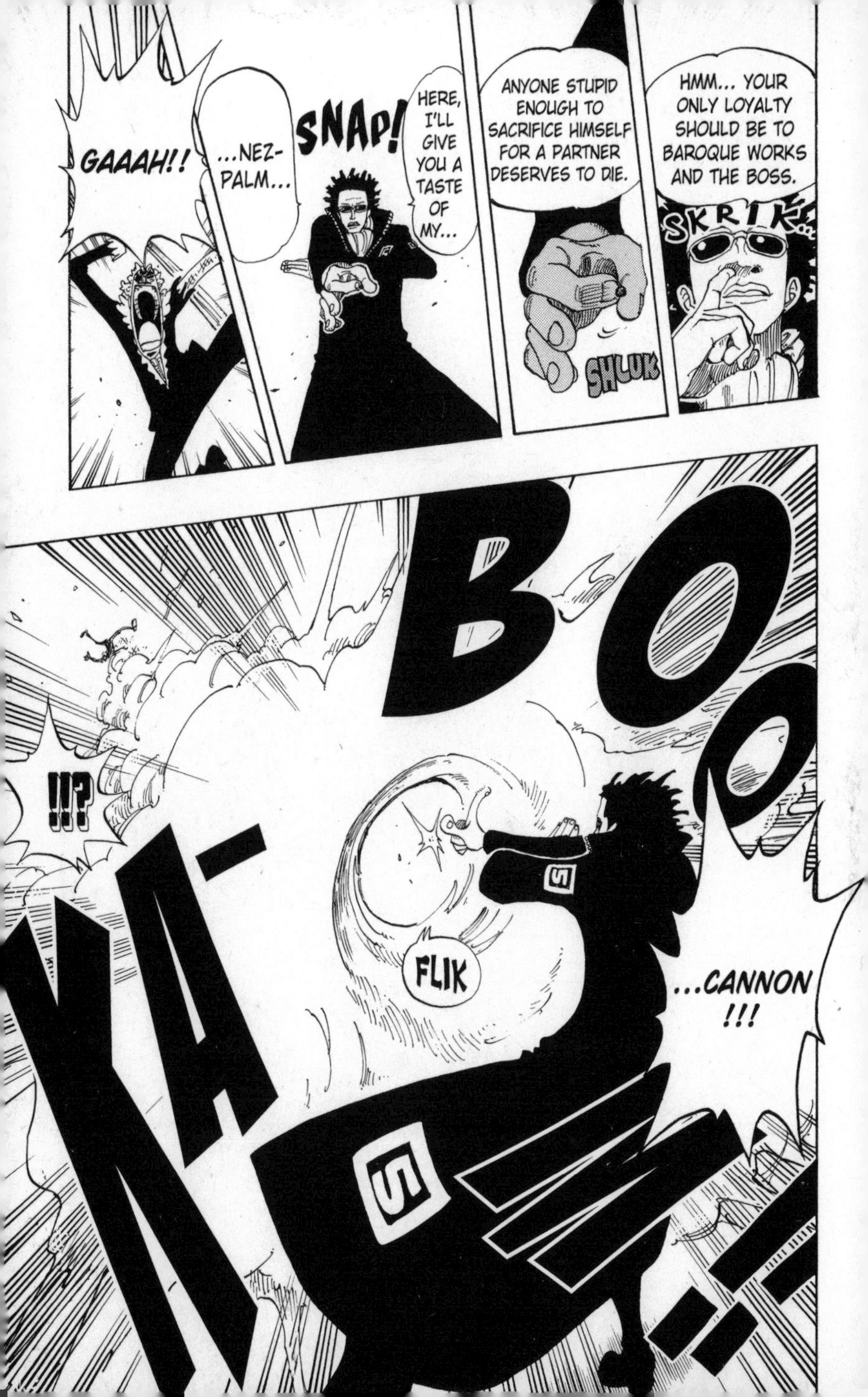

HMM... YOUR ONLY LOYALTY SHOULD BE TO BAROQUE WORKS AND THE BOSS.
SKRIK...
ANYONE STUPID ENOUGH TO SACRIFICE HIMSELF FOR A PARTNER DESERVES TO DIE.
SHLUK
HERE, I'LL GIVE YOU A TASTE OF MY...
SNAP!
...NEZ-PALM...
GAAAH!!
...CANNON !!!
FLIK
!!?
KA-BOOM!!

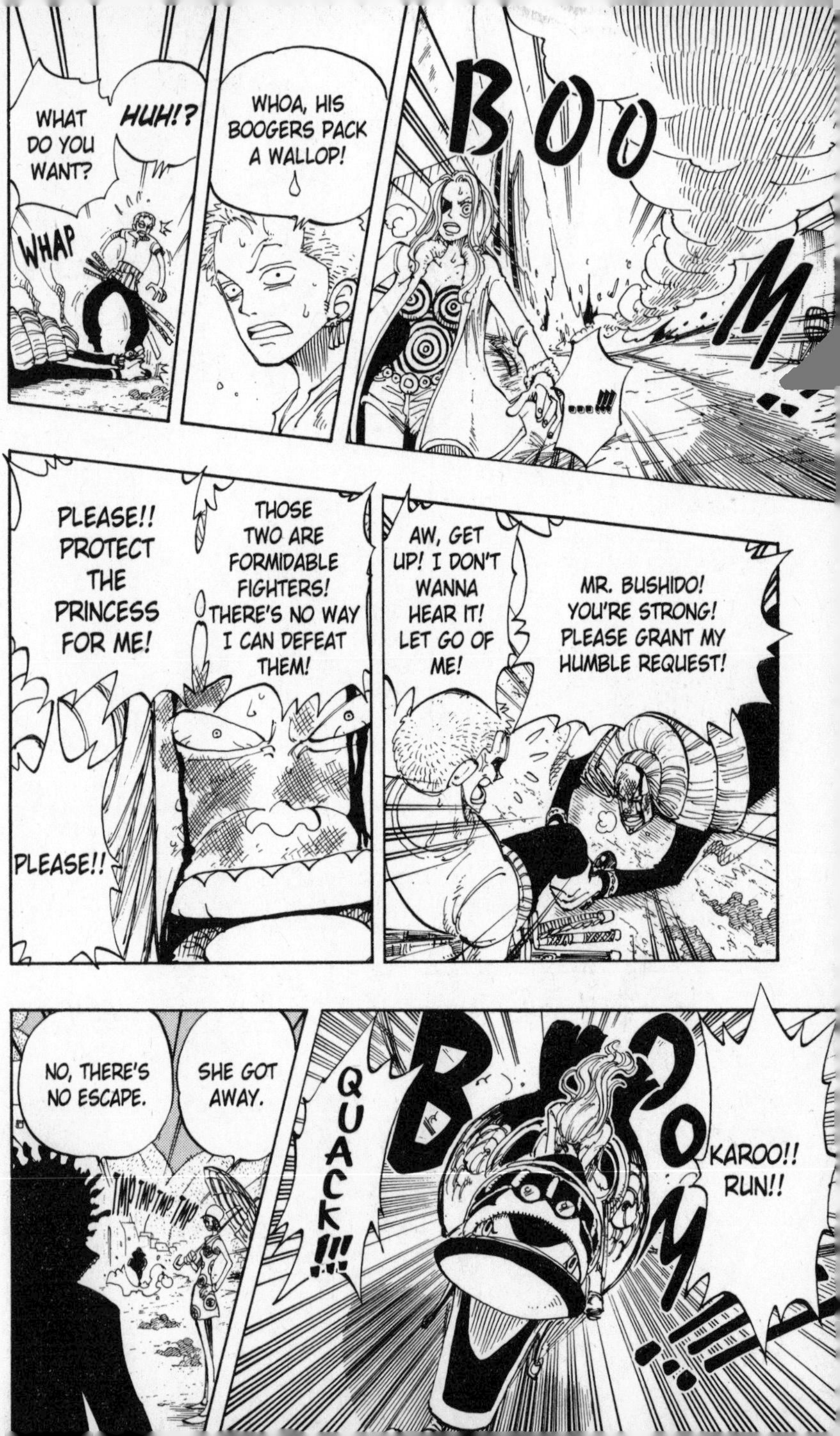
BOOOM...!!!
WHOA, HIS BOOGERS PACK A WALLOP!
HUH!?
WHAT DO YOU WANT?
WHAP
MR. BUSHIDO! YOU'RE STRONG! PLEASE GRANT MY HUMBLE REQUEST!
AW, GET UP! I DON'T WANNA HEAR IT! LET GO OF ME!
THOSE TWO ARE FORMIDABLE FIGHTERS! THERE'S NO WAY I CAN DEFEAT THEM!
PLEASE!! PROTECT THE PRINCESS FOR ME!
PLEASE!!
KAROO!! RUN!!
QUACK!!!
SHE GOT AWAY.
NO, THERE'S NO ESCAPE.
TMP TMP TMP TMP

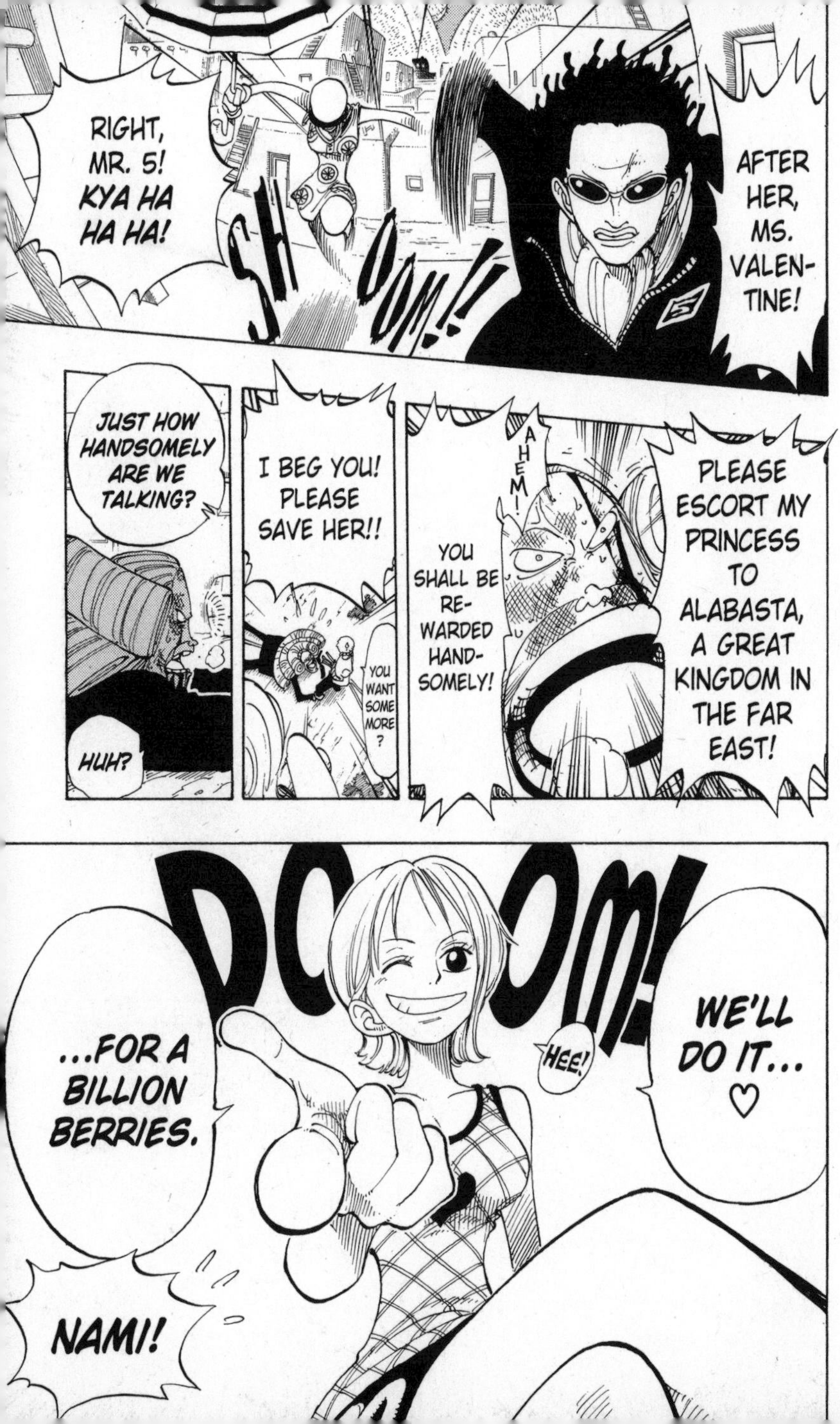

AFTER HER, MS. VALEN-TINE!
SHOOM!!
RIGHT, MR. 5! KYA HA HA HA!
PLEASE ESCORT MY PRINCESS TO ALABASTA, A GREAT KINGDOM IN THE FAR EAST!
AHEM!
YOU SHALL BE RE-WARDED HAND-SOMELY!
I BEG YOU! PLEASE SAVE HER!!
YOU WANT SOME MORE?
JUST HOW HANDSOMELY ARE WE TALKING?
HUH?
WE'LL DO IT... ♡
DOOM!
HEE!
...FOR A BILLION BERRIES.
NAMI!

THE SECRET CRIMINAL ORGANIZATION

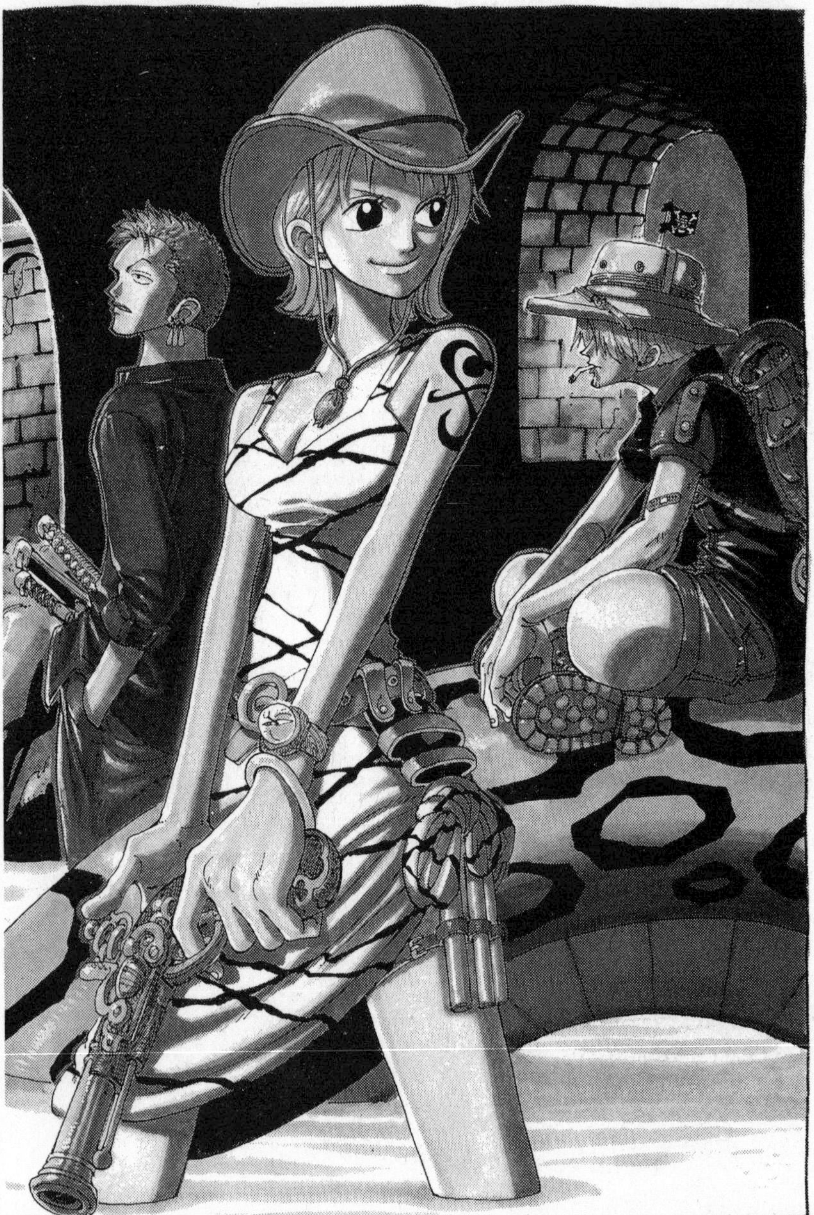

Chapter 111:

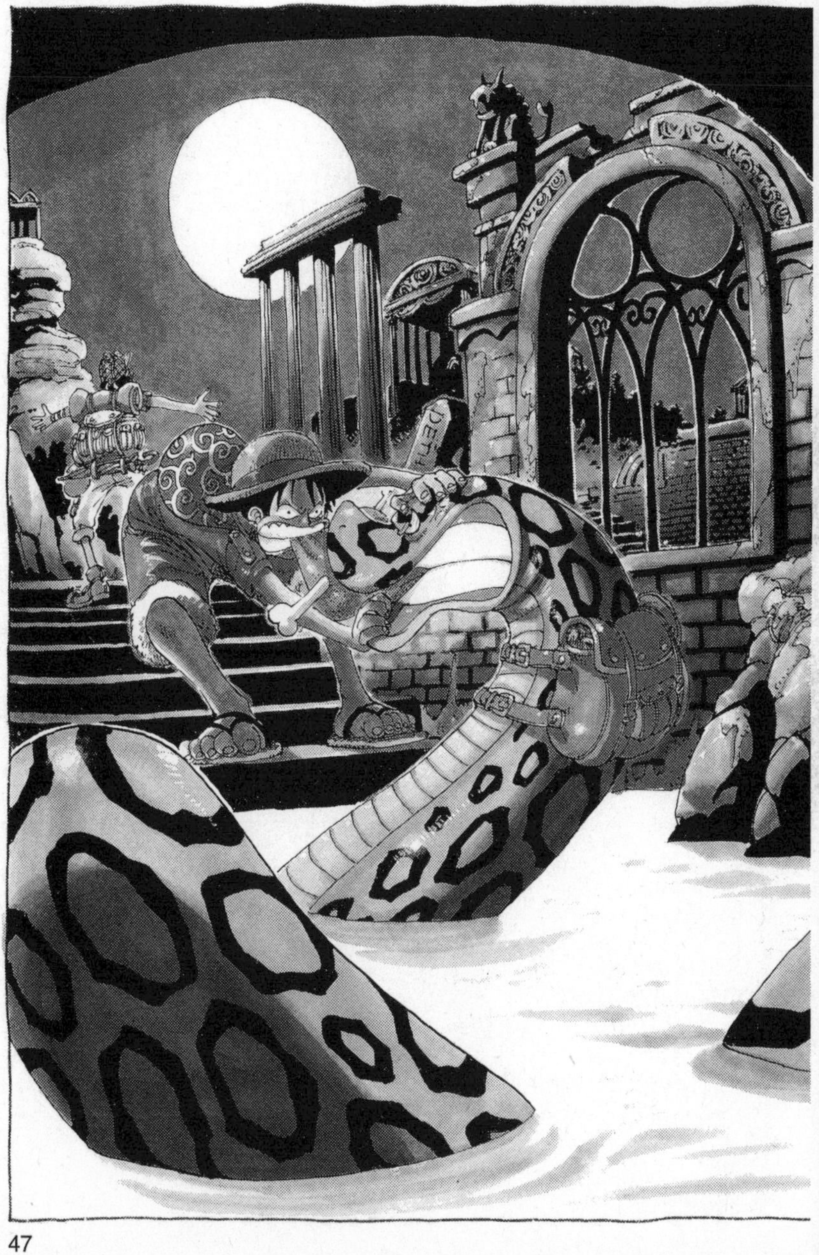

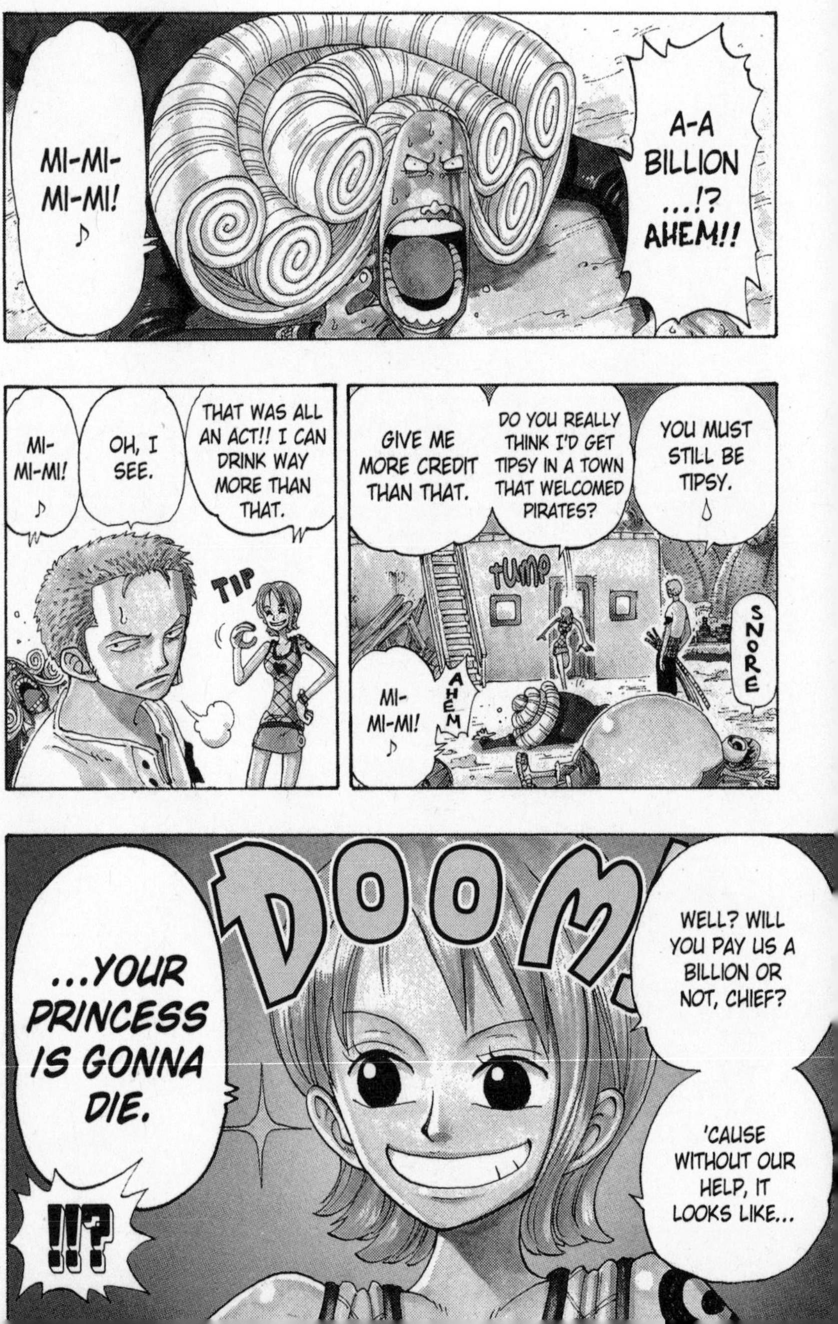
A-A BILLION ...!? AHEM!!
MI-MI-MI-MI! ♪
YOU MUST STILL BE TIPSY.
DO YOU REALLY THINK I'D GET TIPSY IN A TOWN THAT WELCOMED PIRATES?
GIVE ME MORE CREDIT THAN THAT.
TUMP
SNORE
AHEM
MI-MI-MI! ♪
THAT WAS ALL AN ACT!! I CAN DRINK WAY MORE THAN THAT.
OH, I SEE.
MI-MI-MI! ♪
TIP
WELL? WILL YOU PAY US A BILLION OR NOT, CHIEF?
'CAUSE WITHOUT OUR HELP, IT LOOKS LIKE...
DOOM
...YOUR PRINCESS IS GONNA DIE.
!!?

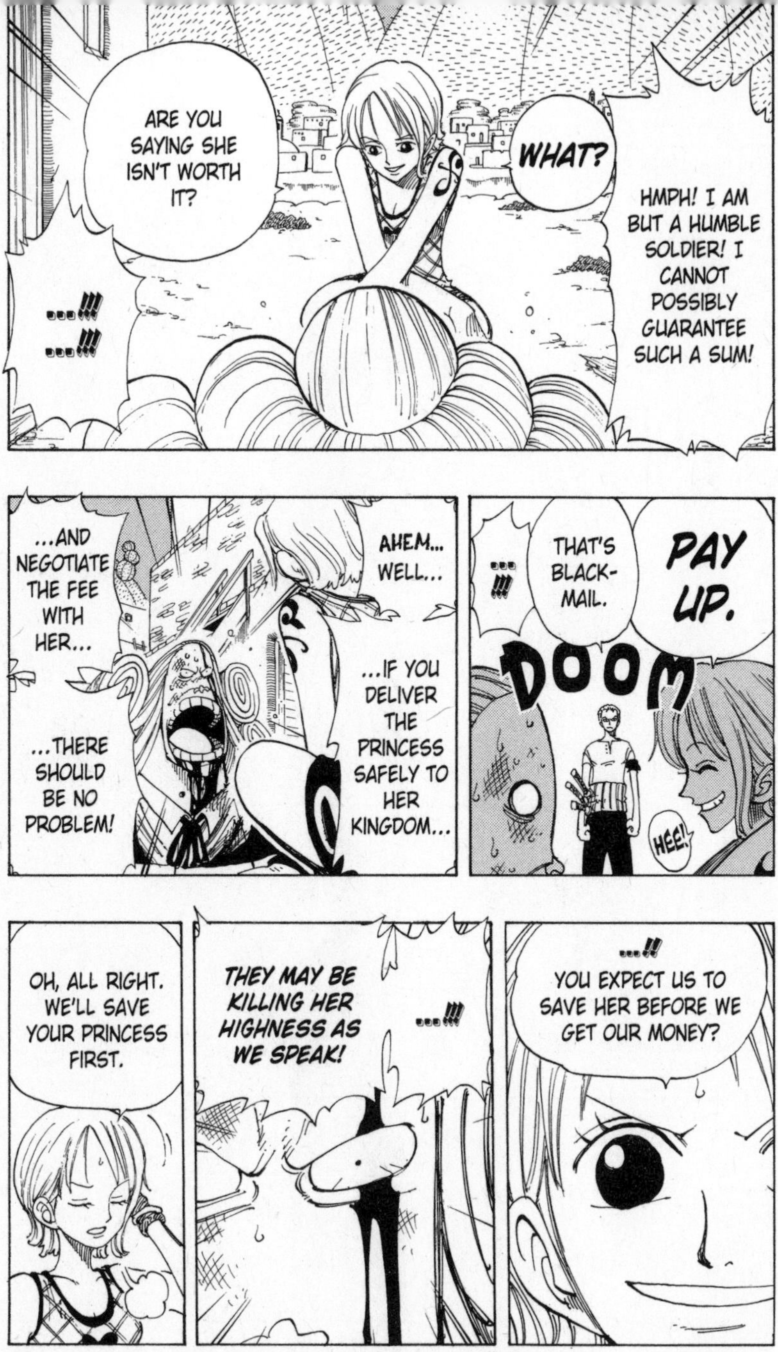
HMPH! I AM BUT A HUMBLE SOLDIER! I CANNOT POSSIBLY GUARANTEE SUCH A SUM!
WHAT?
ARE YOU SAYING SHE ISN'T WORTH IT?
...!!!
...!!!
PAY UP.
THAT'S BLACK-MAIL.
...!!!
DOOM
HEE!
AHEM... WELL...
...IF YOU DELIVER THE PRINCESS SAFELY TO HER KINGDOM...
...AND NEGOTIATE THE FEE WITH HER...
...THERE SHOULD BE NO PROBLEM!
...!!
YOU EXPECT US TO SAVE HER BEFORE WE GET OUR MONEY?
...!!!
THEY MAY BE KILLING HER HIGHNESS AS WE SPEAK!
OH, ALL RIGHT. WE'LL SAVE YOUR PRINCESS FIRST.

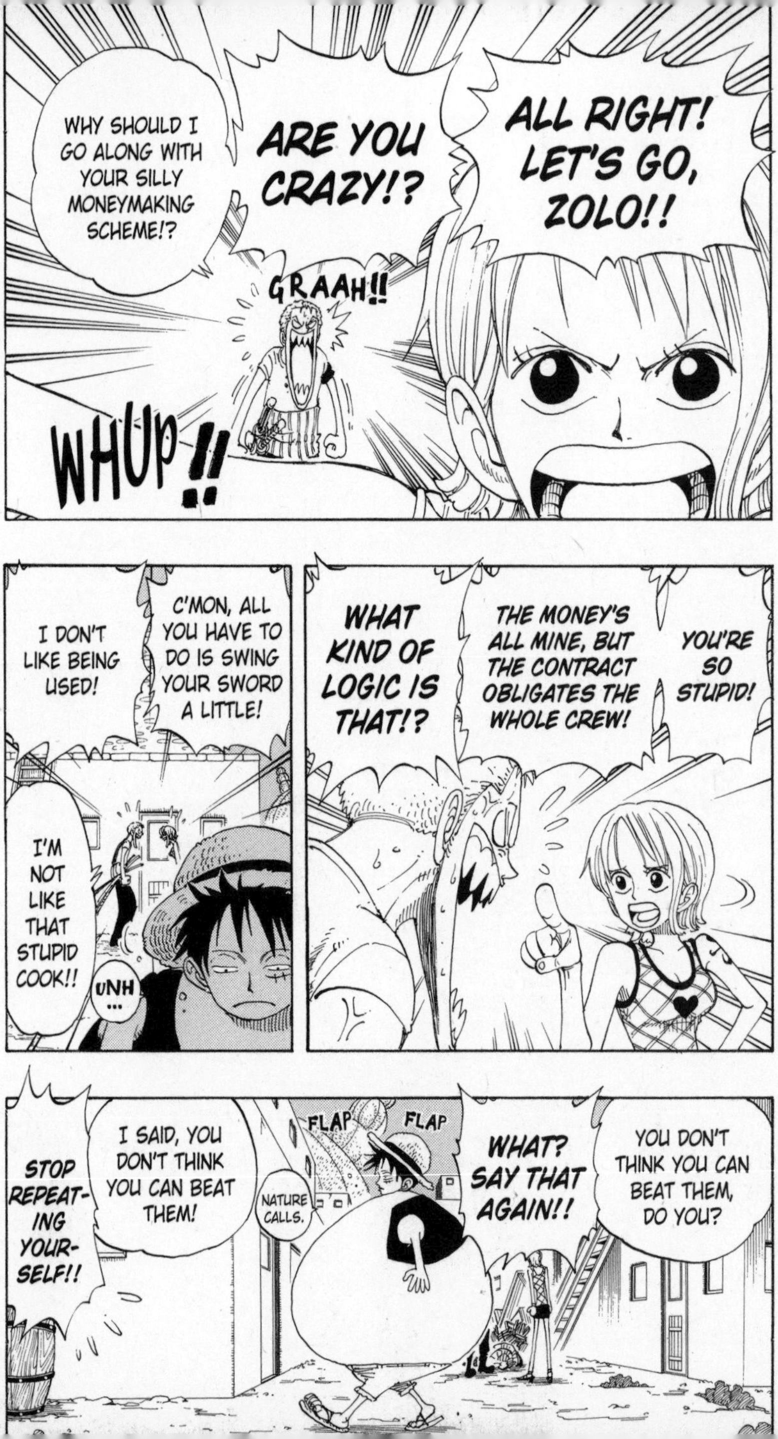
ALL RIGHT! LET'S GO, ZOLO!!
ARE YOU CRAZY!?
GRAAH!!
WHY SHOULD I GO ALONG WITH YOUR SILLY MONEYMAKING SCHEME!?
WHUP!!
YOU'RE SO STUPID!
THE MONEY'S ALL MINE, BUT THE CONTRACT OBLIGATES THE WHOLE CREW!
WHAT KIND OF LOGIC IS THAT!?
C'MON, ALL YOU HAVE TO DO IS SWING YOUR SWORD A LITTLE!
I DON'T LIKE BEING USED!
I'M NOT LIKE THAT STUPID COOK!!
UNH...
YOU DON'T THINK YOU CAN BEAT THEM, DO YOU?
WHAT? SAY THAT AGAIN!!
FLAP FLAP
NATURE CALLS.
I SAID, YOU DON'T THINK YOU CAN BEAT THEM!
STOP REPEATING YOURSELF!!

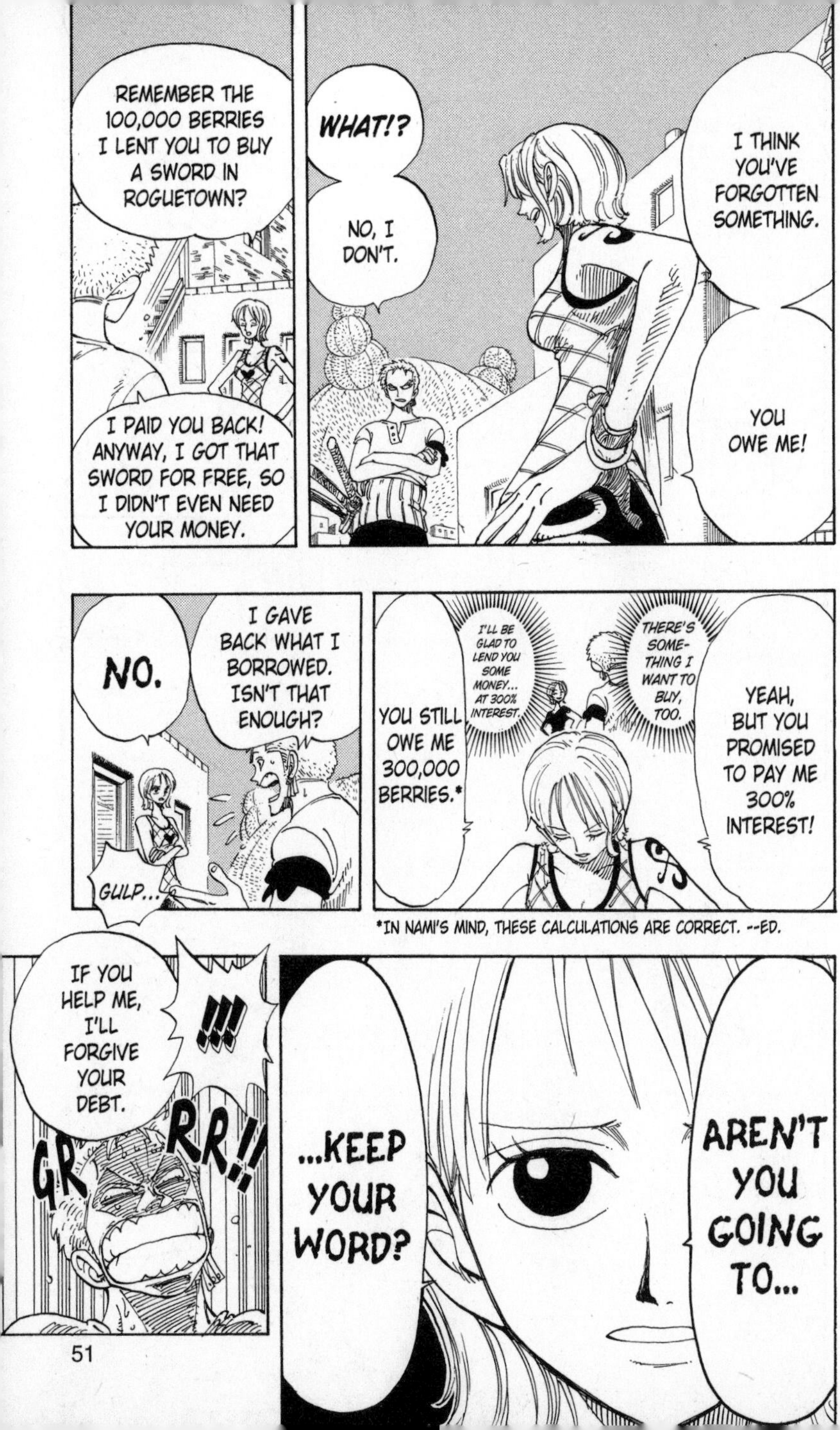
I THINK YOU'VE FORGOTTEN SOMETHING.
YOU OWE ME!
WHAT!?
NO, I DON'T.
REMEMBER THE 100,000 BERRIES I LENT YOU TO BUY A SWORD IN ROGUETOWN?
I PAID YOU BACK! ANYWAY, I GOT THAT SWORD FOR FREE, SO I DIDN'T EVEN NEED YOUR MONEY.
YEAH, BUT YOU PROMISED TO PAY ME 300% INTEREST!
THERE'S SOME-THING I WANT TO BUY, TOO.
I'LL BE GLAD TO LEND YOU SOME MONEY... AT 300% INTEREST.
YOU STILL OWE ME 300,000 BERRIES.*
I GAVE BACK WHAT I BORROWED. ISN'T THAT ENOUGH?
NO.
GULP...
*IN NAMI'S MIND, THESE CALCULATIONS ARE CORRECT. --ED.
AREN'T YOU GOING TO...
...KEEP YOUR WORD?
IF YOU HELP ME, I'LL FORGIVE YOUR DEBT.
!!!
GRRR!!

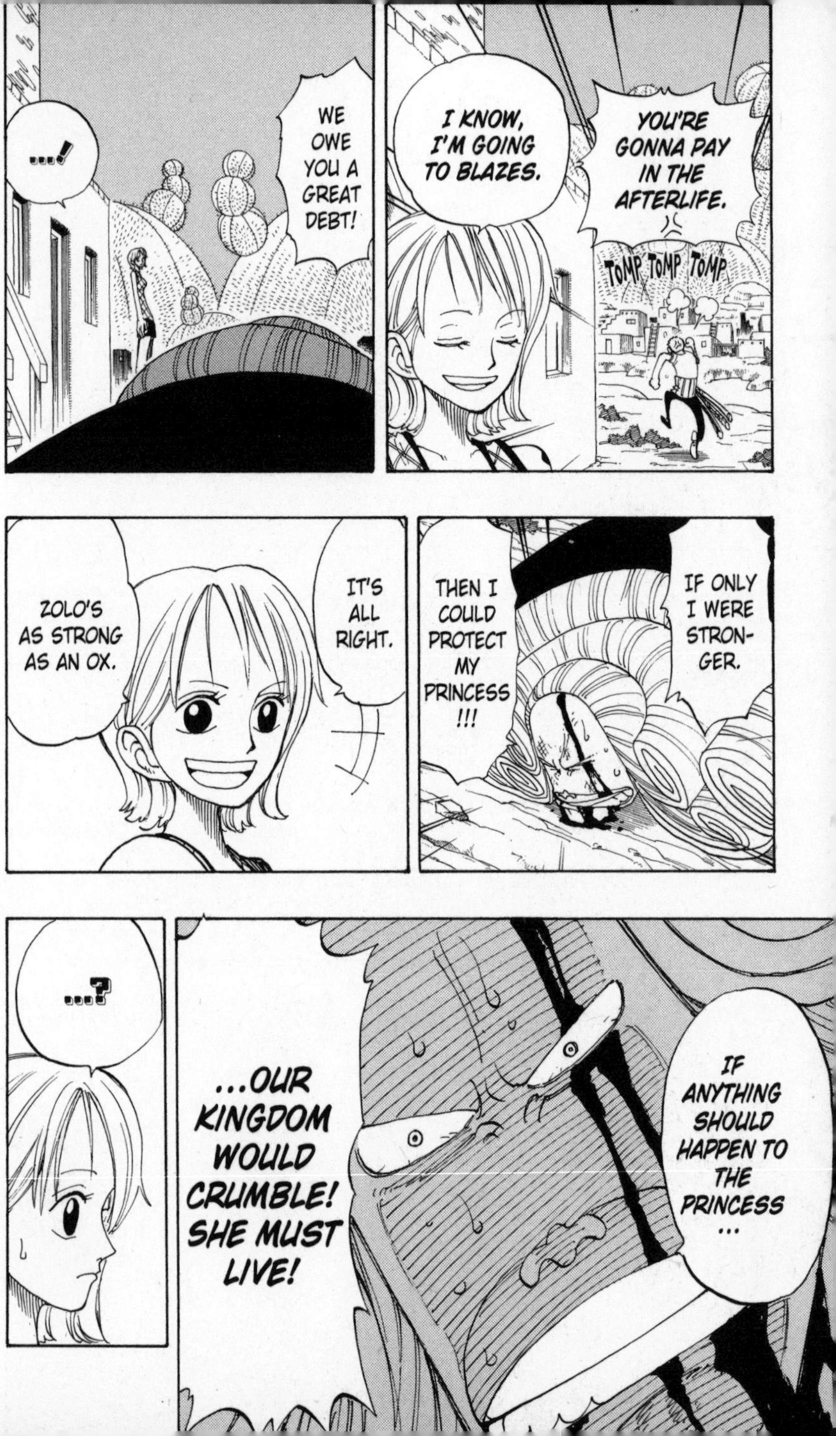
YOU'RE GONNA PAY IN THE AFTERLIFE.
TOMP TOMP TOMP
I KNOW, I'M GOING TO BLAZES.
WE OWE YOU A GREAT DEBT!
...!
IF ONLY I WERE STRON-GER.
THEN I COULD PROTECT MY PRINCESS !!!
IT'S ALL RIGHT.
ZOLO'S AS STRONG AS AN OX.
IF ANYTHING SHOULD HAPPEN TO THE PRINCESS ...
...OUR KINGDOM WOULD CRUMBLE! SHE MUST LIVE!
...?

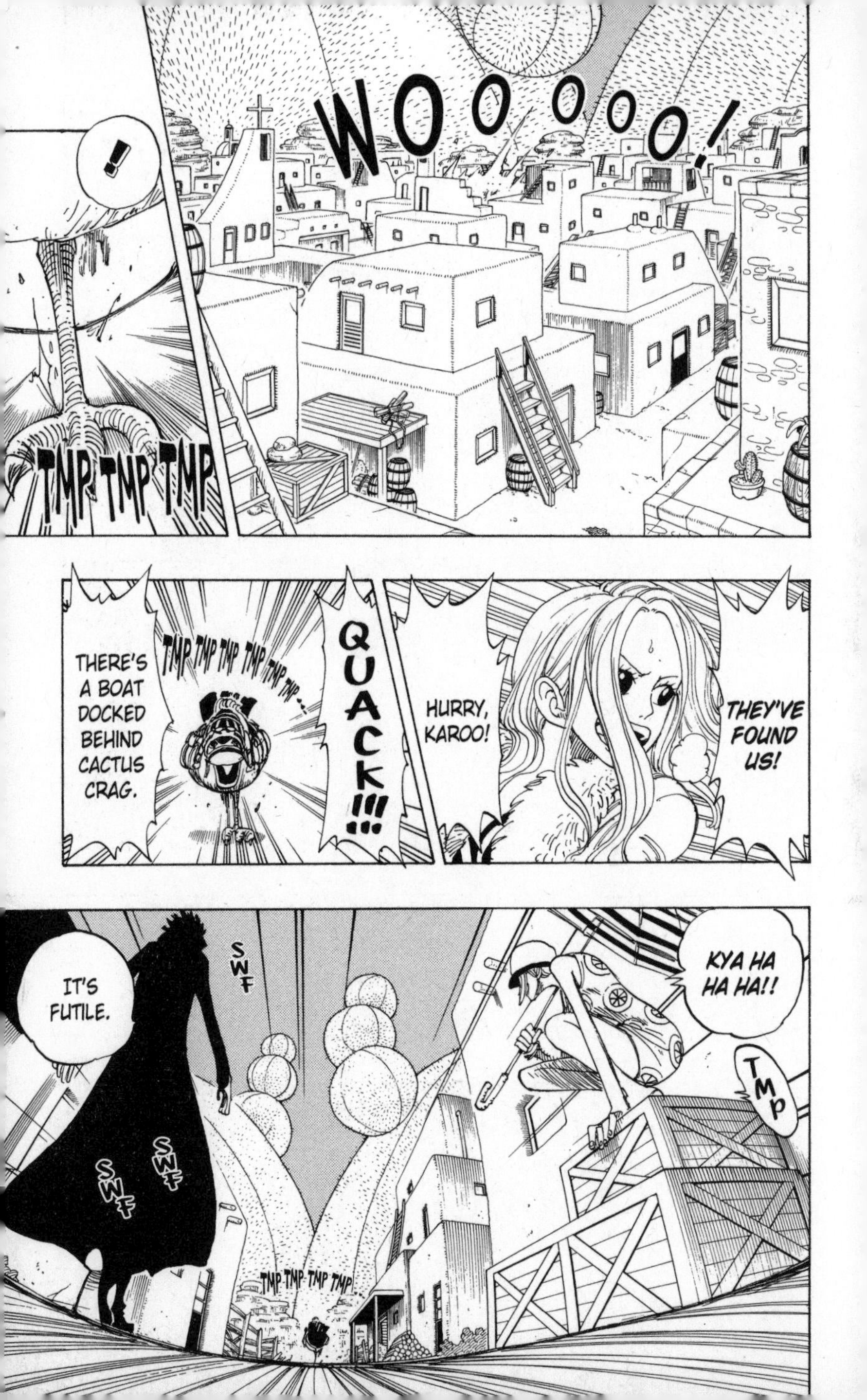
WOOOOO!
!
TMP TMP TMP
THEY'VE FOUND US!
HURRY, KAROO!
QUACK!!!
TMP TMP TMP TMP TMP TMP...
THERE'S A BOAT DOCKED BEHIND CACTUS CRAG.
KYA HA HA HA!!
TMP
SWF
IT'S FUTILE.
SWF
SWF
TMP TMP TMP TMP

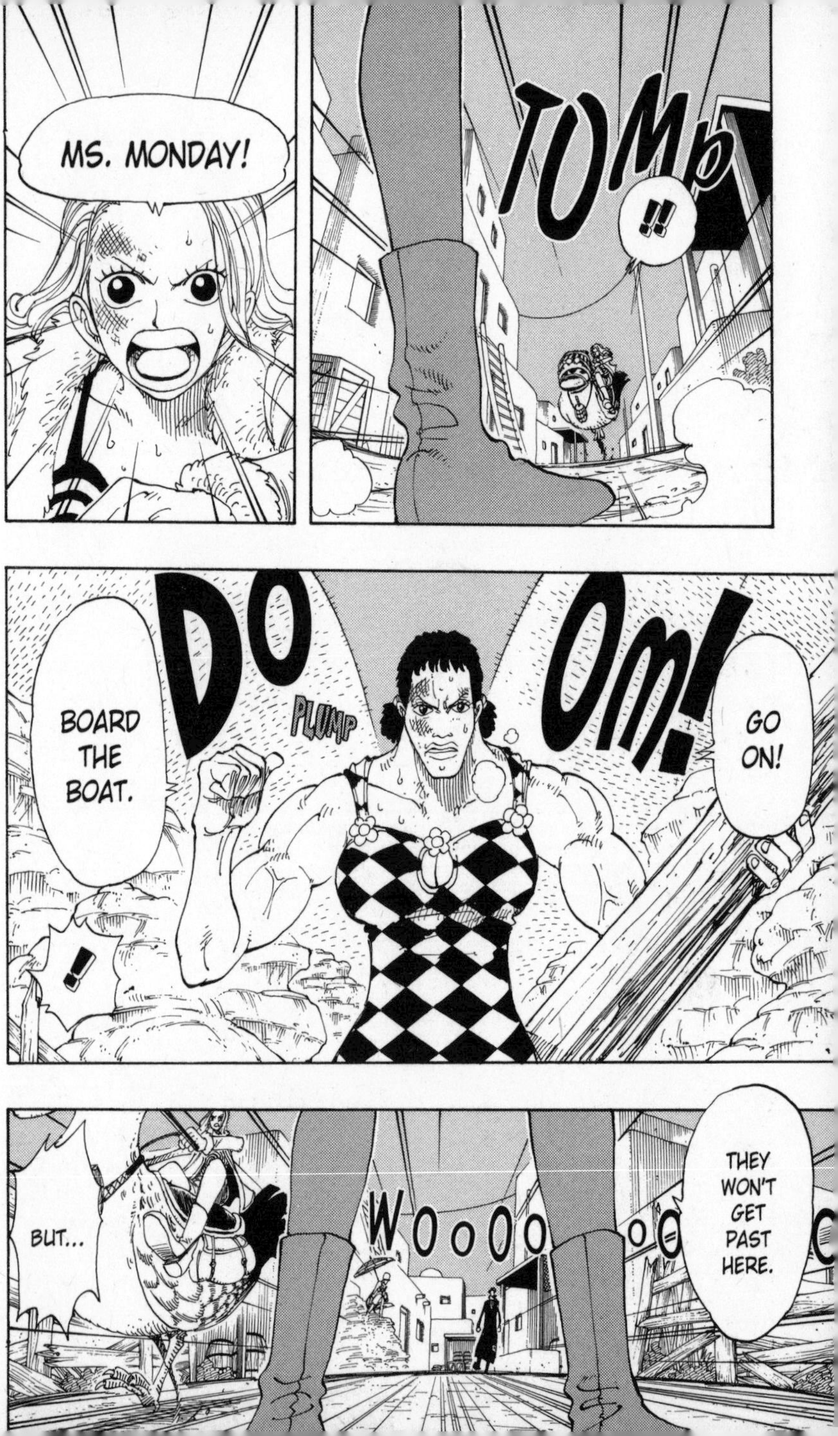
TOMP
!!
MS. MONDAY!
GO ON!
OM!
DO
PLUMP
BOARD THE BOAT.
!
THEY WON'T GET PAST HERE.
WOOOOOOOO
BUT...

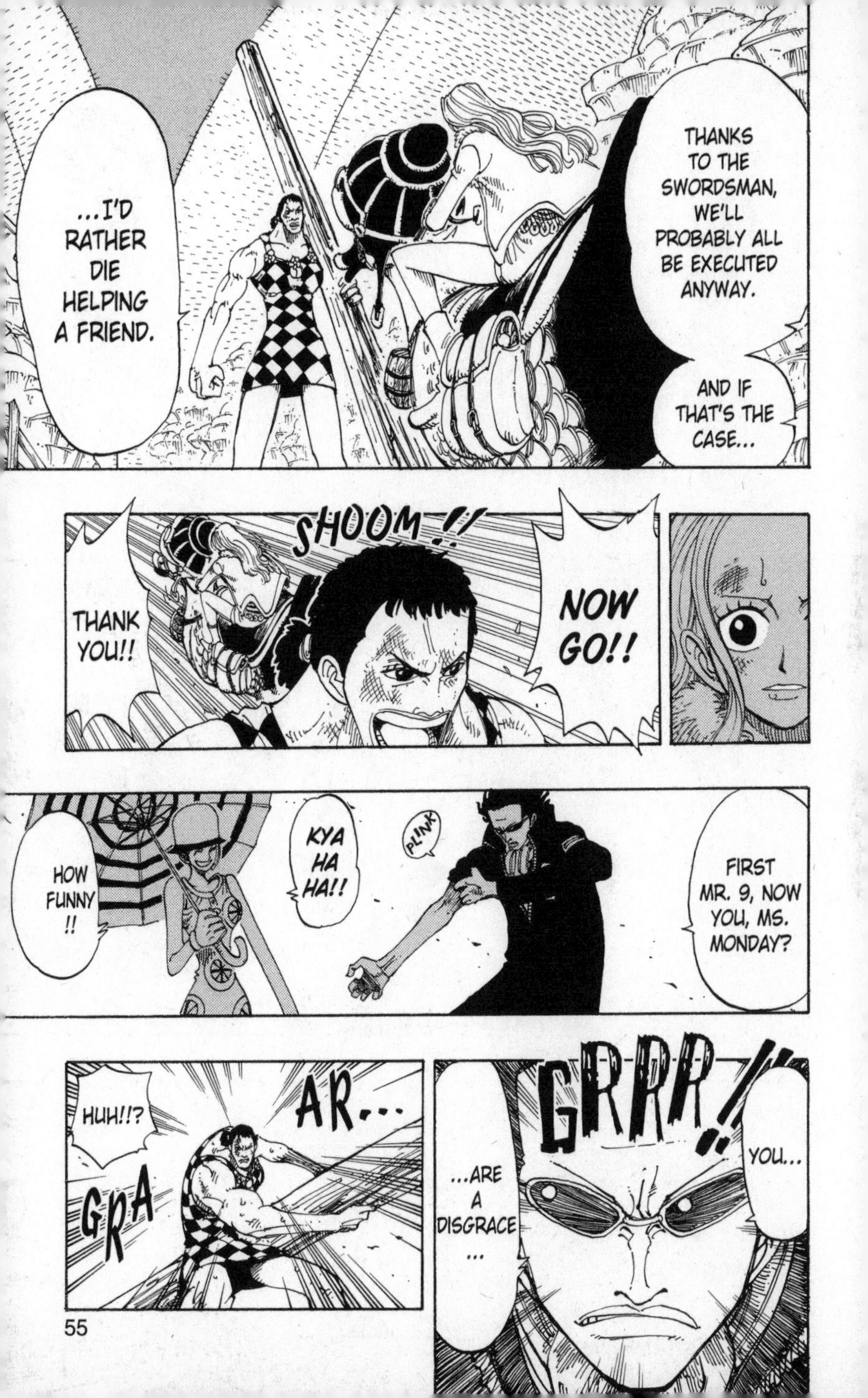
THANKS TO THE SWORDSMAN, WE'LL PROBABLY ALL BE EXECUTED ANYWAY.
AND IF THAT'S THE CASE...
...I'D RATHER DIE HELPING A FRIEND.
NOW GO!!
SHOOM!!
THANK YOU!!
FIRST MR. 9, NOW YOU, MS. MONDAY?
PLINK
KYA HA HA!!
HOW FUNNY!!
GRRR!!
YOU...
...ARE A DISGRACE...
AR...
HUH!!?
GRA

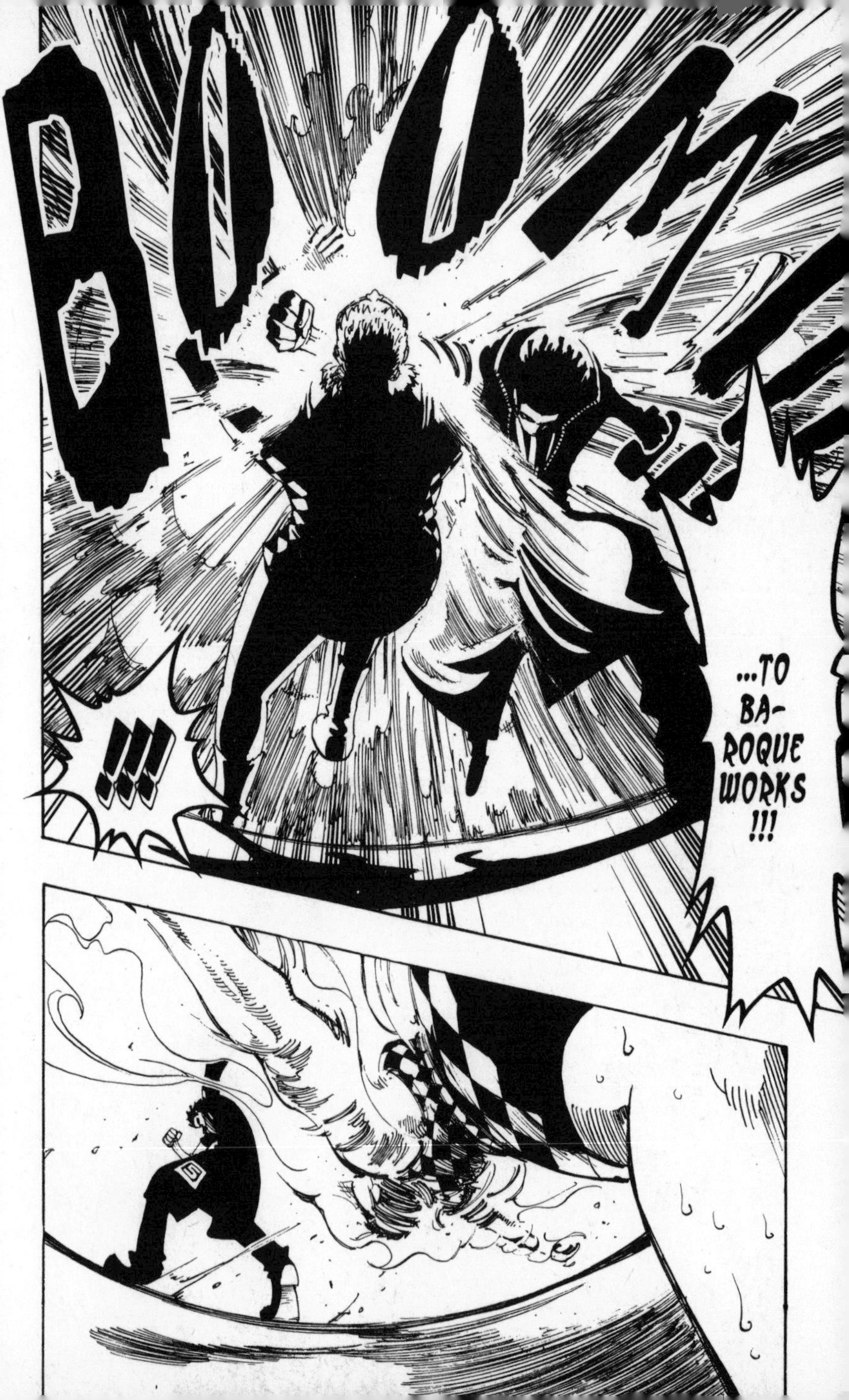
BOOM!!!
...TO BAROQUE WORKS!!!

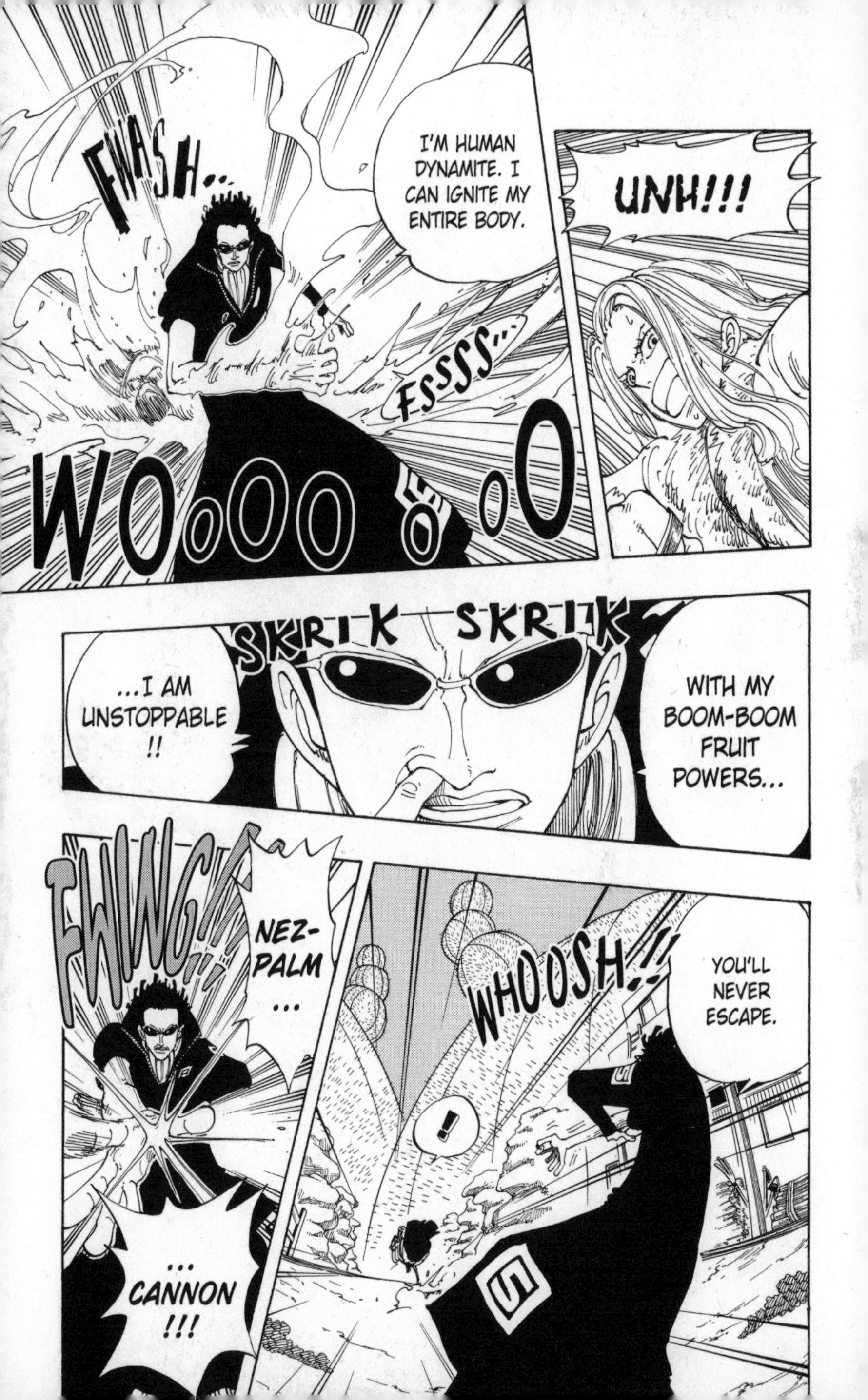
UNH!!!
I'M HUMAN DYNAMITE. I CAN IGNITE MY ENTIRE BODY.
FWASH..
FSSSS..
WOOOOOO
WITH MY BOOM-BOOM FRUIT POWERS...
SKRIK SKRIK
...I AM UNSTOPPABLE !!
YOU'LL NEVER ESCAPE.
WHOOSH..!!
!
FWING!!
NEZ-PALM ...
... CANNON !!!

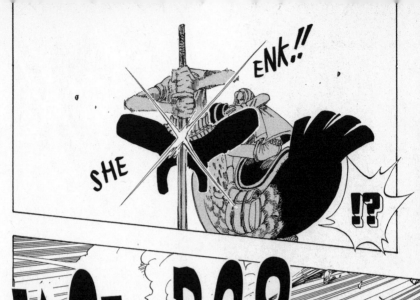

ENK!!

SHE

!?

KA-BOO

HAH!

WHO IS THAT GUY?

RRMM BB.

HEY! THE ROAD!

MR. BUSHIDO!

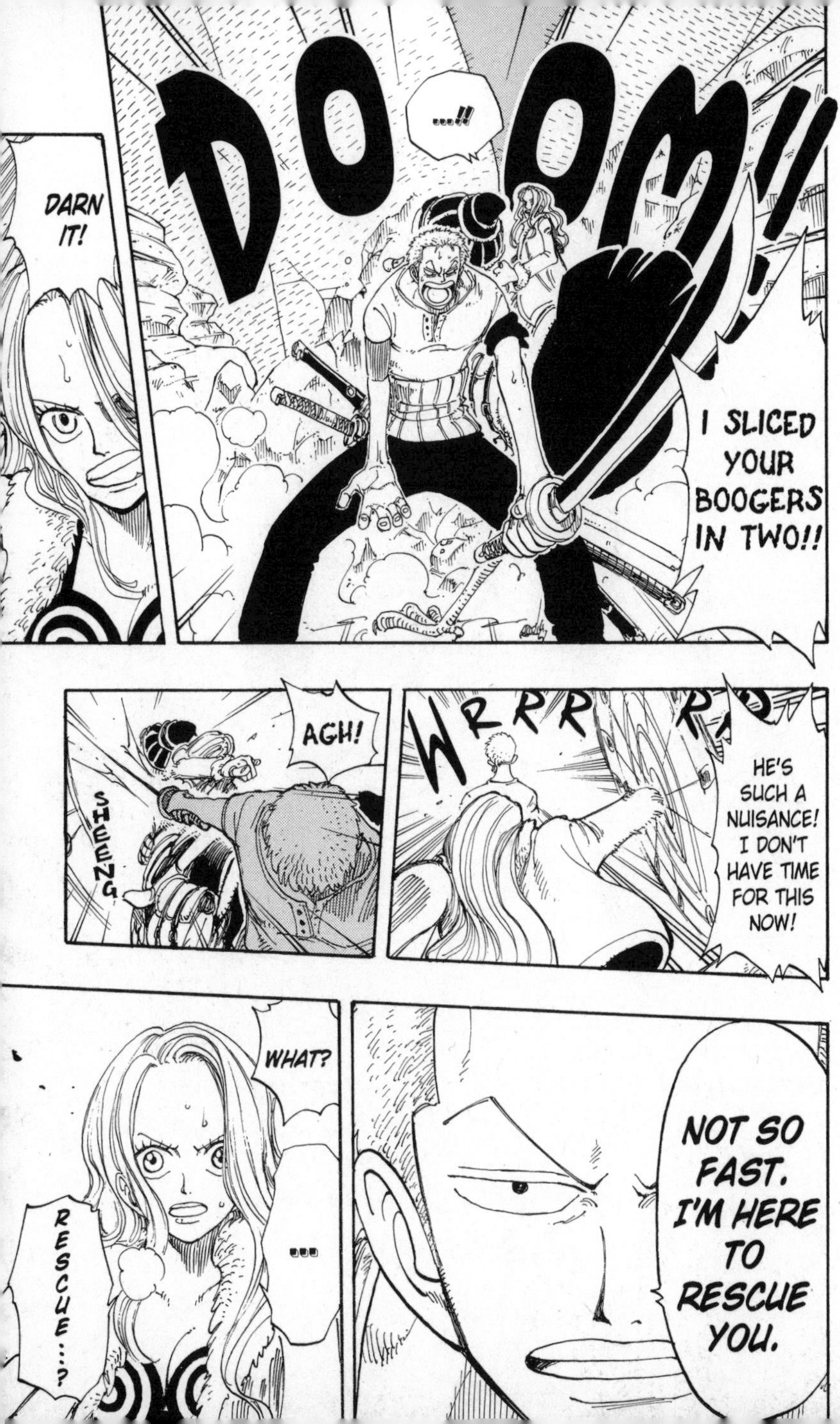
...!!
DOOM!!
I SLICED YOUR BOOGERS IN TWO!!
DARN IT!
WRRR
HE'S SUCH A NUISANCE! I DON'T HAVE TIME FOR THIS NOW!
AGH!
SHEENG
NOT SO FAST. I'M HERE TO RESCUE YOU.
WHAT?
...
RESCUE...?

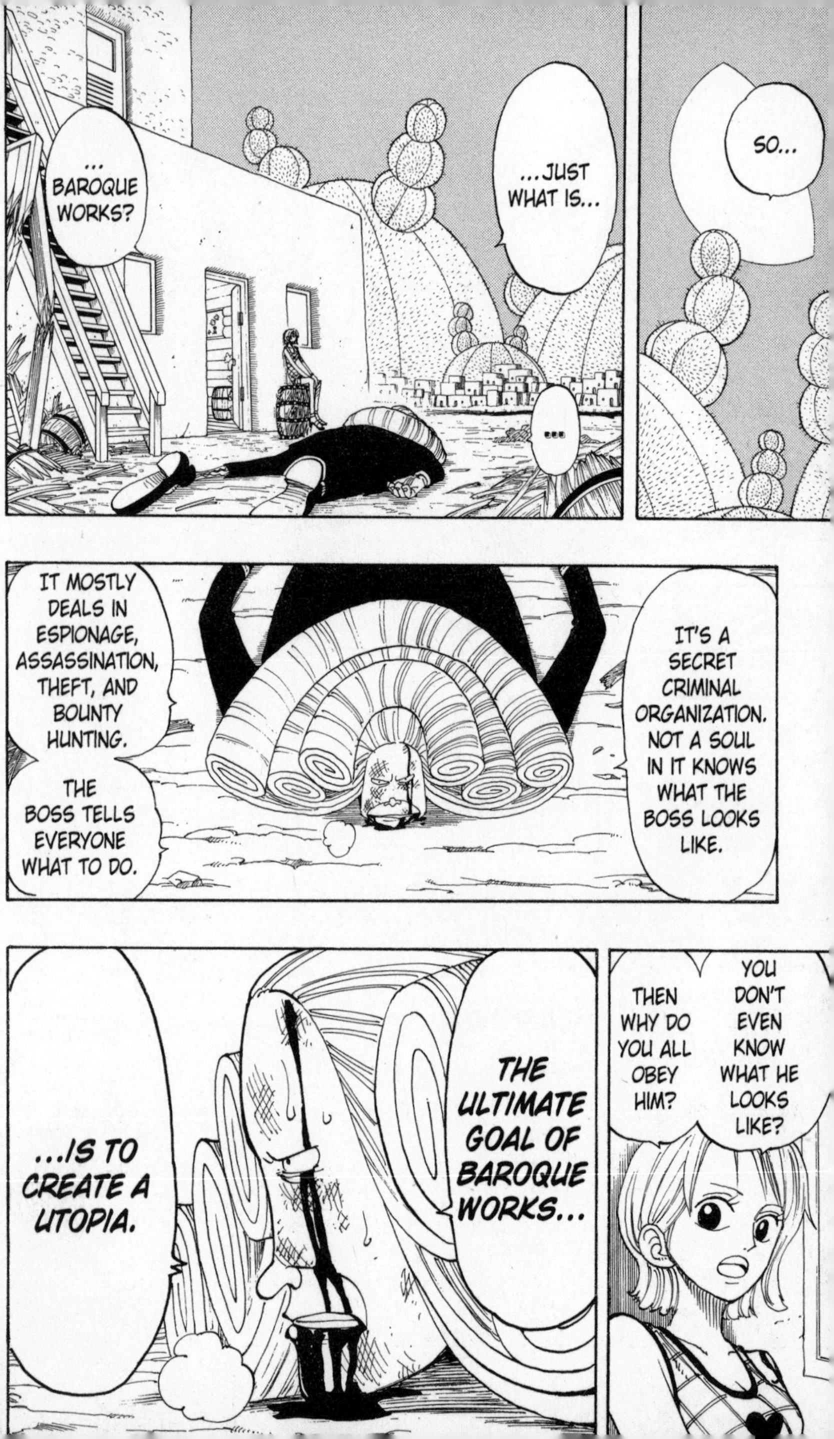
SO...
...JUST WHAT IS...
... BAROQUE WORKS?
...
IT'S A SECRET CRIMINAL ORGANIZATION. NOT A SOUL IN IT KNOWS WHAT THE BOSS LOOKS LIKE.
IT MOSTLY DEALS IN ESPIONAGE, ASSASSINATION, THEFT, AND BOUNTY HUNTING.
THE BOSS TELLS EVERYONE WHAT TO DO.
YOU DON'T EVEN KNOW WHAT HE LOOKS LIKE?
THEN WHY DO YOU ALL OBEY HIM?
THE ULTIMATE GOAL OF BAROQUE WORKS...
...IS TO CREATE A UTOPIA.

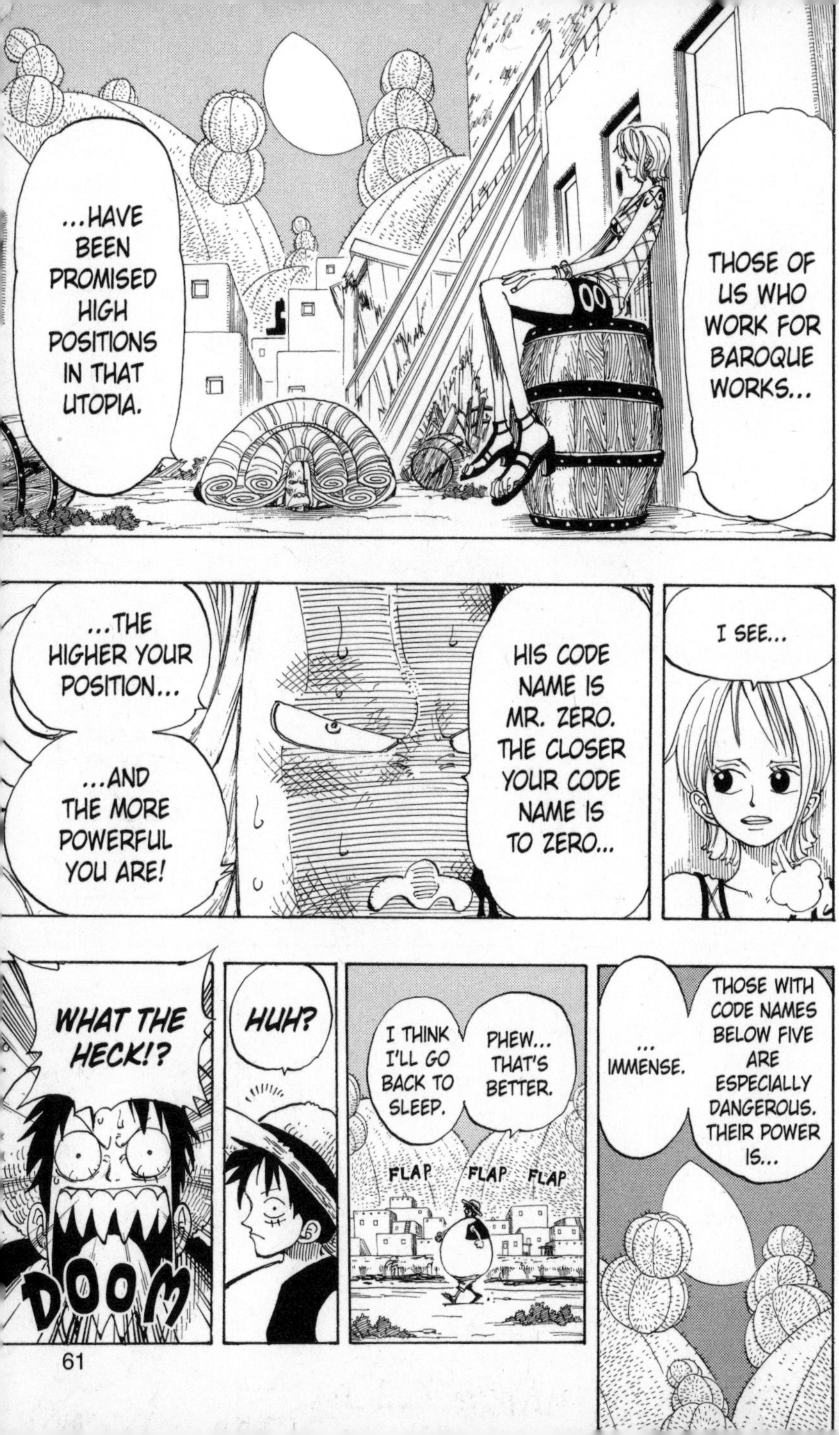
THOSE OF US WHO WORK FOR BAROQUE WORKS...
...HAVE BEEN PROMISED HIGH POSITIONS IN THAT UTOPIA.
I SEE...
HIS CODE NAME IS MR. ZERO. THE CLOSER YOUR CODE NAME IS TO ZERO...
...THE HIGHER YOUR POSITION...
...AND THE MORE POWERFUL YOU ARE!
THOSE WITH CODE NAMES BELOW FIVE ARE ESPECIALLY DANGEROUS. THEIR POWER IS...
...IMMENSE.
PHEW... THAT'S BETTER.
I THINK I'LL GO BACK TO SLEEP.
FLAP FLAP FLAP
HUH?
WHAT THE HECK!?
DOOM

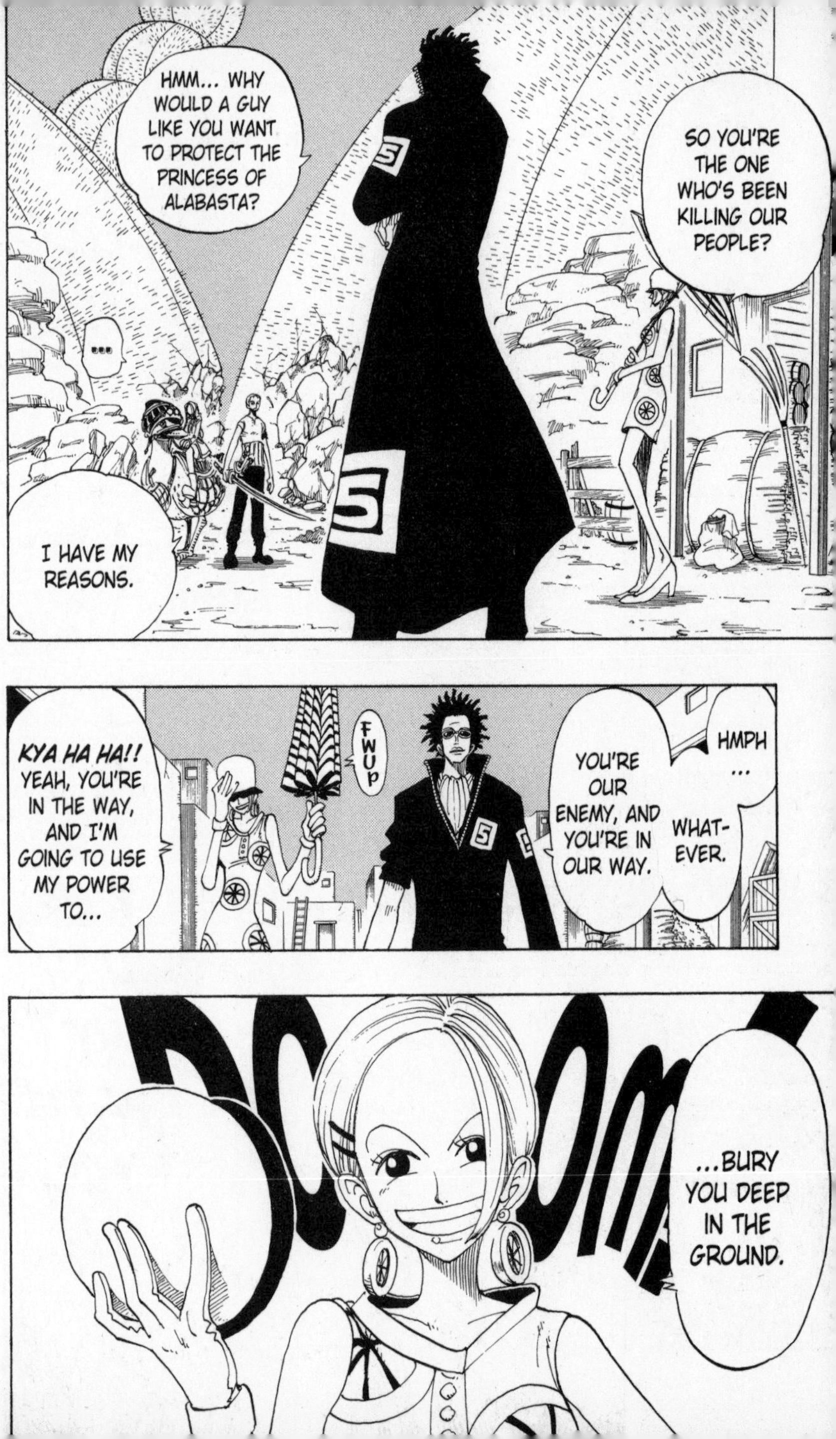
SO YOU'RE THE ONE WHO'S BEEN KILLING OUR PEOPLE?
HMM... WHY WOULD A GUY LIKE YOU WANT TO PROTECT THE PRINCESS OF ALABASTA?
...
I HAVE MY REASONS.
HMPH... WHAT-EVER.
YOU'RE OUR ENEMY, AND YOU'RE IN OUR WAY.
FWUP
KYA HA HA!! YEAH, YOU'RE IN THE WAY, AND I'M GOING TO USE MY POWER TO...
...BURY YOU DEEP IN THE GROUND.

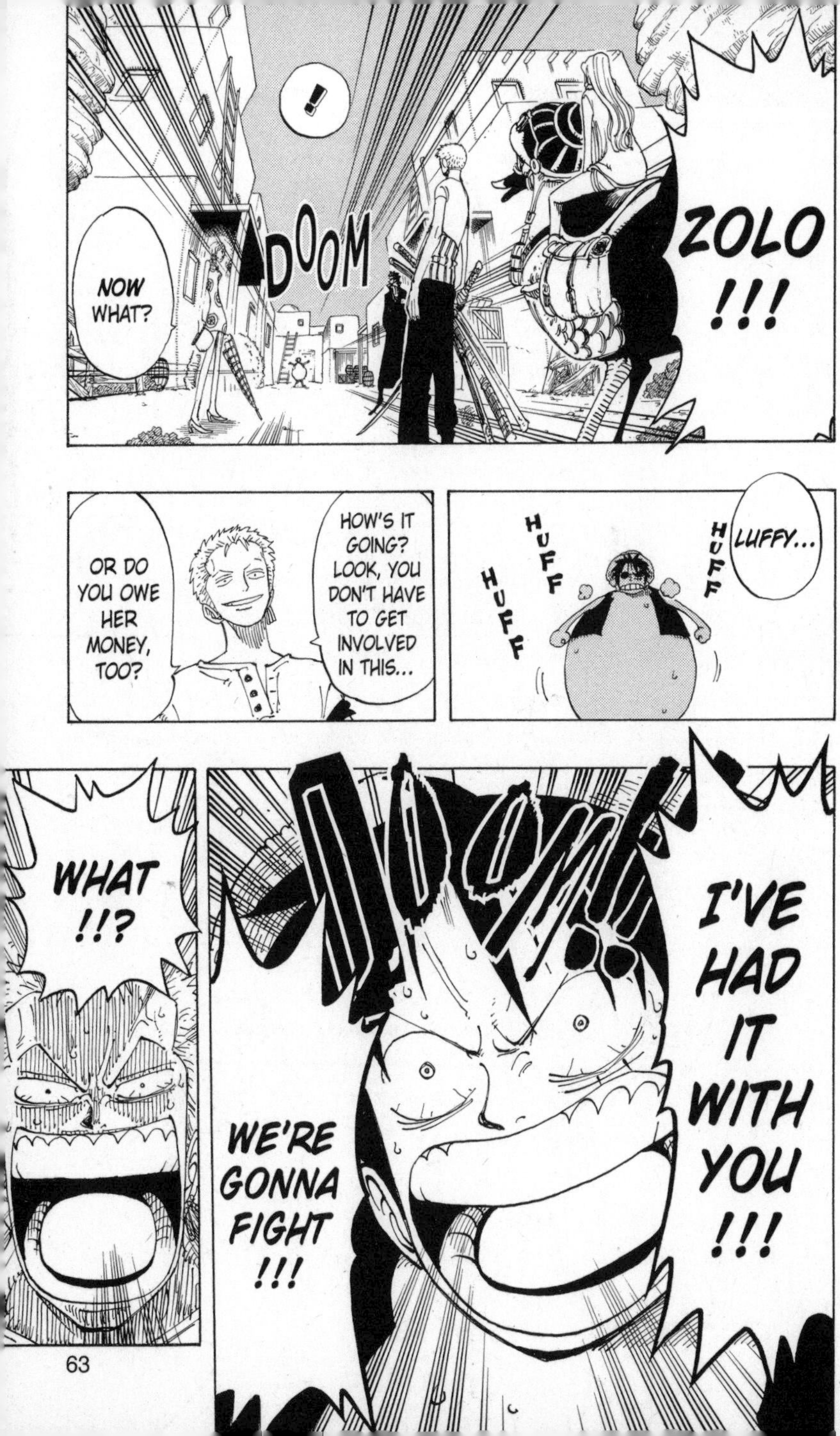
ZOLO !!!
!
DOOM
NOW WHAT?
LUFFY...
HUFF HUFF
HUFF
HUFF
HOW'S IT GOING? LOOK, YOU DON'T HAVE TO GET INVOLVED IN THIS...
OR DO YOU OWE HER MONEY, TOO?
DOOM
I'VE HAD IT WITH YOU !!!
WE'RE GONNA FIGHT !!!
WHAT !!?

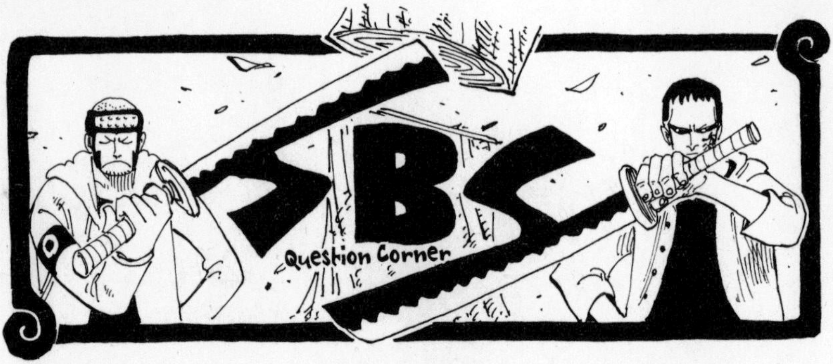
SBS
Question Corner

Q: I heard that someone suggested you for the voice of Panda Man. All opposed, please raise your hand and tell us why you're against it. --Class President

A: Oh, that sounds nice! Me, the voice of Panda Man? Sounds good. All right, let's ask Toei Animation about it. Hey, but Panda Man doesn't say anything.

Q: Question: In SBS, "S" stands for *shitsumon* (questions), "B" for *boshu* (solicit), and "S" for *suru* (for). Oh! I forgot my question. *Ah ha ha ha ha ha! Cackle! Cackle! Ha ha ha ha ha! Wa ha ha ha ha ha…*

A: That laugh! Is that Arlong!?

Q:

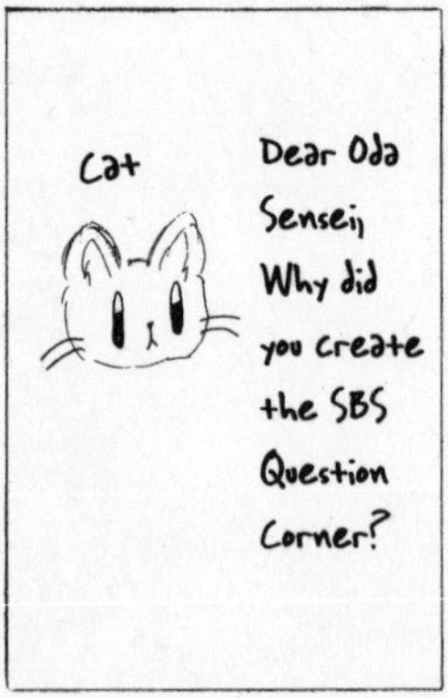
Cat
Dear Oda Sensei,
Why did you create the SBS Question Corner?

A: "Cat"? "Cat"?
Why did I create it? Hmm... Lots of manga used to have sections like this. As a reader, I always liked them, so when I became a manga artist, I decided to include a question and answer column. That's why I created it.
But "Cat," huh...?

Q: Is Hatchan a champion *takoyaki* eater? (Takoyaki are octopus fritters.)

A: "Cat," huh...? Oh...what? A tako...?

Chapter 112:

LUFFY VS. ZOLO

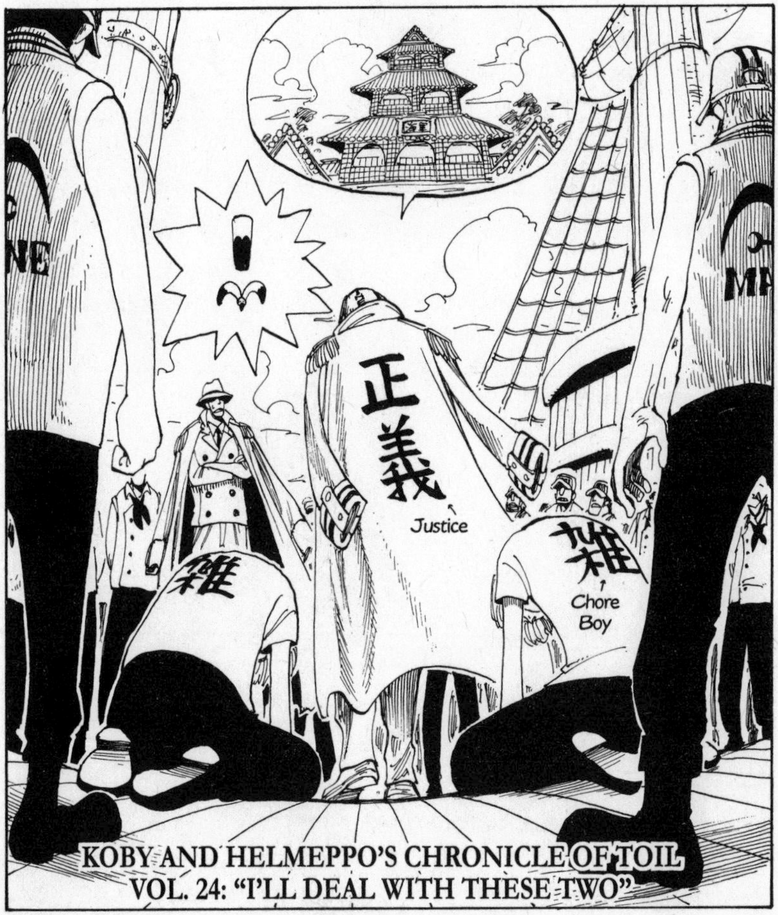
!
正義
Justice
雑
雑
Chore Boy
KOBY AND HELMEPPO'S CHRONICLE OF TOIL
VOL. 24: "I'LL DEAL WITH THESE TWO"

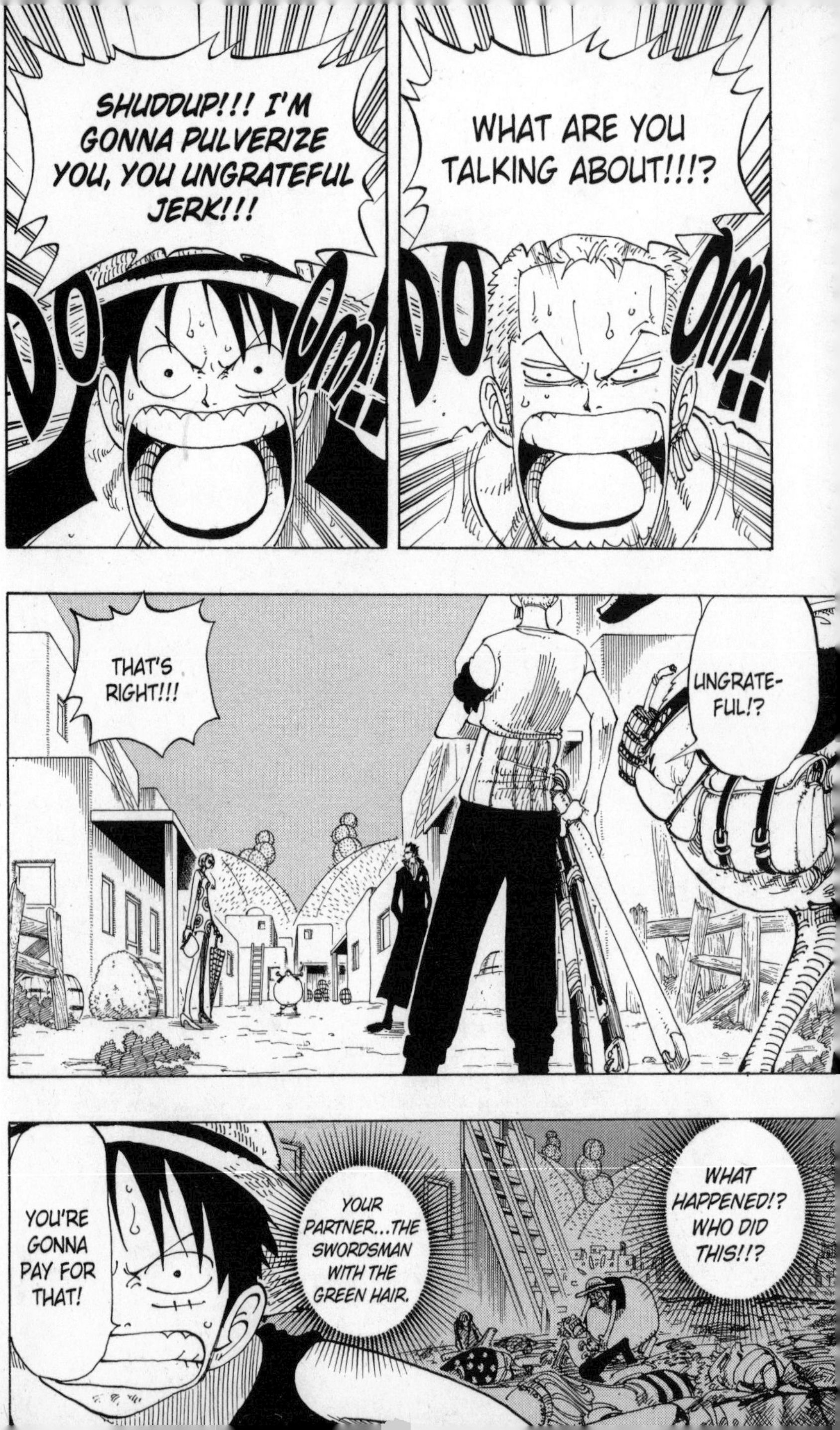
WHAT ARE YOU TALKING ABOUT!!!?
DOOM!!
SHUDDUP!!! I'M GONNA PULVERIZE YOU, YOU UNGRATEFUL JERK!!!
DOOM!!
UNGRATE-FUL!?
THAT'S RIGHT!!!
WHAT HAPPENED!? WHO DID THIS!!?
YOUR PARTNER...THE SWORDSMAN WITH THE GREEN HAIR.
YOU'RE GONNA PAY FOR THAT!

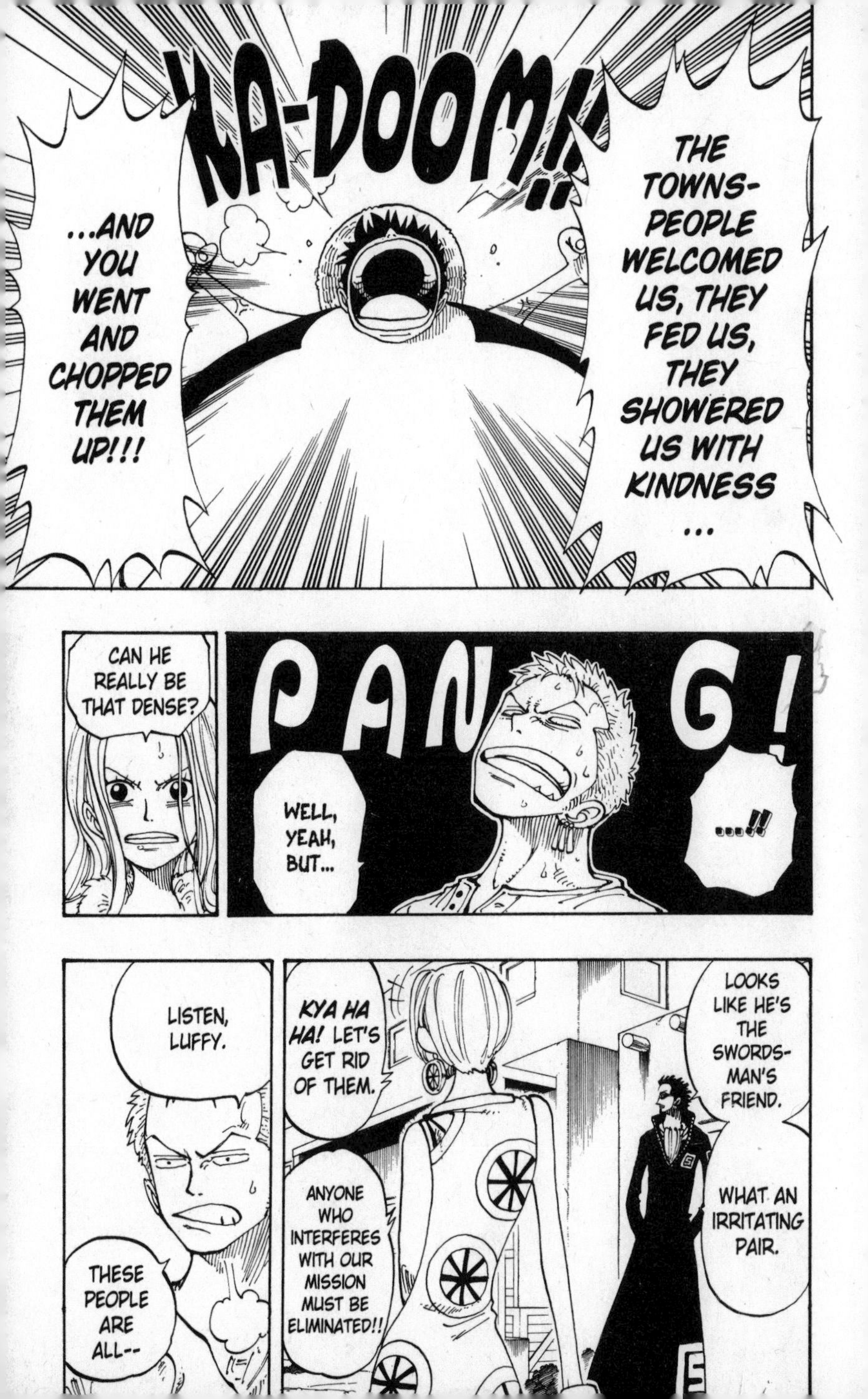
THE TOWNSPEOPLE WELCOMED US, THEY FED US, THEY SHOWERED US WITH KINDNESS ...
KA-DOOM!!
...AND YOU WENT AND CHOPPED THEM UP!!!
PANG!
...!!
WELL, YEAH, BUT...
CAN HE REALLY BE THAT DENSE?
LOOKS LIKE HE'S THE SWORDSMAN'S FRIEND.
KYA HA HA! LET'S GET RID OF THEM.
WHAT AN IRRITATING PAIR.
ANYONE WHO INTERFERES WITH OUR MISSION MUST BE ELIMINATED!!
LISTEN, LUFFY.
THESE PEOPLE ARE ALL--

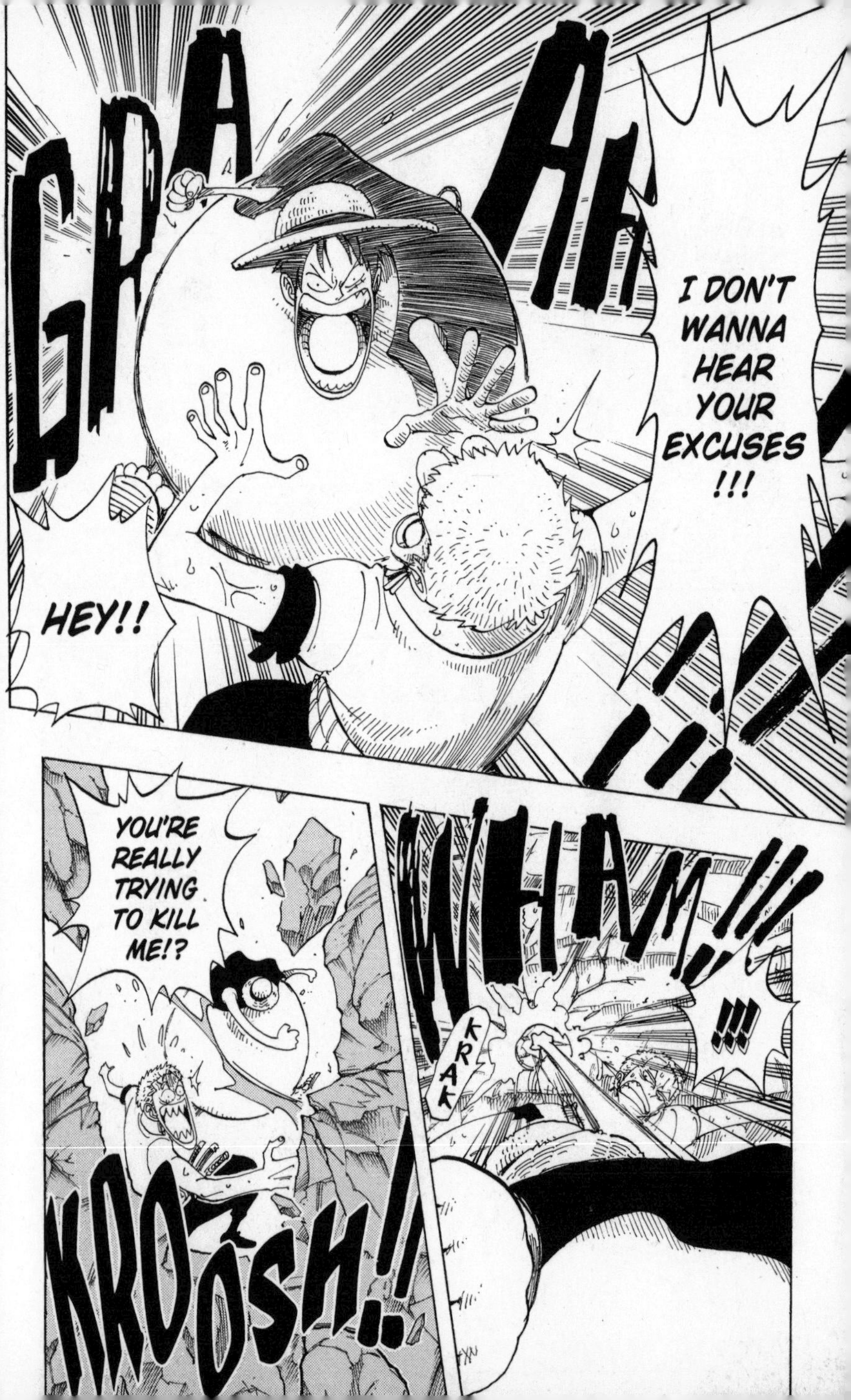

I DON'T WANNA HEAR YOUR EXCUSES !!!
GRAAAH!!!
HEY!!
WHAM!!!
KRAK
YOU'RE REALLY TRYING TO KILL ME!?
KROOSH!!

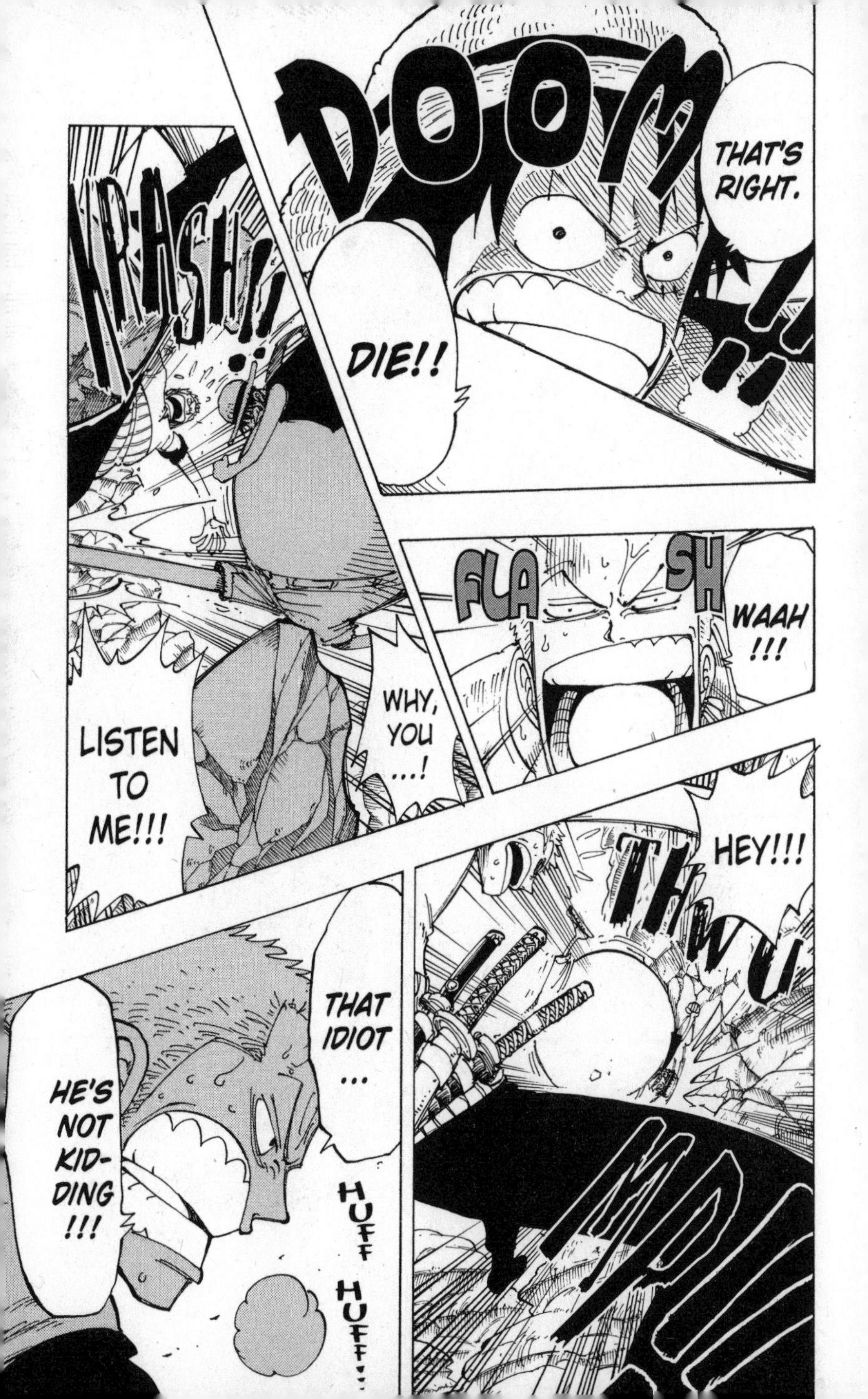
D-O-O-M!!
THAT'S RIGHT.
DIE!!
KRASH!!
WHY, YOU ...!
LISTEN TO ME!!!
FLA SH
WAAH !!!
HEY!!!
THAT IDIOT ...
HE'S NOT KID-DING !!!
HUFF HUFF...

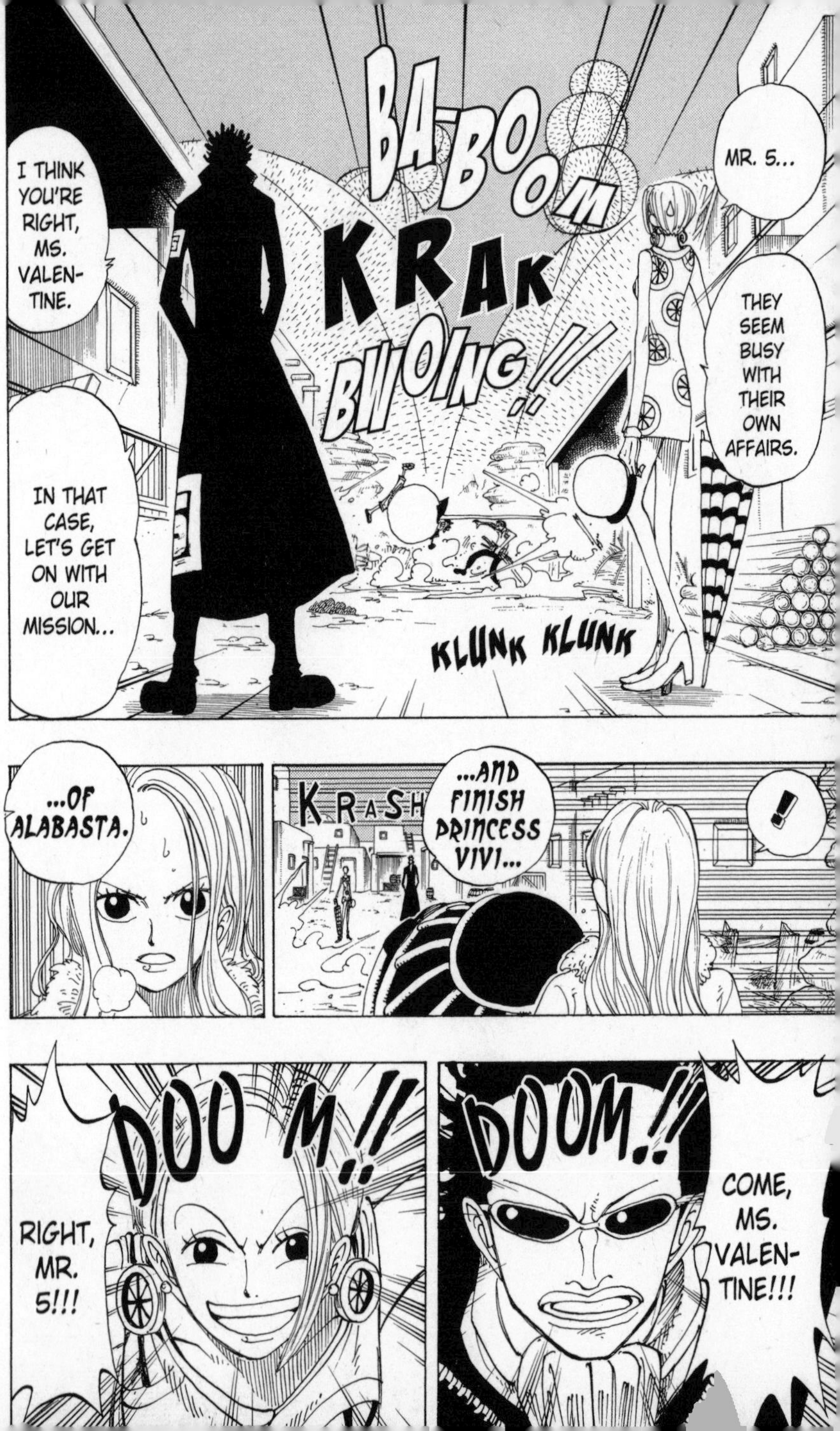
MR. 5...
THEY SEEM BUSY WITH THEIR OWN AFFAIRS.
BA-BOOM
KRAK
BWOING!!
I THINK YOU'RE RIGHT, MS. VALEN-TINE.
IN THAT CASE, LET'S GET ON WITH OUR MISSION...
KLUNK KLUNK
!
...AND FINISH PRINCESS VIVI...
KRASH
...OF ALABASTA.
DOOM!!
COME, MS. VALEN-TINE!!!
DOO M!!
RIGHT, MR. 5!!!

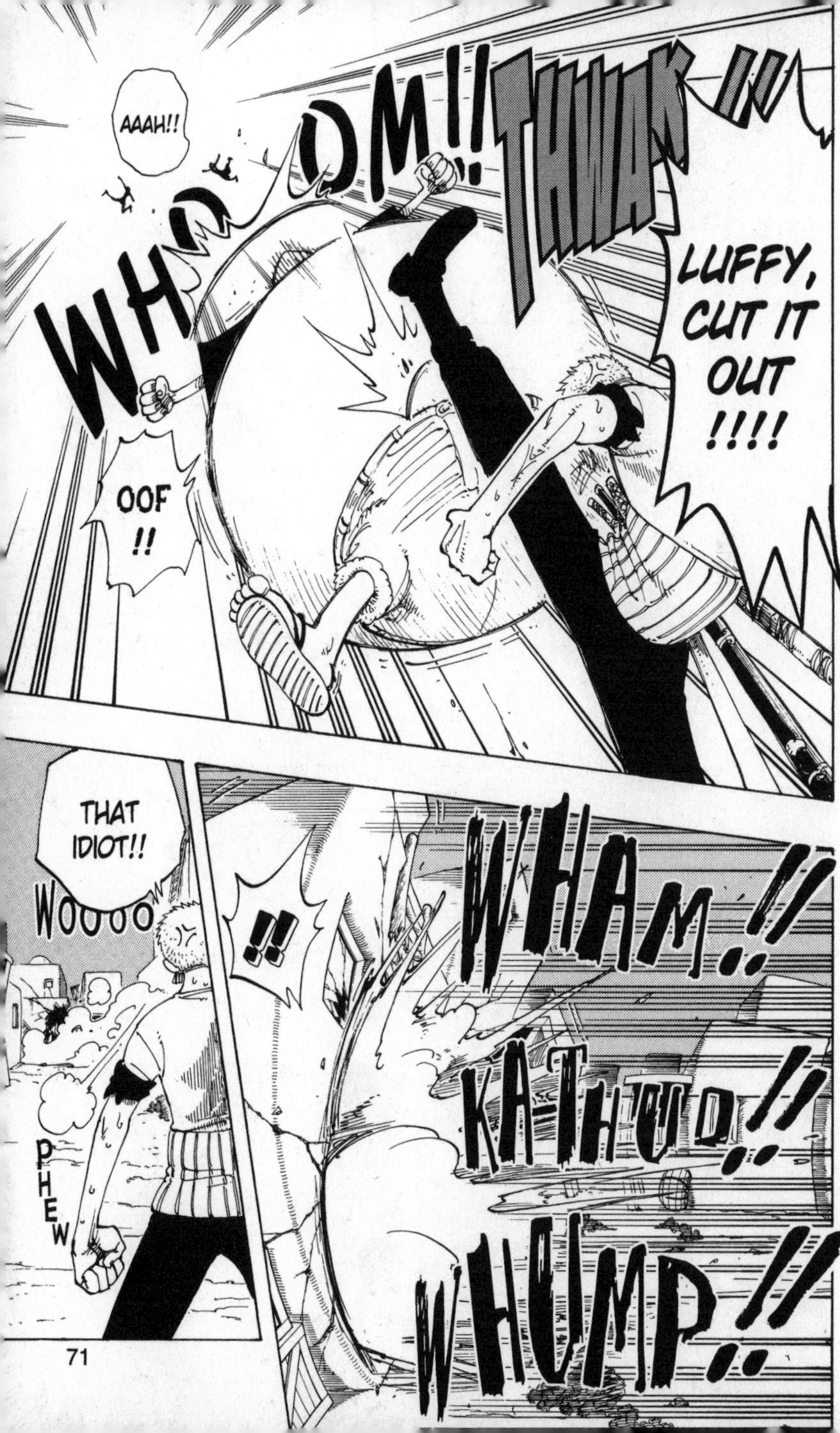
THWAK !!
LUFFY, CUT IT OUT !!!!
AAAH!!
OOF !!
WHAM!!
KATHUD!!
WHUMP!!
!!
THAT IDIOT!!
WOOOO
PHEW

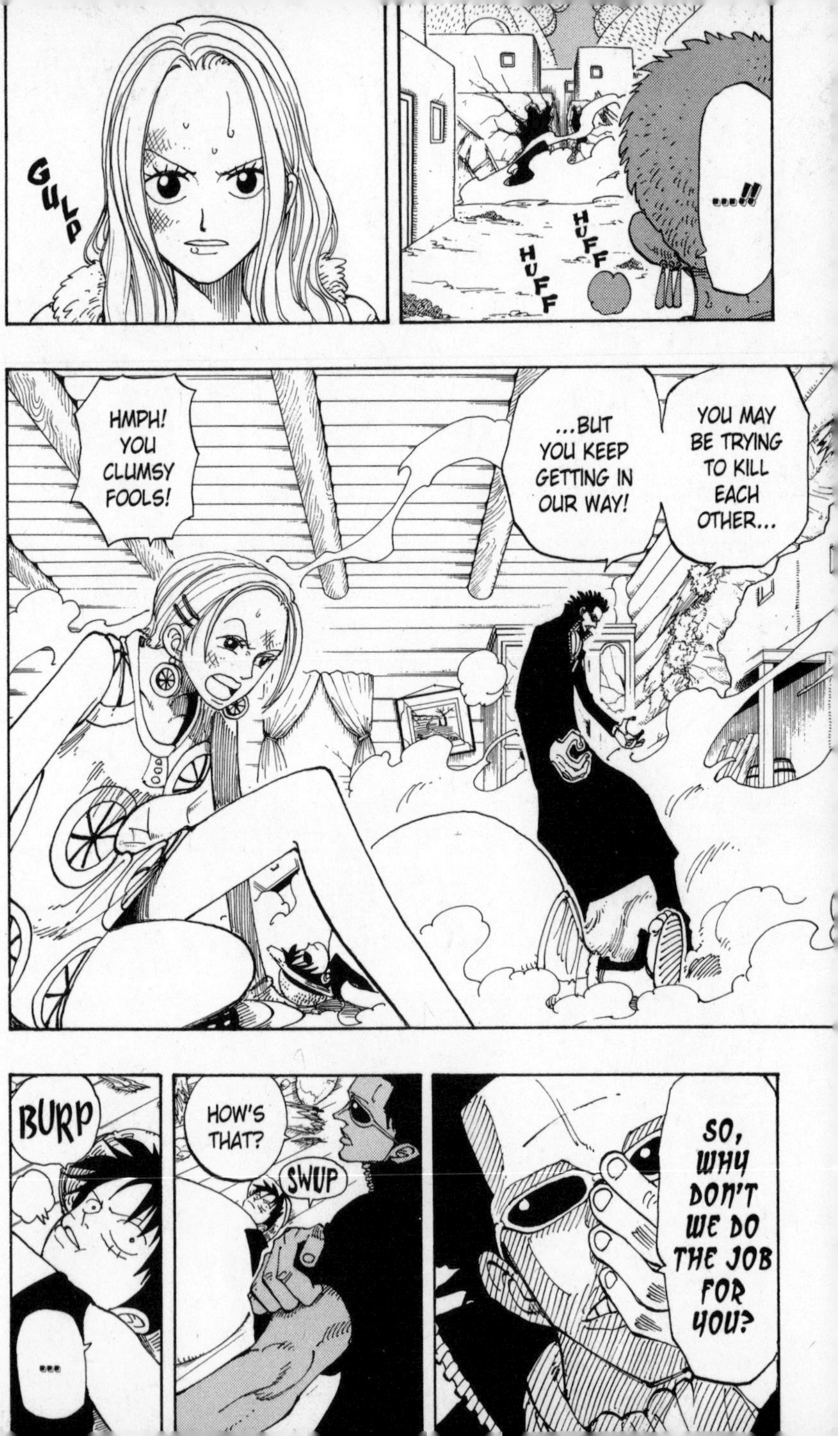
...!!
HUFF
HUFF
GULP
YOU MAY BE TRYING TO KILL EACH OTHER...
...BUT YOU KEEP GETTING IN OUR WAY!
HMPH! YOU CLUMSY FOOLS!
SO, WHY DON'T WE DO THE JOB FOR YOU?
HOW'S THAT?
SWUP
BURP
...

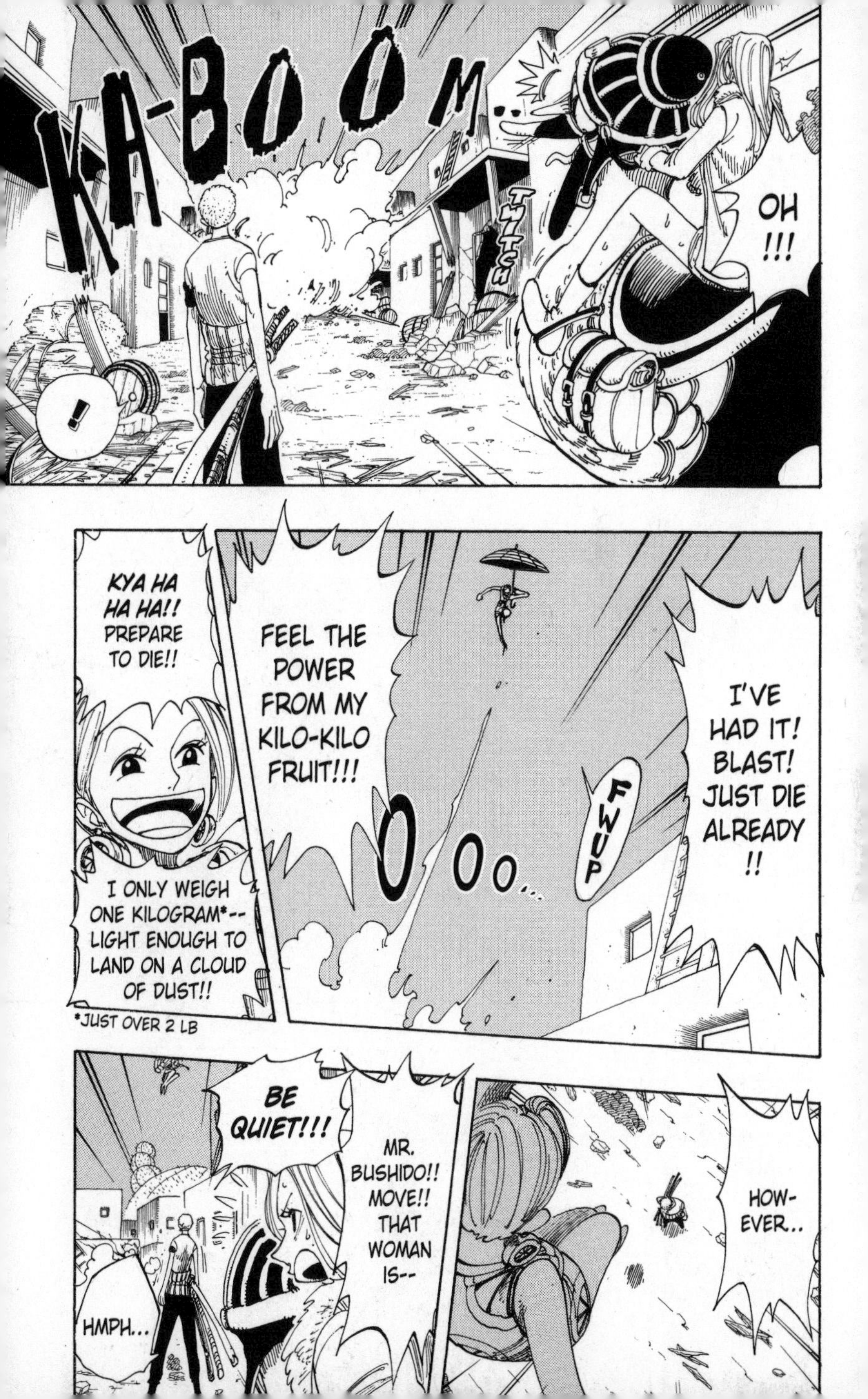
OH !!!
KA-BOOM
TWITCH
!
I'VE HAD IT! BLAST! JUST DIE ALREADY !!
FWUP
FEEL THE POWER FROM MY KILO-KILO FRUIT!!!
OOo...
KYA HA HA HA!! PREPARE TO DIE!!
I ONLY WEIGH ONE KILOGRAM*-- LIGHT ENOUGH TO LAND ON A CLOUD OF DUST!!
*JUST OVER 2 LB
HOW-EVER...
MR. BUSHIDO!! MOVE!! THAT WOMAN IS--
BE QUIET!!!
HMPH...

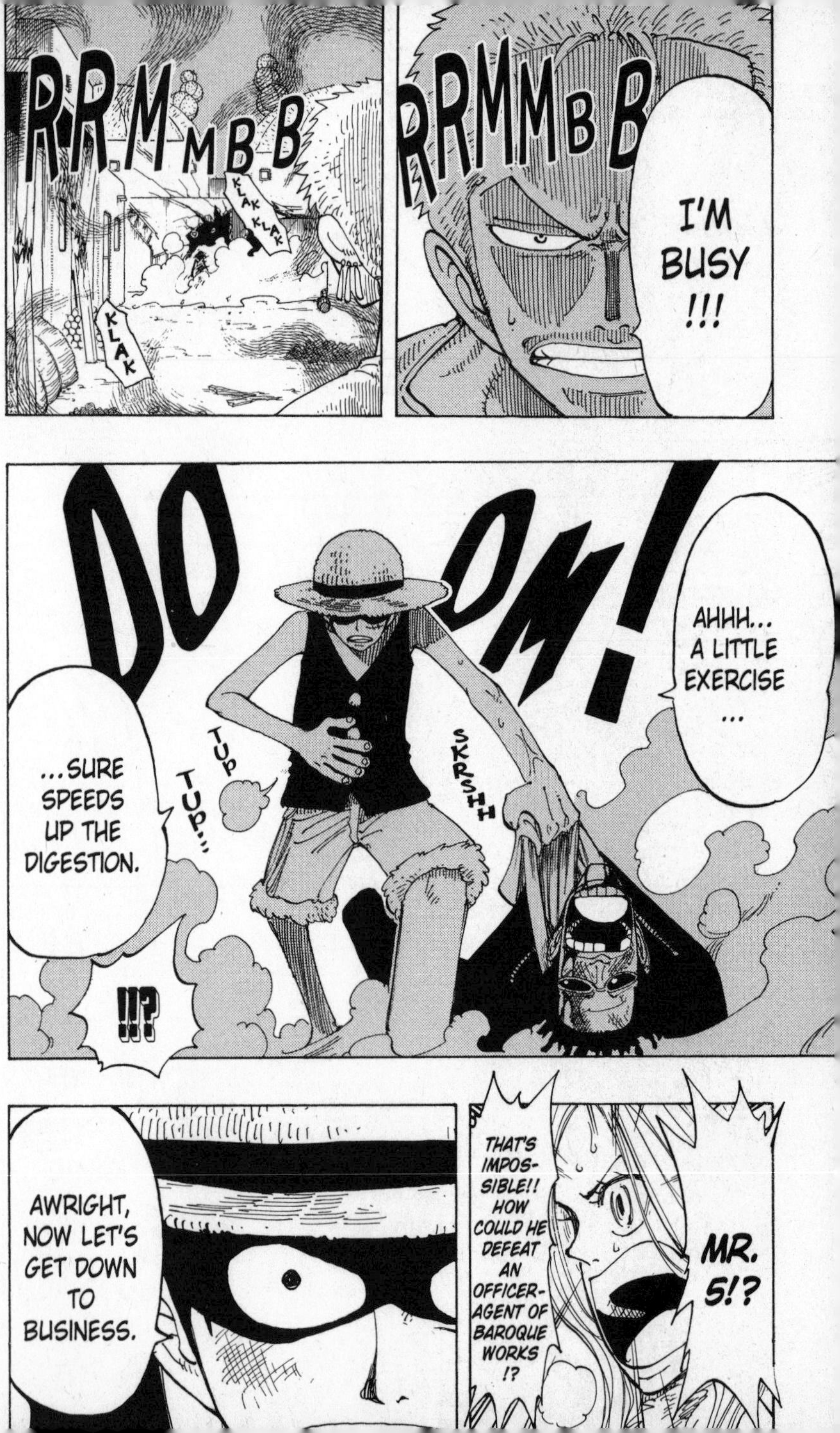
RRMMBB
I'M BUSY!!!
R-R-MMBB
KLAK KLAK
KLAK
DOOM!
AHHH... A LITTLE EXERCISE...
SKRSHH
TUP TUP...
...SURE SPEEDS UP THE DIGESTION.
!!?
THAT'S IMPOSSIBLE!! HOW COULD HE DEFEAT AN OFFICER-AGENT OF BAROQUE WORKS!?
MR. 5!?
AWRIGHT, NOW LET'S GET DOWN TO BUSINESS.

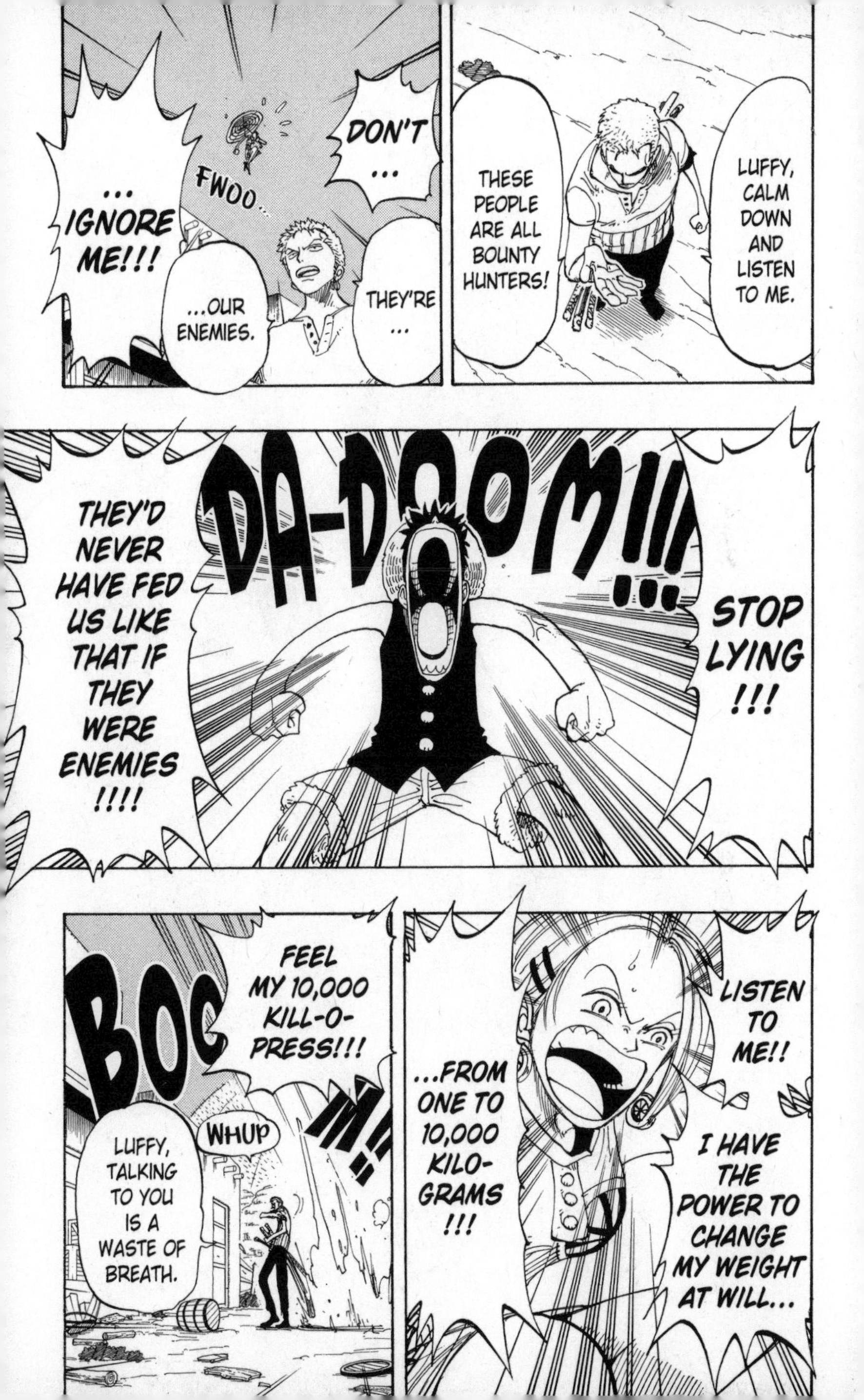
LUFFY, CALM DOWN AND LISTEN TO ME.
THESE PEOPLE ARE ALL BOUNTY HUNTERS!
THEY'RE ...
...OUR ENEMIES.
DON'T ...
FWOO...
... IGNORE ME!!!
STOP LYING!!!
DA-DOOM!!!
THEY'D NEVER HAVE FED US LIKE THAT IF THEY WERE ENEMIES!!!!
LISTEN TO ME!!
I HAVE THE POWER TO CHANGE MY WEIGHT AT WILL...
...FROM ONE TO 10,000 KILO-GRAMS!!!
FEEL MY 10,000 KILL-O-PRESS!!!
BOOM!!
WHUP
LUFFY, TALKING TO YOU IS A WASTE OF BREATH.

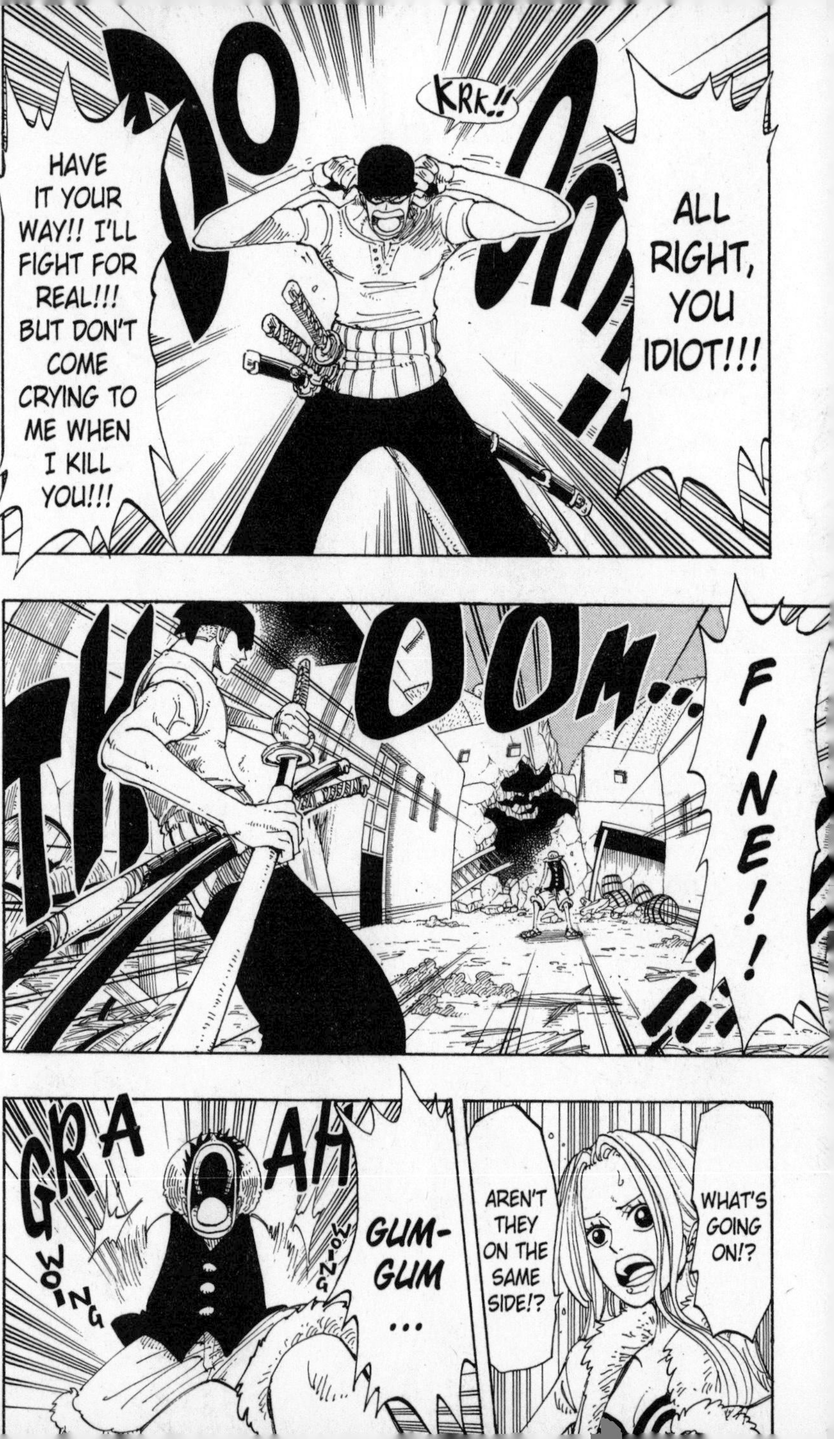
ALL RIGHT, YOU IDIOT!!!
KRK!!
HAVE IT YOUR WAY!! I'LL FIGHT FOR REAL!!! BUT DON'T COME CRYING TO ME WHEN I KILL YOU!!!
FINE!!!
WHAT'S GOING ON!?
AREN'T THEY ON THE SAME SIDE!?
GUM-GUM ...
WOING
WOING

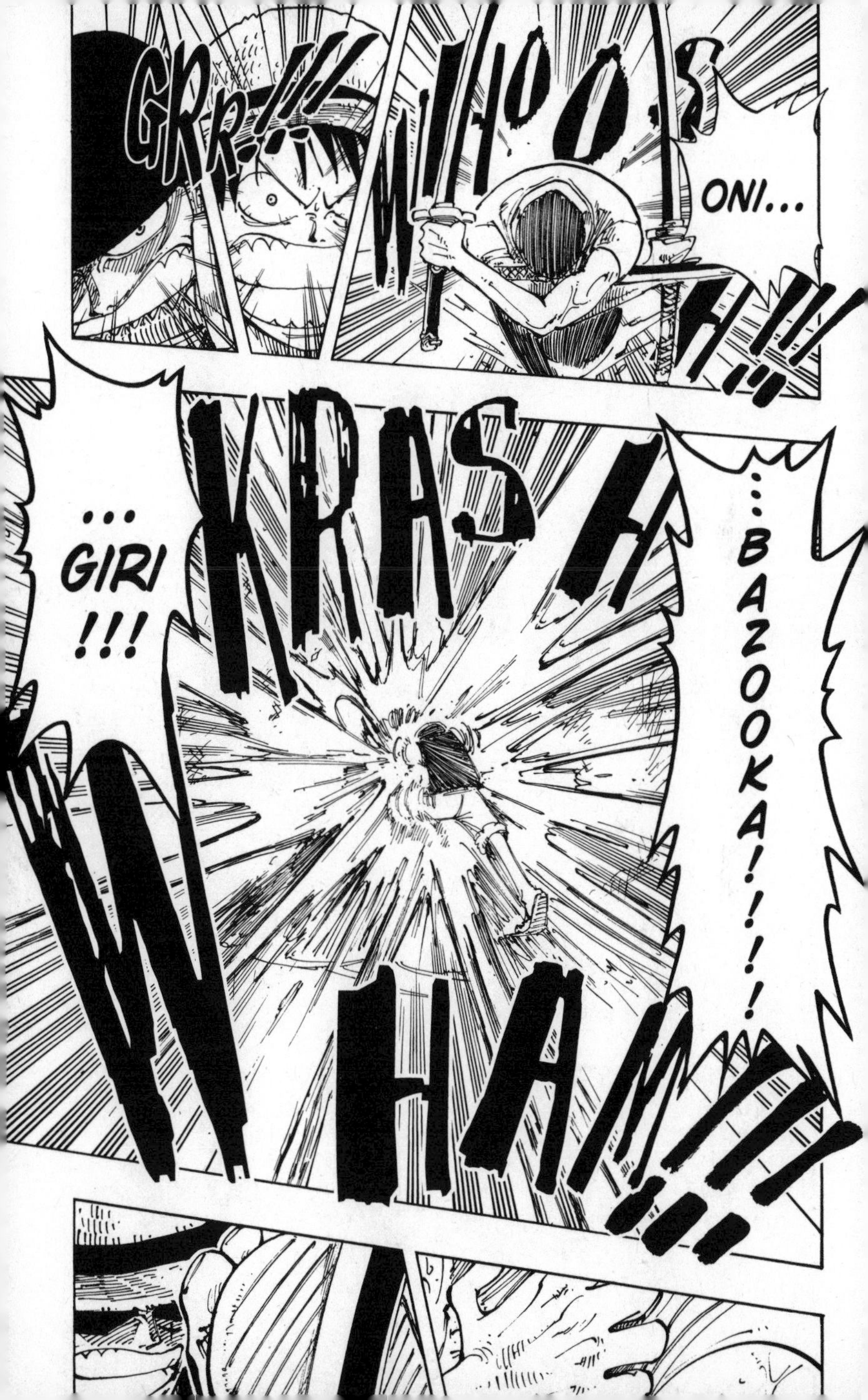

ONI...
WHOOSH!!!
GRR!!!
...BAZOOKA!!!!
...GIRI!!!
KRASH
WHAM!!!

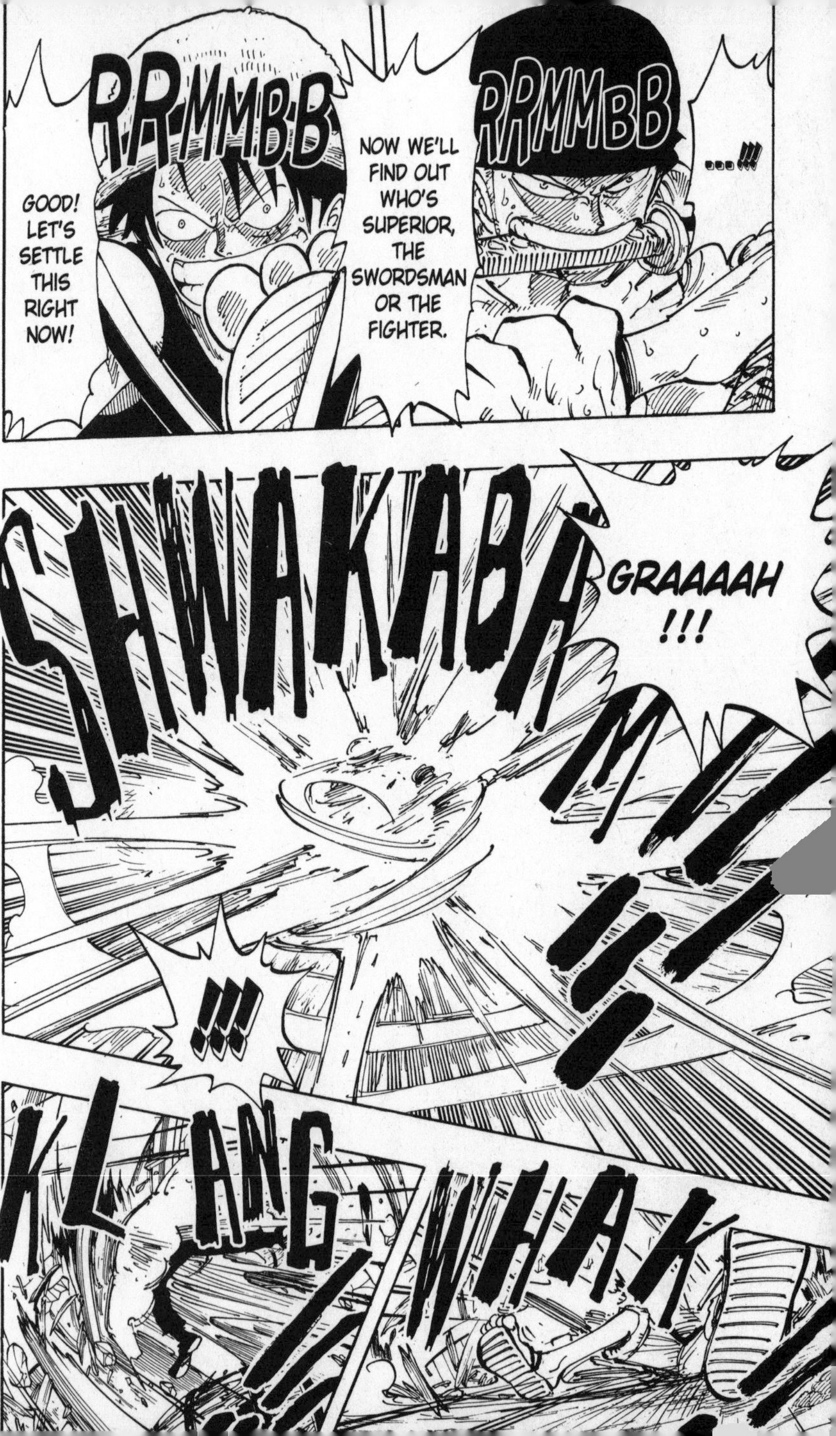
RRMMBB
...!!!
NOW WE'LL FIND OUT WHO'S SUPERIOR, THE SWORDSMAN OR THE FIGHTER.
RRMMBB
GOOD! LET'S SETTLE THIS RIGHT NOW!
GRAAAAH !!!
SHWAKABAM
!!!
WHAK
KLANG

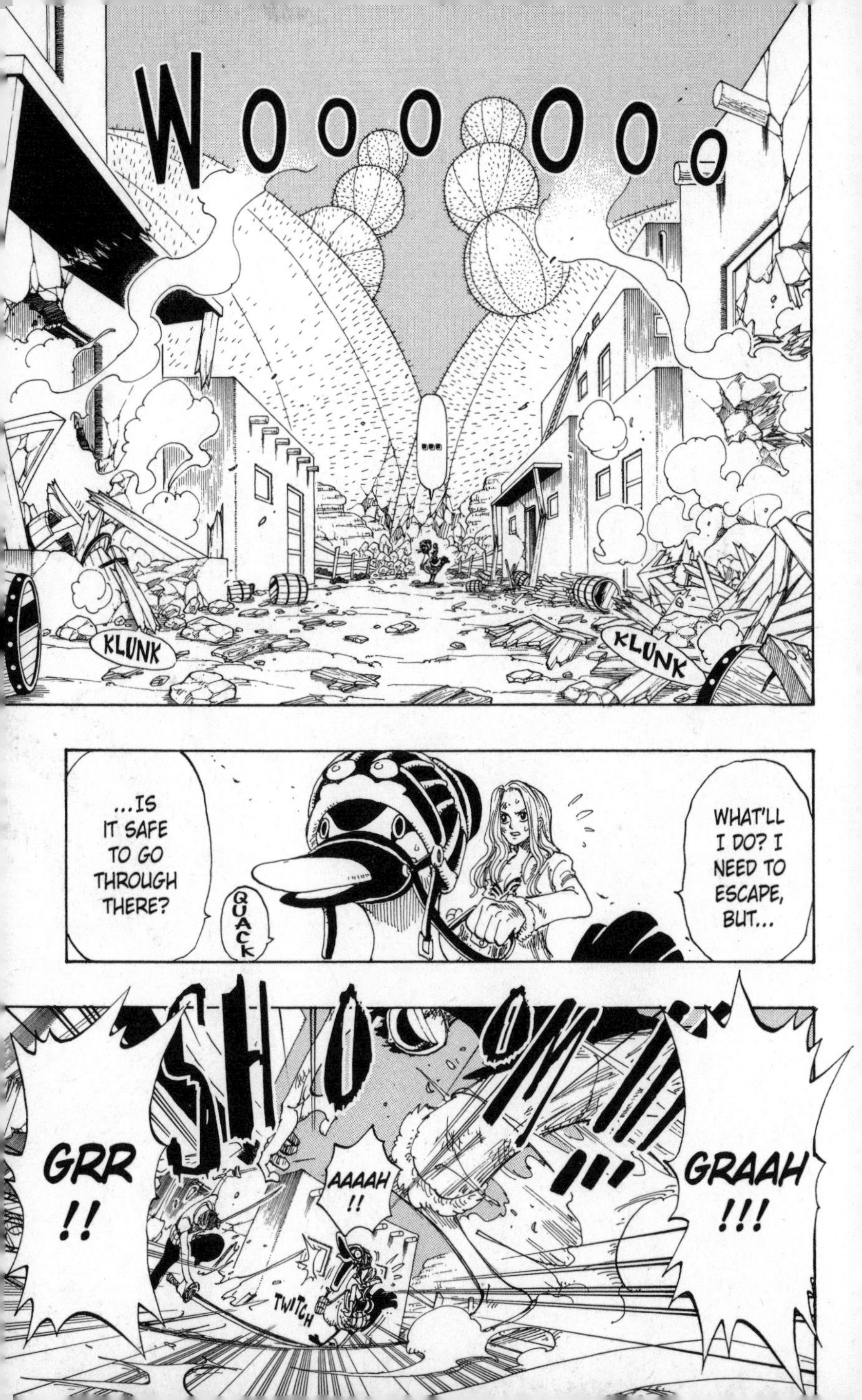
WOOOOOOO
KLUNK
KLUNK
WHAT'LL I DO? I NEED TO ESCAPE, BUT...
...IS IT SAFE TO GO THROUGH THERE?
QUACK
SHOOM!!!
GRAAH!!!
AAAAH!!
GRR!!
TWITCH

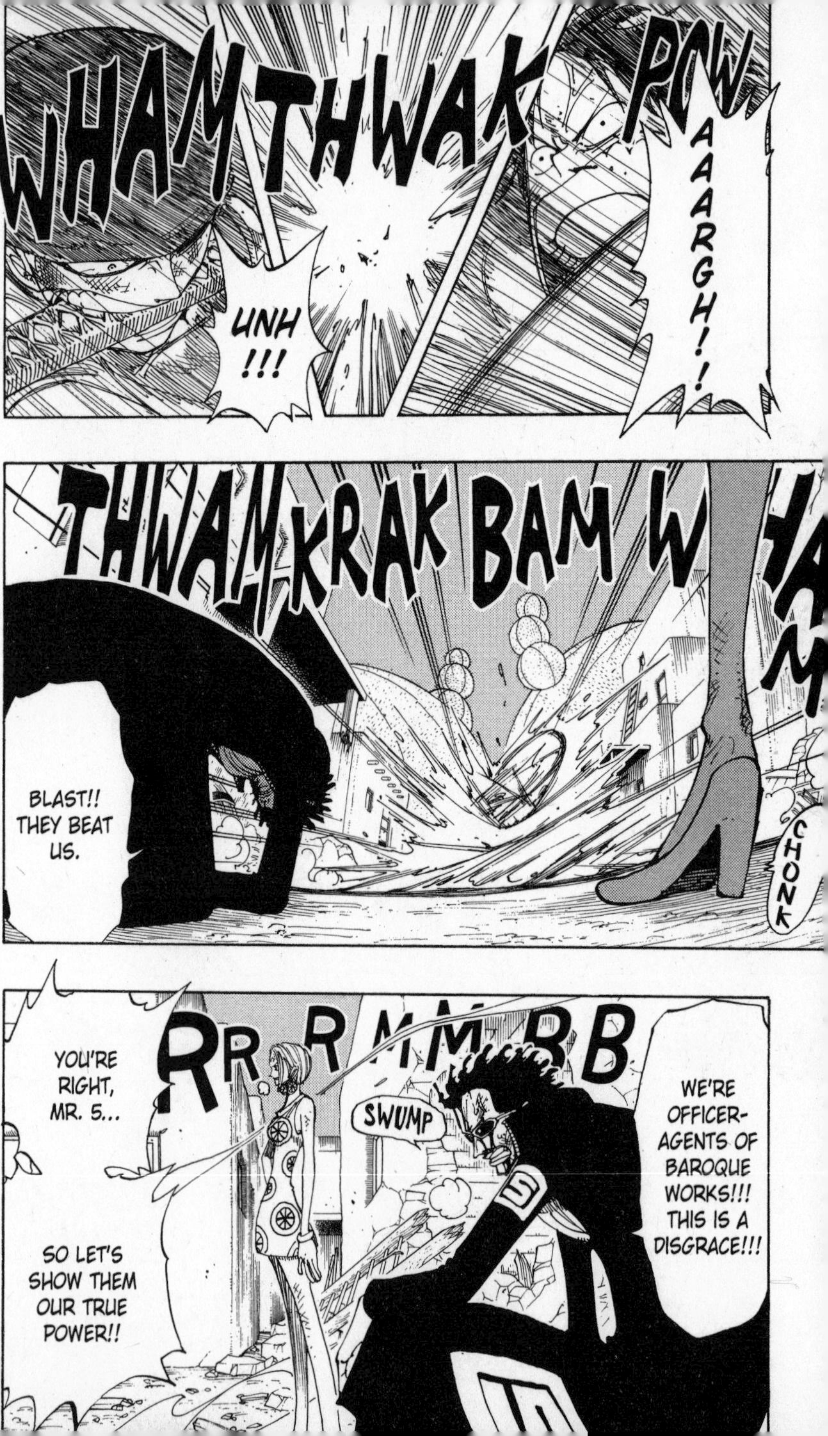
WHAM THWAK POW
AAARGH!!
UNH!!!
THWAM KRAK BAM WHAM
CHONK
BLAST!! THEY BEAT US.
RRRMMBB
WE'RE OFFICER-AGENTS OF BAROQUE WORKS!!! THIS IS A DISGRACE!!!
SWUMP
YOU'RE RIGHT, MR. 5...
SO LET'S SHOW THEM OUR TRUE POWER!!

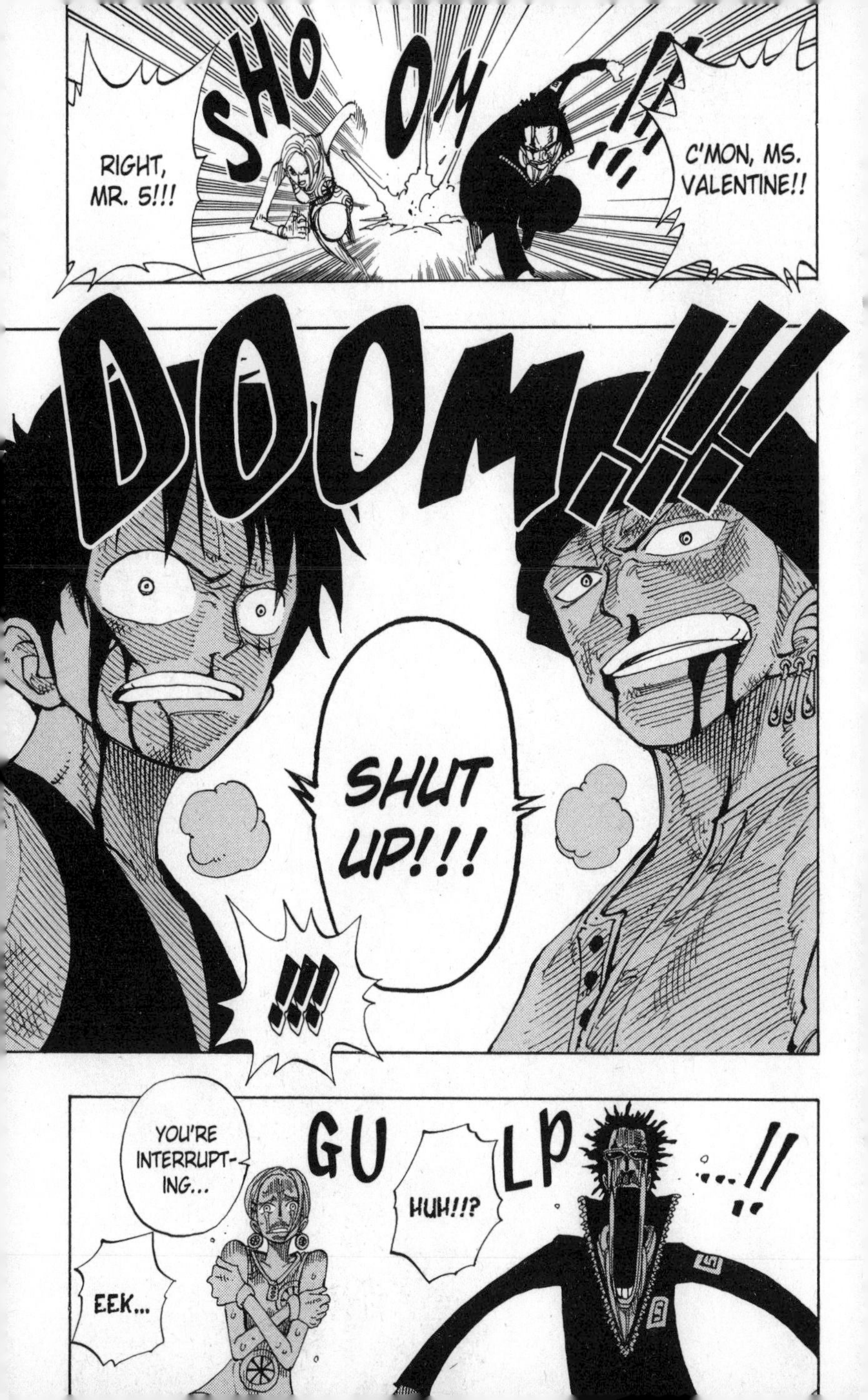
C'MON, MS. VALENTINE!!
SHO OM
!!!
RIGHT, MR. 5!!!
DOOM!!!
SHUT UP!!!
!!!
...!!
GU LP
HUH!!?
YOU'RE INTERRUPT-ING...
EEK...

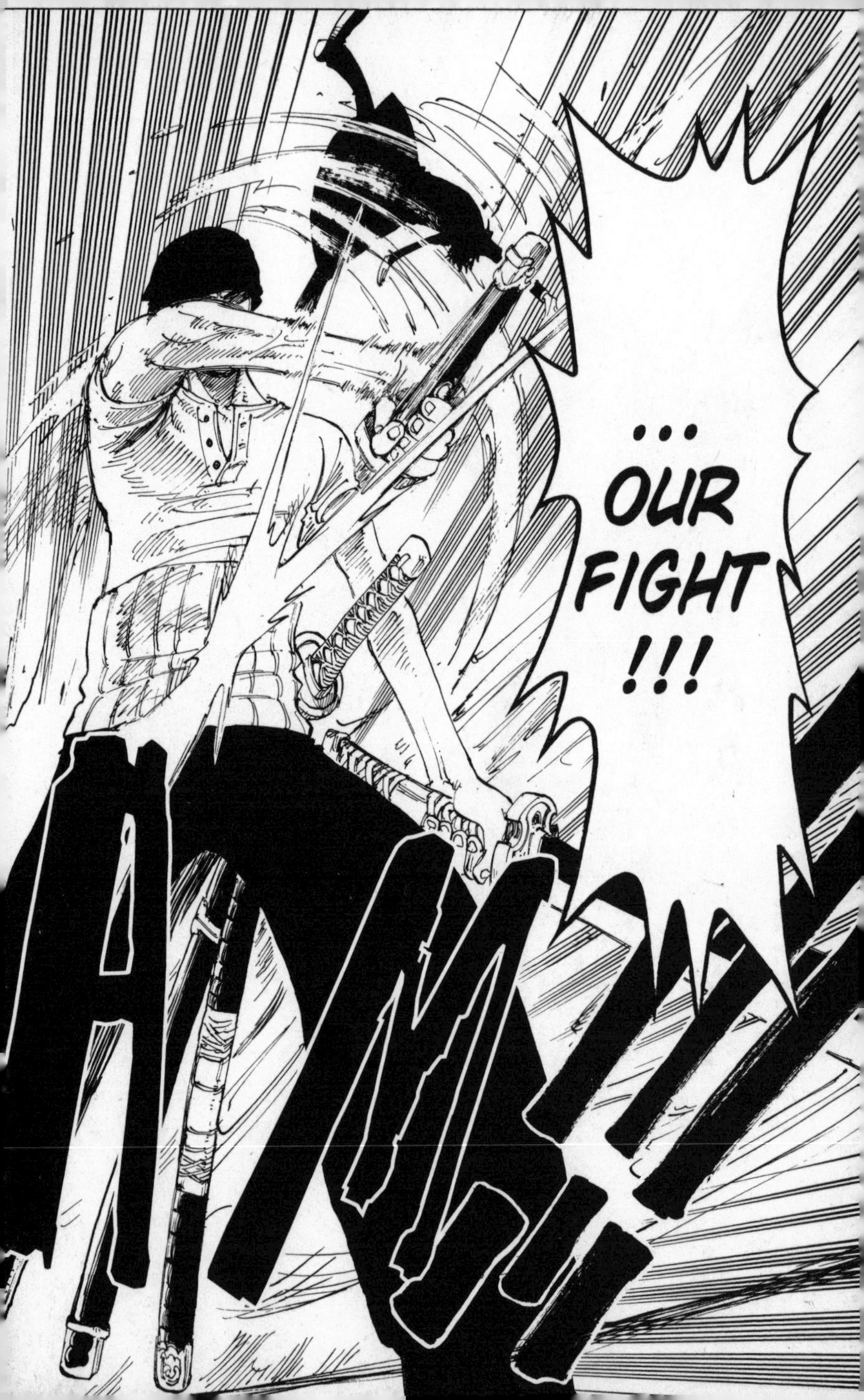
...OUR FIGHT!!!

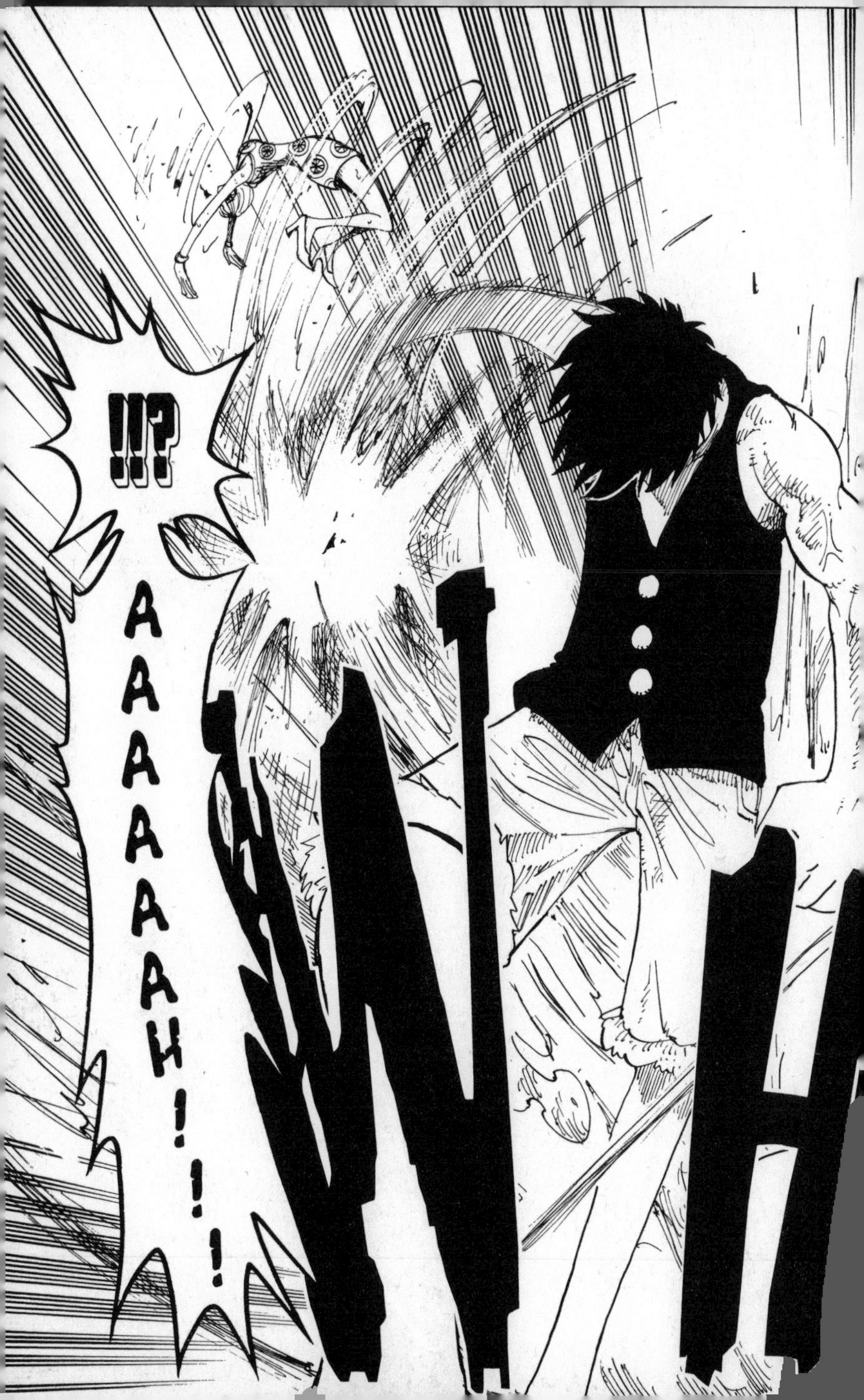
!!?
AAAAAAH!!!

Q: Can you tell me what "21 Excellent Grade" means? And what's this about Yubashiri (Snow Chaser) having a blade with *midareba*. What does it all mean? Huh???? I don't get it.

A: Oh, that. Maybe you don't understand exactly what they are, but if you get the idea that they're something awesome, that's good enough. But let me explain a little about swords.

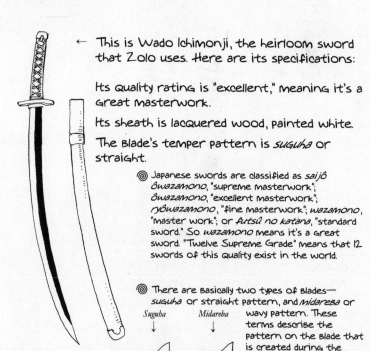

← This is Wado Ichimonji, the heirloom sword that Zolo uses. Here are its specifications:

Its quality rating is "excellent," meaning it's a great masterwork.

Its sheath is lacquered wood, painted white.

The blade's temper pattern is *suguha* or straight.

◎ Japanese swords are classified as *saijō ōwazamono*, "supreme masterwork"; *ōwazamono*, "excellent masterwork"; *ryōwazamono*, "fine masterwork"; *wazamono*, "master work"; or *futsū no katana*, "standard sword." So *wazamono* means it's a great sword. "Twelve Supreme Grade" means that 12 swords of this quality exist in the world.

◎ There are basically two types of blades— *suguha* or straight pattern, and *midareba* or wavy pattern. These terms describe the pattern on the blade that is created during the tempering process. There are various types of *midareba* as well.

Suguha
↓

Midareba
↓

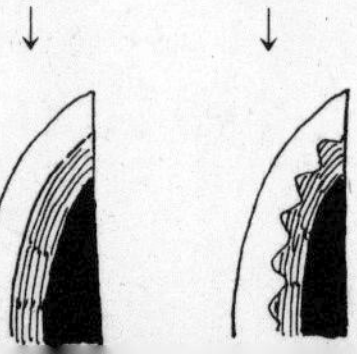

Chapter 113:
IT'S ALL RIGHT

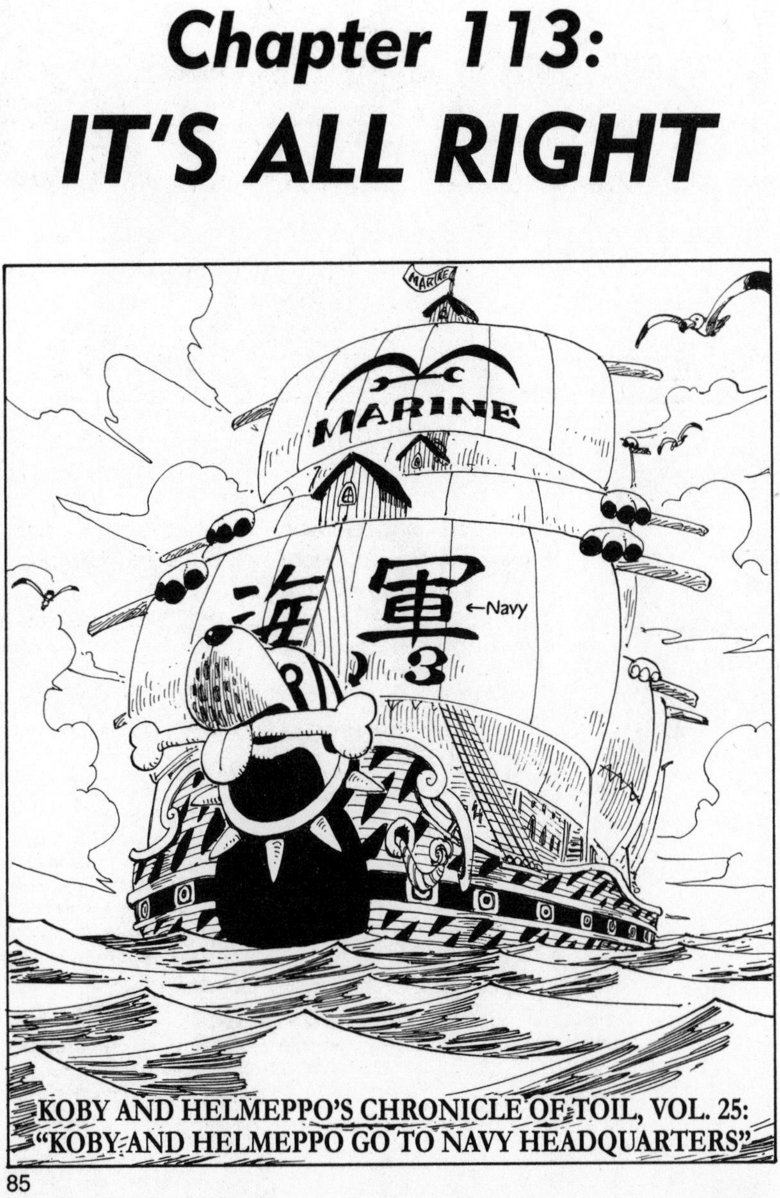
MARINE
MARINE
海軍 ←Navy
3

KOBY AND HELMEPPO'S CHRONICLE OF TOIL, VOL. 25:
"KOBY AND HELMEPPO GO TO NAVY HEADQUARTERS"

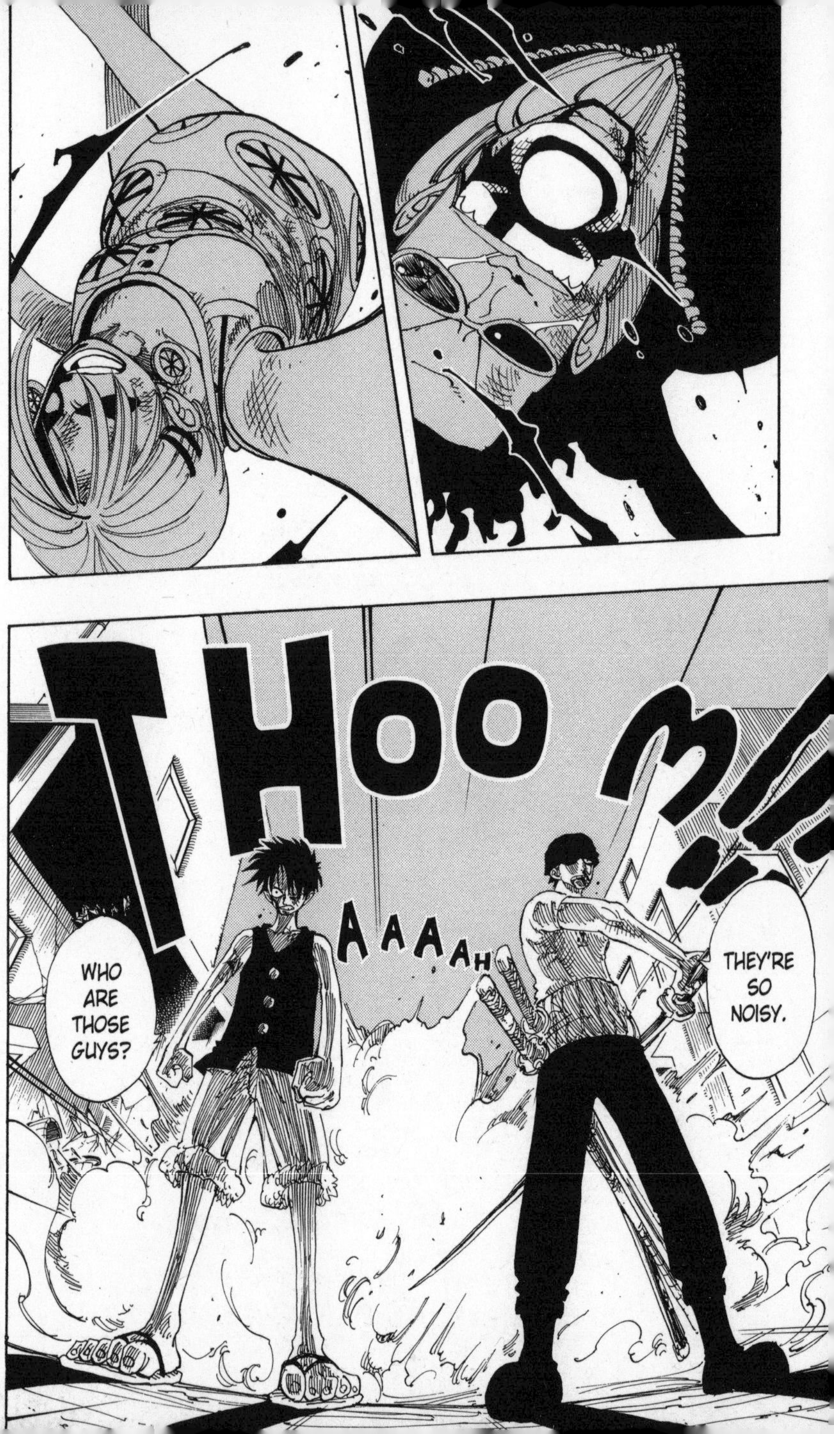
THOOM!!
THEY'RE SO NOISY.
AAAAH
WHO ARE THOSE GUYS?

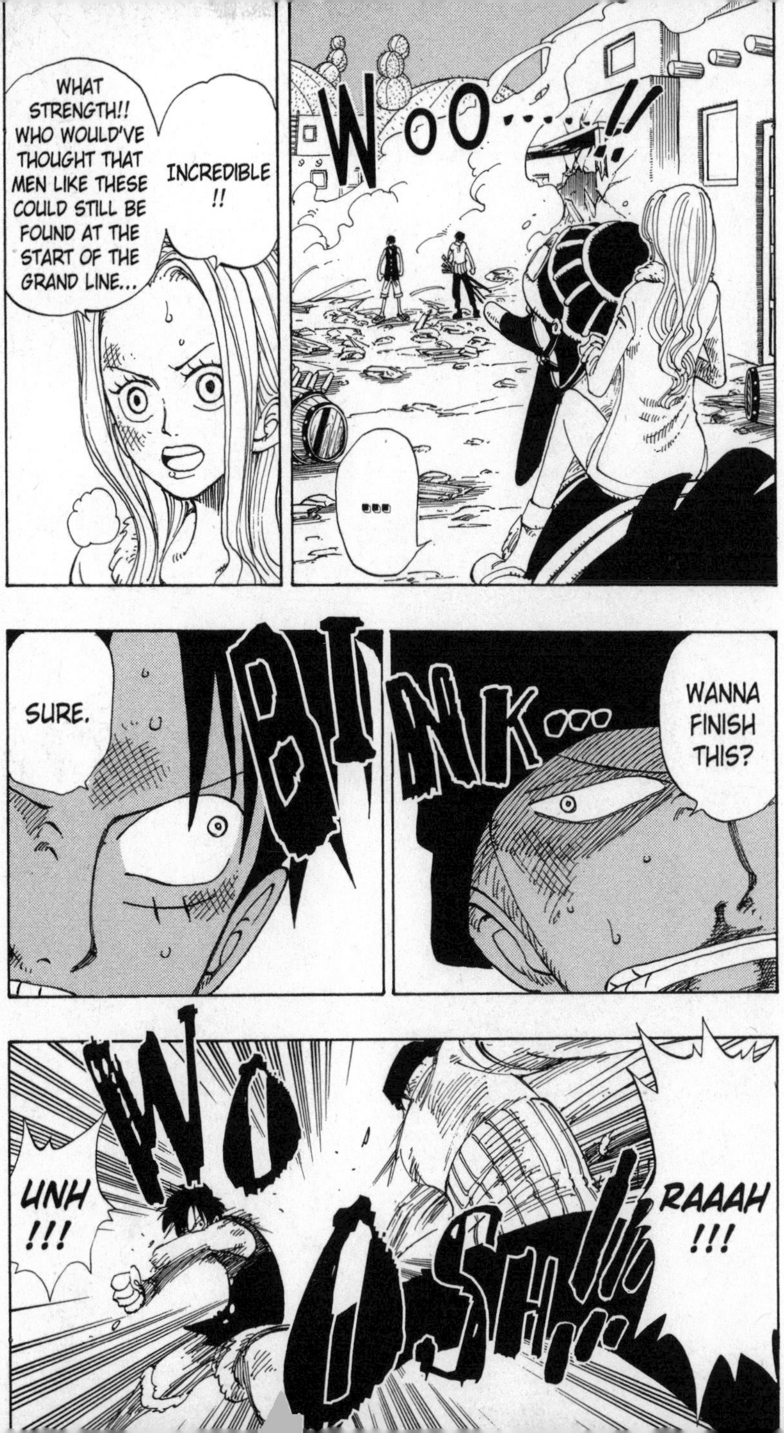
WOO...!!
...
INCREDIBLE!!
WHAT STRENGTH!! WHO WOULD'VE THOUGHT THAT MEN LIKE THESE COULD STILL BE FOUND AT THE START OF THE GRAND LINE...
WANNA FINISH THIS?
BLINK...
SURE.
RAAAH!!!
WOOSH...
UNH!!!

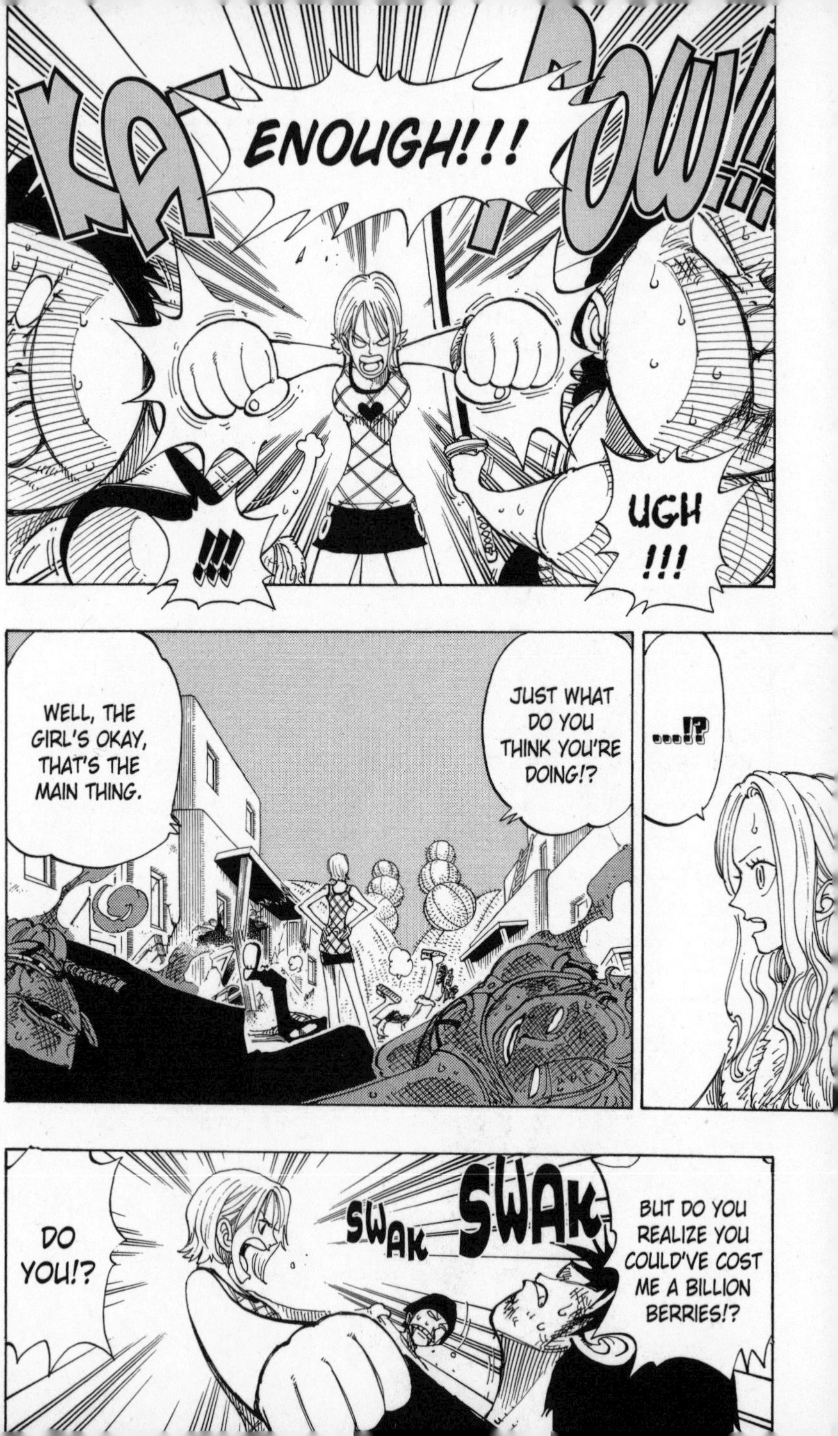
KA POW!!!
ENOUGH!!!
UGH !!!
!!!
...!?
JUST WHAT DO YOU THINK YOU'RE DOING!?
WELL, THE GIRL'S OKAY, THAT'S THE MAIN THING.
BUT DO YOU REALIZE YOU COULD'VE COST ME A BILLION BERRIES!?
SWAK SWAK
DO YOU!?

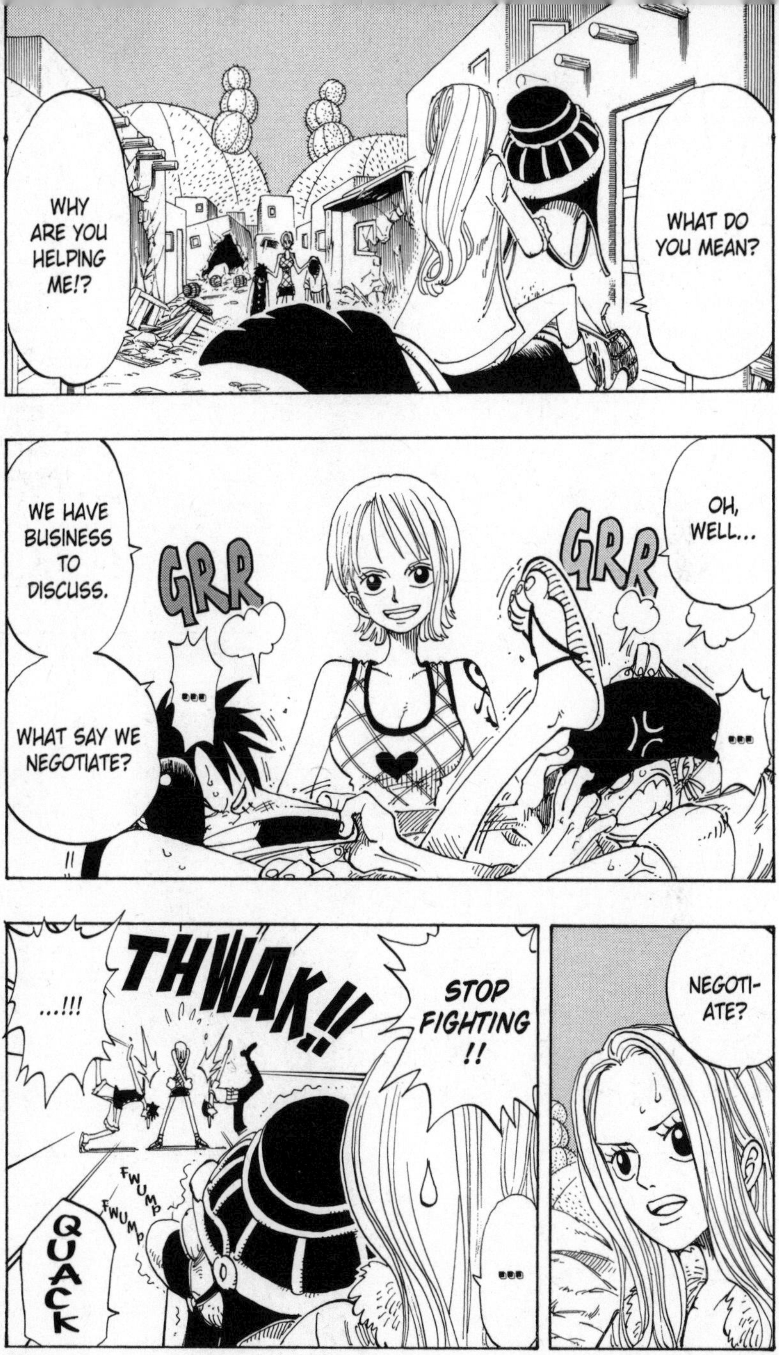
WHAT DO YOU MEAN?
WHY ARE YOU HELPING ME!?
OH, WELL...
GRR
...
WE HAVE BUSINESS TO DISCUSS.
WHAT SAY WE NEGOTIATE?
GRR
...
!!
NEGOTI- ATE?
STOP FIGHTING !!
THWAK!!
...!!!
...
FWUMP
FWUMP
QUACK

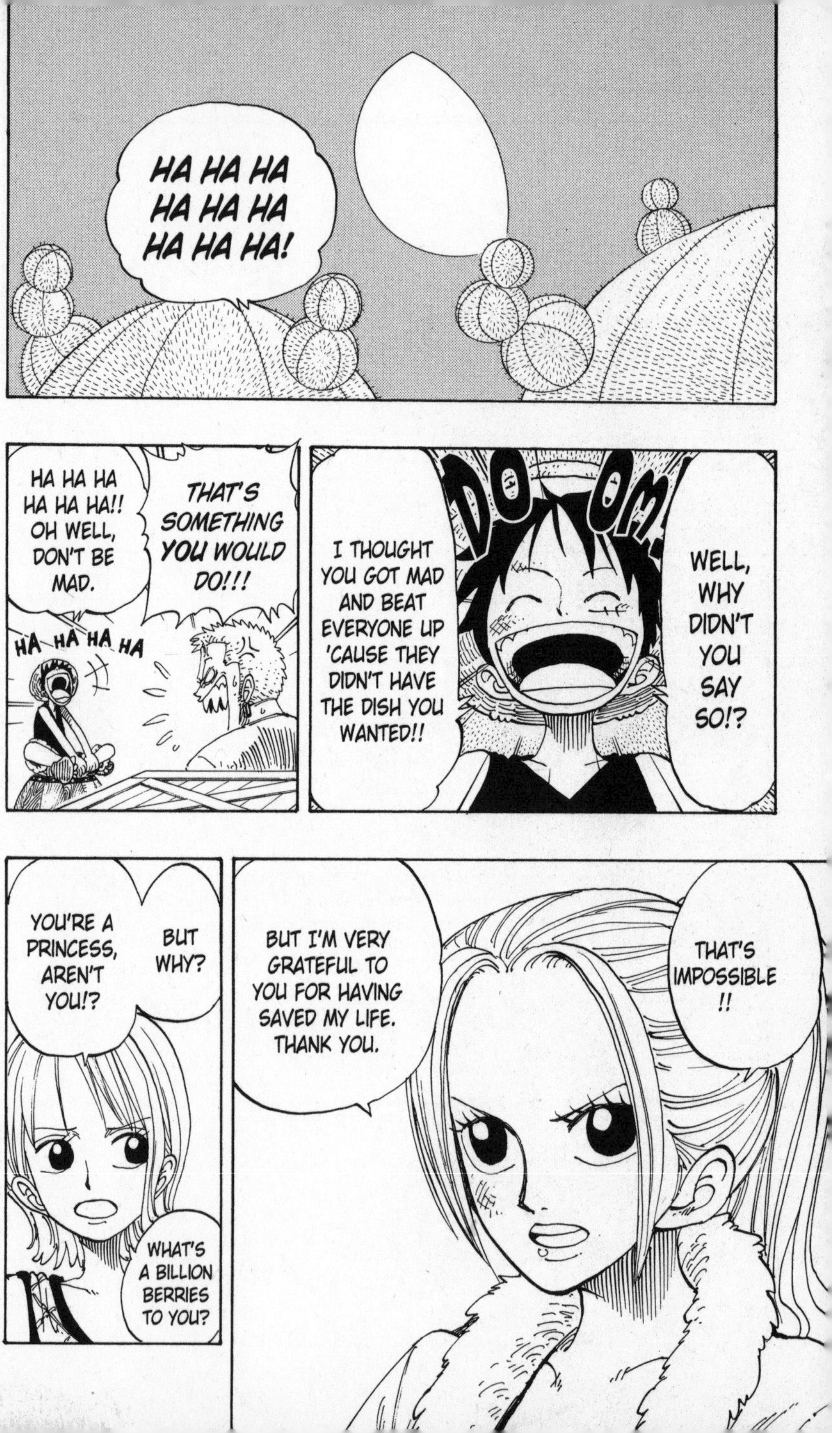
HA HA HA HA HA HA HA HA HA!
WELL, WHY DIDN'T YOU SAY SO!?
DOOM!
I THOUGHT YOU GOT MAD AND BEAT EVERYONE UP 'CAUSE THEY DIDN'T HAVE THE DISH YOU WANTED!!
THAT'S SOMETHING YOU WOULD DO!!!
HA HA HA HA HA HA!! OH WELL, DON'T BE MAD.
HA HA HA HA
THAT'S IMPOSSIBLE!!
BUT I'M VERY GRATEFUL TO YOU FOR HAVING SAVED MY LIFE. THANK YOU.
BUT WHY?
YOU'RE A PRINCESS, AREN'T YOU!?
WHAT'S A BILLION BERRIES TO YOU?

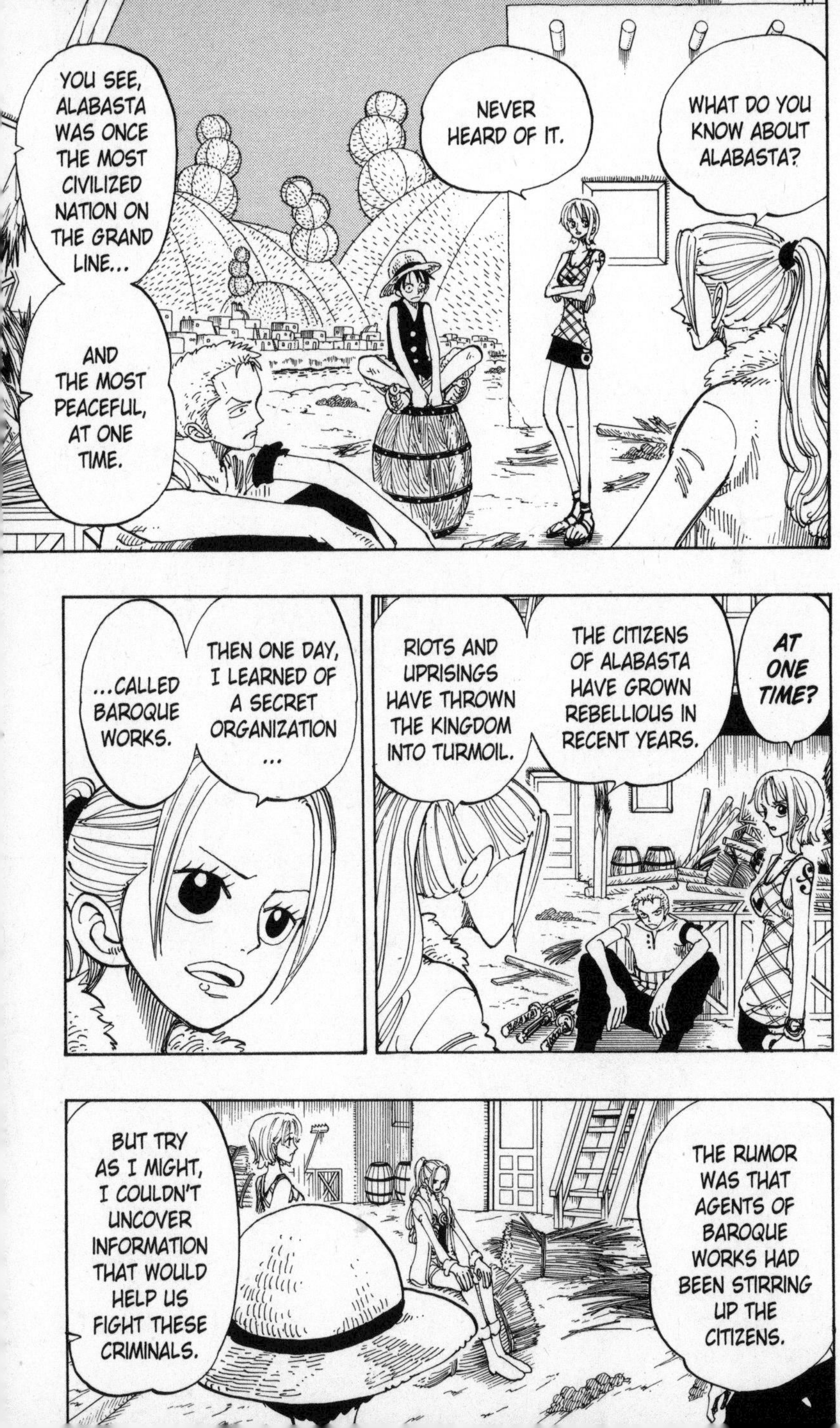
WHAT DO YOU KNOW ABOUT ALABASTA?
NEVER HEARD OF IT.
YOU SEE, ALABASTA WAS ONCE THE MOST CIVILIZED NATION ON THE GRAND LINE...
AND THE MOST PEACEFUL, AT ONE TIME.
AT ONE TIME?
THE CITIZENS OF ALABASTA HAVE GROWN REBELLIOUS IN RECENT YEARS.
RIOTS AND UPRISINGS HAVE THROWN THE KINGDOM INTO TURMOIL.
THEN ONE DAY, I LEARNED OF A SECRET ORGANIZATION ...
...CALLED BAROQUE WORKS.
THE RUMOR WAS THAT AGENTS OF BAROQUE WORKS HAD BEEN STIRRING UP THE CITIZENS.
BUT TRY AS I MIGHT, I COULDN'T UNCOVER INFORMATION THAT WOULD HELP US FIGHT THESE CRIMINALS.

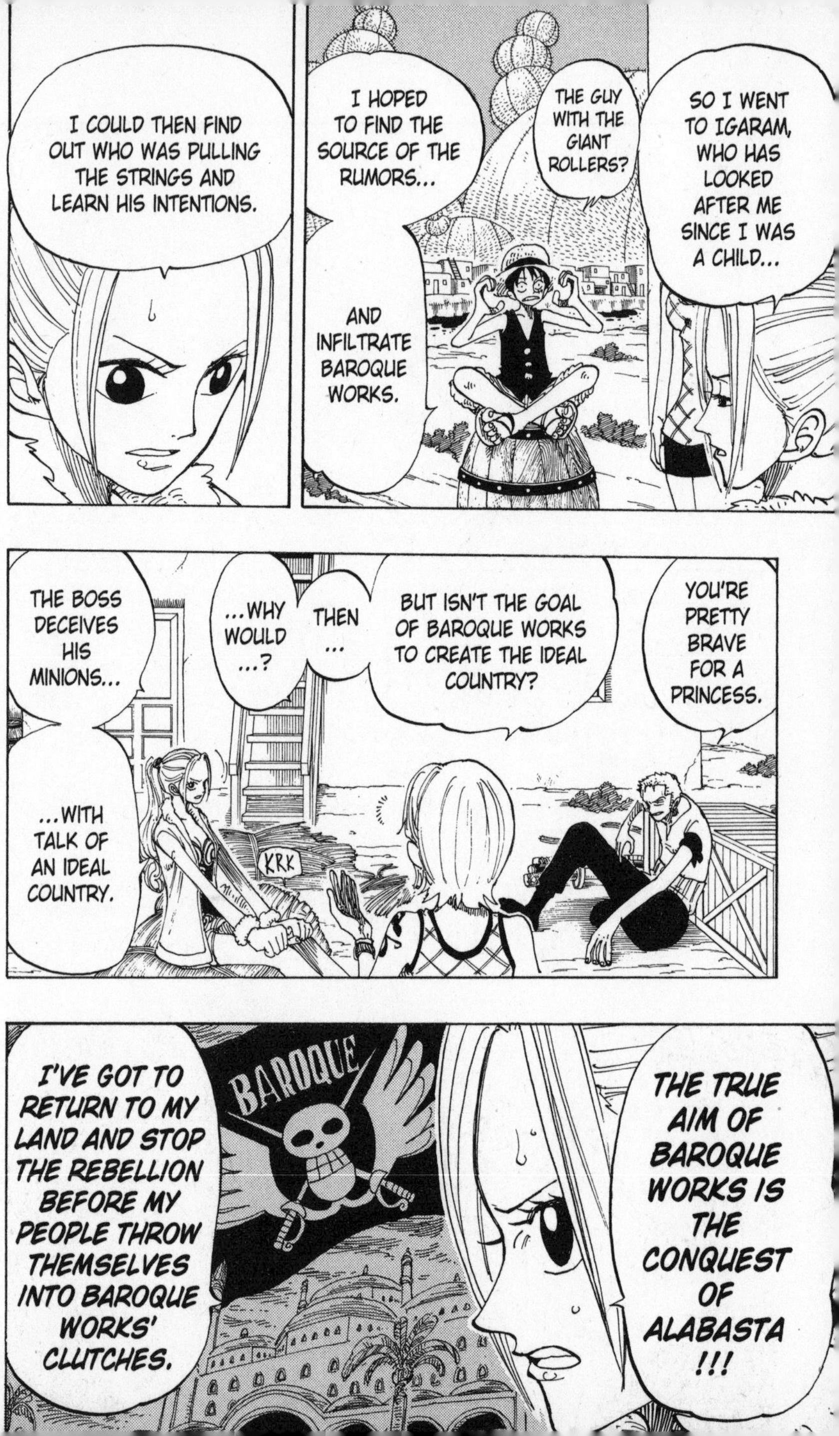

SO I WENT TO IGARAM, WHO HAS LOOKED AFTER ME SINCE I WAS A CHILD...
THE GUY WITH THE GIANT ROLLERS?
I HOPED TO FIND THE SOURCE OF THE RUMORS...
AND INFILTRATE BAROQUE WORKS.
I COULD THEN FIND OUT WHO WAS PULLING THE STRINGS AND LEARN HIS INTENTIONS.
YOU'RE PRETTY BRAVE FOR A PRINCESS.
BUT ISN'T THE GOAL OF BAROQUE WORKS TO CREATE THE IDEAL COUNTRY?
THEN ...
...WHY WOULD ...?
THE BOSS DECEIVES HIS MINIONS...
...WITH TALK OF AN IDEAL COUNTRY.
KRK
THE TRUE AIM OF BAROQUE WORKS IS THE CONQUEST OF ALABASTA !!!
BAROQUE
I'VE GOT TO RETURN TO MY LAND AND STOP THE REBELLION BEFORE MY PEOPLE THROW THEMSELVES INTO BAROQUE WORKS' CLUTCHES.

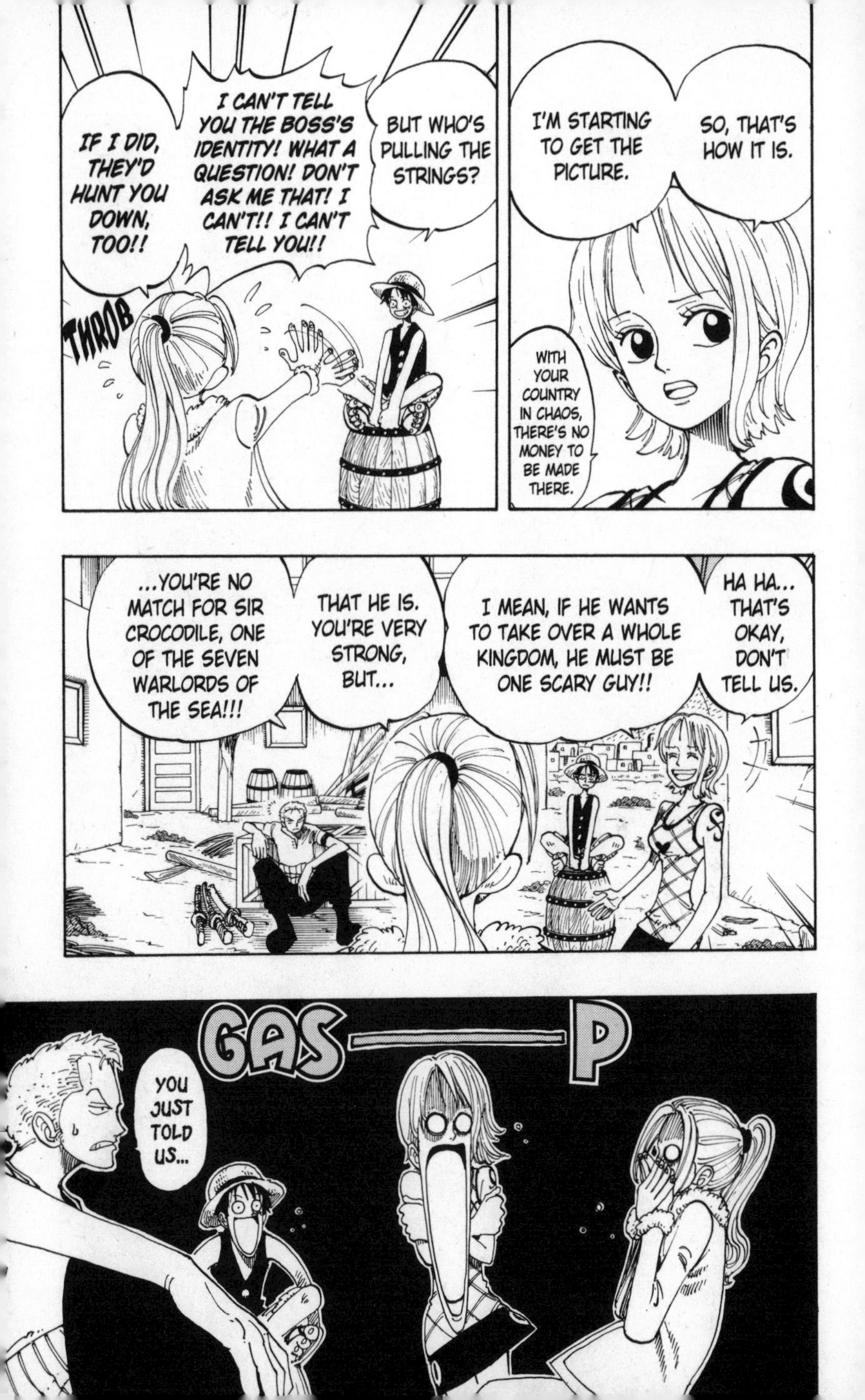
SO, THAT'S HOW IT IS.
I'M STARTING TO GET THE PICTURE.
WITH YOUR COUNTRY IN CHAOS, THERE'S NO MONEY TO BE MADE THERE.
BUT WHO'S PULLING THE STRINGS?
I CAN'T TELL YOU THE BOSS'S IDENTITY! WHAT A QUESTION! DON'T ASK ME THAT! I CAN'T!! I CAN'T TELL YOU!!
IF I DID, THEY'D HUNT YOU DOWN, TOO!!
THROB
HA HA... THAT'S OKAY, DON'T TELL US.
I MEAN, IF HE WANTS TO TAKE OVER A WHOLE KINGDOM, HE MUST BE ONE SCARY GUY!!
THAT HE IS. YOU'RE VERY STRONG, BUT...
...YOU'RE NO MATCH FOR SIR CROCODILE, ONE OF THE SEVEN WARLORDS OF THE SEA!!!
GAS—P
YOU JUST TOLD US...

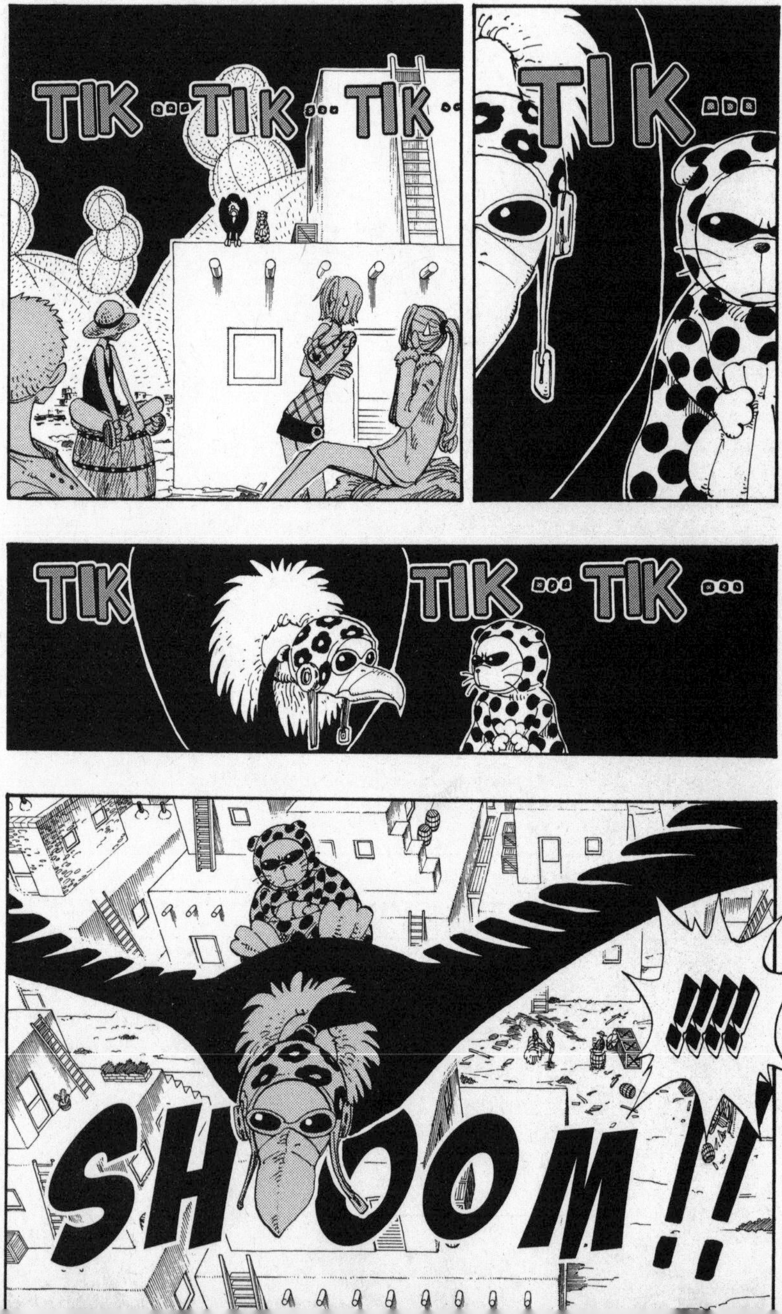
TIK...
TIK... TIK... TIK...
TIK
TIK... TIK...
!!!!
SHOOM!!

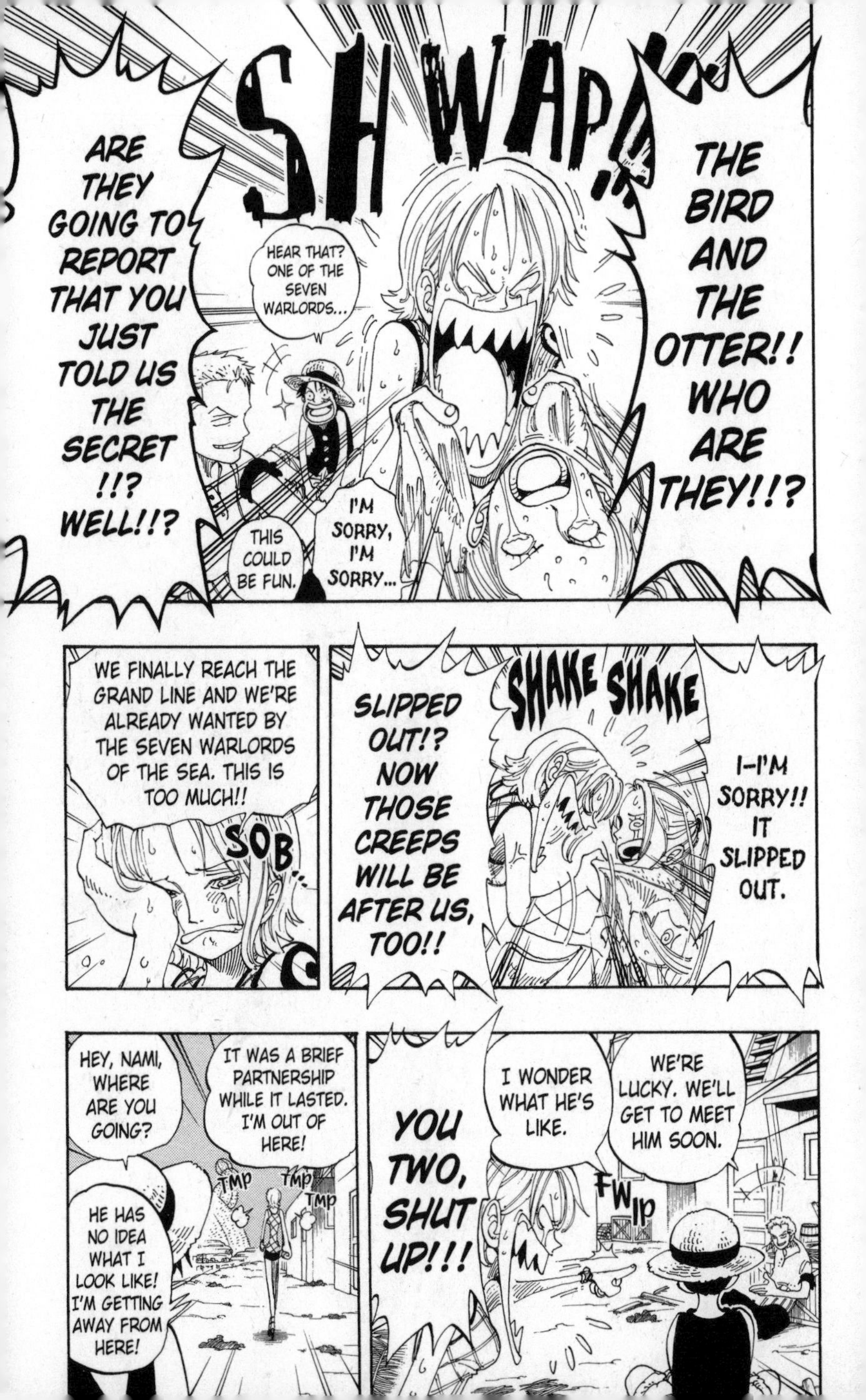
SHWAP!!
THE BIRD AND THE OTTER!! WHO ARE THEY!!?
HEAR THAT? ONE OF THE SEVEN WARLORDS...
ARE THEY GOING TO REPORT THAT YOU JUST TOLD US THE SECRET!!? WELL!!?
I'M SORRY, I'M SORRY...
THIS COULD BE FUN.
SHAKE SHAKE
I-I'M SORRY!! IT SLIPPED OUT.
SLIPPED OUT!? NOW THOSE CREEPS WILL BE AFTER US, TOO!!
WE FINALLY REACH THE GRAND LINE AND WE'RE ALREADY WANTED BY THE SEVEN WARLORDS OF THE SEA. THIS IS TOO MUCH!!
SOB...
WE'RE LUCKY. WE'LL GET TO MEET HIM SOON.
I WONDER WHAT HE'S LIKE.
FWIP
YOU TWO, SHUT UP!!!
IT WAS A BRIEF PARTNERSHIP WHILE IT LASTED. I'M OUT OF HERE!
HEY, NAMI, WHERE ARE YOU GOING?
TMP TMP TMP
HE HAS NO IDEA WHAT I LOOK LIKE! I'M GETTING AWAY FROM HERE!

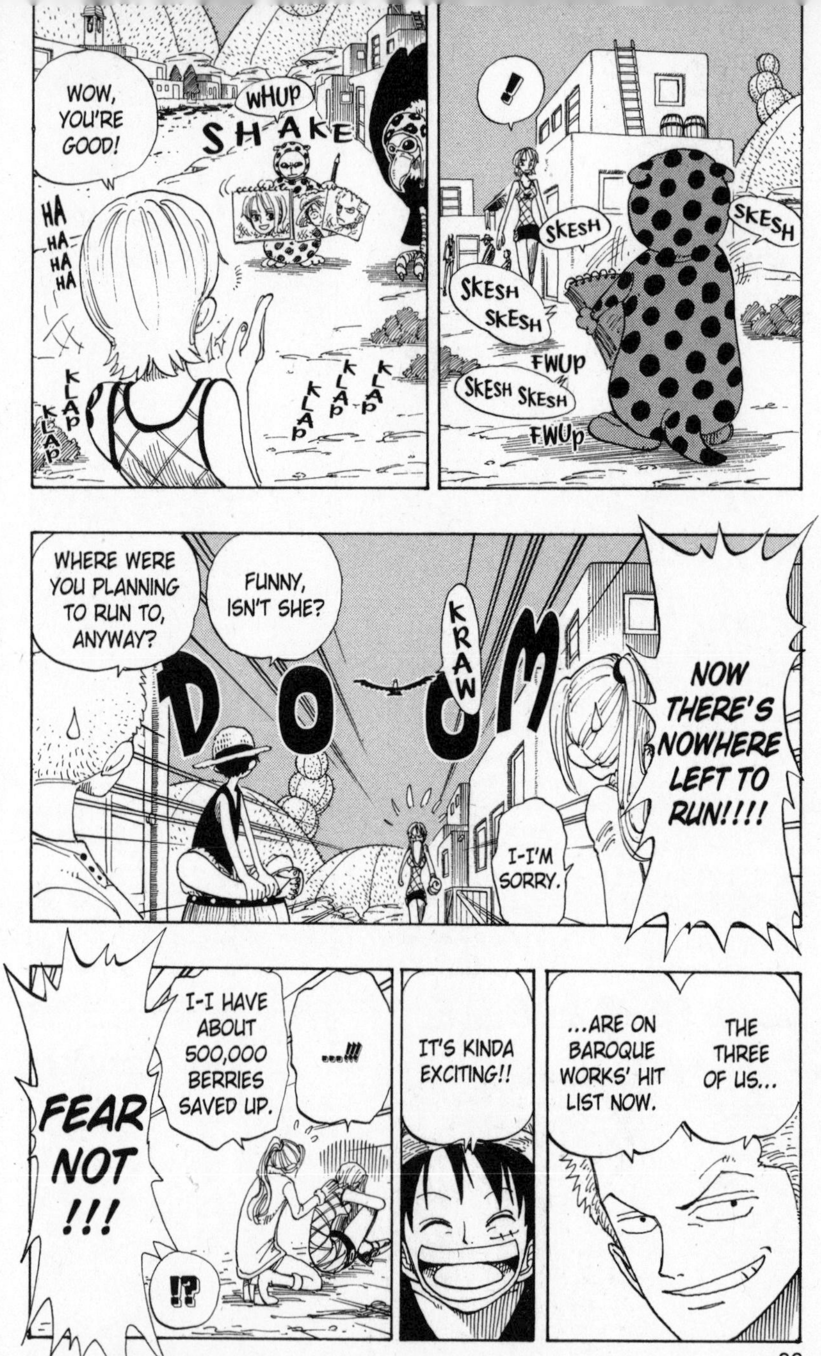
!
SKESH
SKESH
SKESH SKESH
FWUp
SKESH SKESH
FWUp
WOW, YOU'RE GOOD!
WHUP
SHAKE
HA HA HA HA
KLAP KLAP KLAP KLAP KLAP KLAP
NOW THERE'S NOWHERE LEFT TO RUN!!!!
I-I'M SORRY.
KRAW
DOOM
FUNNY, ISN'T SHE?
WHERE WERE YOU PLANNING TO RUN TO, ANYWAY?
THE THREE OF US...
...ARE ON BAROQUE WORKS' HIT LIST NOW.
IT'S KINDA EXCITING!!
...!!!
I-I HAVE ABOUT 500,000 BERRIES SAVED UP.
FEAR NOT!!!
!?

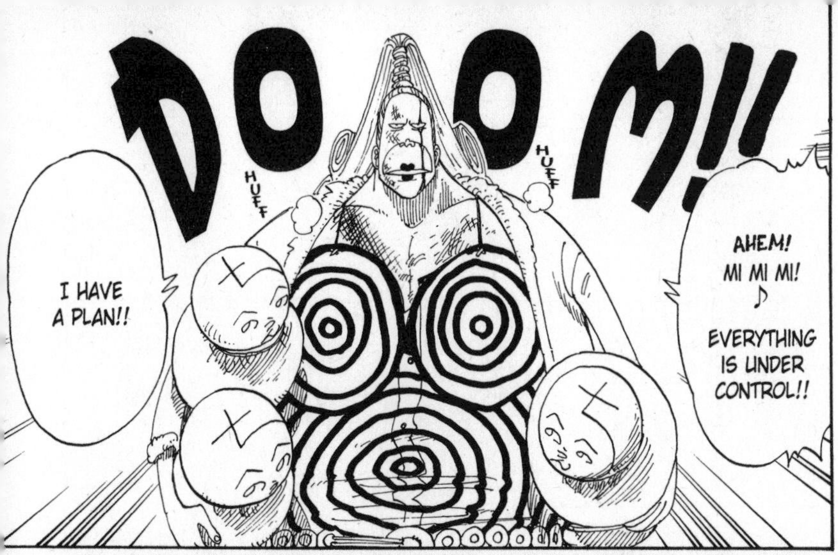
DOOM!!
HUFF
HUFF
AHEM! MI MI MI! ♪
EVERYTHING IS UNDER CONTROL!!
I HAVE A PLAN!!

THE DUMMIES' FACES ARE MADE UP OF JAPANESE TEXT. THEY DON'T TRANSLATE TO ANYTHING, THOUGH.

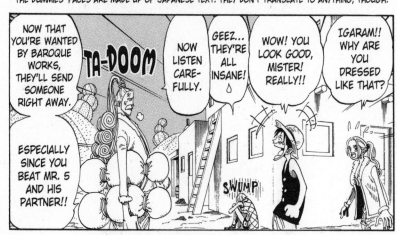

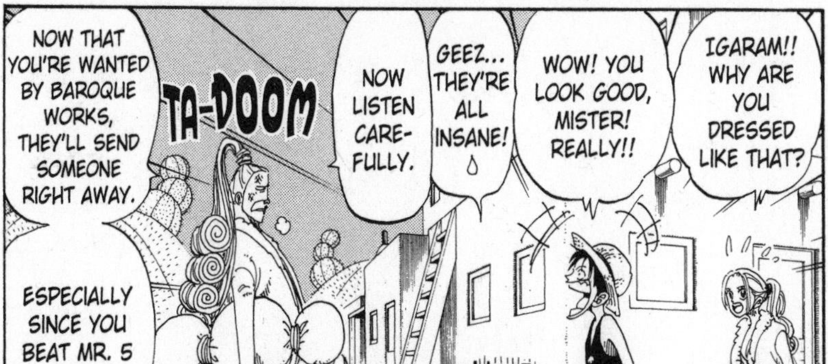
IGARAM!! WHY ARE YOU DRESSED LIKE THAT?
WOW! YOU LOOK GOOD, MISTER! REALLY!!
GEEZ... THEY'RE ALL INSANE!
NOW LISTEN CAREFULLY.
TA-DOOM
NOW THAT YOU'RE WANTED BY BAROQUE WORKS, THEY'LL SEND SOMEONE RIGHT AWAY.
ESPECIALLY SINCE YOU BEAT MR. 5 AND HIS PARTNER!!
SWUMP

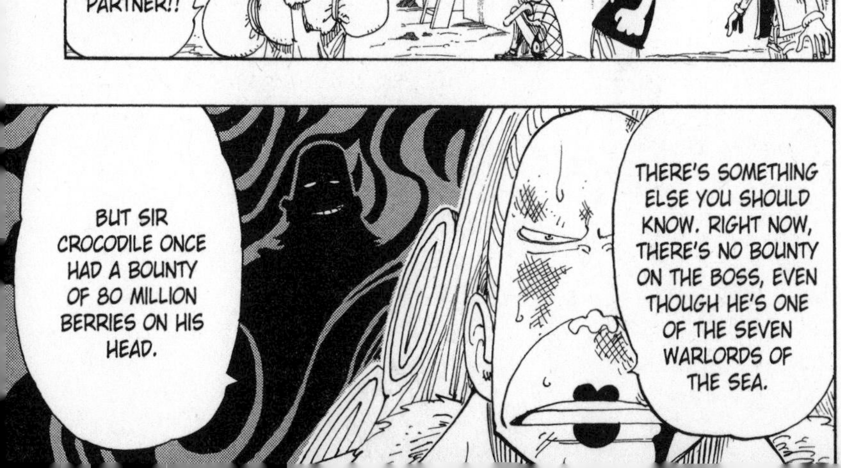
THERE'S SOMETHING ELSE YOU SHOULD KNOW. RIGHT NOW, THERE'S NO BOUNTY ON THE BOSS, EVEN THOUGH HE'S ONE OF THE SEVEN WARLORDS OF THE SEA.
BUT SIR CROCODILE ONCE HAD A BOUNTY OF 80 MILLION BERRIES ON HIS HEAD.

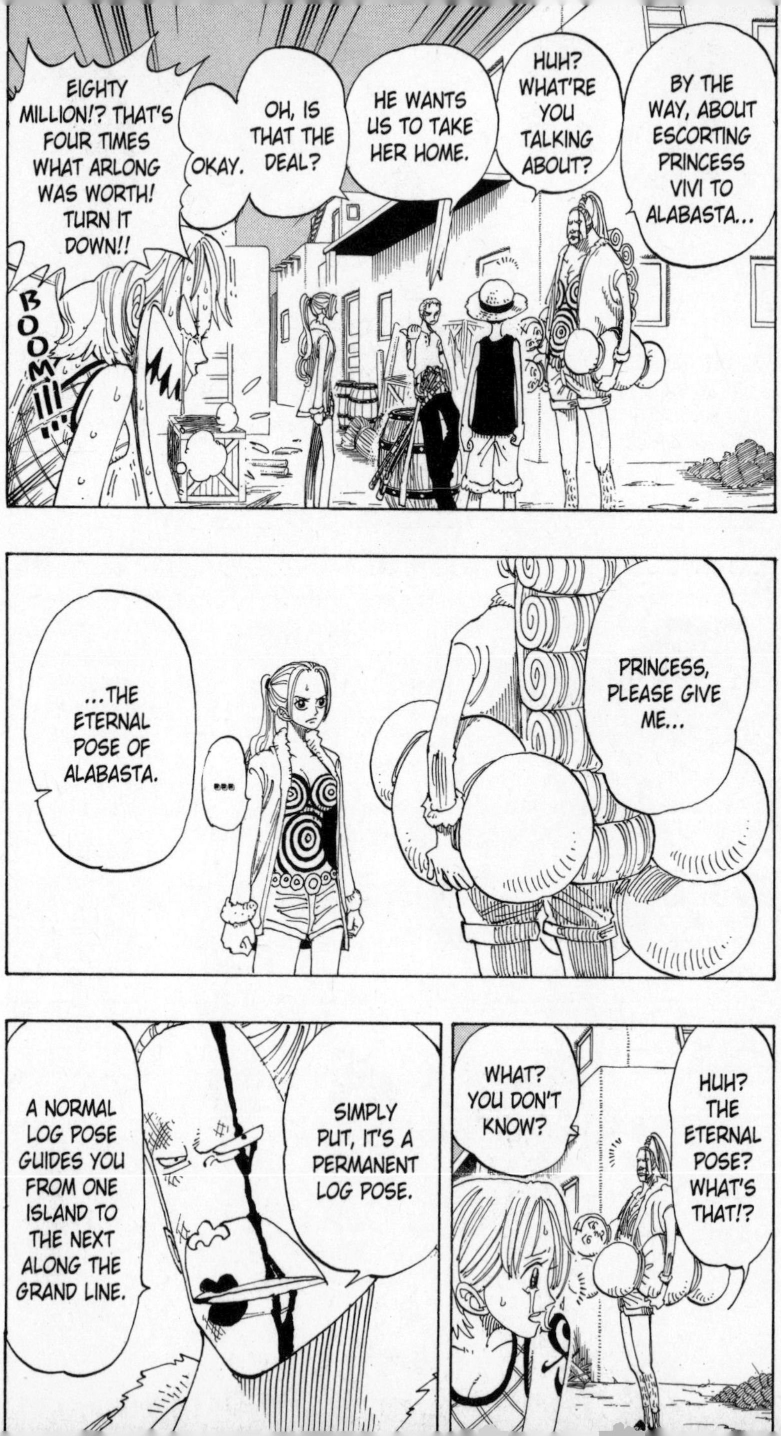
BY THE WAY, ABOUT ESCORTING PRINCESS VIVI TO ALABASTA...
HUH? WHAT'RE YOU TALKING ABOUT?
HE WANTS US TO TAKE HER HOME.
OH, IS THAT THE DEAL?
OKAY.
EIGHTY MILLION!? THAT'S FOUR TIMES WHAT ARLONG WAS WORTH! TURN IT DOWN!!
BOOM!!!
PRINCESS, PLEASE GIVE ME...
...
...THE ETERNAL POSE OF ALABASTA.
HUH? THE ETERNAL POSE? WHAT'S THAT!?
WHAT? YOU DON'T KNOW?
SIMPLY PUT, IT'S A PERMANENT LOG POSE.
A NORMAL LOG POSE GUIDES YOU FROM ONE ISLAND TO THE NEXT ALONG THE GRAND LINE.

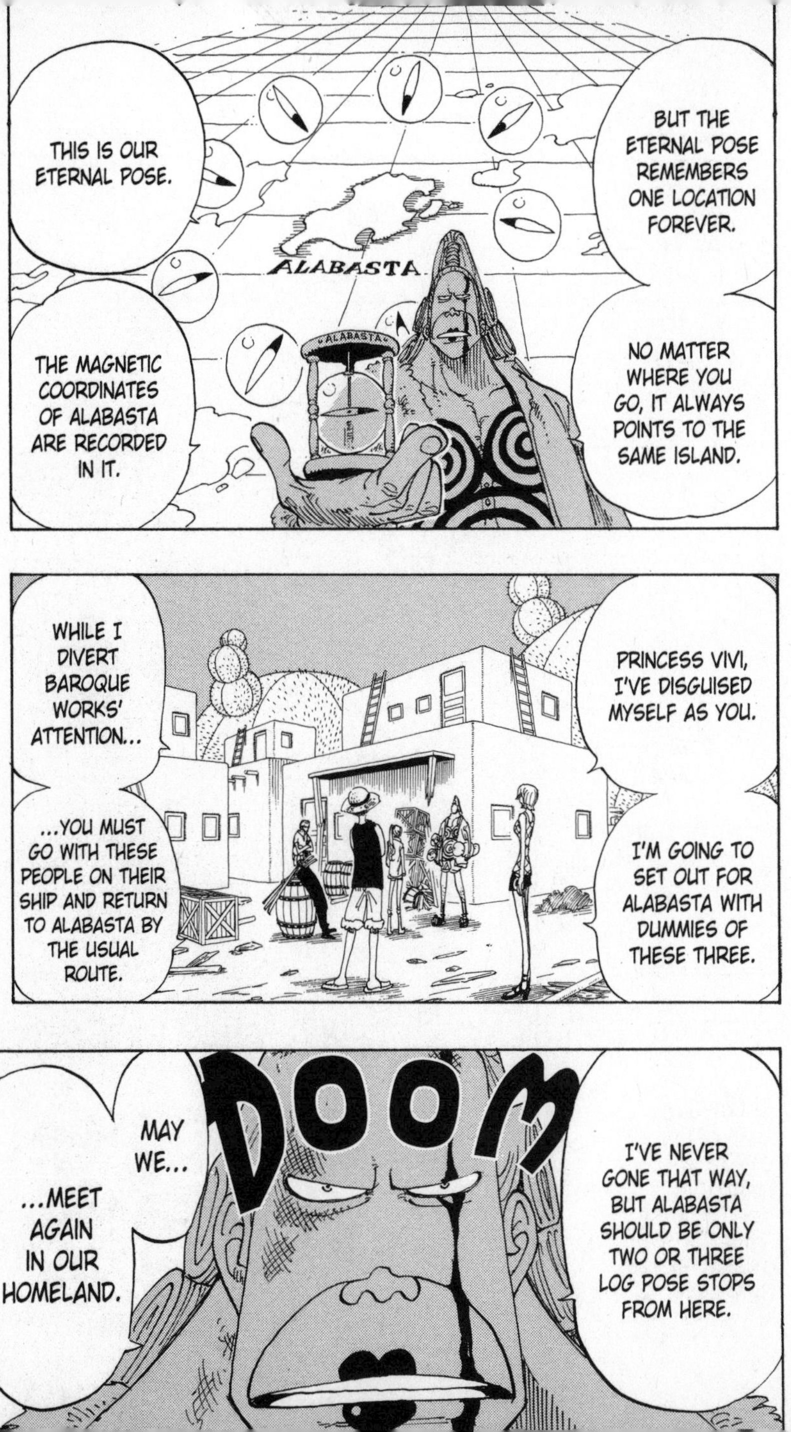
BUT THE ETERNAL POSE REMEMBERS ONE LOCATION FOREVER.
NO MATTER WHERE YOU GO, IT ALWAYS POINTS TO THE SAME ISLAND.
THIS IS OUR ETERNAL POSE.
THE MAGNETIC COORDINATES OF ALABASTA ARE RECORDED IN IT.
ALABASTA
ALABASTA
PRINCESS VIVI, I'VE DISGUISED MYSELF AS YOU.
I'M GOING TO SET OUT FOR ALABASTA WITH DUMMIES OF THESE THREE.
WHILE I DIVERT BAROQUE WORKS' ATTENTION...
...YOU MUST GO WITH THESE PEOPLE ON THEIR SHIP AND RETURN TO ALABASTA BY THE USUAL ROUTE.
I'VE NEVER GONE THAT WAY, BUT ALABASTA SHOULD BE ONLY TWO OR THREE LOG POSE STOPS FROM HERE.
DOOM
MAY WE...
...MEET AGAIN IN OUR HOMELAND.

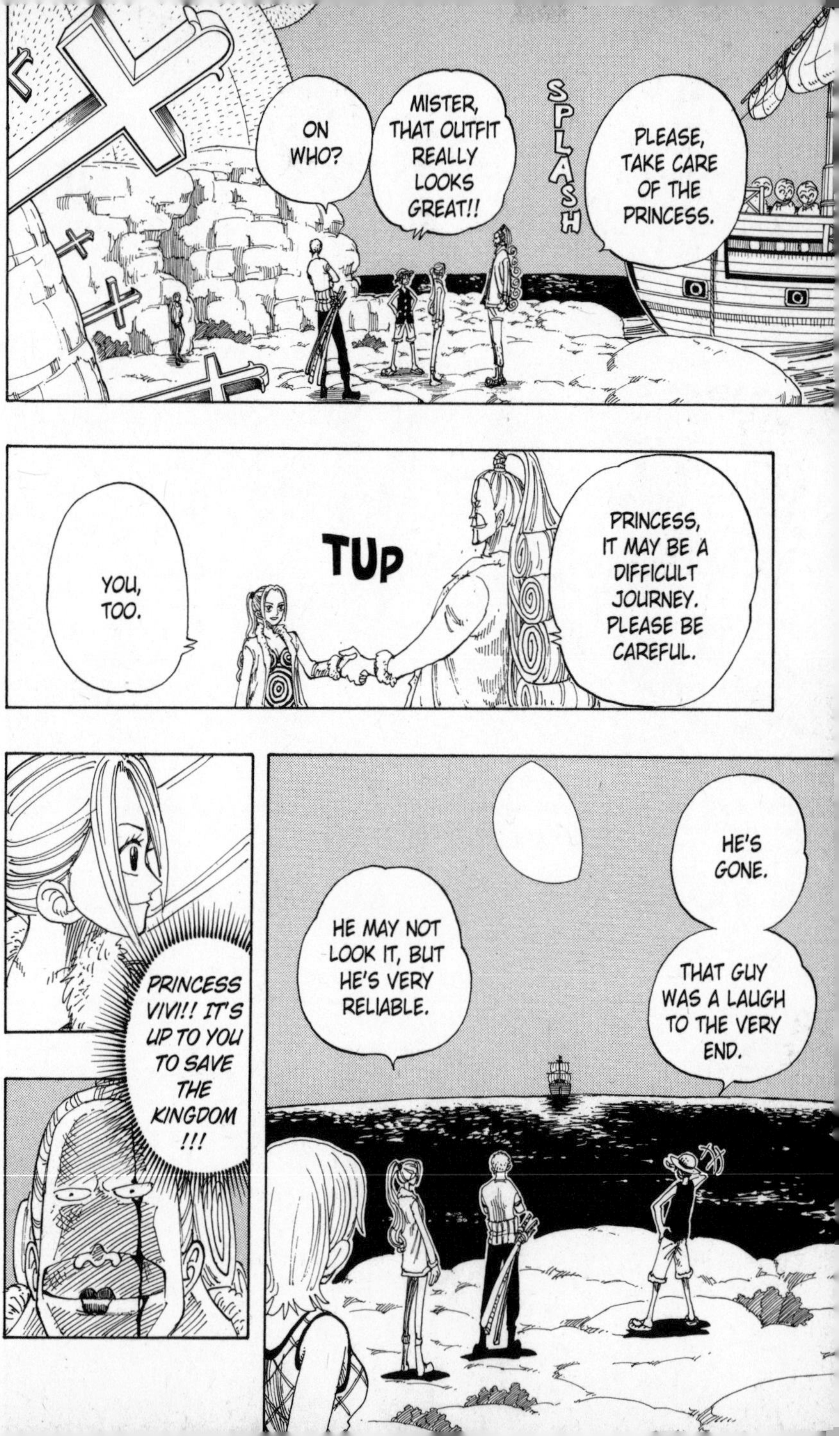
PLEASE, TAKE CARE OF THE PRINCESS.
SPLASH
MISTER, THAT OUTFIT REALLY LOOKS GREAT!!
ON WHO?
PRINCESS, IT MAY BE A DIFFICULT JOURNEY. PLEASE BE CAREFUL.
TUP
YOU, TOO.
HE'S GONE.
THAT GUY WAS A LAUGH TO THE VERY END.
HE MAY NOT LOOK IT, BUT HE'S VERY RELIABLE.
PRINCESS VIVI!! IT'S UP TO YOU TO SAVE THE KINGDOM!!!

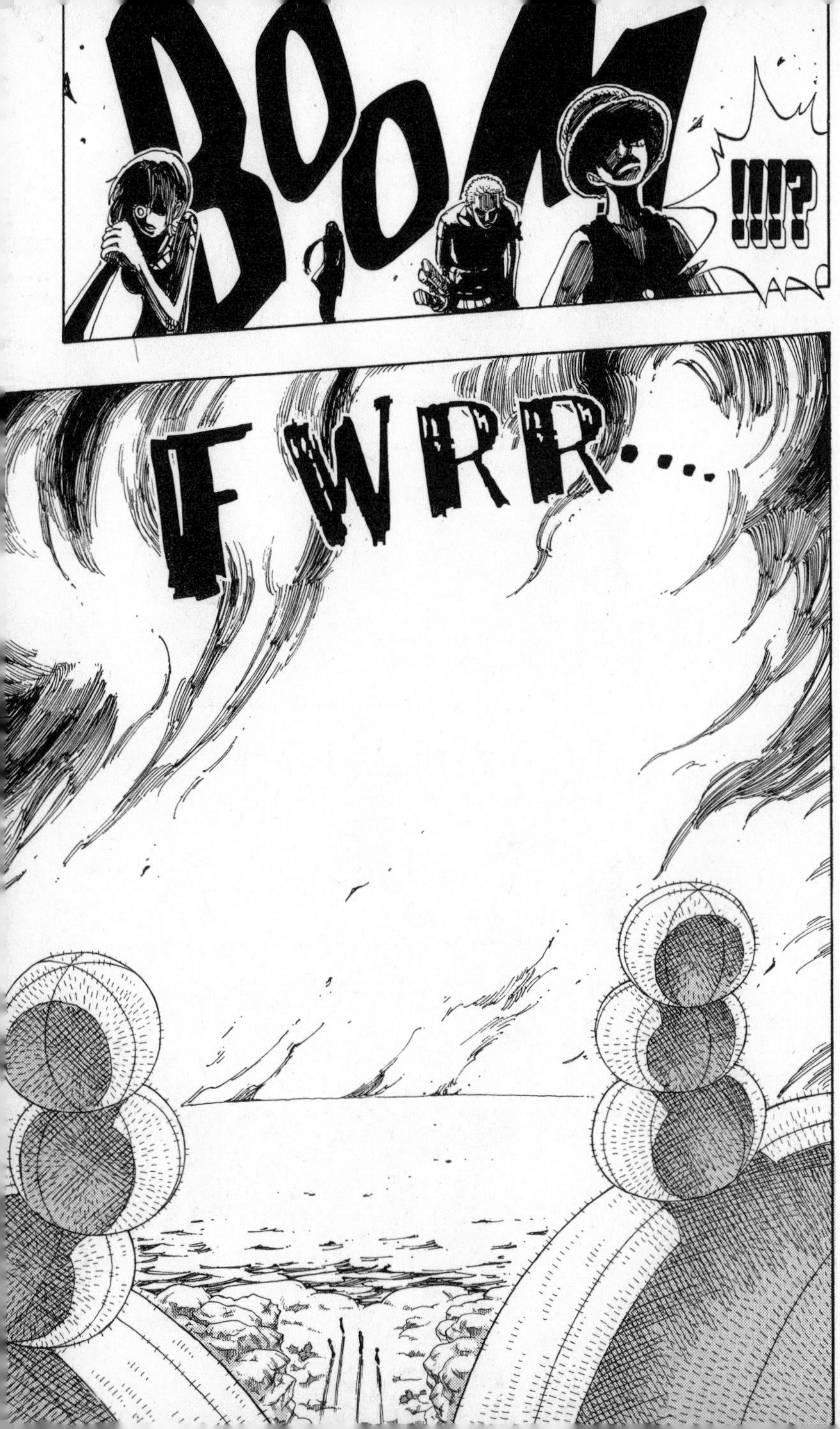
!!!?
BOOM
FWRR...

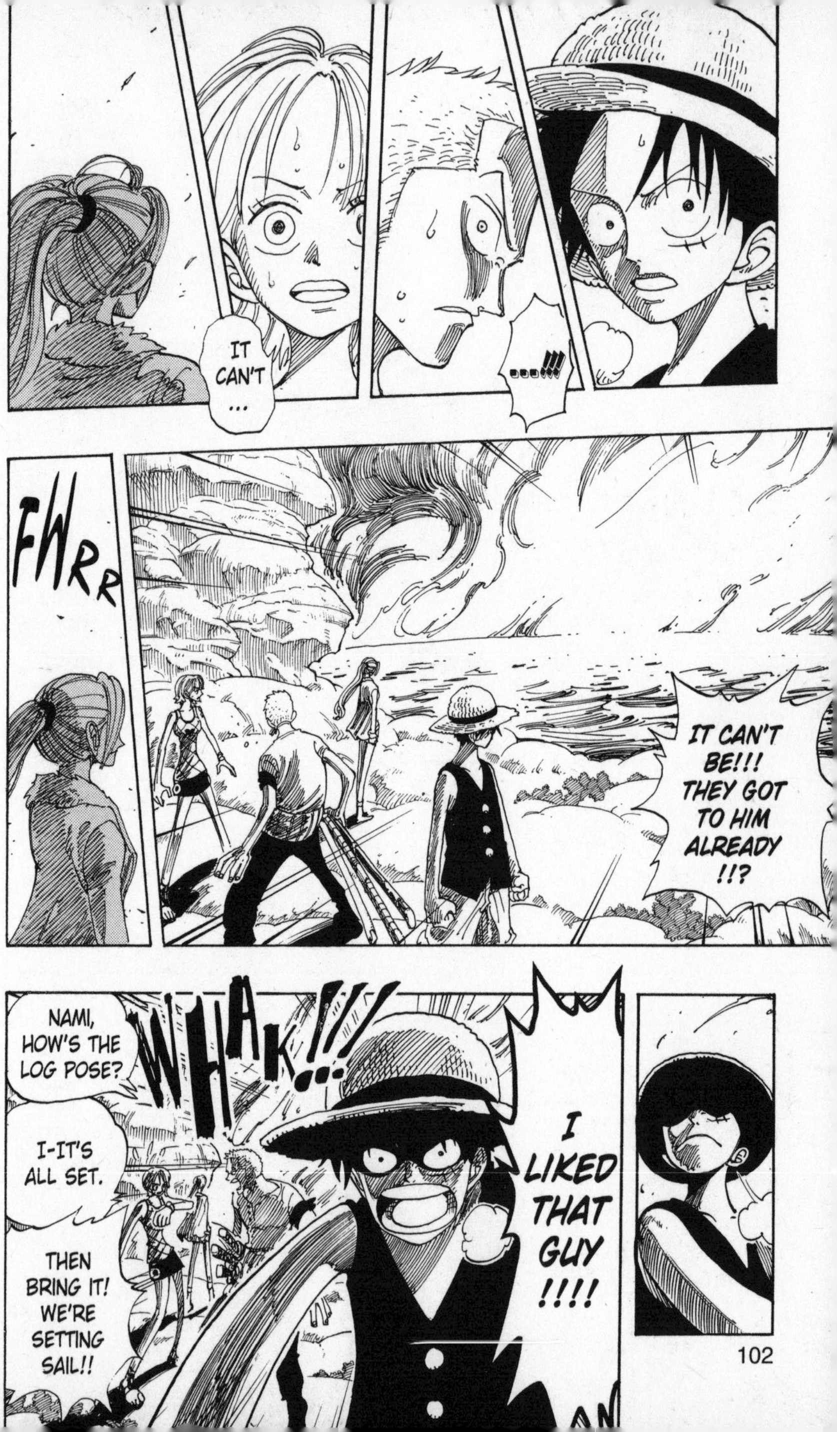
...!!!
IT CAN'T ...
IT CAN'T BE!!! THEY GOT TO HIM ALREADY !!?
FWRRR
I LIKED THAT GUY !!!!
WHAK!!!
NAMI, HOW'S THE LOG POSE?
I-IT'S ALL SET.
THEN BRING IT! WE'RE SETTING SAIL!!

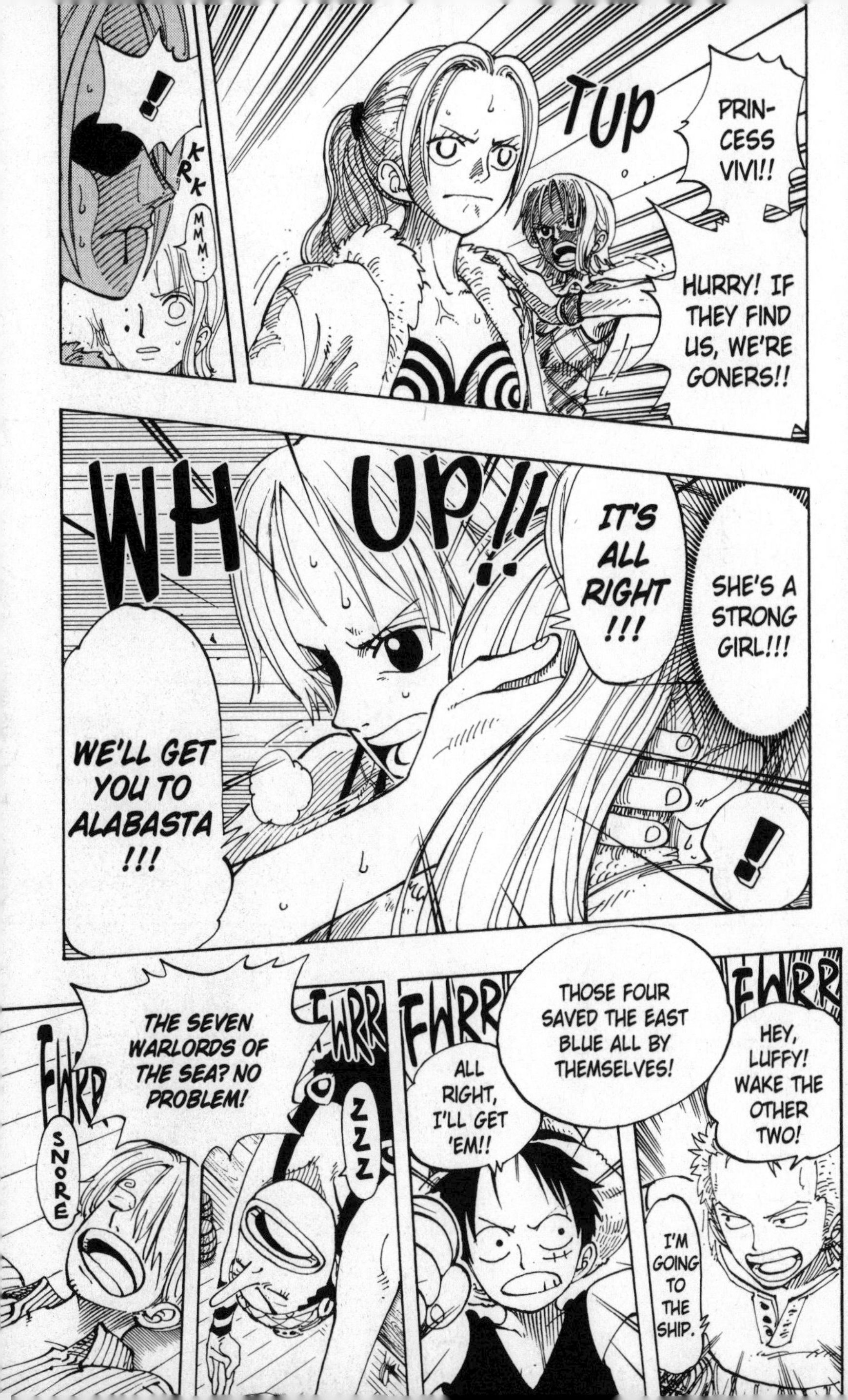
PRIN-CESS VIVI!!
TUP
HURRY! IF THEY FIND US, WE'RE GONERS!!
!
KRK
MMM...
SHE'S A STRONG GIRL!!!
!
IT'S ALL RIGHT!!!
WH UP!!
WE'LL GET YOU TO ALABASTA!!!
FWRR
HEY, LUFFY! WAKE THE OTHER TWO!
I'M GOING TO THE SHIP.
THOSE FOUR SAVED THE EAST BLUE ALL BY THEMSELVES!
ALL RIGHT, I'LL GET 'EM!!
FWRR
FWRR
ZZZ
THE SEVEN WARLORDS OF THE SEA? NO PROBLEM!
FWRR
SNORE

SBS
Question Corner

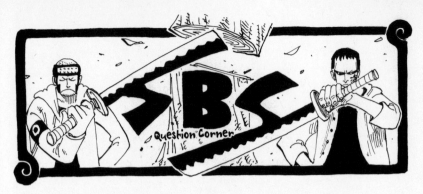

Q: What are those glasses that Usopp wears when he fights?

A: They're Sniper Goggles.
At first, Usopp wore regular goggles, but in Roguetown he got hold of some brand-new North Blue goggles.
To the right is a scene that got cut from the start of chapter 98 in volume 11, due to page restrictions.
These goggles are like sunglasses that deflect light when Usopp makes his sniper attacks. He really likes them because they flip up and down.

HUH?
FWIP
FWIP
HMM ...
HMM ...
FWIP FWIP FWIP
DOOM
OH!!
HEY LADY, I LIKE THESE GOGGLES.
YOU HAVE GOOD TASTE. THEY'RE THE LATEST NORTH BLUE GOGGLES.
THE NAVY PUTS OUT A NEW MODEL ONCE A YEAR.
SAME WITH THIS WATCH.
AND THIS COMPASS.
OH YEAH, DO YOU HAVE ANY RAW EGGS!?
TRY A SUPER-MARKET!!
JUNK SHOP

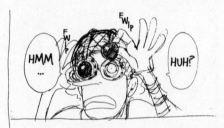

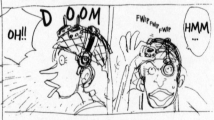

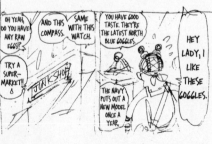

Q: Hello, Oda Sensei. I'm confused, so please clarify something. Is that thing you draw on Sanji's chin a goatee or a shadow or what? If it's a goatee, can I shave it?

A: It's a goatee! And no, you can't shave it!!

This is the end of SBS!!

The end...the end...the end...

Chapter 114: THE COURSE

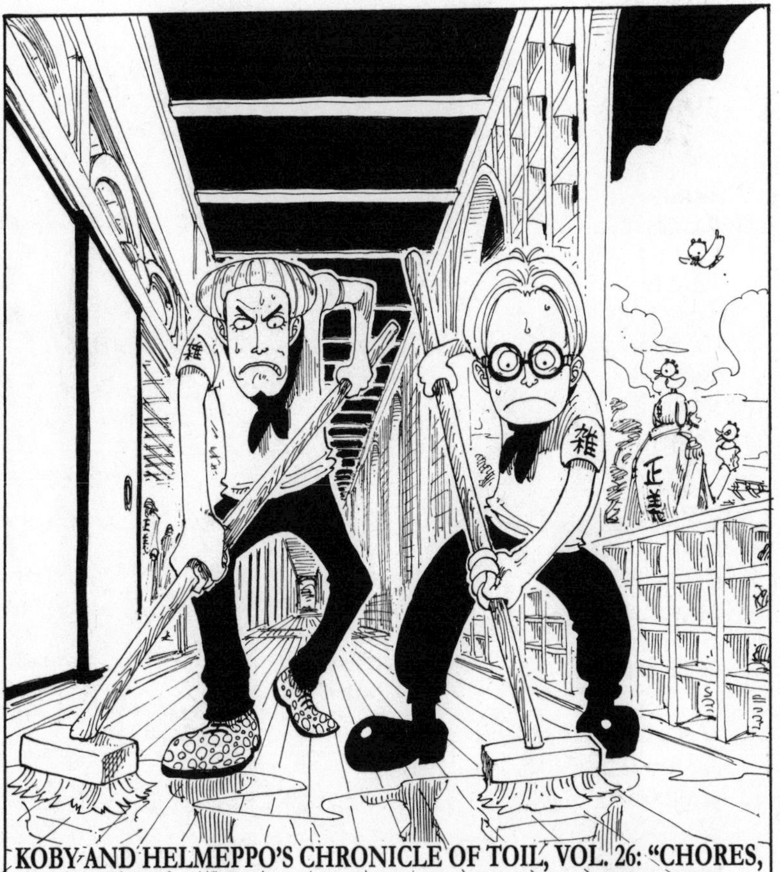

KOBY AND HELMEPPO'S CHRONICLE OF TOIL, VOL. 26: "CHORES, CHORES, AND MORE CHORES AT NAVY HEADQUARTERS"

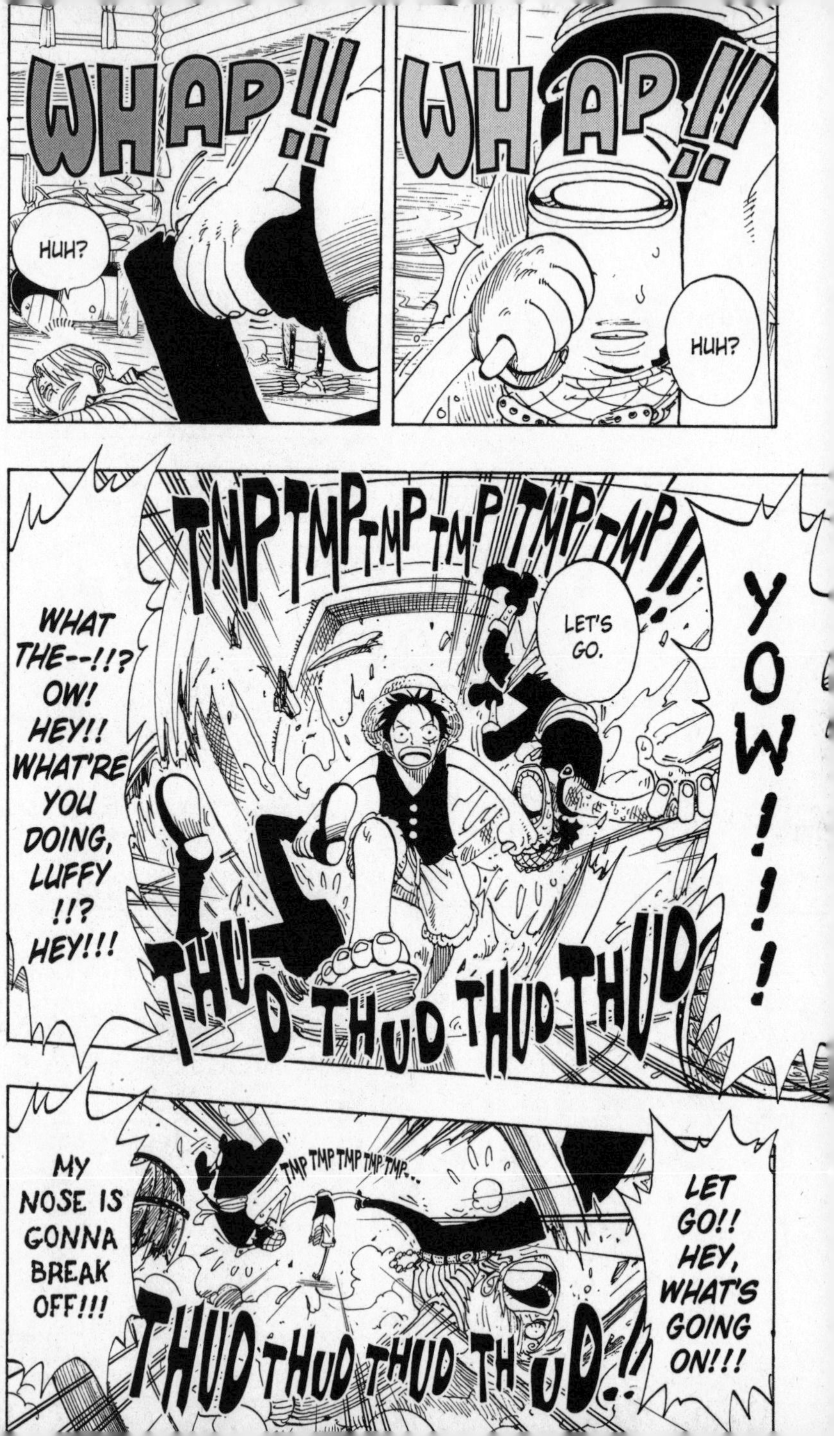
WHAP!!
HUH?
WHAP!!
HUH?
YOW!!!!!
LET'S GO.
TMP TMP TMP TMP TMP TMP!!
WHAT THE--!!? OW! HEY!! WHAT'RE YOU DOING, LUFFY !!? HEY!!!
THUD THUD THUD THUD
LET GO!! HEY, WHAT'S GOING ON!!!
TMP TMP TMP TMP TMP...
MY NOSE IS GONNA BREAK OFF!!!
THUD THUD THUD THUD!!

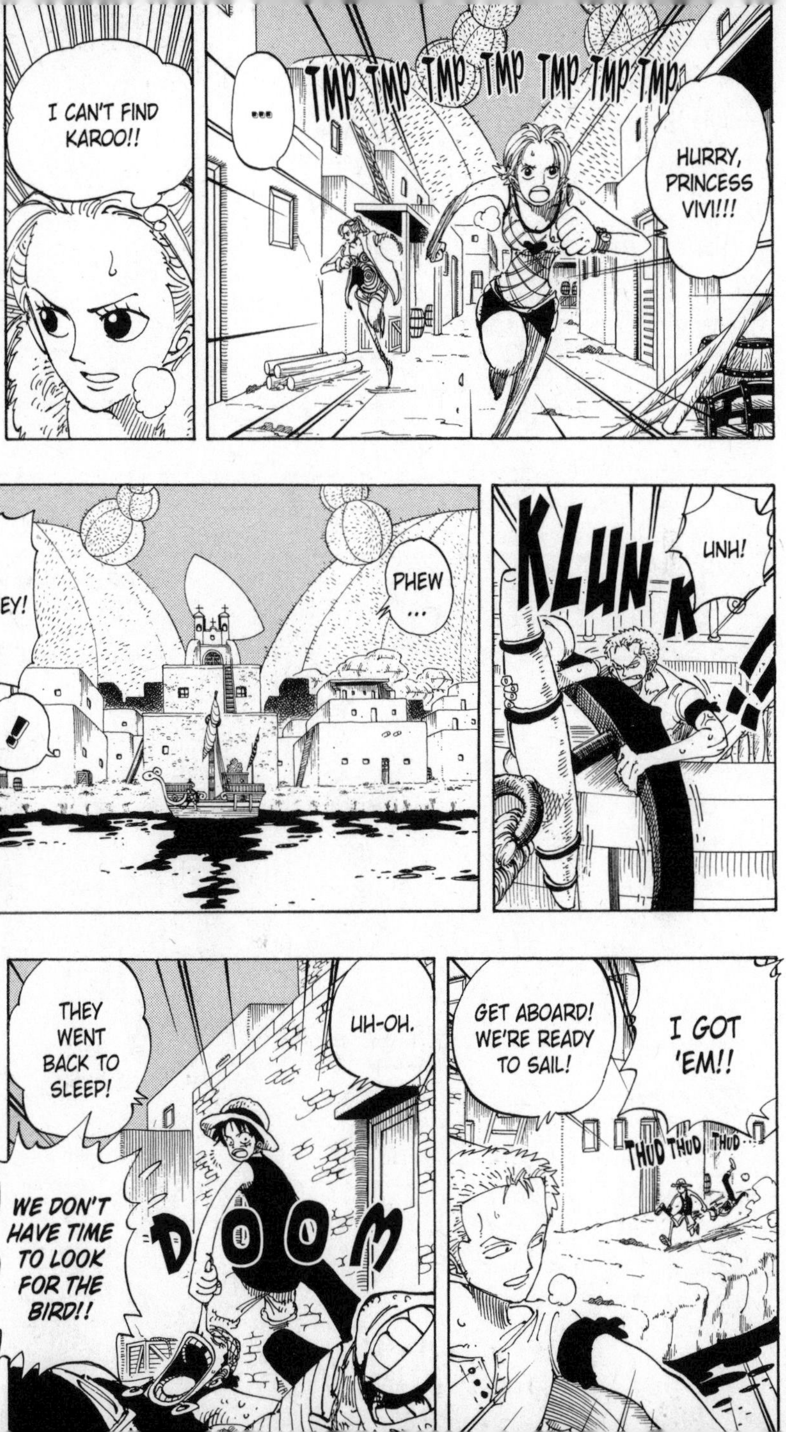
TMP TMP TMP TMP TMP TMP TMP
HURRY, PRINCESS VIVI!!!
...
I CAN'T FIND KAROO!!
KLUNK!!
UNH!
PHEW...
HEY!
!
I GOT 'EM!!
GET ABOARD! WE'RE READY TO SAIL!
THUD THUD THUD
UH-OH.
THEY WENT BACK TO SLEEP!
DOOM
WE DON'T HAVE TIME TO LOOK FOR THE BIRD!!

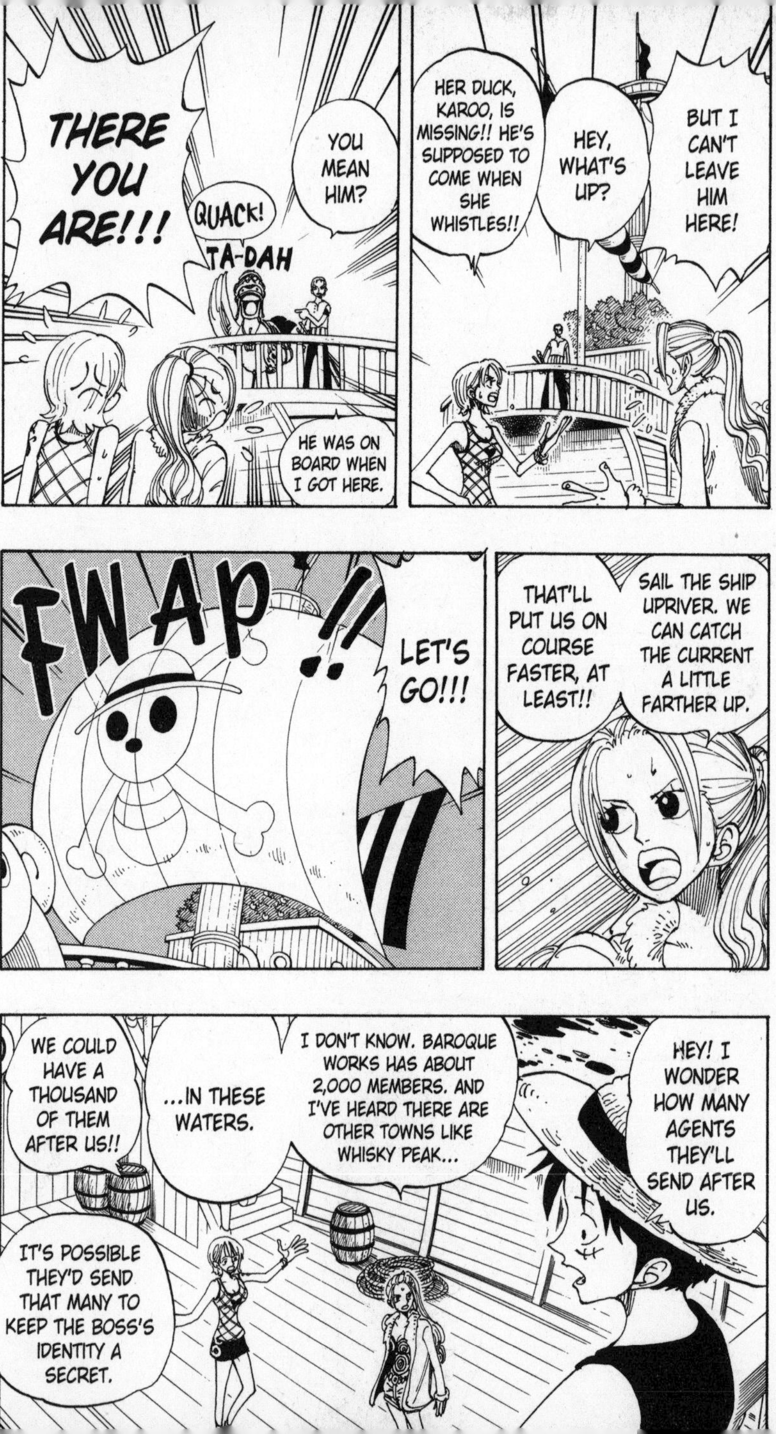
BUT I CAN'T LEAVE HIM HERE!
HEY, WHAT'S UP?
HER DUCK, KAROO, IS MISSING!! HE'S SUPPOSED TO COME WHEN SHE WHISTLES!!
YOU MEAN HIM?
THERE YOU ARE!!!
QUACK!
TA-DAH
HE WAS ON BOARD WHEN I GOT HERE.
SAIL THE SHIP UPRIVER. WE CAN CATCH THE CURRENT A LITTLE FARTHER UP.
THAT'LL PUT US ON COURSE FASTER, AT LEAST!!
LET'S GO!!!
FWAP!!
HEY! I WONDER HOW MANY AGENTS THEY'LL SEND AFTER US.
I DON'T KNOW. BAROQUE WORKS HAS ABOUT 2,000 MEMBERS. AND I'VE HEARD THERE ARE OTHER TOWNS LIKE WHISKY PEAK...
...IN THESE WATERS.
WE COULD HAVE A THOUSAND OF THEM AFTER US!!
IT'S POSSIBLE THEY'D SEND THAT MANY TO KEEP THE BOSS'S IDENTITY A SECRET.

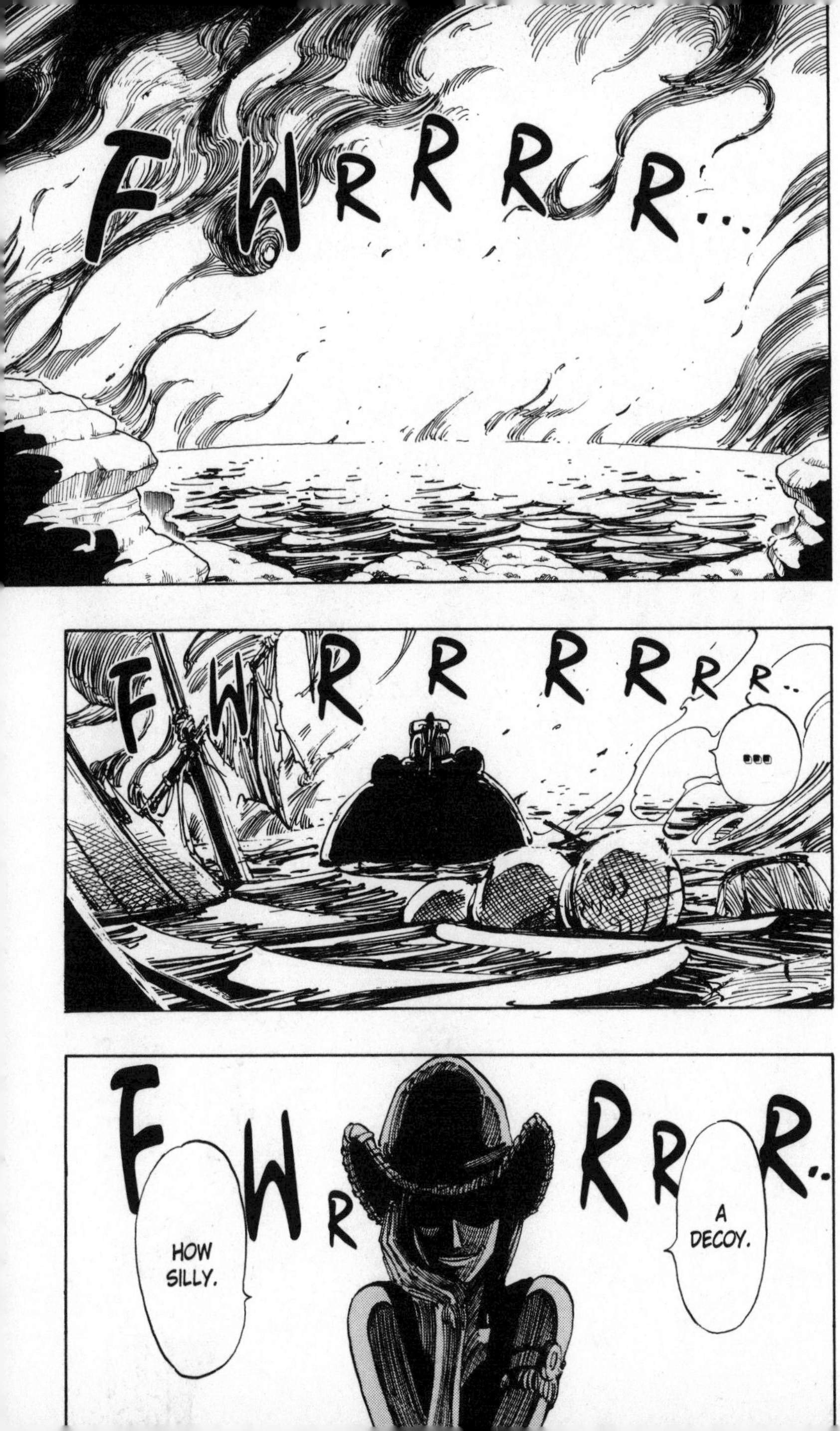
FWRRRR...
FWRRRRRR..
...
FWRRRR..
A DECOY.
HOW SILLY.

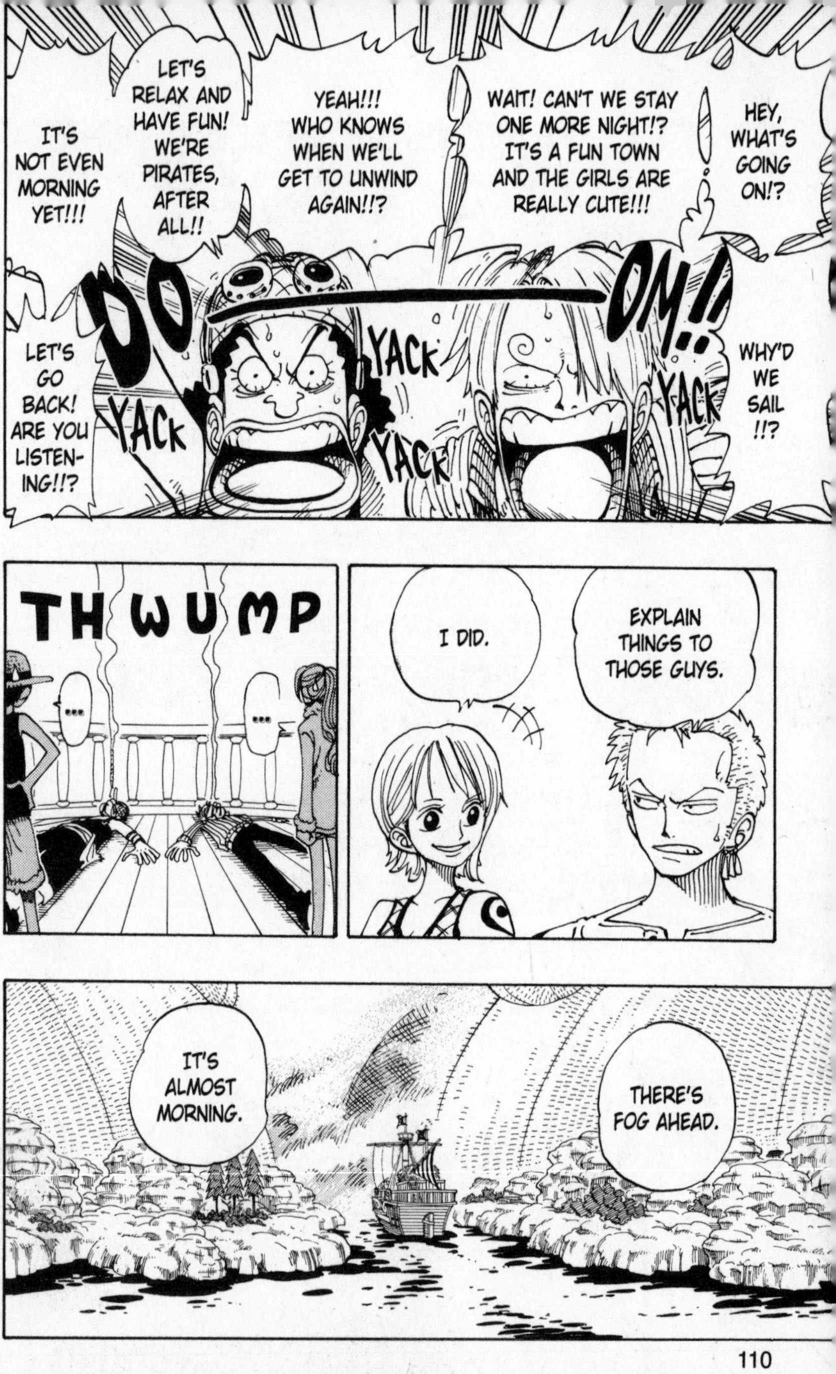
HEY, WHAT'S GOING ON!?
WAIT! CAN'T WE STAY ONE MORE NIGHT!? IT'S A FUN TOWN AND THE GIRLS ARE REALLY CUTE!!!
YEAH!!! WHO KNOWS WHEN WE'LL GET TO UNWIND AGAIN!!?
LET'S RELAX AND HAVE FUN! WE'RE PIRATES, AFTER ALL!!
IT'S NOT EVEN MORNING YET!!!
DOOM!!
WHY'D WE SAIL !!?
YACK
YACK
YACK
YACK
LET'S GO BACK! ARE YOU LISTEN-ING!!?
EXPLAIN THINGS TO THOSE GUYS.
I DID.
THWUMP
...
...
THERE'S FOG AHEAD.
IT'S ALMOST MORNING.

READ THIS WAY

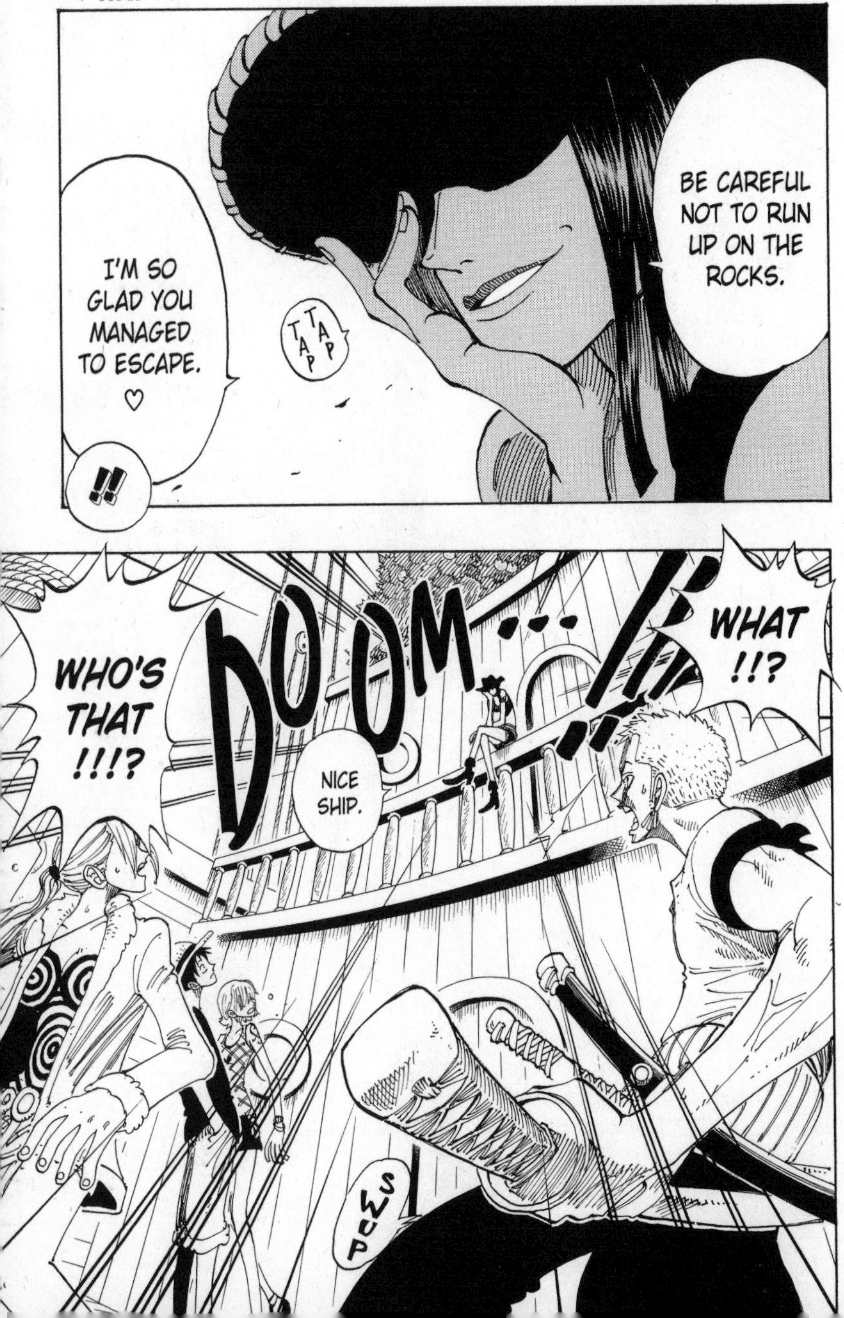
BE CAREFUL NOT TO RUN UP ON THE ROCKS.
TAP TAP
I'M SO GLAD YOU MANAGED TO ESCAPE. ♡
!!
WHAT!!?
DOOM...!!
NICE SHIP.
WHO'S THAT!!!?
SWUP

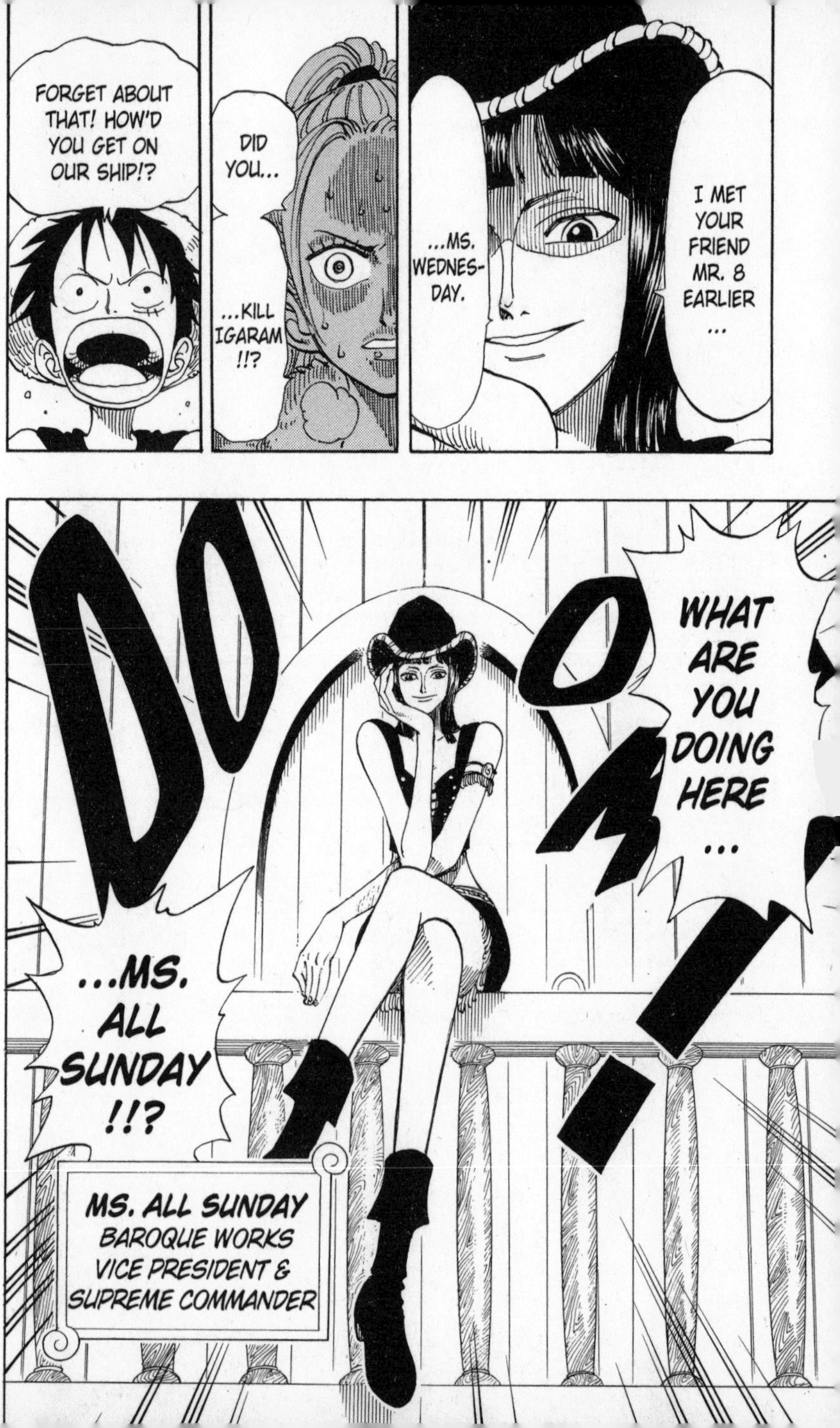
I MET YOUR FRIEND MR. 8 EARLIER ...
...MS. WEDNES-DAY.
DID YOU...
...KILL IGARAM !!?
FORGET ABOUT THAT! HOW'D YOU GET ON OUR SHIP!?
WHAT ARE YOU DOING HERE ...
DOOM!
...MS. ALL SUNDAY !!?
MS. ALL SUNDAY
BAROQUE WORKS VICE PRESIDENT & SUPREME COMMANDER

READ THIS WAY

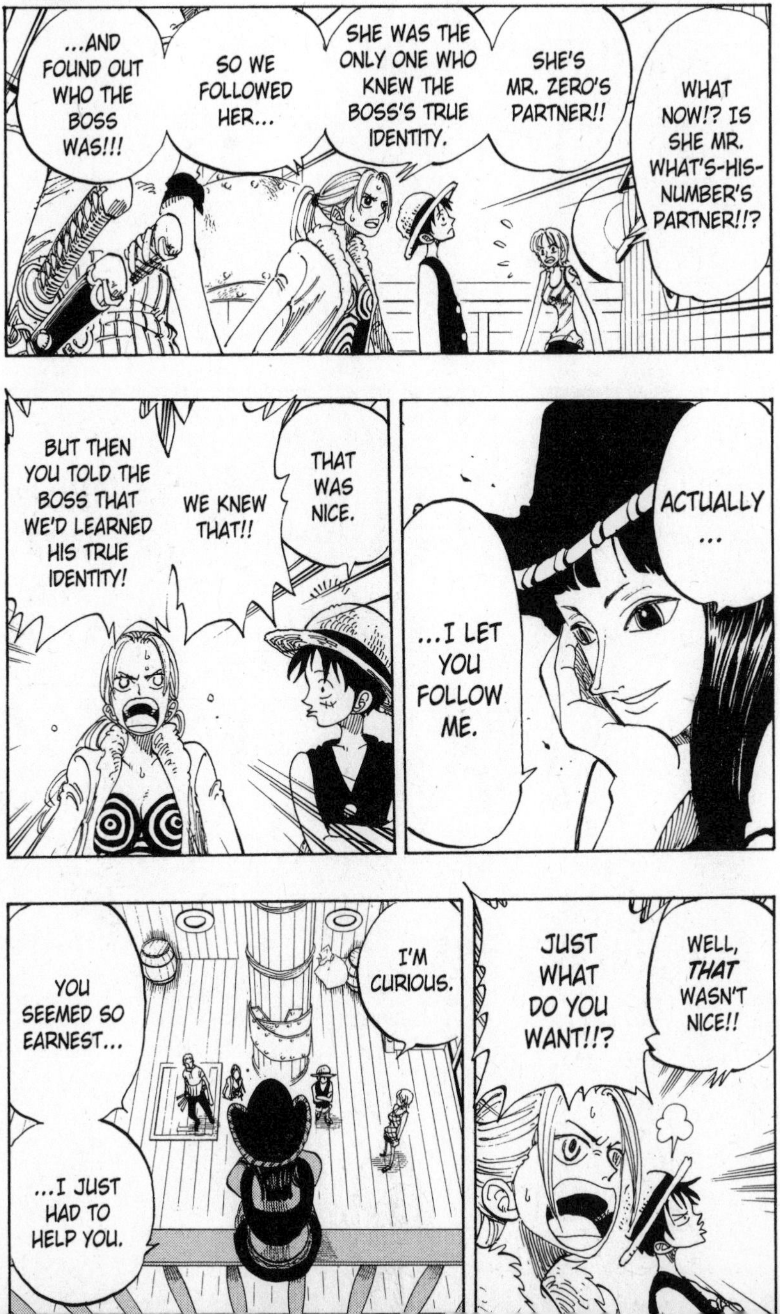
WHAT NOW!? IS SHE MR. WHAT'S-HIS-NUMBER'S PARTNER!!?
SHE'S MR. ZERO'S PARTNER!!
SHE WAS THE ONLY ONE WHO KNEW THE BOSS'S TRUE IDENTITY.
SO WE FOLLOWED HER...
...AND FOUND OUT WHO THE BOSS WAS!!!
ACTUALLY...
...I LET YOU FOLLOW ME.
THAT WAS NICE.
WE KNEW THAT!!
BUT THEN YOU TOLD THE BOSS THAT WE'D LEARNED HIS TRUE IDENTITY!
WELL, *THAT* WASN'T NICE!!
JUST WHAT DO YOU WANT!!?
I'M CURIOUS.
YOU SEEMED SO EARNEST...
...I JUST HAD TO HELP YOU.

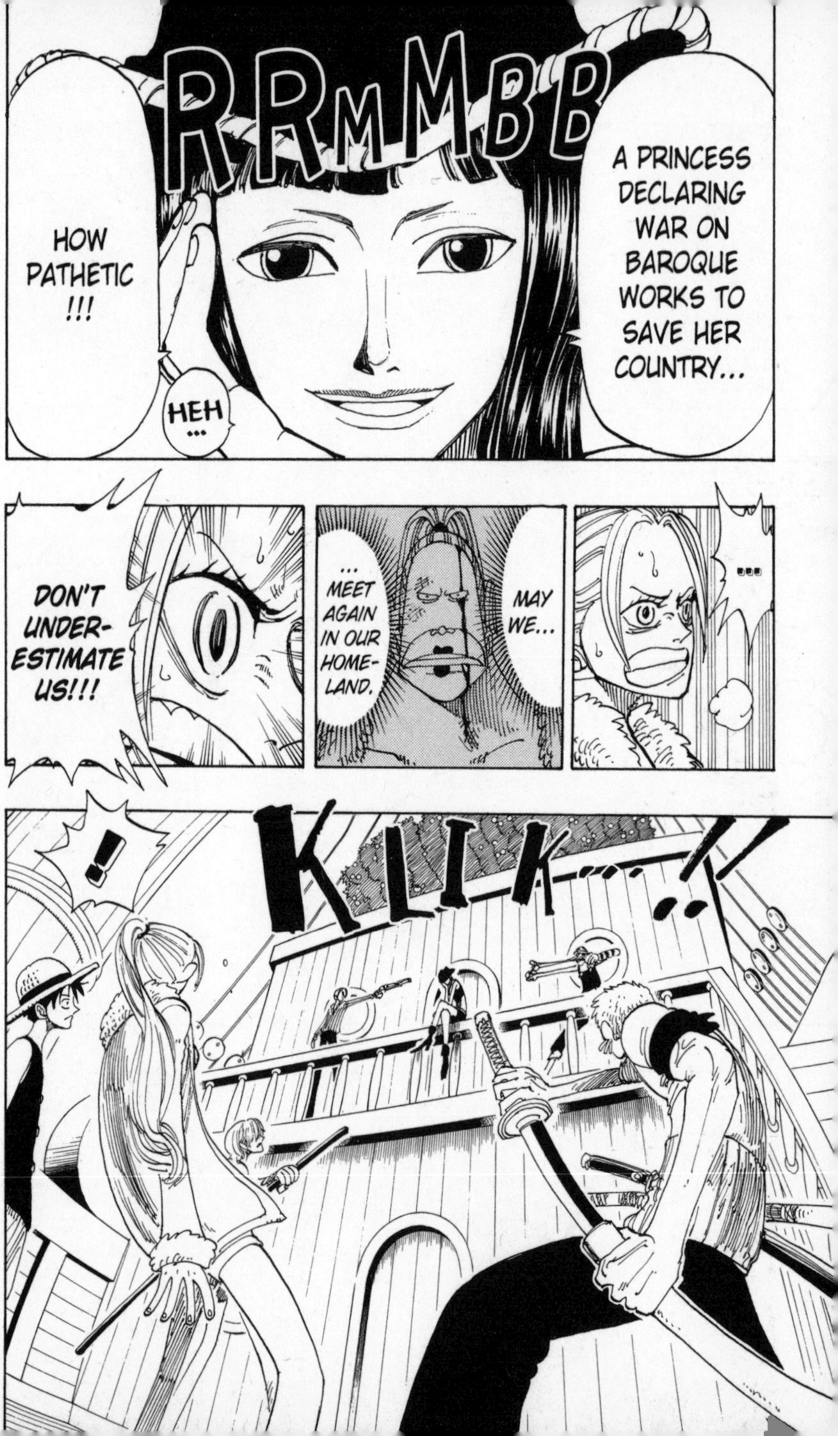
RRMMBB
A PRINCESS DECLARING WAR ON BAROQUE WORKS TO SAVE HER COUNTRY...
HOW PATHETIC!!!
HEH...
...
MAY WE...
...MEET AGAIN IN OUR HOME-LAND.
DON'T UNDER-ESTIMATE US!!!
KLIK...K..
!

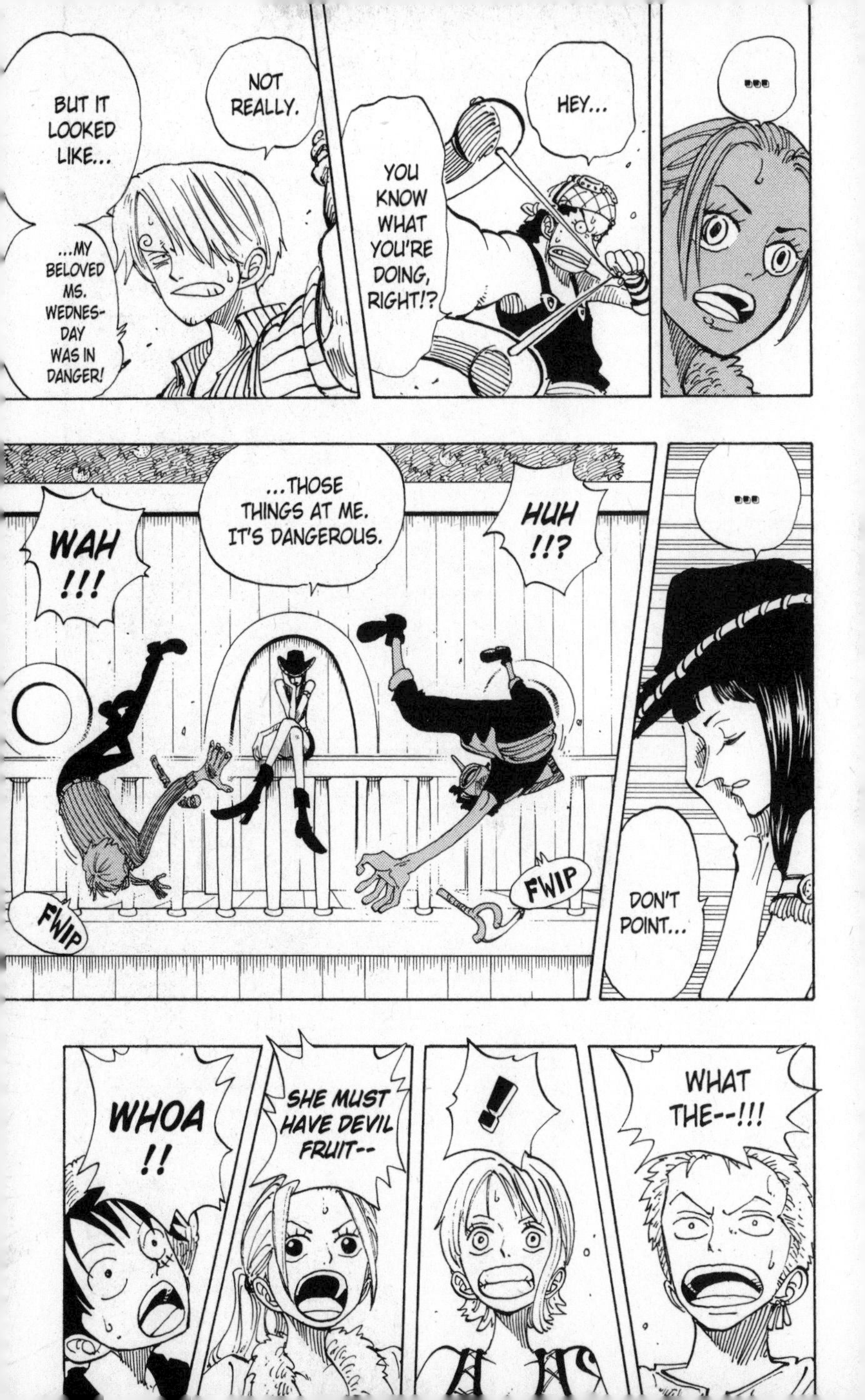
...
HEY...
YOU KNOW WHAT YOU'RE DOING, RIGHT!?
NOT REALLY.
BUT IT LOOKED LIKE...
...MY BELOVED MS. WEDNES-DAY WAS IN DANGER!
...
DON'T POINT...
HUH!!?
...THOSE THINGS AT ME. IT'S DANGEROUS.
WAH!!!
FWIP
FWIP
WHAT THE--!!!
!
SHE MUST HAVE DEVIL FRUIT--
WHOA!!

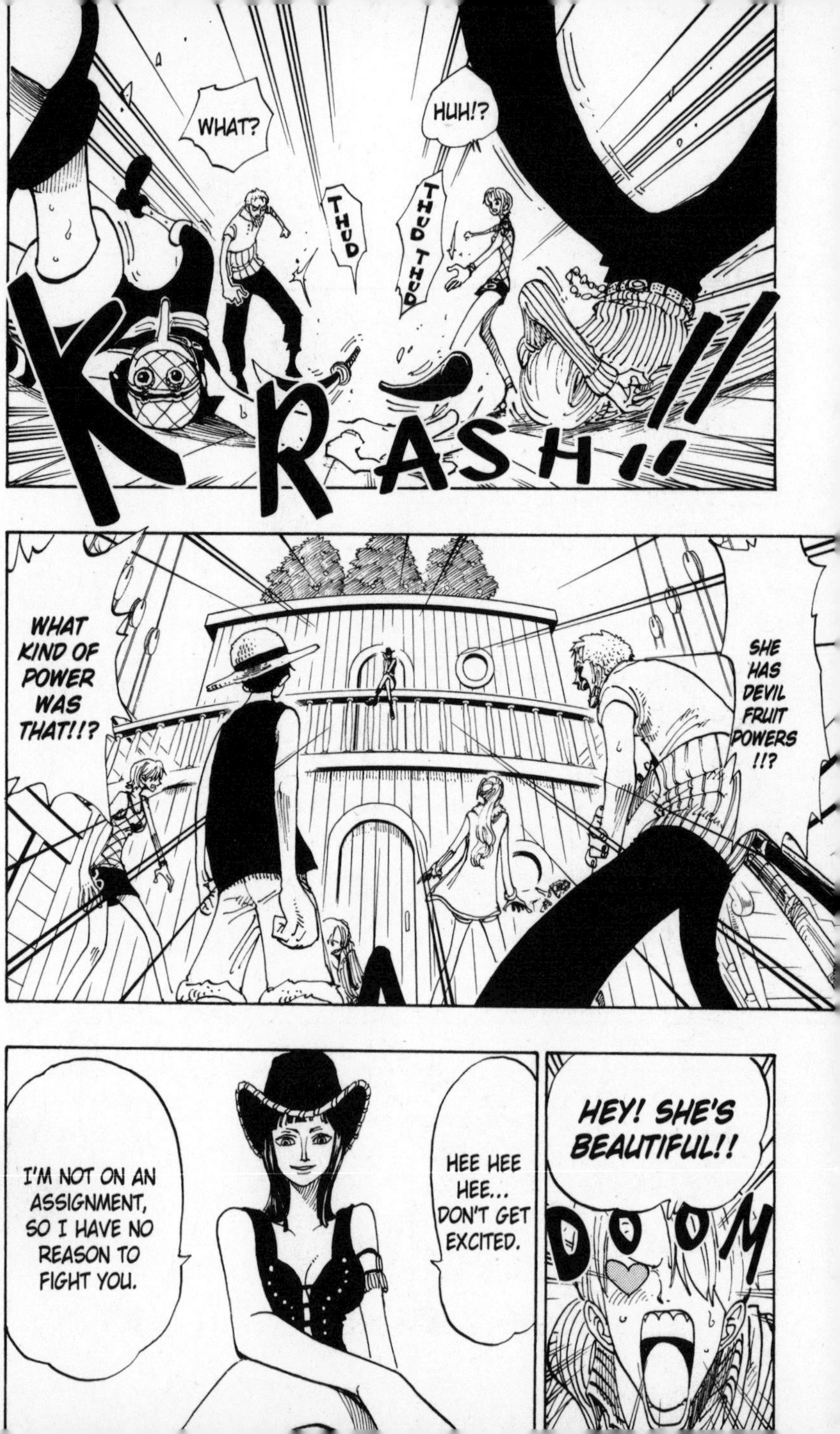
HUH!?
WHAT?
THUD THUD
THUD
KRASH!!
SHE HAS DEVIL FRUIT POWERS!!?
WHAT KIND OF POWER WAS THAT!!?
HEY! SHE'S BEAUTIFUL!!
DOOM
HEE HEE HEE... DON'T GET EXCITED.
I'M NOT ON AN ASSIGNMENT, SO I HAVE NO REASON TO FIGHT YOU.

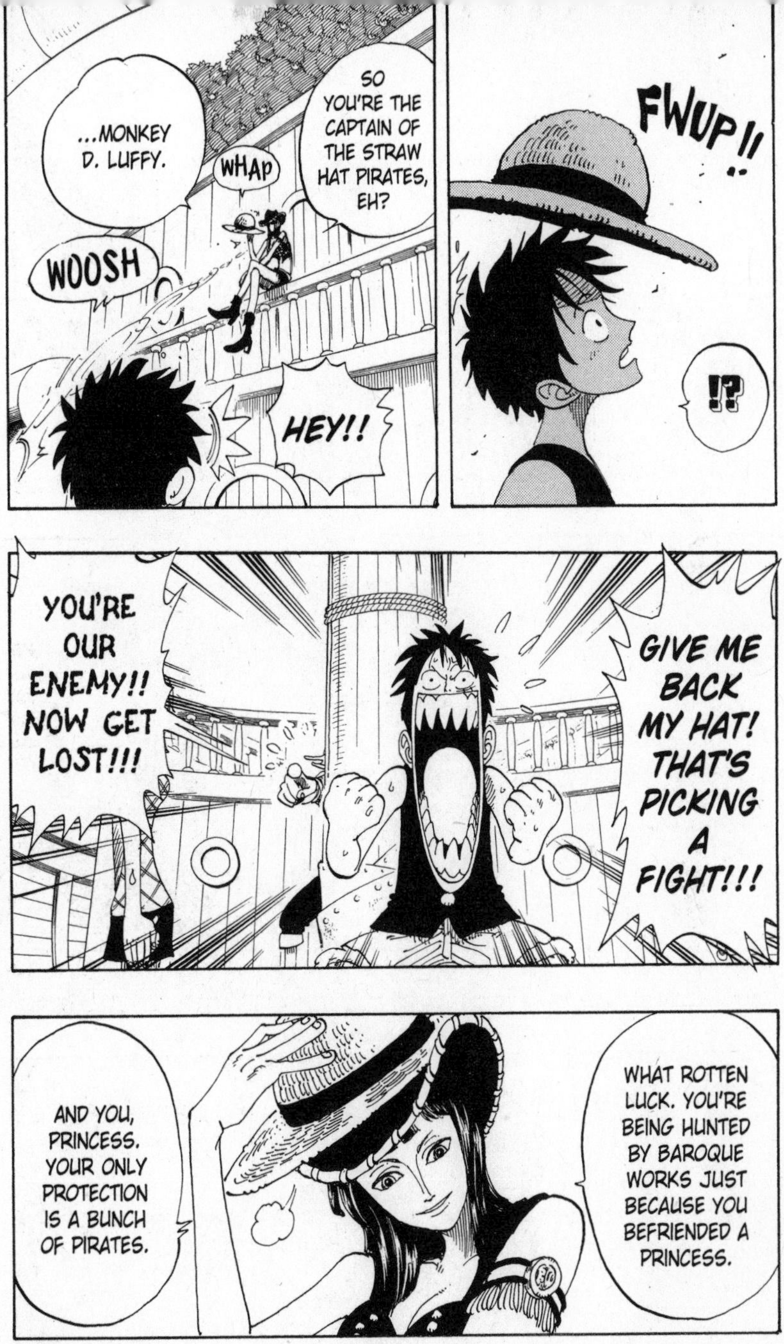
FWUP!!
!?
SO YOU'RE THE CAPTAIN OF THE STRAW HAT PIRATES, EH?
WHAp
...MONKEY D. LUFFY.
WOOSH
HEY!!
GIVE ME BACK MY HAT! THAT'S PICKING A FIGHT!!!
YOU'RE OUR ENEMY!! NOW GET LOST!!!
WHAT ROTTEN LUCK. YOU'RE BEING HUNTED BY BAROQUE WORKS JUST BECAUSE YOU BEFRIENDED A PRINCESS.
AND YOU, PRINCESS. YOUR ONLY PROTECTION IS A BUNCH OF PIRATES.

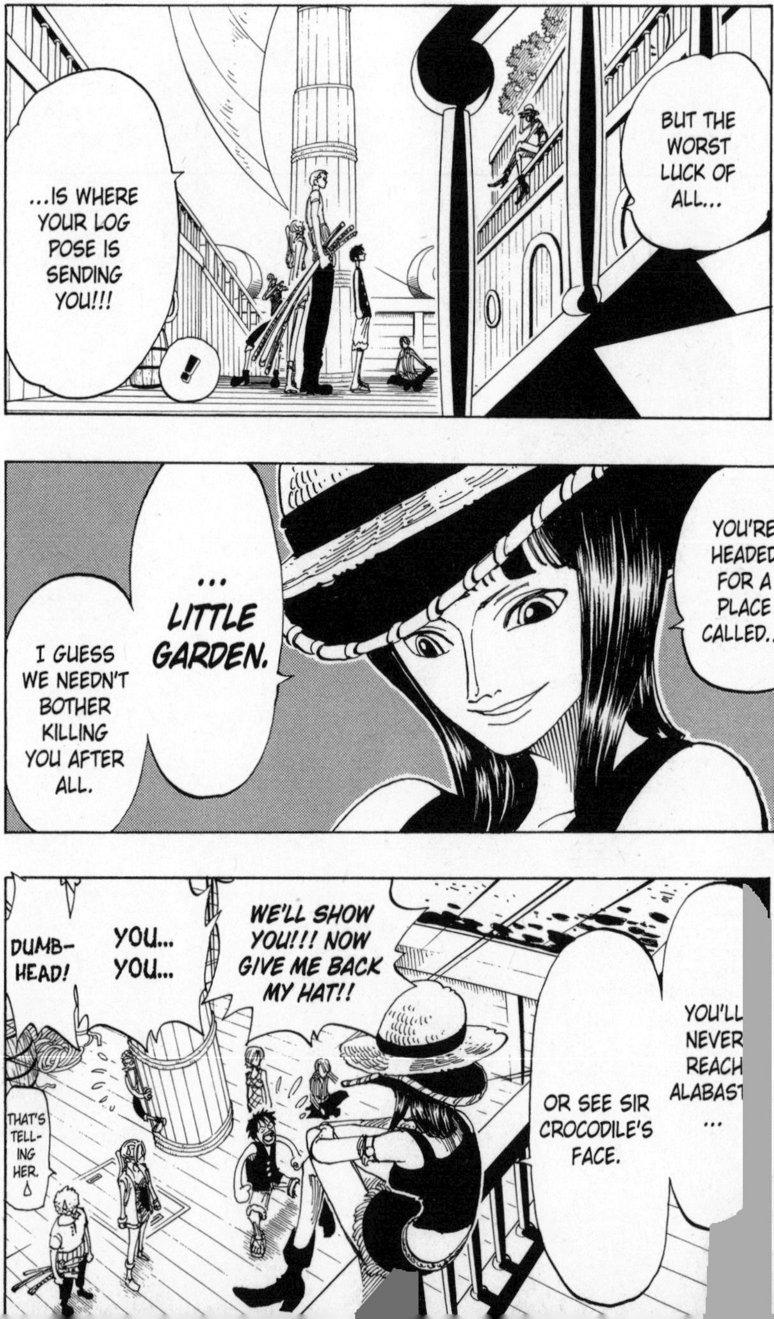
BUT THE WORST LUCK OF ALL...
...IS WHERE YOUR LOG POSE IS SENDING YOU!!!
!
YOU'RE HEADED FOR A PLACE CALLED...
... LITTLE GARDEN.
I GUESS WE NEEDN'T BOTHER KILLING YOU AFTER ALL.
YOU'LL NEVER REACH ALABAST ...
OR SEE SIR CROCODILE'S FACE.
WE'LL SHOW YOU!!! NOW GIVE ME BACK MY HAT!!
YOU... YOU...
DUMB-HEAD!
THAT'S TELL-ING HER.

READ THIS WAY

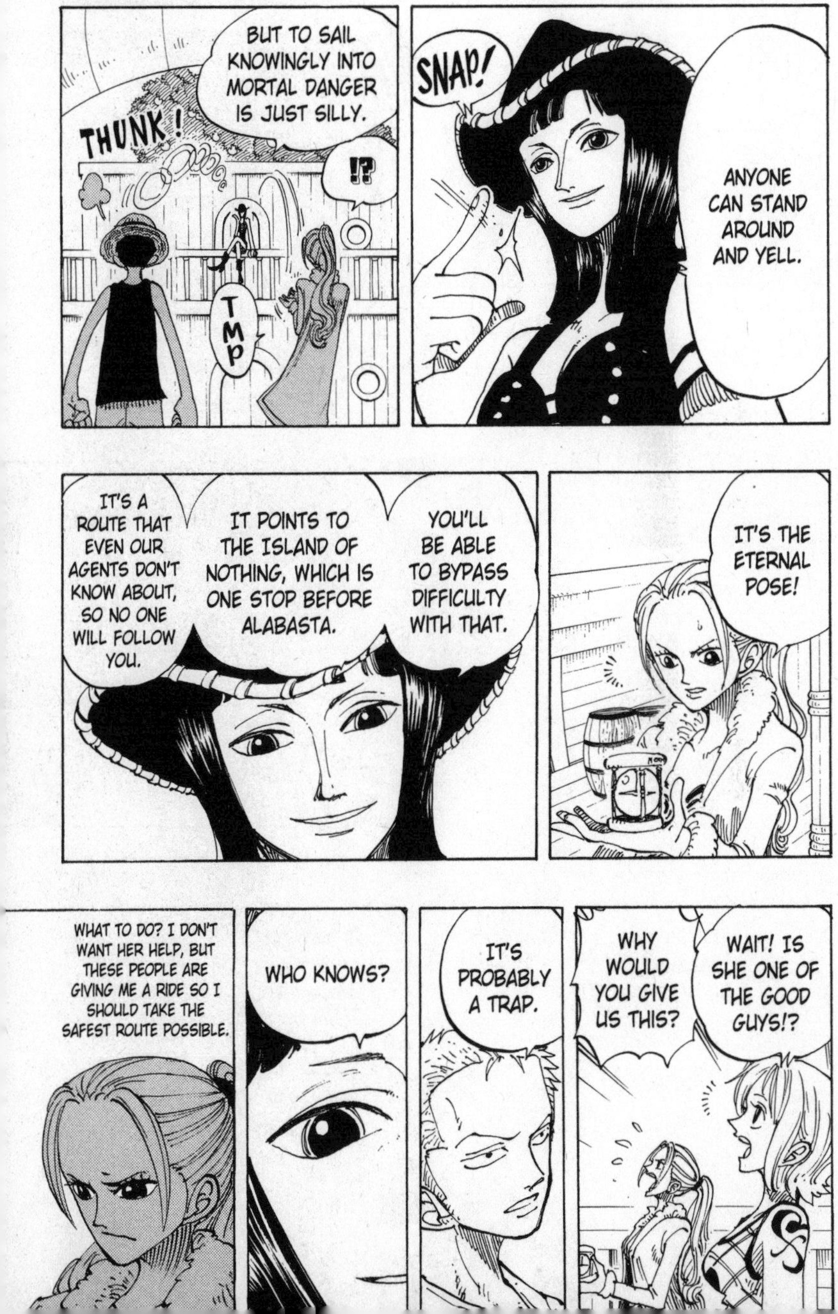
ANYONE CAN STAND AROUND AND YELL.
SNAP!
BUT TO SAIL KNOWINGLY INTO MORTAL DANGER IS JUST SILLY.
THUNK!
!?
TMP
IT'S THE ETERNAL POSE!
YOU'LL BE ABLE TO BYPASS DIFFICULTY WITH THAT.
IT POINTS TO THE ISLAND OF NOTHING, WHICH IS ONE STOP BEFORE ALABASTA.
IT'S A ROUTE THAT EVEN OUR AGENTS DON'T KNOW ABOUT, SO NO ONE WILL FOLLOW YOU.
WAIT! IS SHE ONE OF THE GOOD GUYS!?
WHY WOULD YOU GIVE US THIS?
IT'S PROBABLY A TRAP.
WHO KNOWS?
WHAT TO DO? I DON'T WANT HER HELP, BUT THESE PEOPLE ARE GIVING ME A RIDE SO I SHOULD TAKE THE SAFEST ROUTE POSSIBLE.

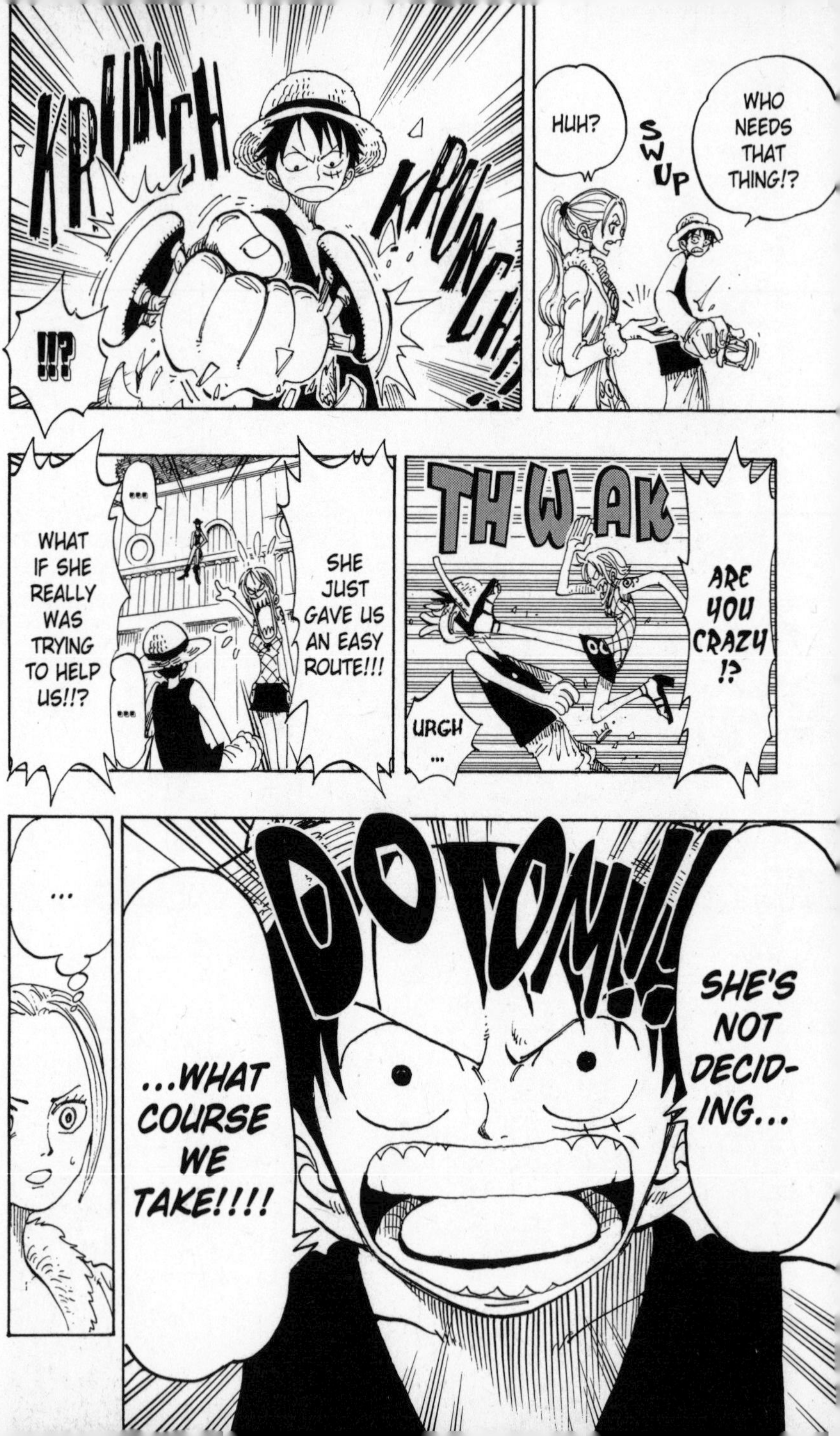
WHO NEEDS THAT THING!?
SWUP
HUH?
KRUNCH
KRUNCH!!
!!?
THWAK
ARE YOU CRAZY!?
URGH ...
SHE JUST GAVE US AN EASY ROUTE!!!
...
WHAT IF SHE REALLY WAS TRYING TO HELP US!!?
...
DOTON!!
SHE'S NOT DECIDING...
...WHAT COURSE WE TAKE!!!!
...

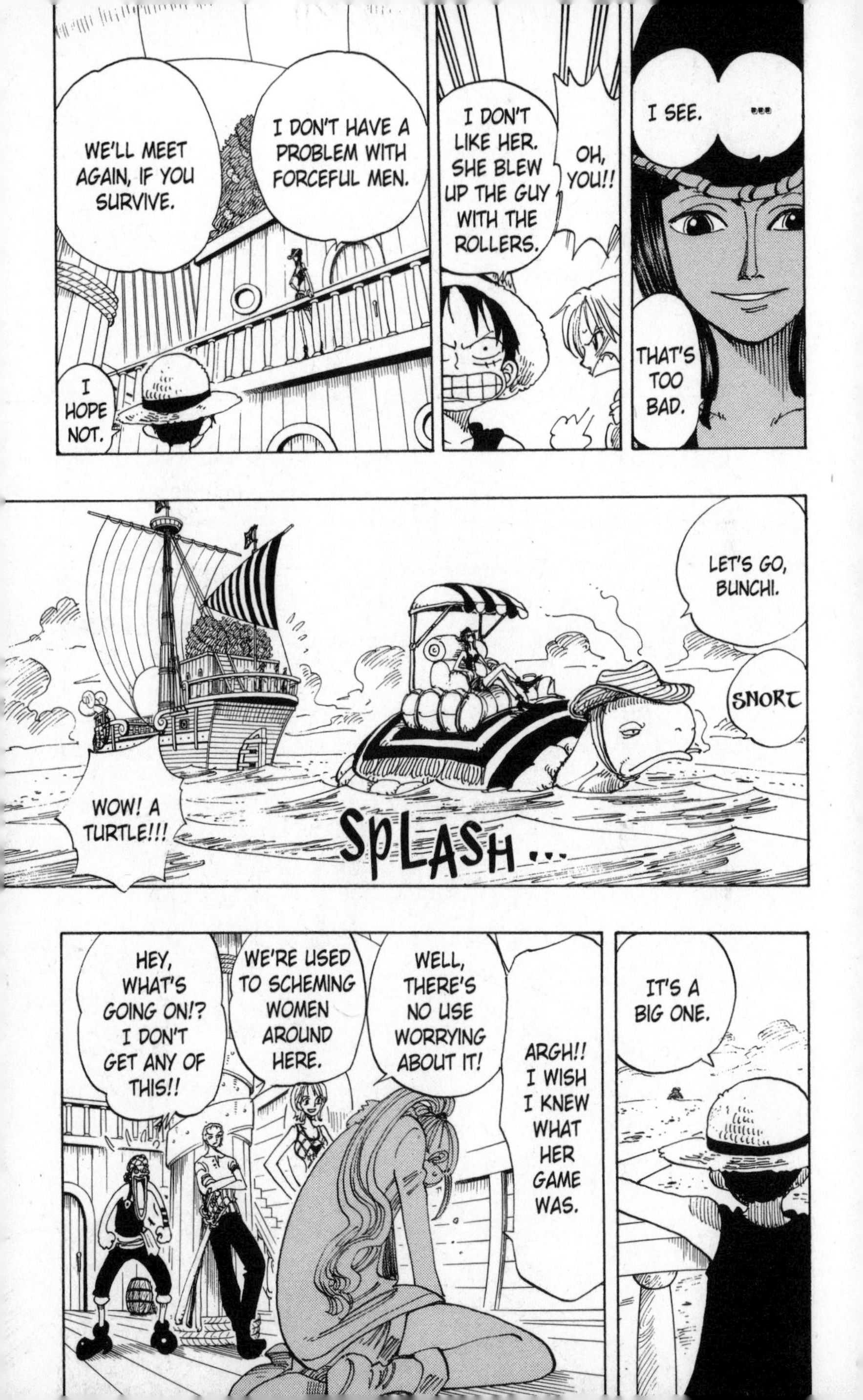
I SEE.
...
THAT'S TOO BAD.
I DON'T LIKE HER. SHE BLEW UP THE GUY WITH THE ROLLERS.
OH, YOU!!
I DON'T HAVE A PROBLEM WITH FORCEFUL MEN.
WE'LL MEET AGAIN, IF YOU SURVIVE.
I HOPE NOT.
LET'S GO, BUNCHI.
SNORT
SPLASH...
WOW! A TURTLE!!!
IT'S A BIG ONE.
ARGH!! I WISH I KNEW WHAT HER GAME WAS.
WELL, THERE'S NO USE WORRYING ABOUT IT!
WE'RE USED TO SCHEMING WOMEN AROUND HERE.
HEY, WHAT'S GOING ON!? I DON'T GET ANY OF THIS!!

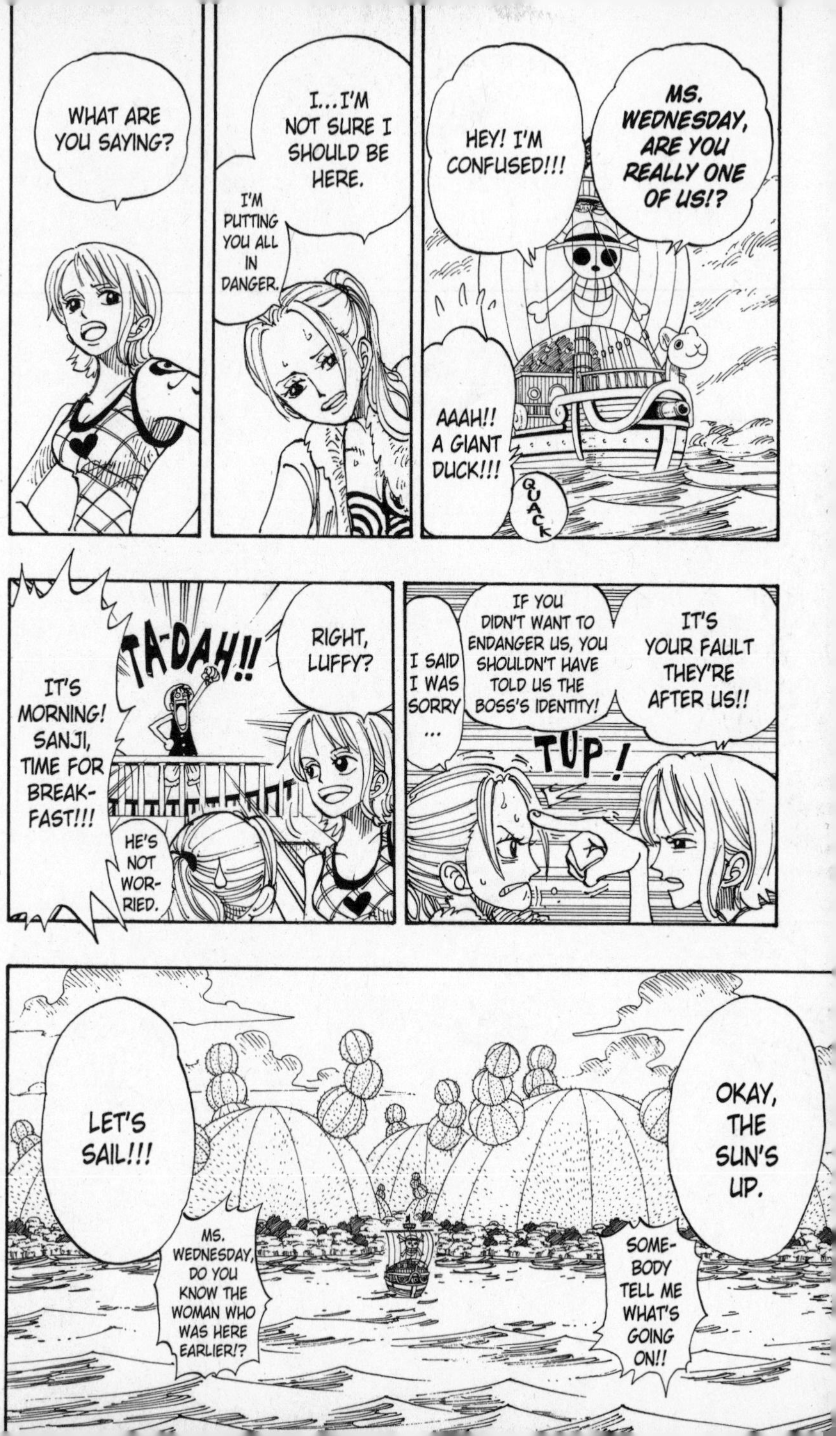
MS. WEDNESDAY, ARE YOU REALLY ONE OF US!?
HEY! I'M CONFUSED!!!
AAAH!! A GIANT DUCK!!!
QUACK
I...I'M NOT SURE I SHOULD BE HERE.
I'M PUTTING YOU ALL IN DANGER.
WHAT ARE YOU SAYING?
IT'S YOUR FAULT THEY'RE AFTER US!!
IF YOU DIDN'T WANT TO ENDANGER US, YOU SHOULDN'T HAVE TOLD US THE BOSS'S IDENTITY!
TUP!
I SAID I WAS SORRY ...
RIGHT, LUFFY?
TA-DAH!!
IT'S MORNING! SANJI, TIME FOR BREAK-FAST!!!
HE'S NOT WOR-RIED.
OKAY, THE SUN'S UP.
LET'S SAIL!!!
SOME-BODY TELL ME WHAT'S GOING ON!!
MS. WEDNESDAY, DO YOU KNOW THE WOMAN WHO WAS HERE EARLIER!?

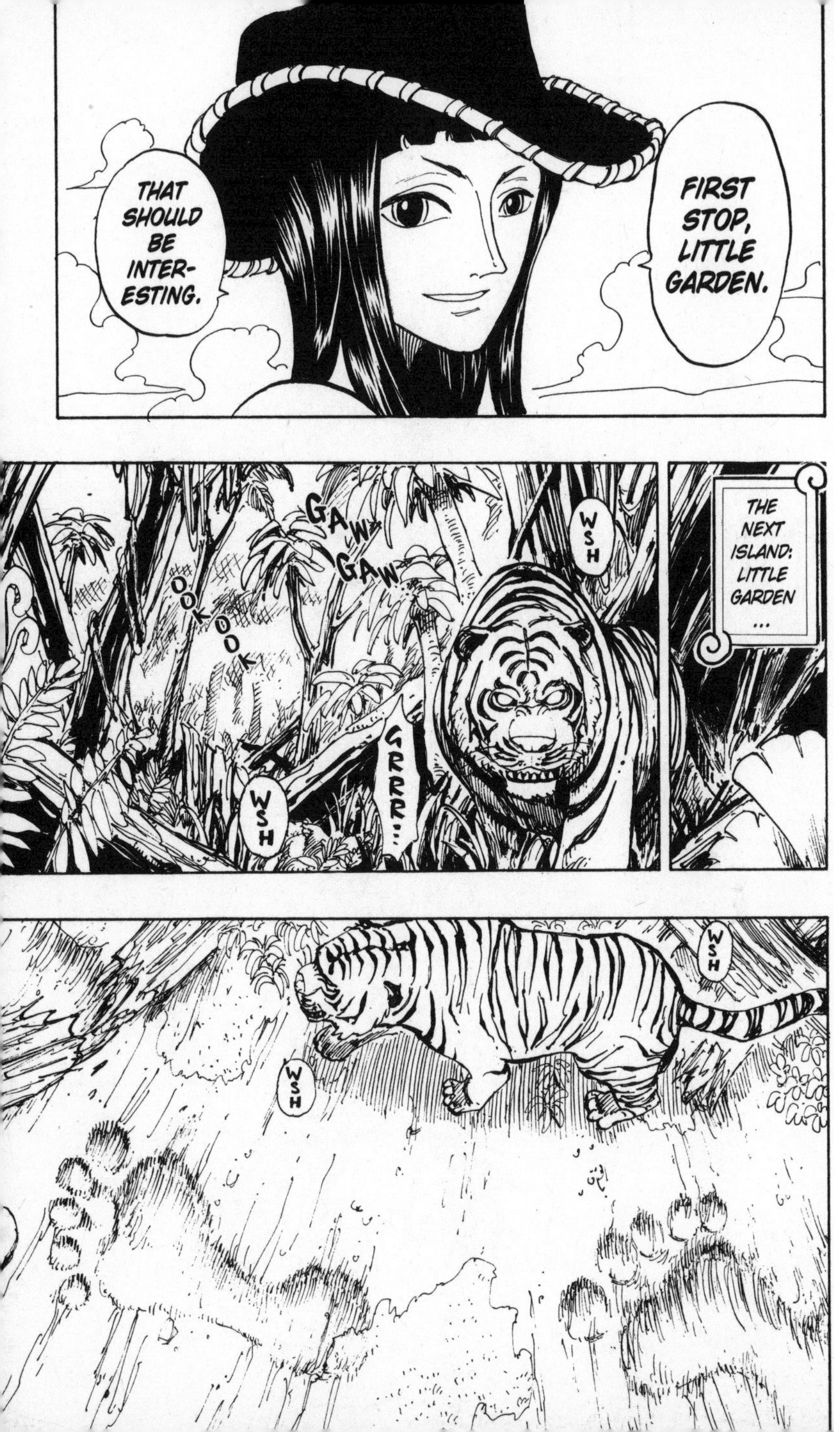
FIRST STOP, LITTLE GARDEN.
THAT SHOULD BE INTER-ESTING.
THE NEXT ISLAND: LITTLE GARDEN ...
WSH
GAW GAW
OOK OOK
GRRR...
WSH
WSH
WSH

CHAPTER 115: LITTLE GARDEN OF ADVENTURE

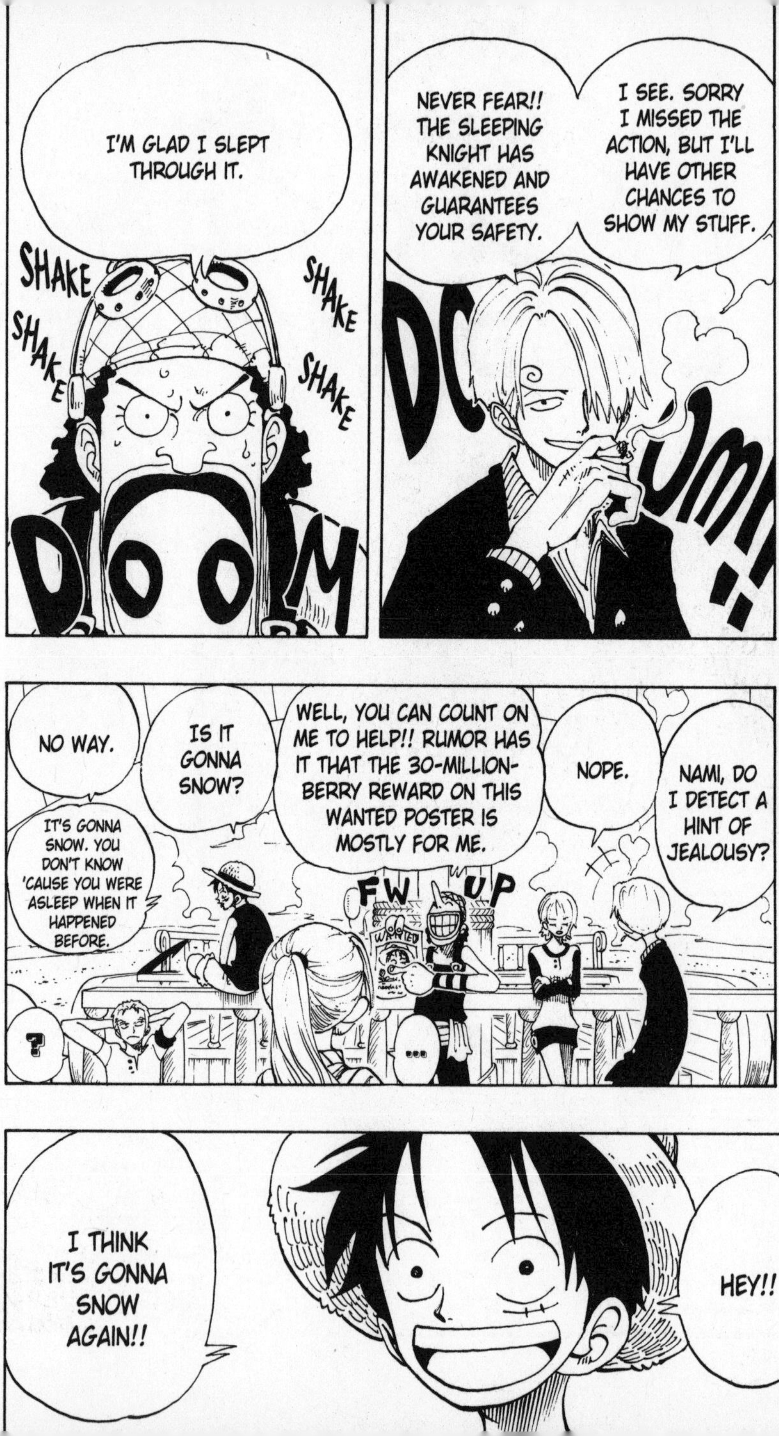
I SEE. SORRY I MISSED THE ACTION, BUT I'LL HAVE OTHER CHANCES TO SHOW MY STUFF.
NEVER FEAR!! THE SLEEPING KNIGHT HAS AWAKENED AND GUARANTEES YOUR SAFETY.
DOOM!!
SHAKE SHAKE
SHAKE SHAKE
I'M GLAD I SLEPT THROUGH IT.
DOOM
NAMI, DO I DETECT A HINT OF JEALOUSY?
NOPE.
WELL, YOU CAN COUNT ON ME TO HELP!! RUMOR HAS IT THAT THE 30-MILLION-BERRY REWARD ON THIS WANTED POSTER IS MOSTLY FOR ME.
FW UP
WANTED
IS IT GONNA SNOW?
NO WAY.
IT'S GONNA SNOW. YOU DON'T KNOW 'CAUSE YOU WERE ASLEEP WHEN IT HAPPENED BEFORE.
...
?
HEY!!
I THINK IT'S GONNA SNOW AGAIN!!

Chapter 115:
LITTLE GARDEN OF ADVENTURE

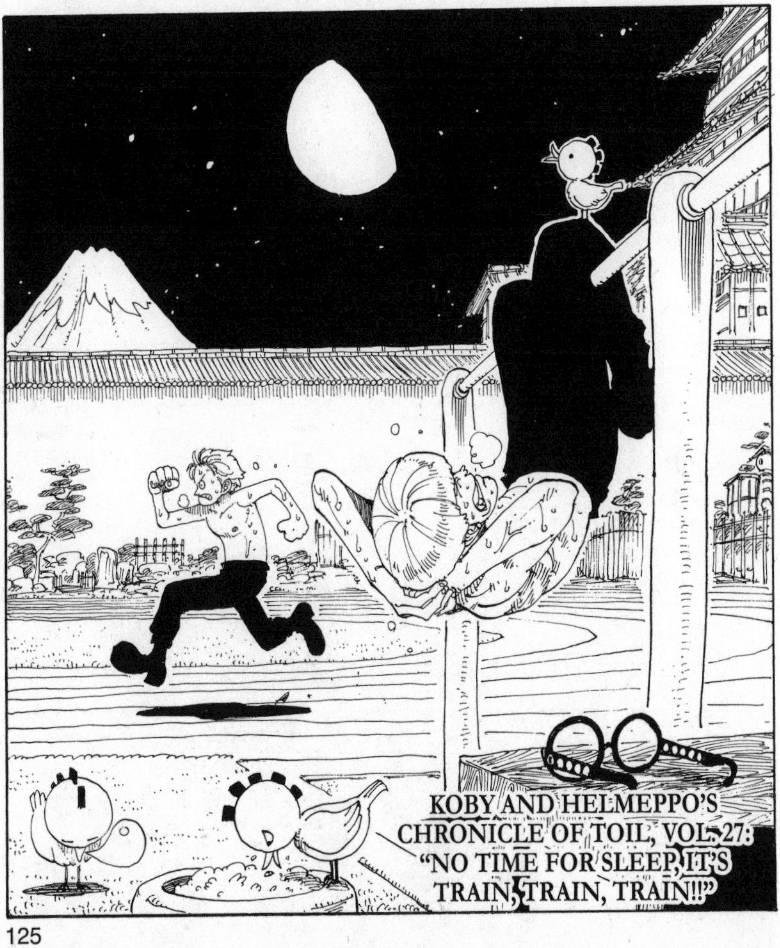
KOBY AND HELMEPPO'S CHRONICLE OF TOIL, VOL. 27:
"NO TIME FOR SLEEP, IT'S TRAIN, TRAIN, TRAIN!!"

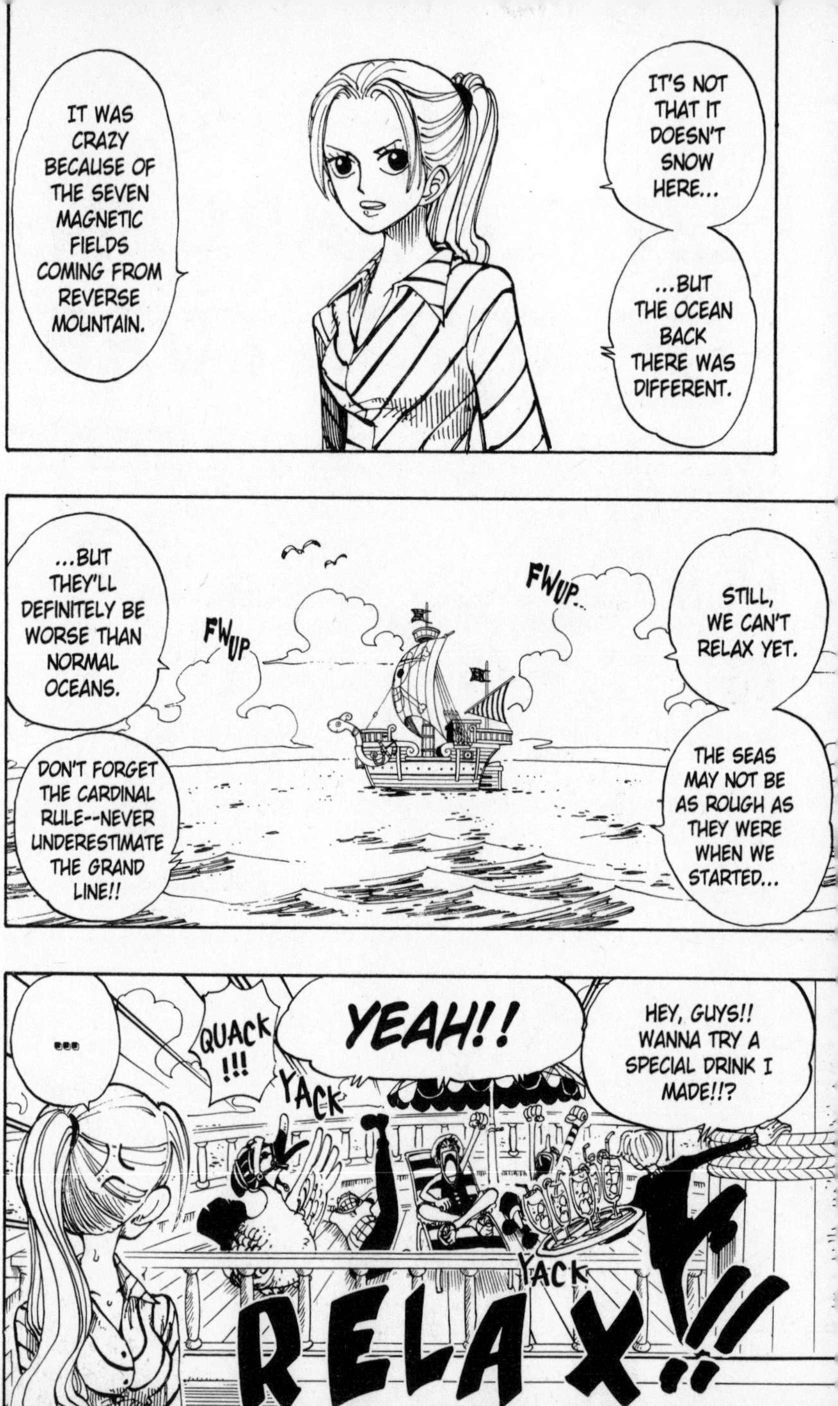
IT'S NOT THAT IT DOESN'T SNOW HERE...
...BUT THE OCEAN BACK THERE WAS DIFFERENT.
IT WAS CRAZY BECAUSE OF THE SEVEN MAGNETIC FIELDS COMING FROM REVERSE MOUNTAIN.
STILL, WE CAN'T RELAX YET.
THE SEAS MAY NOT BE AS ROUGH AS THEY WERE WHEN WE STARTED...
FWUP...
FWUP
...BUT THEY'LL DEFINITELY BE WORSE THAN NORMAL OCEANS.
DON'T FORGET THE CARDINAL RULE--NEVER UNDERESTIMATE THE GRAND LINE!!
HEY, GUYS!! WANNA TRY A SPECIAL DRINK I MADE!!?
YEAH!!
QUACK!!!
YACK
...
YACK
RELAX!!

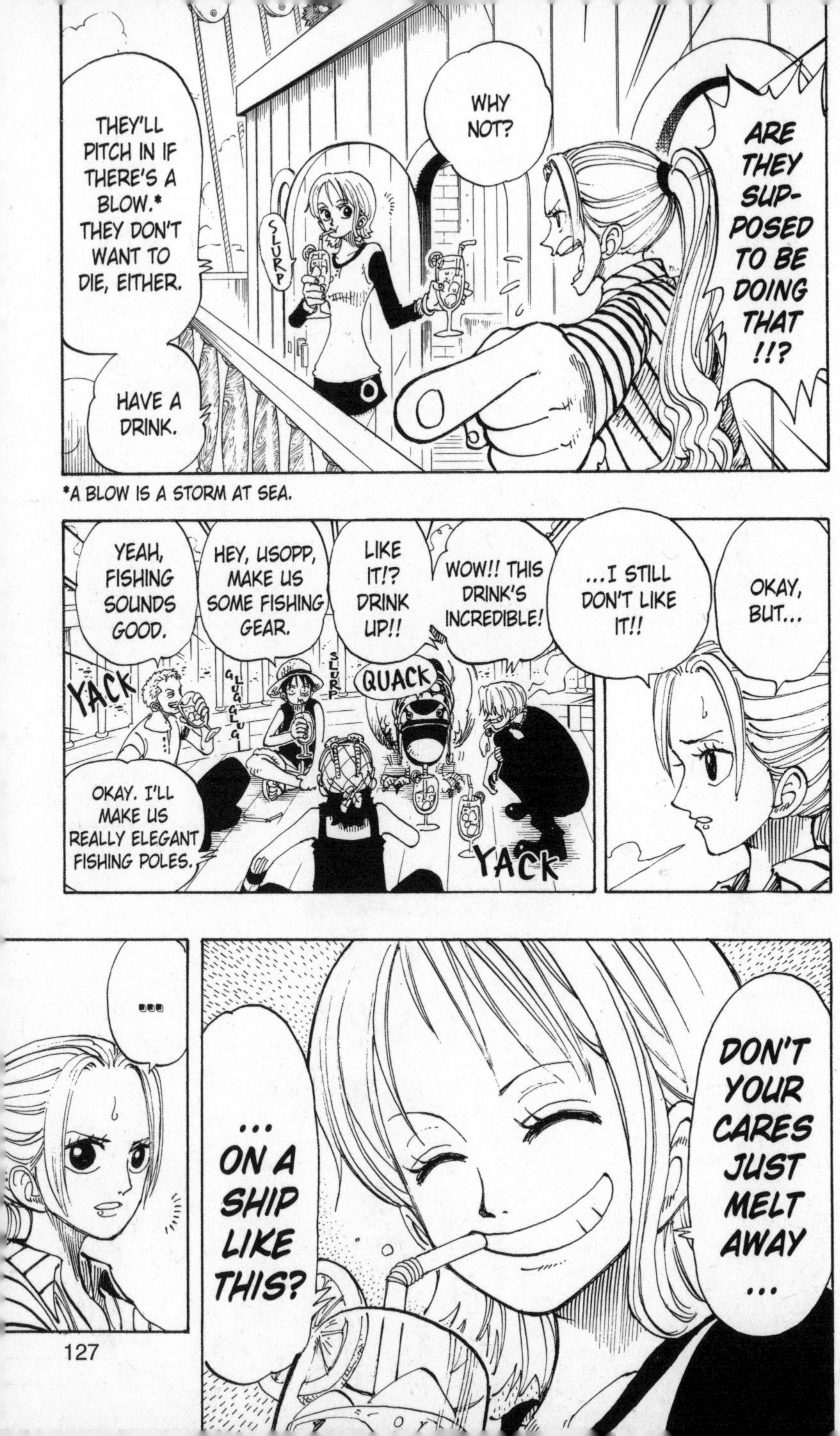
ARE THEY SUPPOSED TO BE DOING THAT!!?
WHY NOT?
SLURP
THEY'LL PITCH IN IF THERE'S A BLOW.* THEY DON'T WANT TO DIE, EITHER.
HAVE A DRINK.
OKAY, BUT...
...I STILL DON'T LIKE IT!!
WOW!! THIS DRINK'S INCREDIBLE!
LIKE IT!? DRINK UP!!
QUACK
SLURP
HEY, USOPP, MAKE US SOME FISHING GEAR.
GLUG GLUG
YEAH, FISHING SOUNDS GOOD.
YACK
OKAY. I'LL MAKE US REALLY ELEGANT FISHING POLES.
YACK
DON'T YOUR CARES JUST MELT AWAY...
...ON A SHIP LIKE THIS?
...

*A BLOW IS A STORM AT SEA.

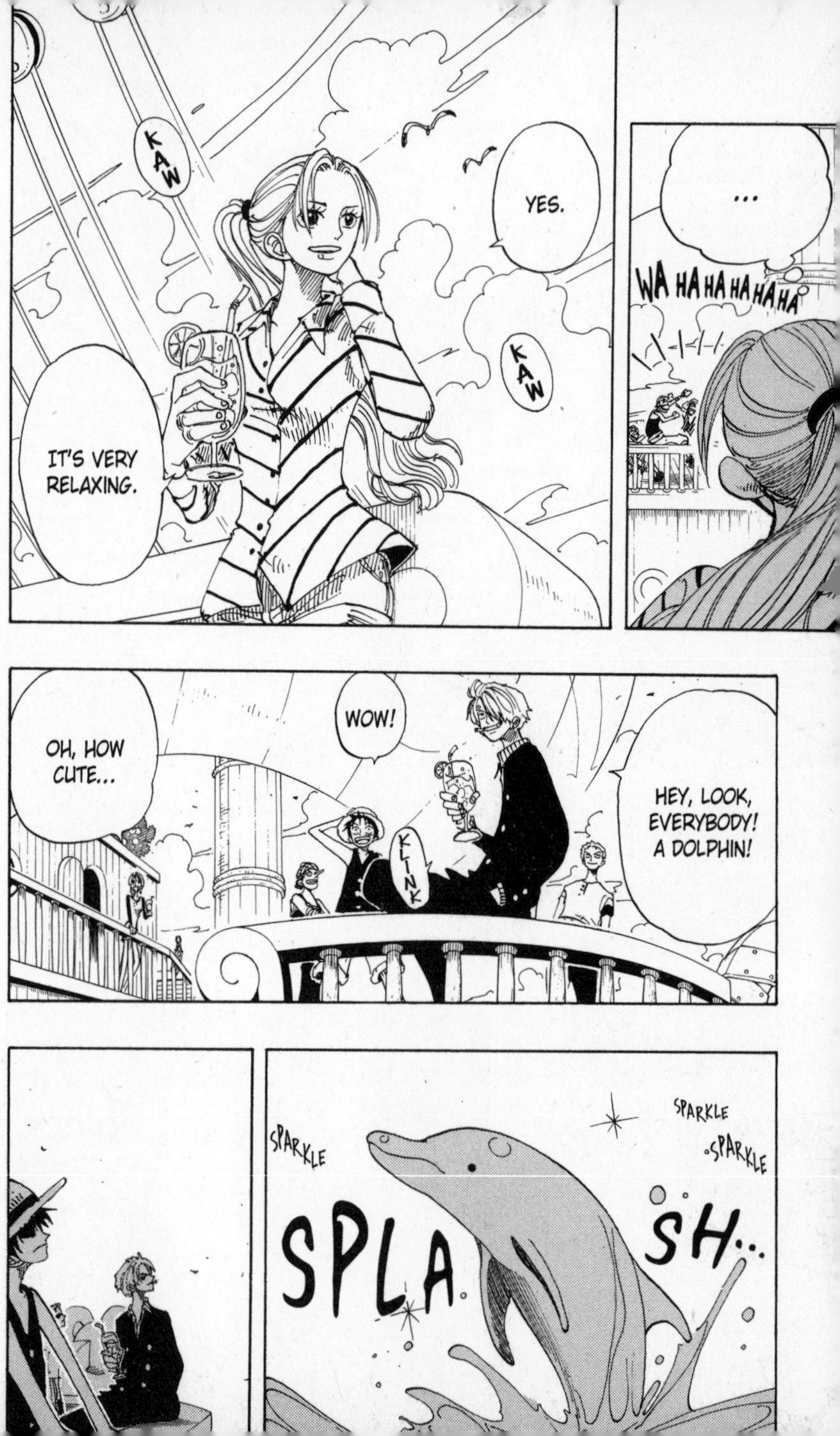
...
WA HA HA HA HA HA
YES.
KAW
KAW
IT'S VERY RELAXING.
HEY, LOOK, EVERYBODY! A DOLPHIN!
WOW!
KLINK
OH, HOW CUTE...
SPARKLE
SPARKLE
SPARKLE
SPLASH...

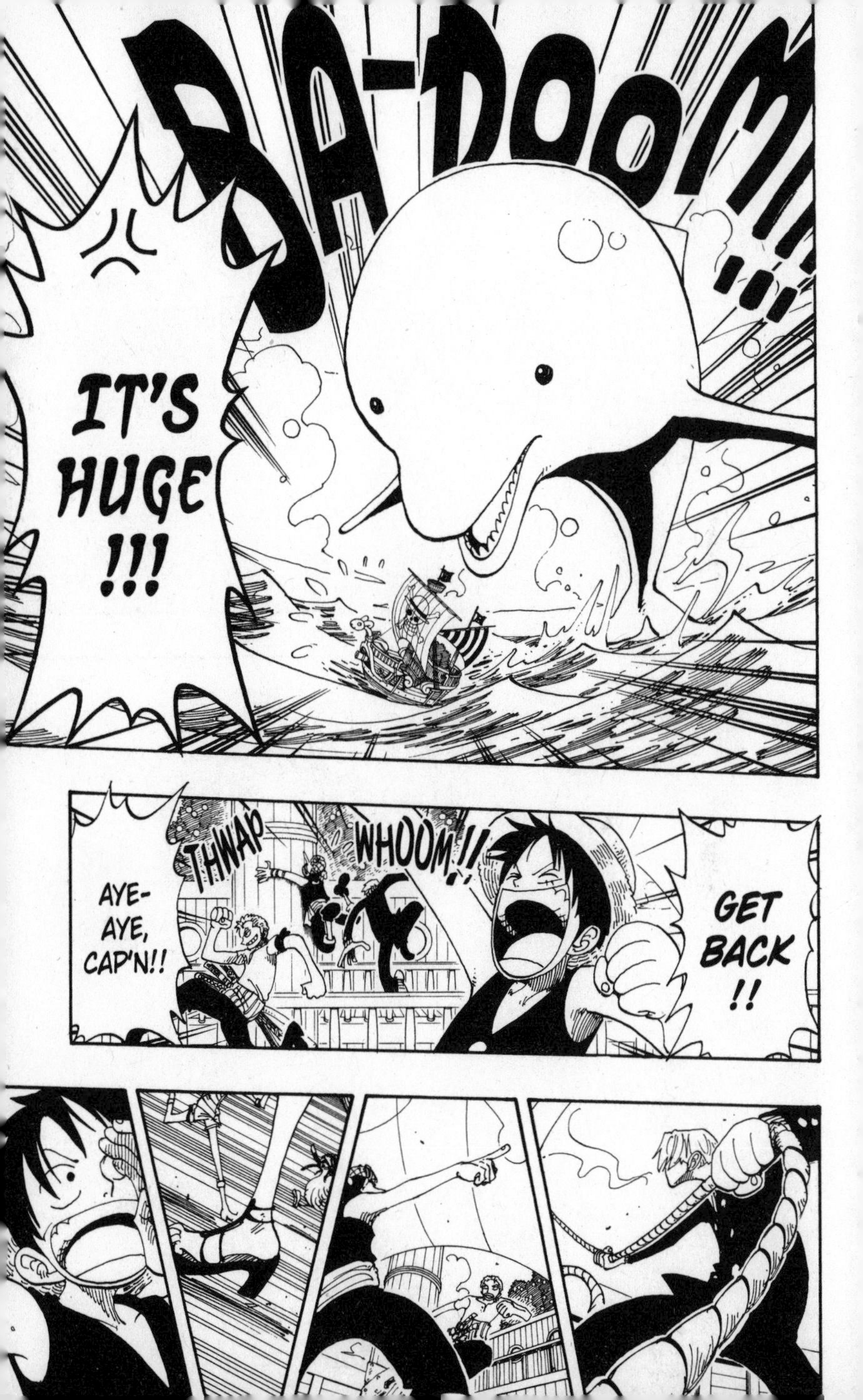
BA-DOOM!!!
IT'S HUGE !!!
GET BACK !!
WHOOM!!
THWAP
AYE-AYE, CAP'N!!

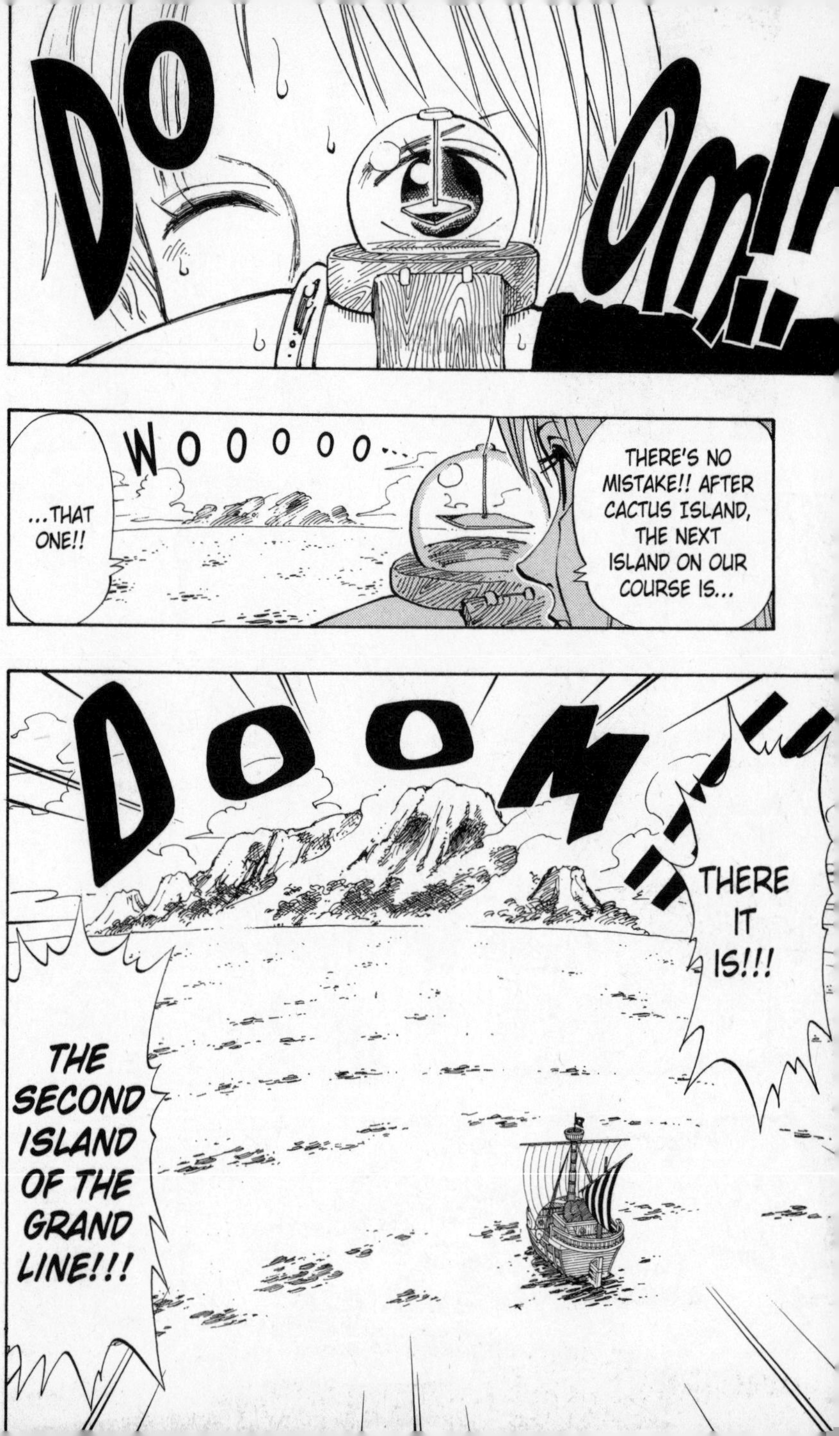
DOOM!!
THERE'S NO MISTAKE!! AFTER CACTUS ISLAND, THE NEXT ISLAND ON OUR COURSE IS...
WOOOOO...
...THAT ONE!!
DOOM!!
THERE IT IS!!!
THE SECOND ISLAND OF THE GRAND LINE!!!

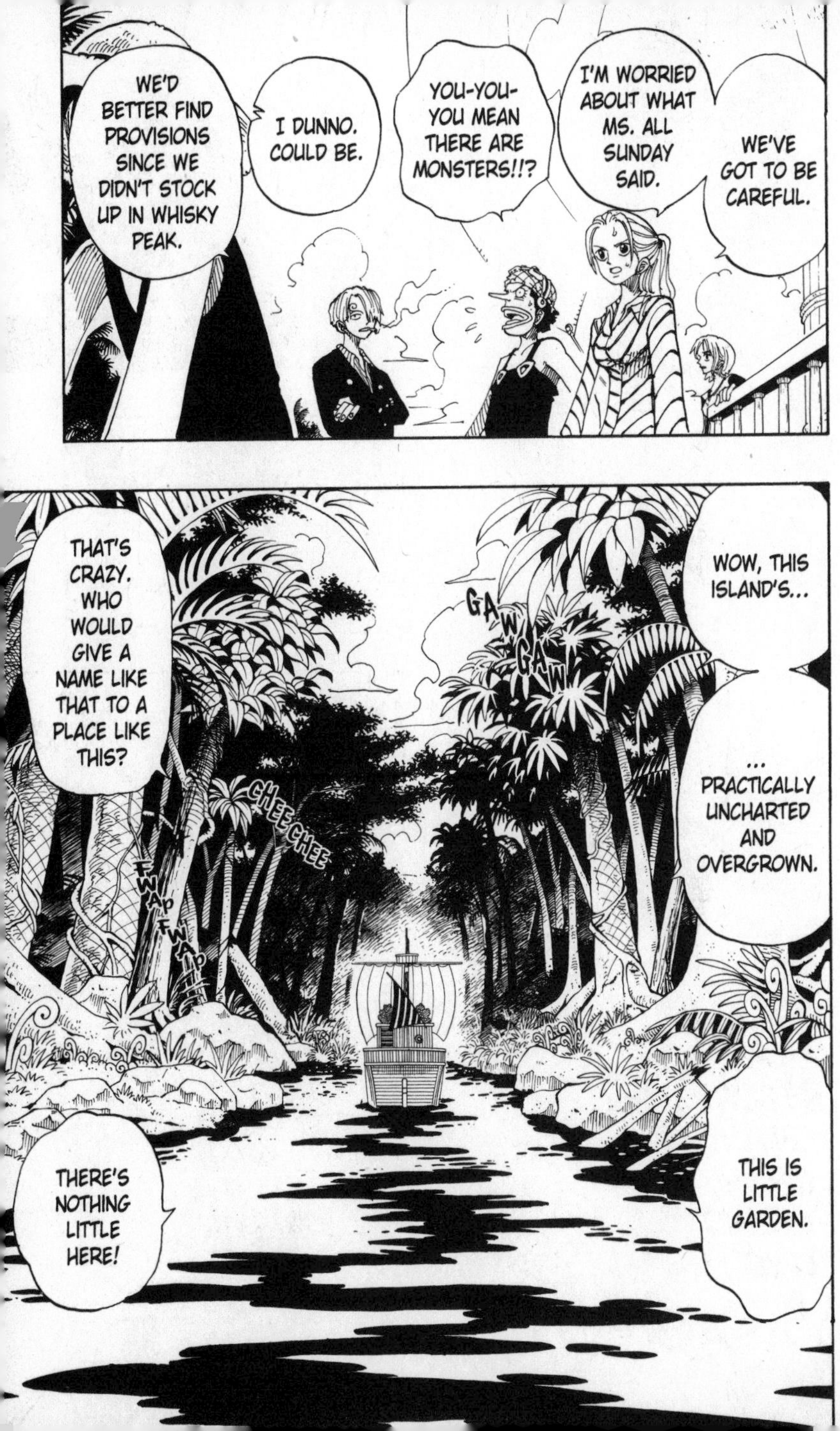
I'M WORRIED ABOUT WHAT MS. ALL SUNDAY SAID.
WE'VE GOT TO BE CAREFUL.
YOU-YOU-YOU MEAN THERE ARE MONSTERS!!?
I DUNNO. COULD BE.
WE'D BETTER FIND PROVISIONS SINCE WE DIDN'T STOCK UP IN WHISKY PEAK.
WOW, THIS ISLAND'S...
... PRACTICALLY UNCHARTED AND OVERGROWN.
GAW GAW
CHEE CHEE
FWAP FWAP
THIS IS LITTLE GARDEN.
THAT'S CRAZY. WHO WOULD GIVE A NAME LIKE THAT TO A PLACE LIKE THIS?
THERE'S NOTHING LITTLE HERE!

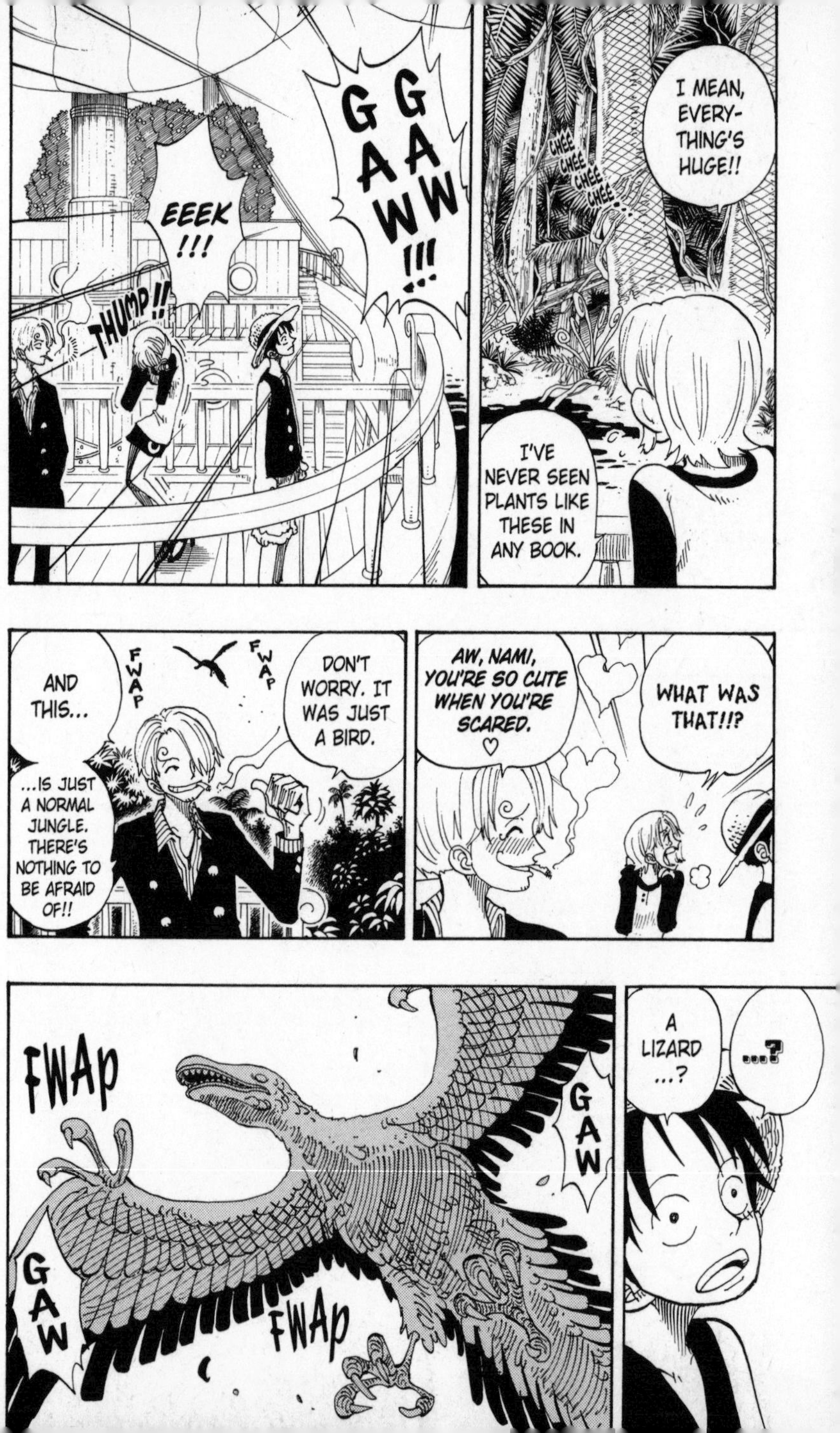
I MEAN, EVERY-THING'S HUGE!!
CHEE CHEE CHEE CHEE
I'VE NEVER SEEN PLANTS LIKE THESE IN ANY BOOK.
GGAAWW!!!
EEEK!!!
THUMP!!
WHAT WAS THAT!!?
AW, NAMI, YOU'RE SO CUTE WHEN YOU'RE SCARED. ♡
DON'T WORRY. IT WAS JUST A BIRD.
FWAP
FWAP
AND THIS...
...IS JUST A NORMAL JUNGLE. THERE'S NOTHING TO BE AFRAID OF!!
...?
A LIZARD ...?
GAW
FWAP
GAW
FWAP

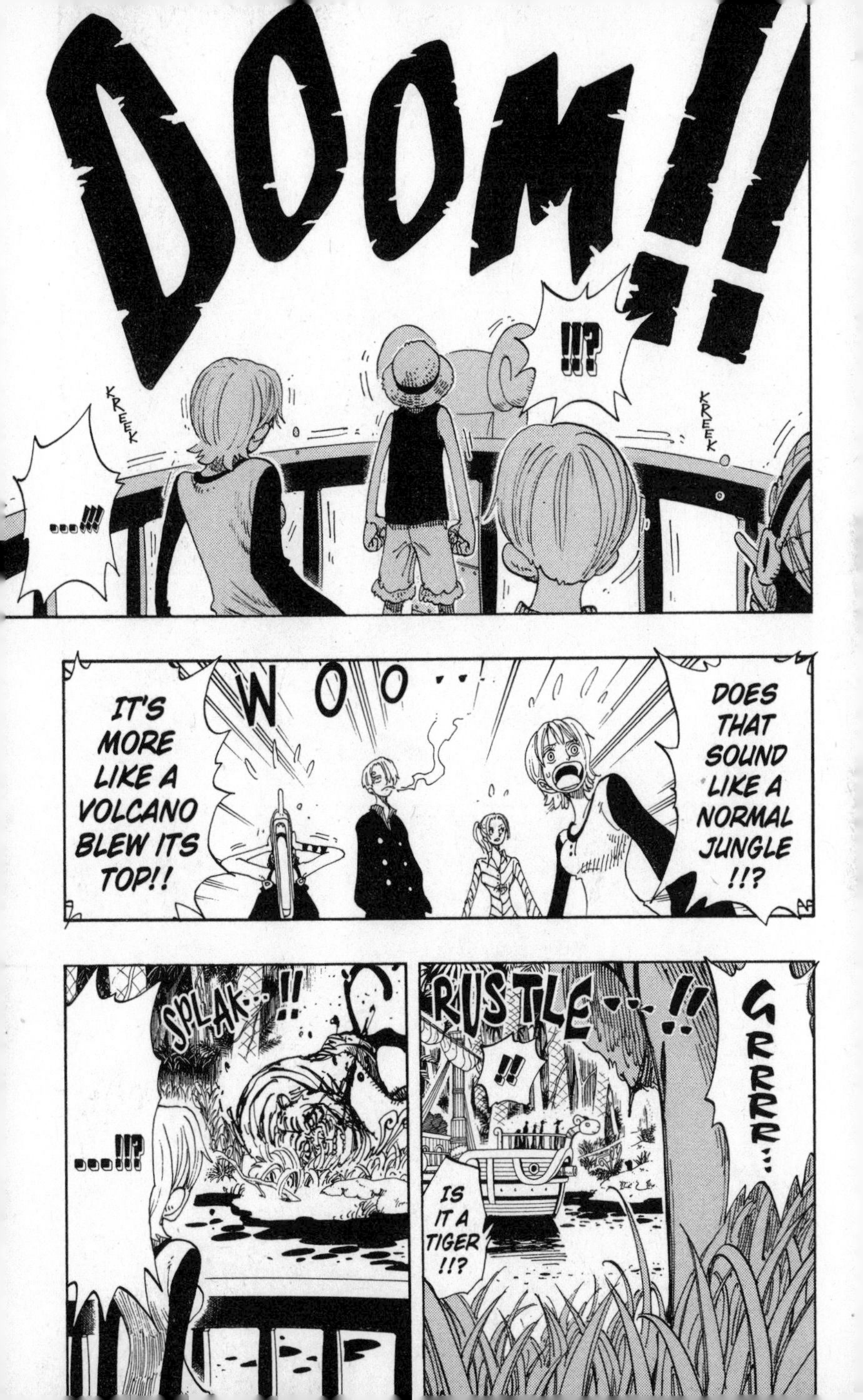
DOOM!!
KREEK
!!?
KREEK
...!!!
DOES THAT SOUND LIKE A NORMAL JUNGLE !!?
WOO...
IT'S MORE LIKE A VOLCANO BLEW ITS TOP!!
GRRRR...
RUSTLE...!!
!!
IS IT A TIGER !!?
SPLAK..!!
...!!?

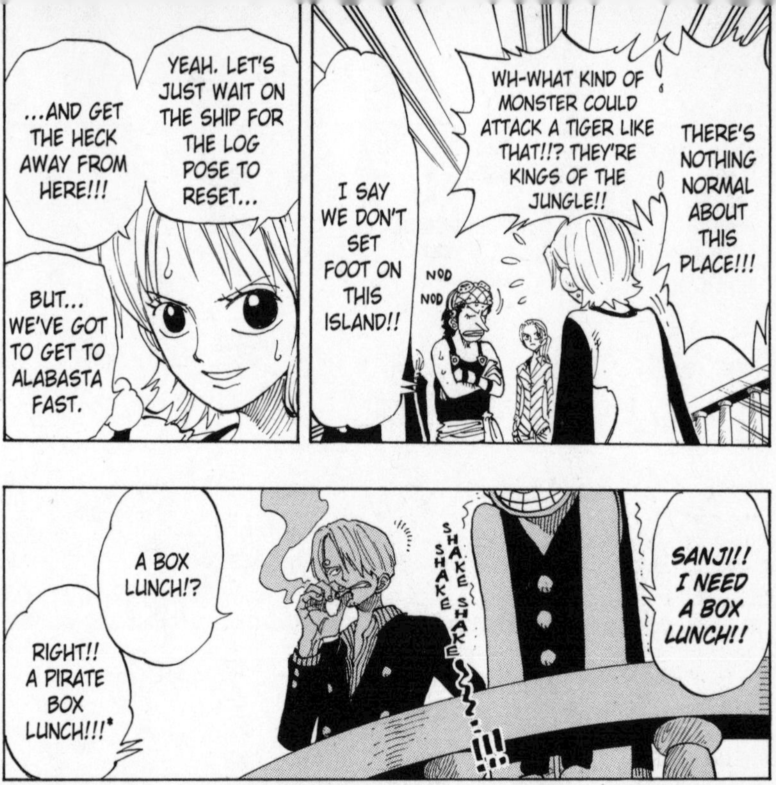
WH-WHAT KIND OF MONSTER COULD ATTACK A TIGER LIKE THAT!!? THEY'RE KINGS OF THE JUNGLE!!
THERE'S NOTHING NORMAL ABOUT THIS PLACE!!!
NOD NOD
I SAY WE DON'T SET FOOT ON THIS ISLAND!!
YEAH. LET'S JUST WAIT ON THE SHIP FOR THE LOG POSE TO RESET...
...AND GET THE HECK AWAY FROM HERE!!!
BUT... WE'VE GOT TO GET TO ALABASTA FAST.
SANJI!! I NEED A BOX LUNCH!!
SHAKE SHAKE SHAKE
A BOX LUNCH!?
RIGHT!! A PIRATE BOX LUNCH!!!*
!!!

*PIRATE BOX LUNCH: A VEGETABLE-FREE BOX LUNCH FOR QUICK ENERGY.

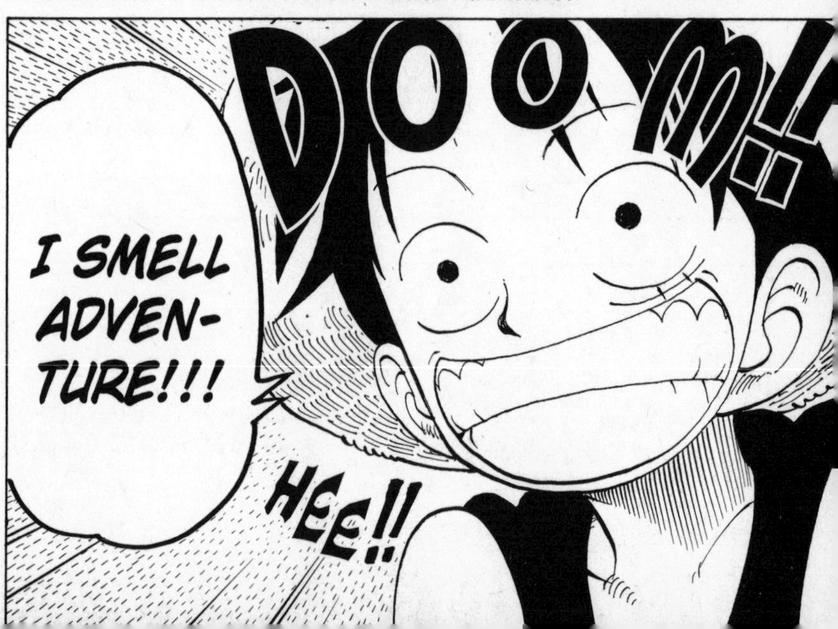
DOOM!!
I SMELL ADVEN-TURE!!!
HEE!!

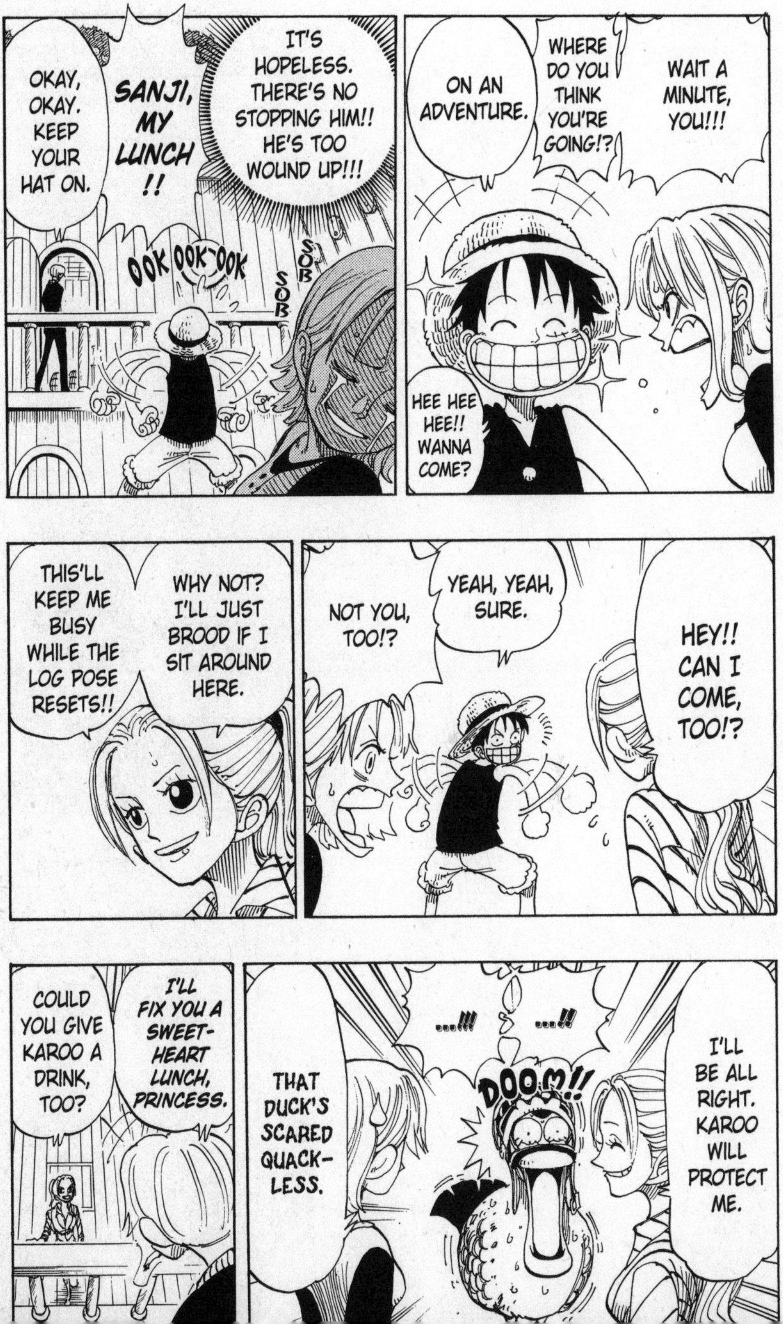
WAIT A MINUTE, YOU!!!
WHERE DO YOU THINK YOU'RE GOING!?
ON AN ADVENTURE.
HEE HEE HEE!! WANNA COME?
IT'S HOPELESS. THERE'S NO STOPPING HIM!! HE'S TOO WOUND UP!!!
SOB SOB
SANJI, MY LUNCH!!
OOK OOK OOK
OKAY, OKAY. KEEP YOUR HAT ON.
HEY!! CAN I COME, TOO!?
YEAH, YEAH, SURE.
NOT YOU, TOO!?
WHY NOT? I'LL JUST BROOD IF I SIT AROUND HERE.
THIS'LL KEEP ME BUSY WHILE THE LOG POSE RESETS!!
I'LL BE ALL RIGHT. KAROO WILL PROTECT ME.
...!!
...!!!
DOOM!!
THAT DUCK'S SCARED QUACK-LESS.
I'LL FIX YOU A SWEET-HEART LUNCH, PRINCESS.
COULD YOU GIVE KAROO A DRINK, TOO?

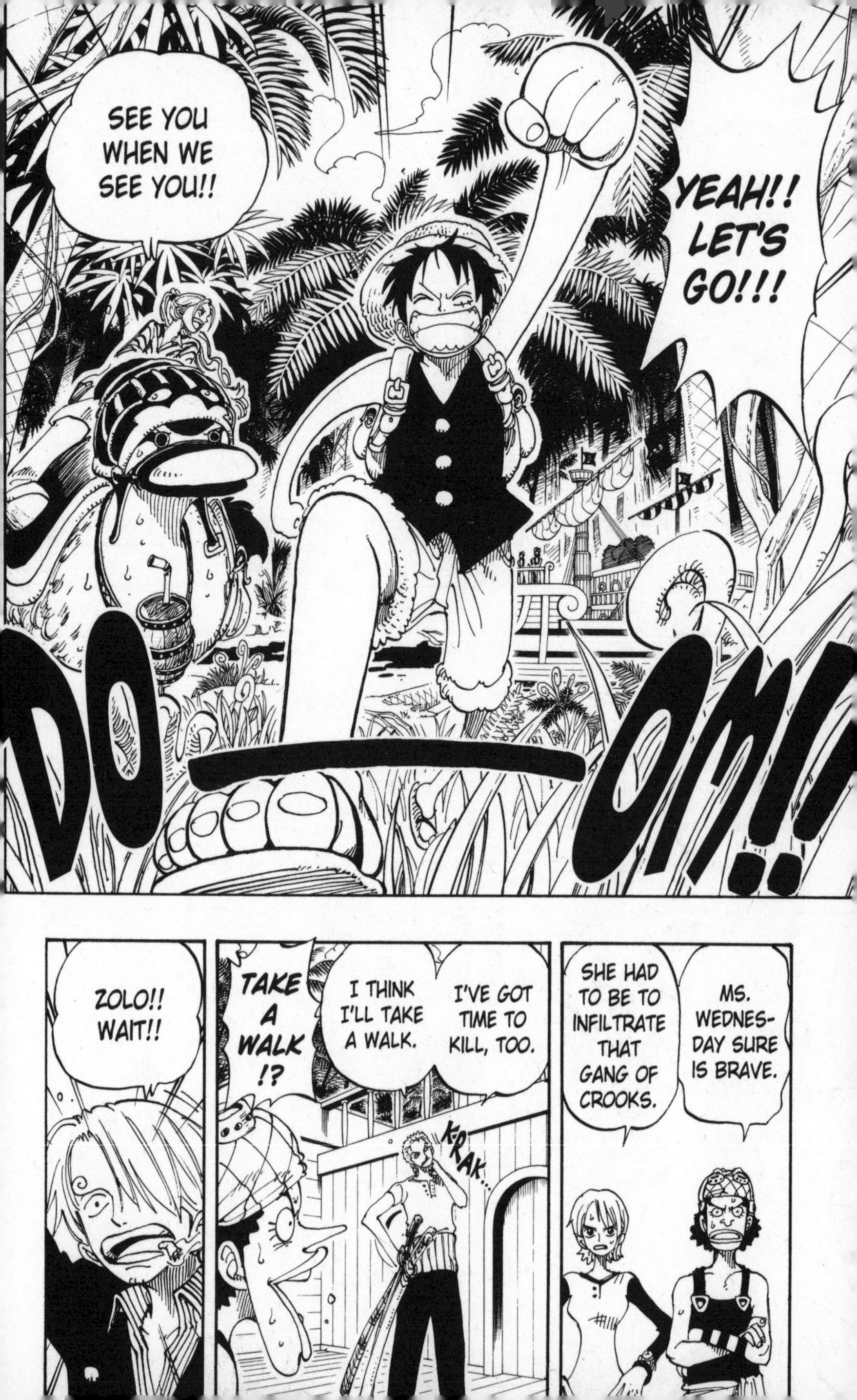
YEAH!! LET'S GO!!!
SEE YOU WHEN WE SEE YOU!!
DO—OM!!
MS. WEDNES-DAY SURE IS BRAVE.
SHE HAD TO BE TO INFILTRATE THAT GANG OF CROOKS.
I'VE GOT TIME TO KILL, TOO.
I THINK I'LL TAKE A WALK.
KRAK...
TAKE A WALK !?
ZOLO!! WAIT!!

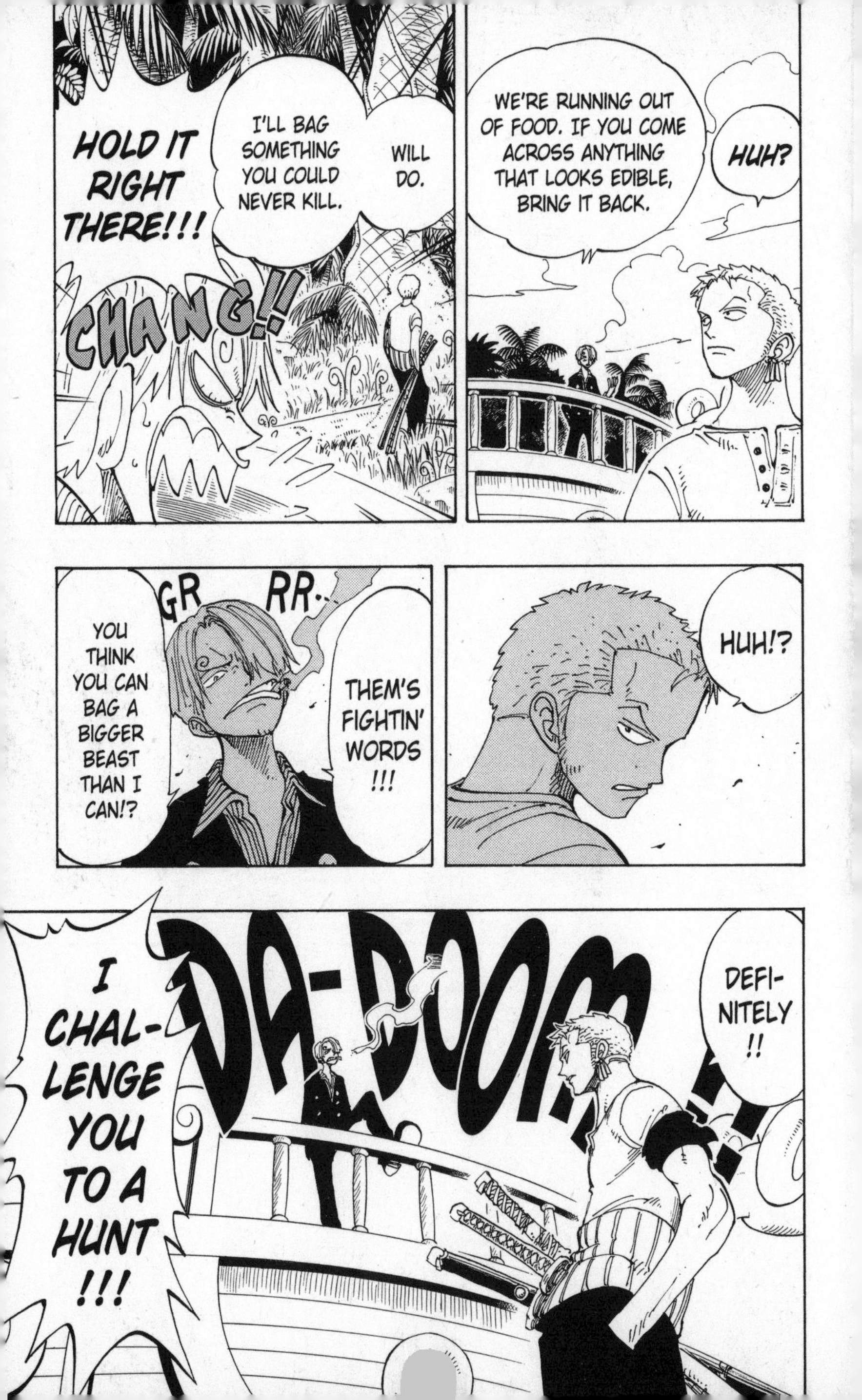
HUH?
WE'RE RUNNING OUT OF FOOD. IF YOU COME ACROSS ANYTHING THAT LOOKS EDIBLE, BRING IT BACK.
WILL DO.
I'LL BAG SOMETHING YOU COULD NEVER KILL.
HOLD IT RIGHT THERE!!!
CHANG!!
HUH!?
GR RR...
THEM'S FIGHTIN' WORDS!!!
YOU THINK YOU CAN BAG A BIGGER BEAST THAN I CAN!?
DEFI-NITELY!!
DA-DOOM!!
I CHAL-LENGE YOU TO A HUNT!!!

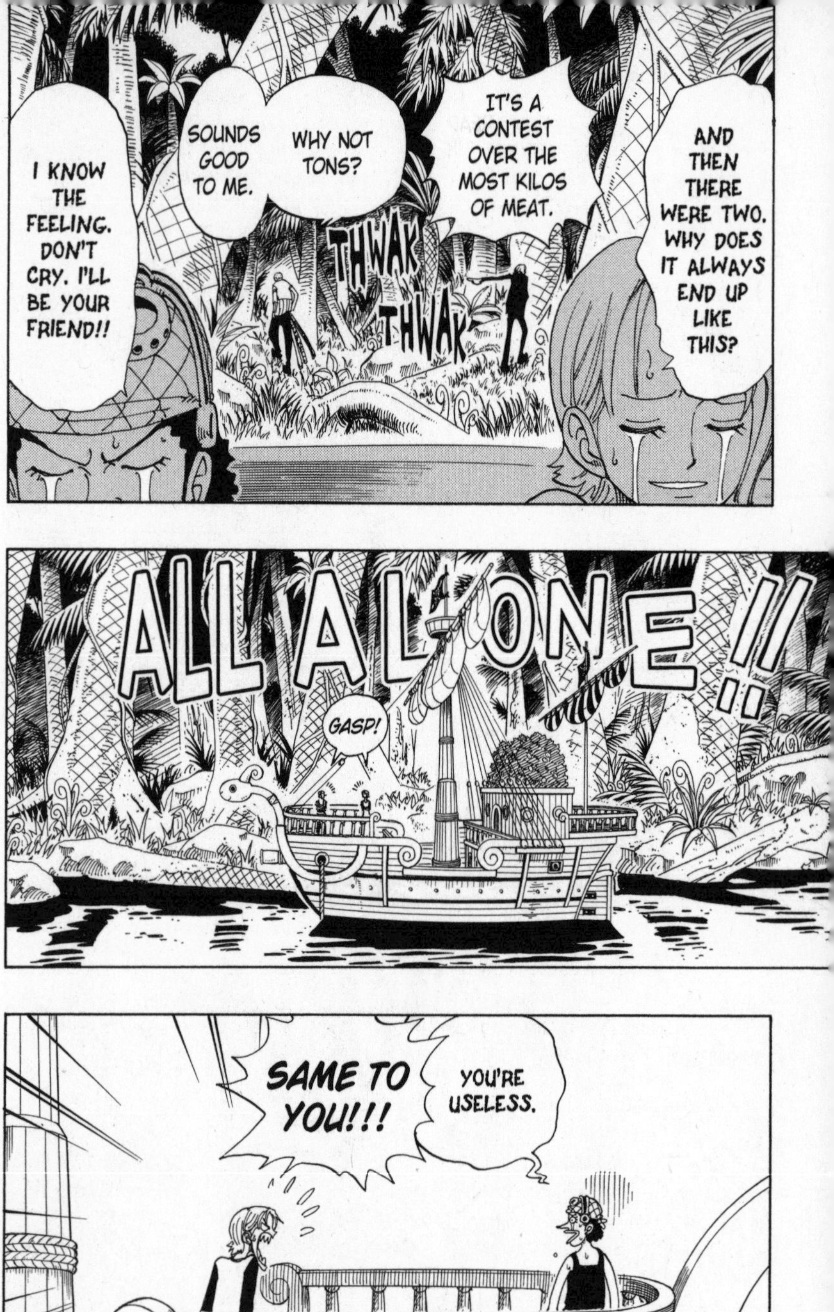
AND THEN THERE WERE TWO. WHY DOES IT ALWAYS END UP LIKE THIS?
IT'S A CONTEST OVER THE MOST KILOS OF MEAT.
WHY NOT TONS?
SOUNDS GOOD TO ME.
THWAK
THWAK
I KNOW THE FEELING. DON'T CRY. I'LL BE YOUR FRIEND!!
ALL ALONE!!
GASP!
YOU'RE USELESS.
SAME TO YOU!!!

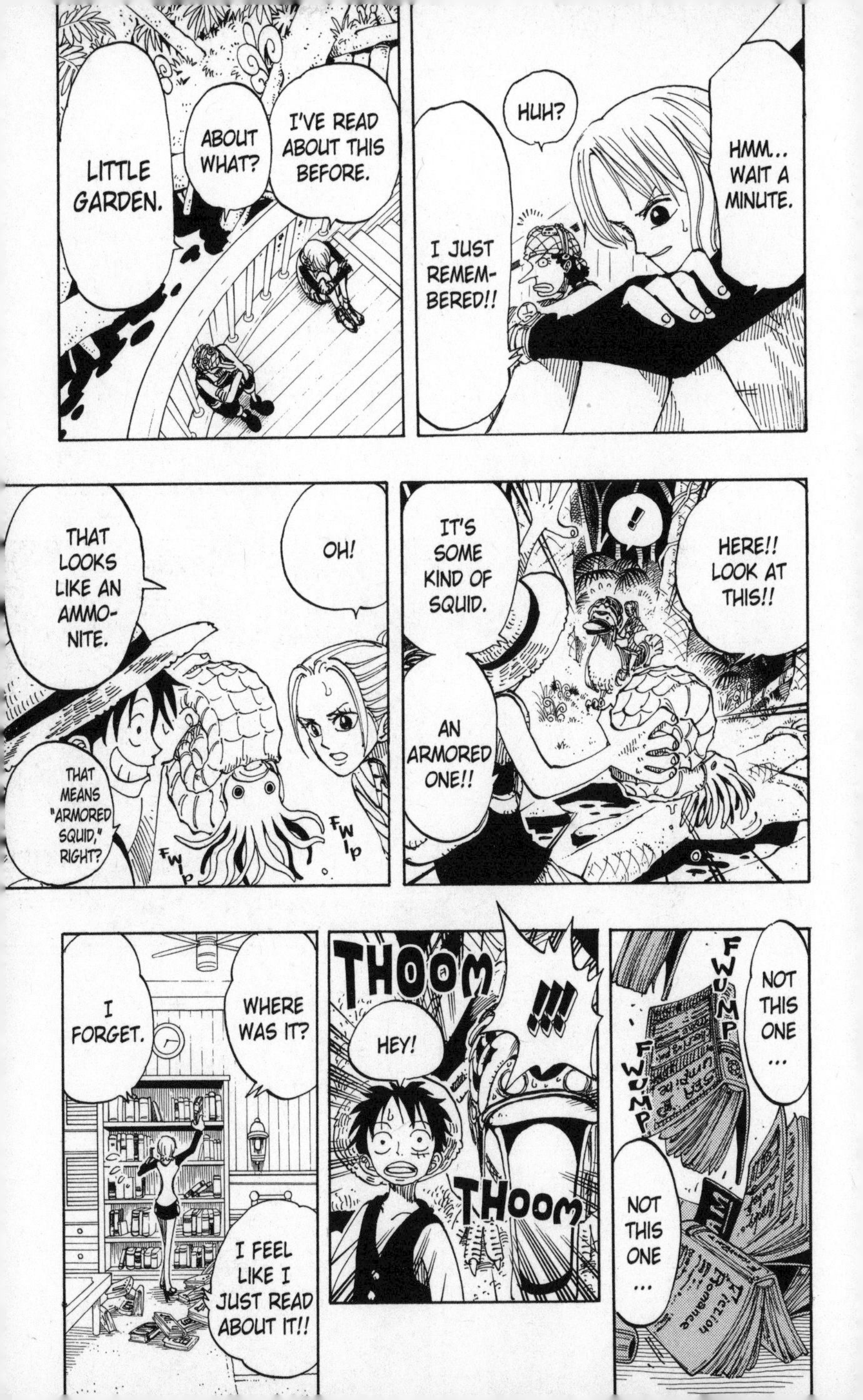
HMM... WAIT A MINUTE.
HUH?
I JUST REMEMBERED!!
I'VE READ ABOUT THIS BEFORE.
ABOUT WHAT?
LITTLE GARDEN.
HERE!! LOOK AT THIS!!
!
IT'S SOME KIND OF SQUID.
AN ARMORED ONE!!
OH!
THAT LOOKS LIKE AN AMMONITE.
THAT MEANS "ARMORED SQUID," RIGHT?
FWIP
FWIP
NOT THIS ONE...
FWUMP
FWUMP
NOT THIS ONE...
THOOM
!!!
HEY!
THOOM
WHERE WAS IT?
I FORGET.
I FEEL LIKE I JUST READ ABOUT IT!!

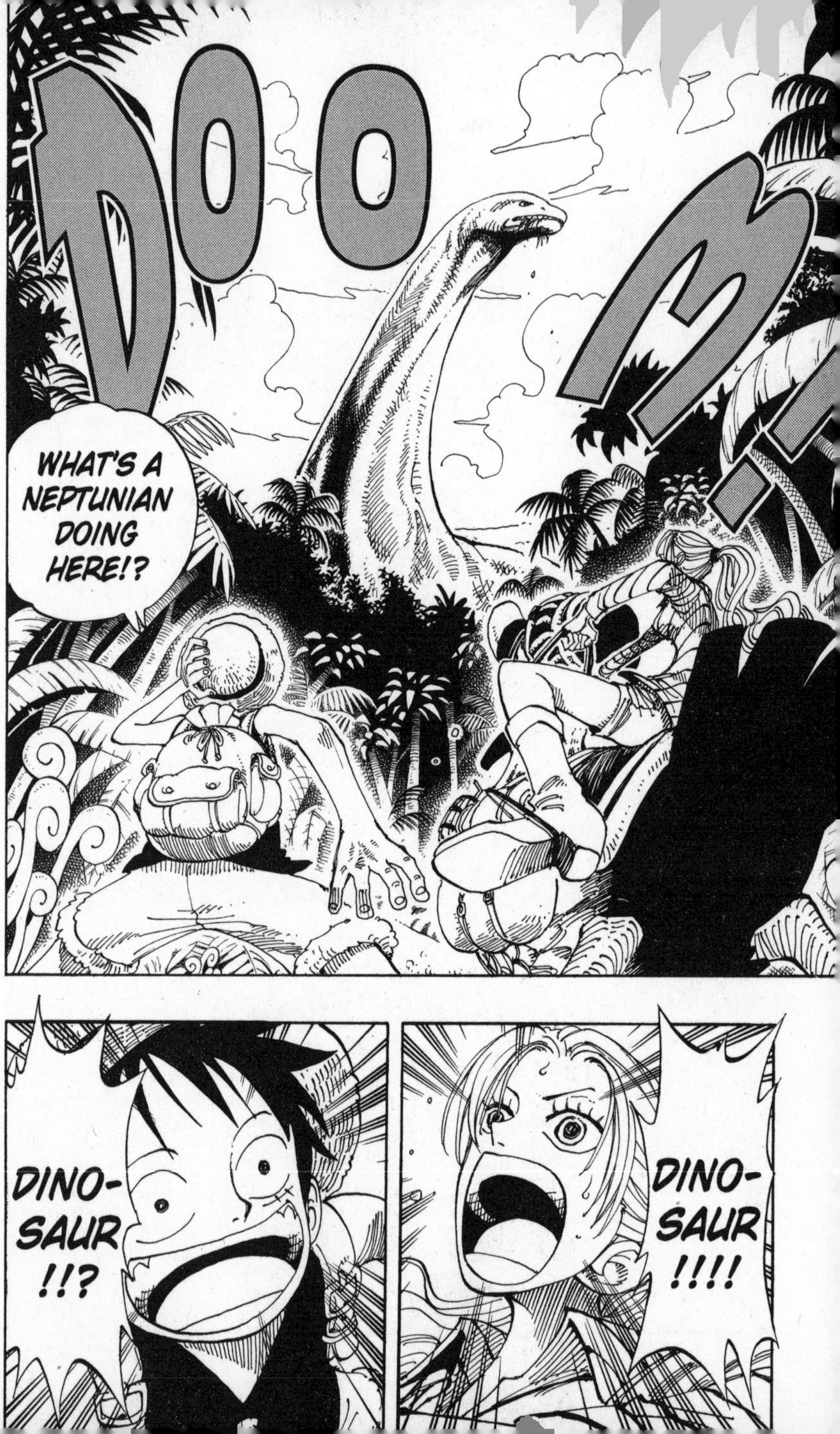
DOOM!!
WHAT'S A NEPTUNIAN DOING HERE!?
DINO-SAUR !!!!
DINO-SAUR !!?

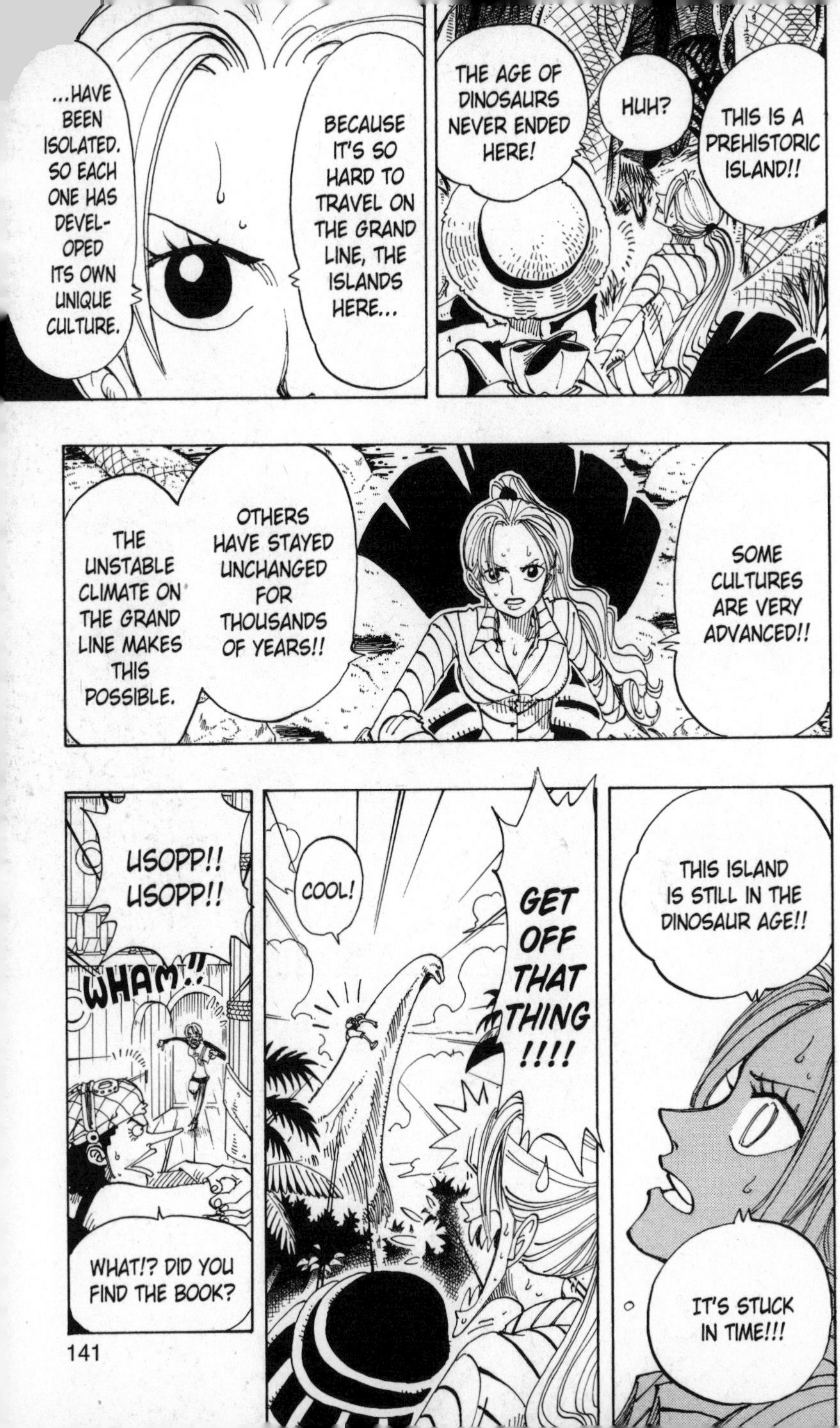
THIS IS A PREHISTORIC ISLAND!!
HUH?
THE AGE OF DINOSAURS NEVER ENDED HERE!
BECAUSE IT'S SO HARD TO TRAVEL ON THE GRAND LINE, THE ISLANDS HERE...
...HAVE BEEN ISOLATED. SO EACH ONE HAS DEVEL-OPED ITS OWN UNIQUE CULTURE.
SOME CULTURES ARE VERY ADVANCED!!
OTHERS HAVE STAYED UNCHANGED FOR THOUSANDS OF YEARS!!
THE UNSTABLE CLIMATE ON THE GRAND LINE MAKES THIS POSSIBLE.
THIS ISLAND IS STILL IN THE DINOSAUR AGE!!
IT'S STUCK IN TIME!!!
GET OFF THAT THING!!!!
COOL!
USOPP!! USOPP!!
WHAM!!
WHAT!? DID YOU FIND THE BOOK?

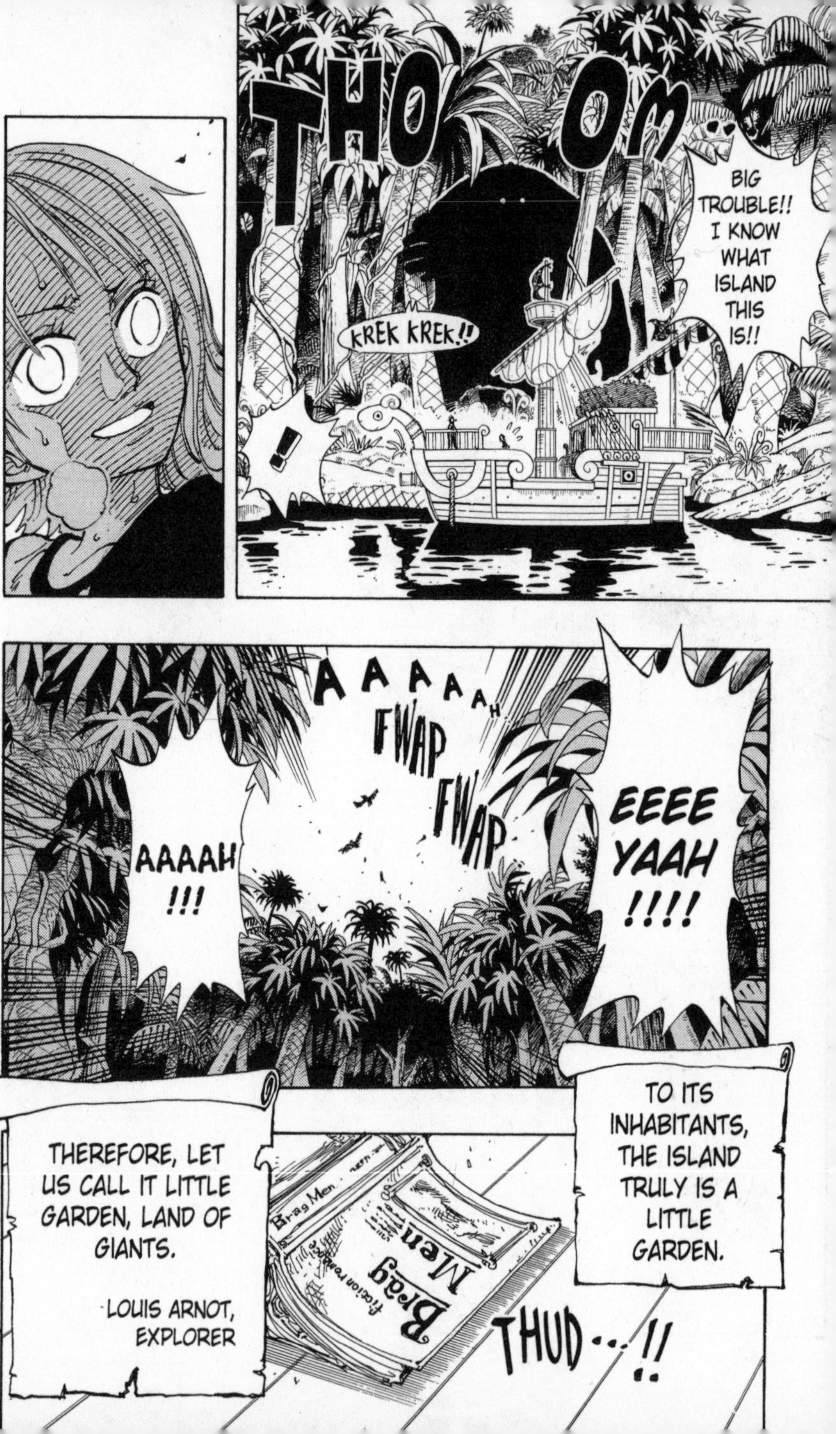
THO OM
BIG TROUBLE!! I KNOW WHAT ISLAND THIS IS!!
KREK KREK!!
!
EEEE YAAH!!!!
FWAP FWAP
AAAAAH
AAAAH!!!
TO ITS INHABITANTS, THE ISLAND TRULY IS A LITTLE GARDEN.
THUD...!!
Brag Men
THEREFORE, LET US CALL IT LITTLE GARDEN, LAND OF GIANTS.
-LOUIS ARNOT, EXPLORER

Chapter 116:
BIG

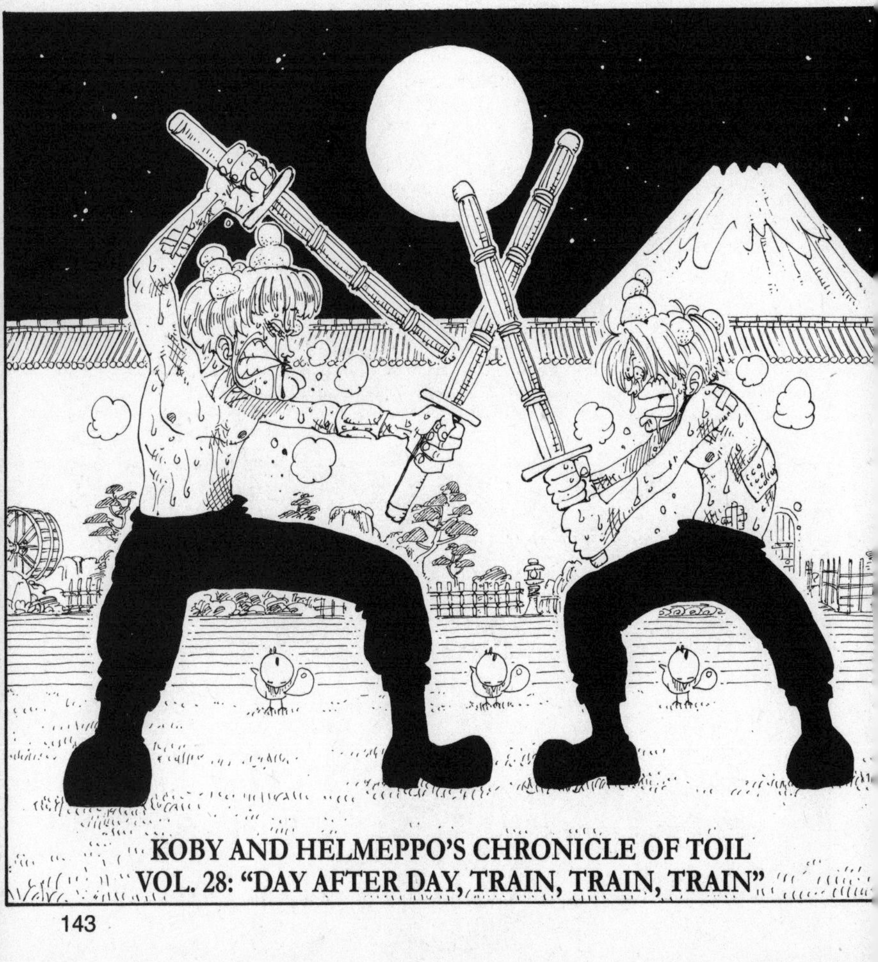
KOBY AND HELMEPPO'S CHRONICLE OF TOIL
VOL. 28: "DAY AFTER DAY, TRAIN, TRAIN, TRAIN"

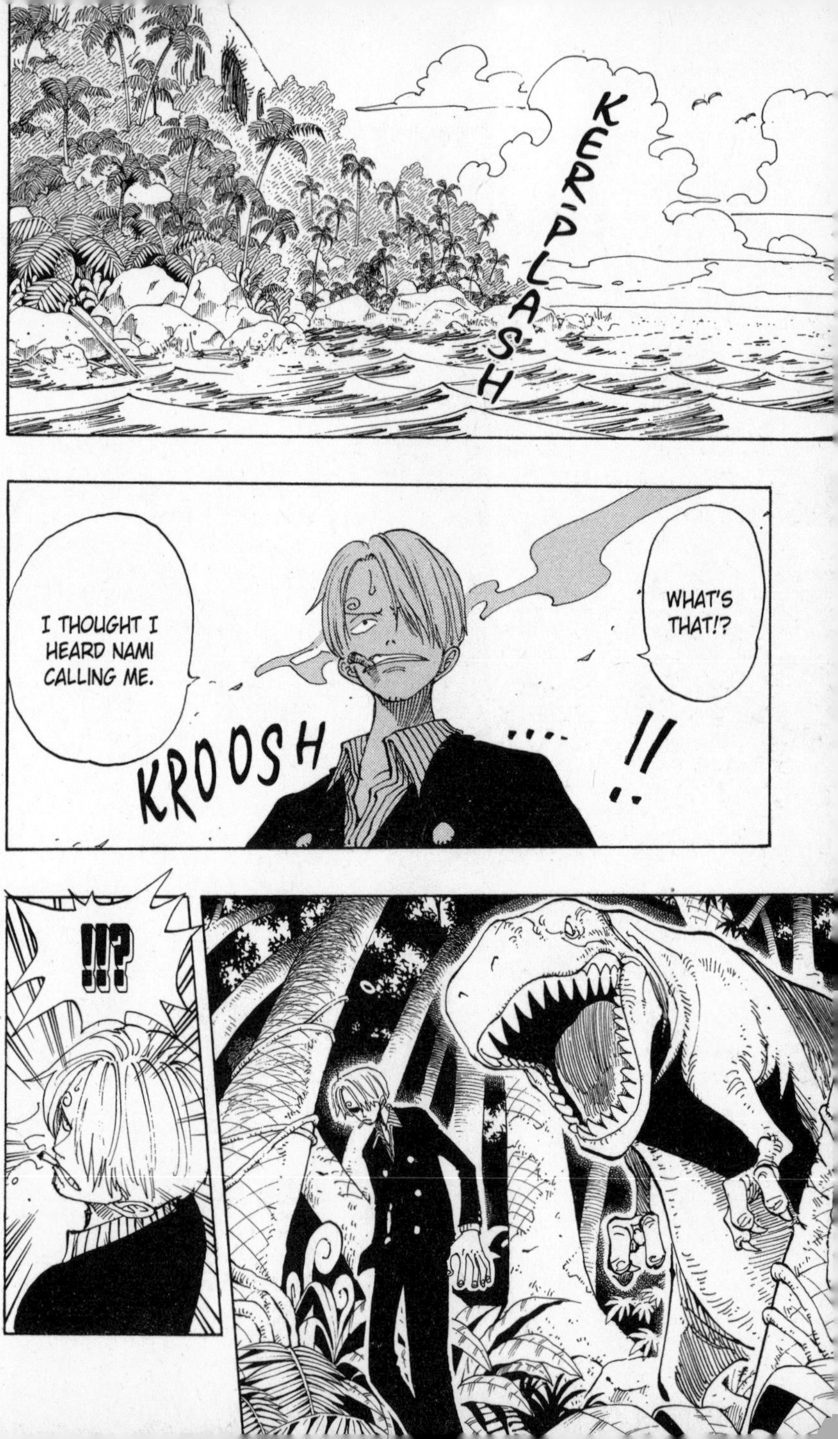
KER'PLASH
WHAT'S THAT!?
...!!
I THOUGHT I HEARD NAMI CALLING ME.
KROOSH
!!?

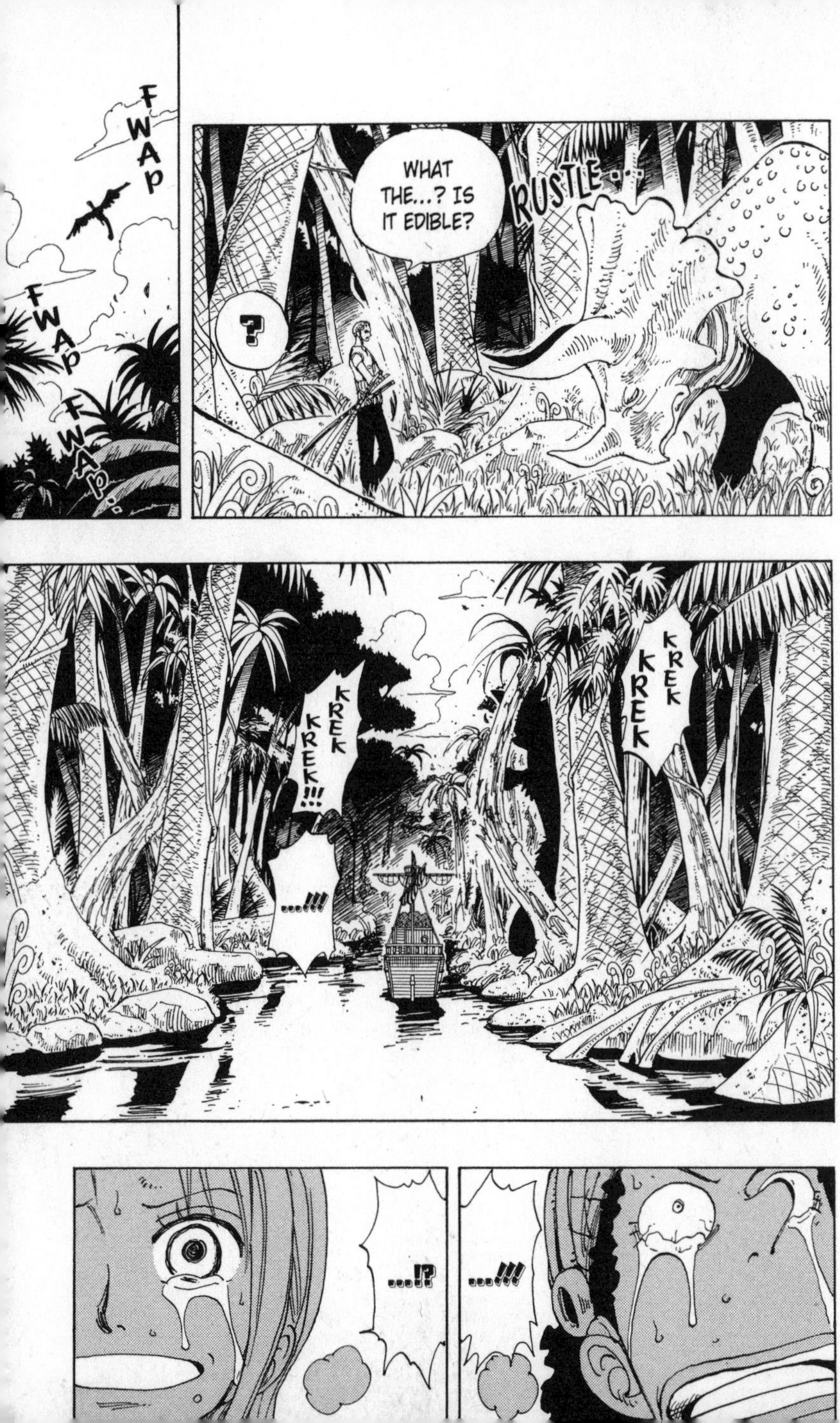
RUSTLE...
WHAT THE...? IS IT EDIBLE?
?
FWAP
FWAP
FWAP
KREK KREK
KREK KREK!!!
...!!!
...!!!
...!?

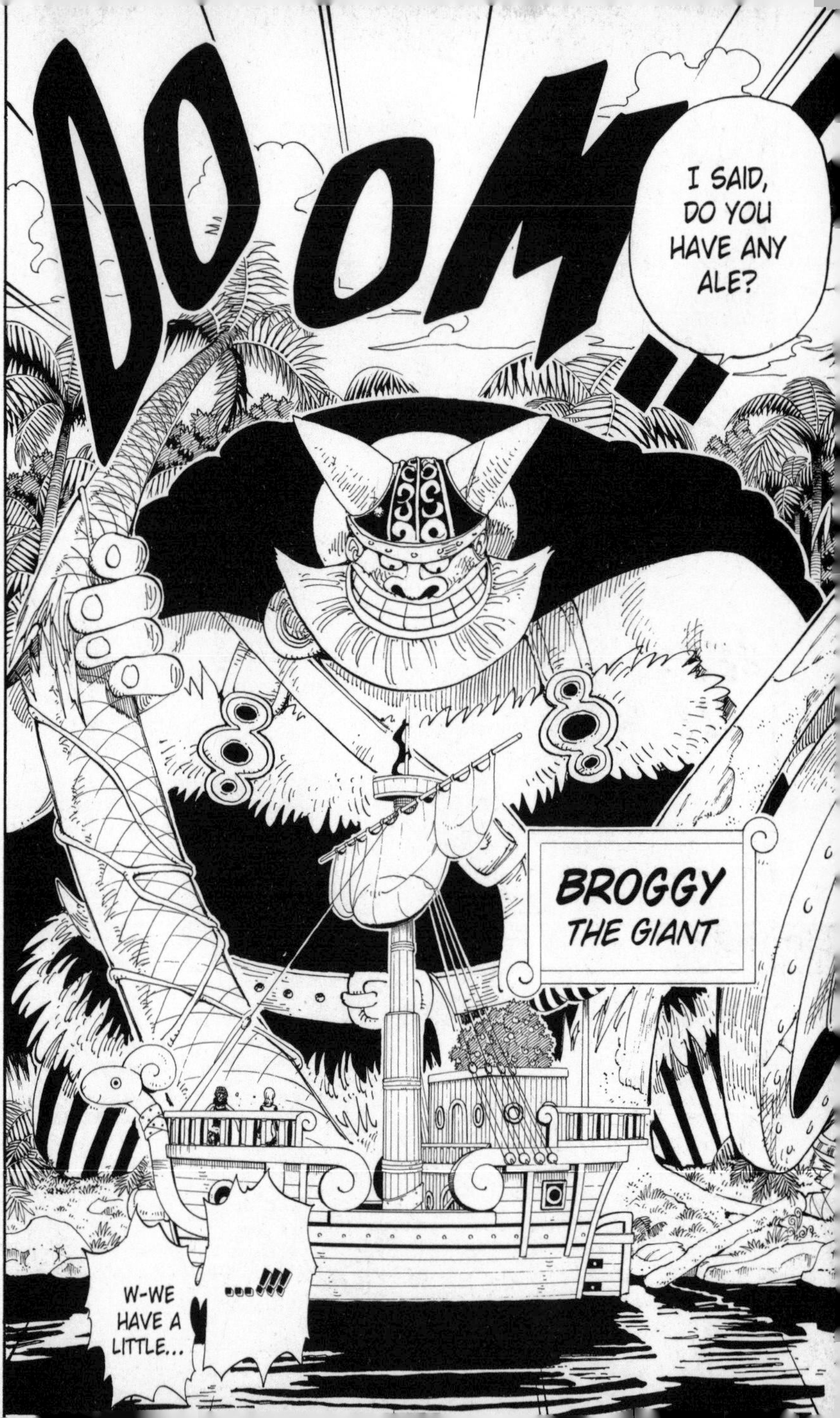
DOOM!!
I SAID, DO YOU HAVE ANY ALE?
BROGGY THE GIANT
...!!!
W-WE HAVE A LITTLE...

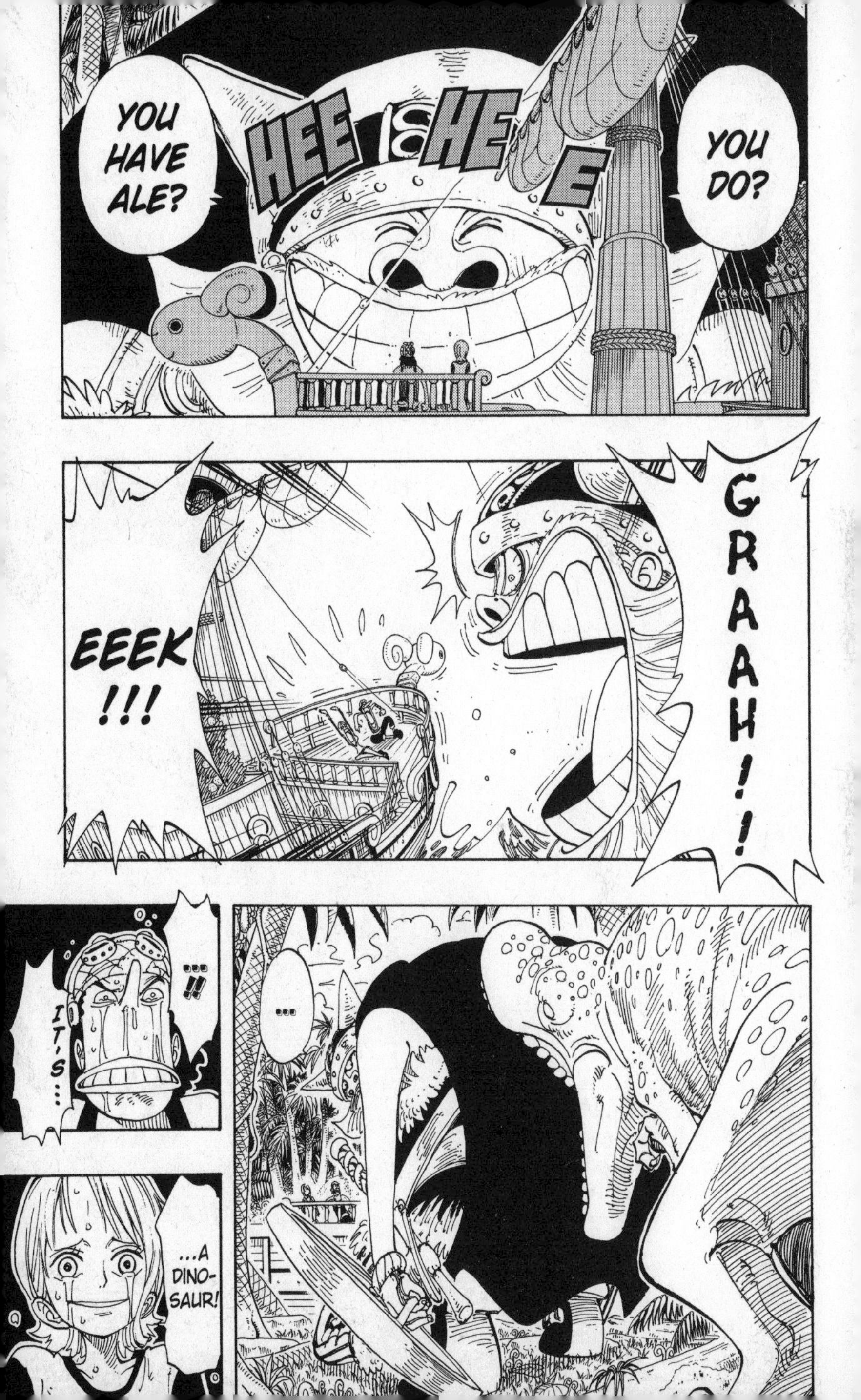
YOU DO?
HEE HE E
YOU HAVE ALE?
GRAAH!!!
EEEK!!!
...
...!!
IT'S...
...A DINO-SAUR!

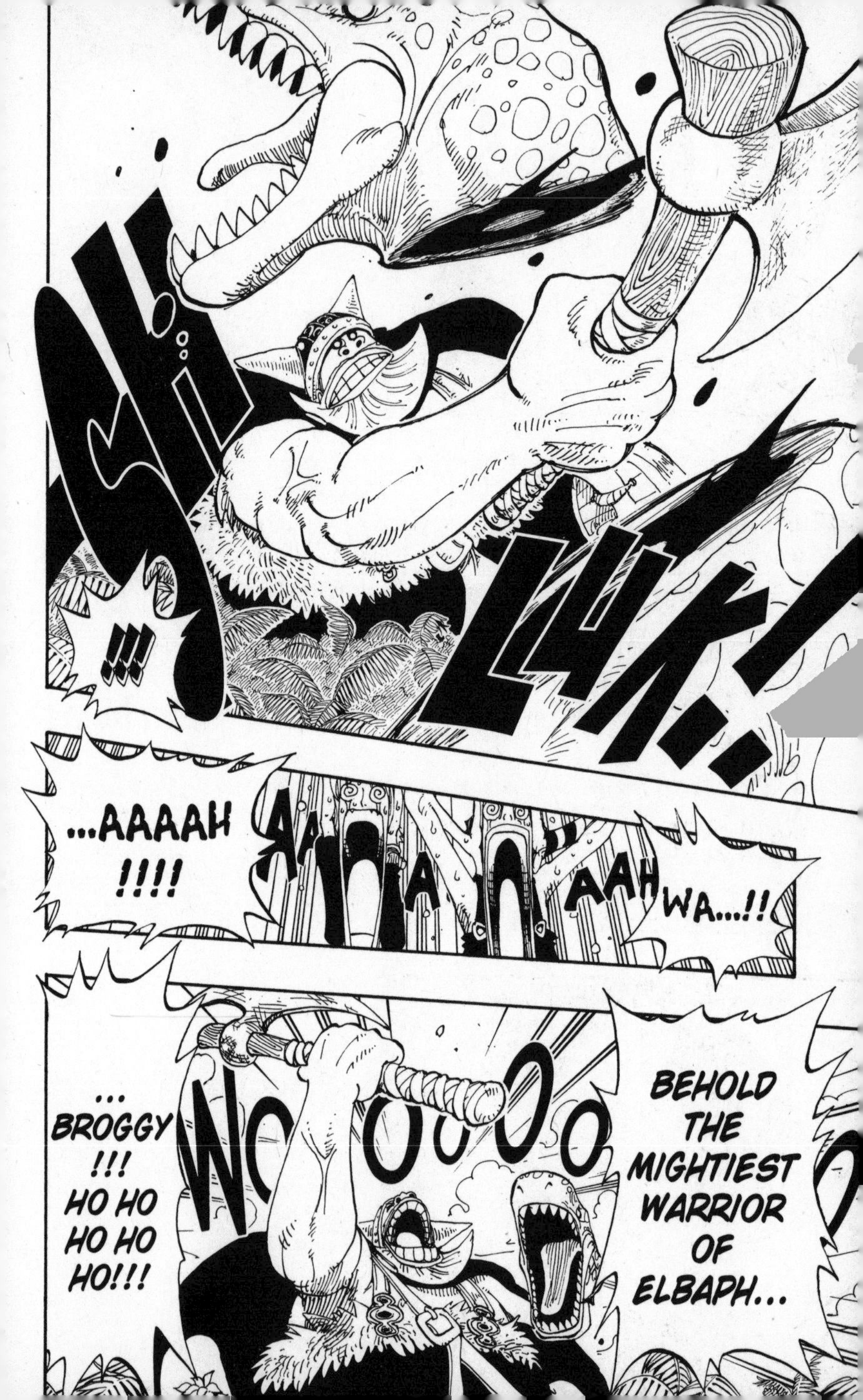
!!!
WA...!!
...AAAAH !!!!
BEHOLD THE MIGHTIEST WARRIOR OF ELBAPH...
...BROGGY!!! HO HO HO HO HO!!!

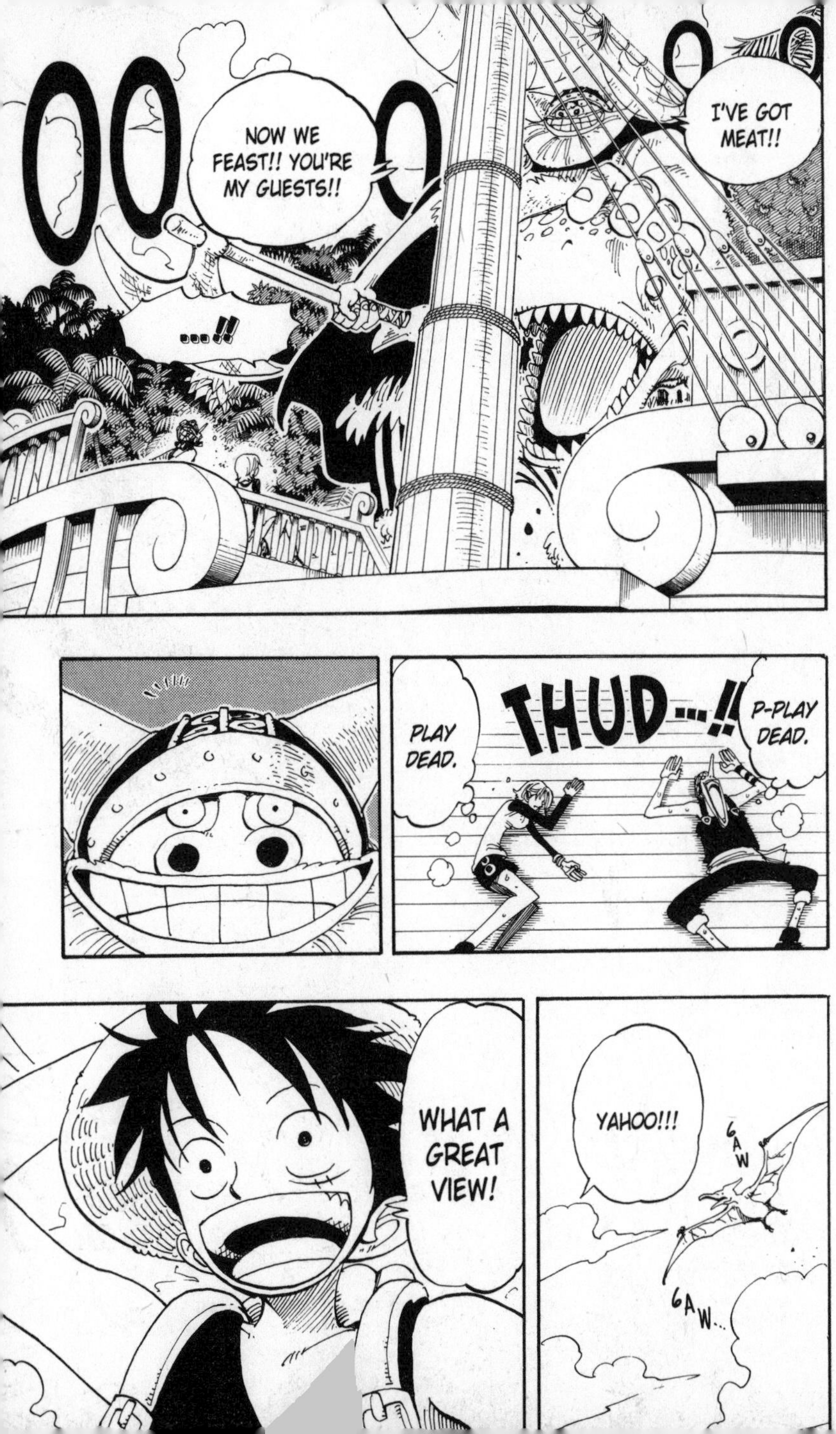
OOOO
I'VE GOT MEAT!!
NOW WE FEAST!! YOU'RE MY GUESTS!!
...!!
P-PLAY DEAD.
THUD...!!
PLAY DEAD.
YAHOO!!!
GAW
GAW...
WHAT A GREAT VIEW!

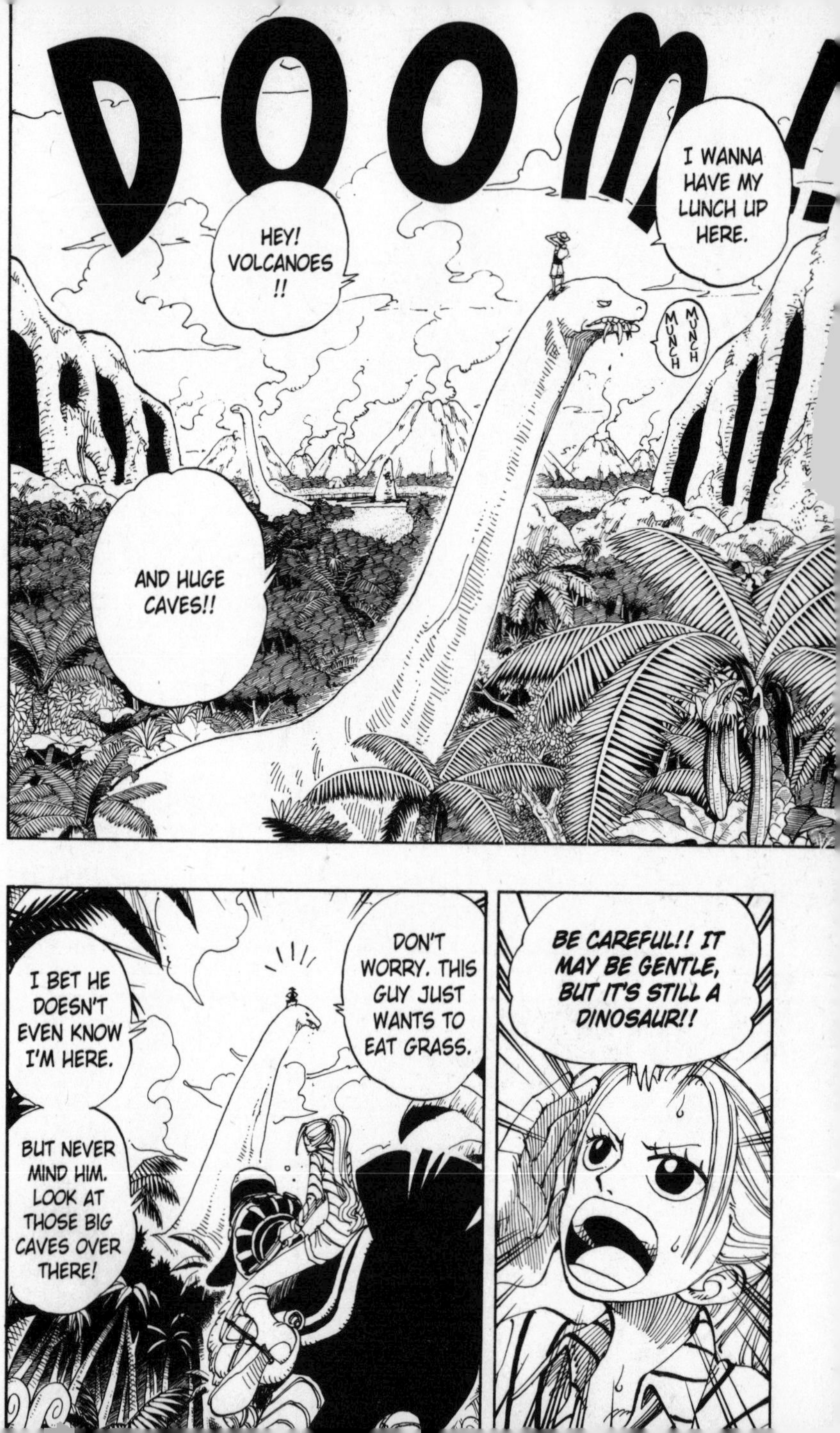
DOOM!
I WANNA HAVE MY LUNCH UP HERE.
MUNCH MUNCH
HEY! VOLCANOES!!
AND HUGE CAVES!!
BE CAREFUL!! IT MAY BE GENTLE, BUT IT'S STILL A DINOSAUR!!
DON'T WORRY. THIS GUY JUST WANTS TO EAT GRASS.
I BET HE DOESN'T EVEN KNOW I'M HERE.
BUT NEVER MIND HIM. LOOK AT THOSE BIG CAVES OVER THERE!

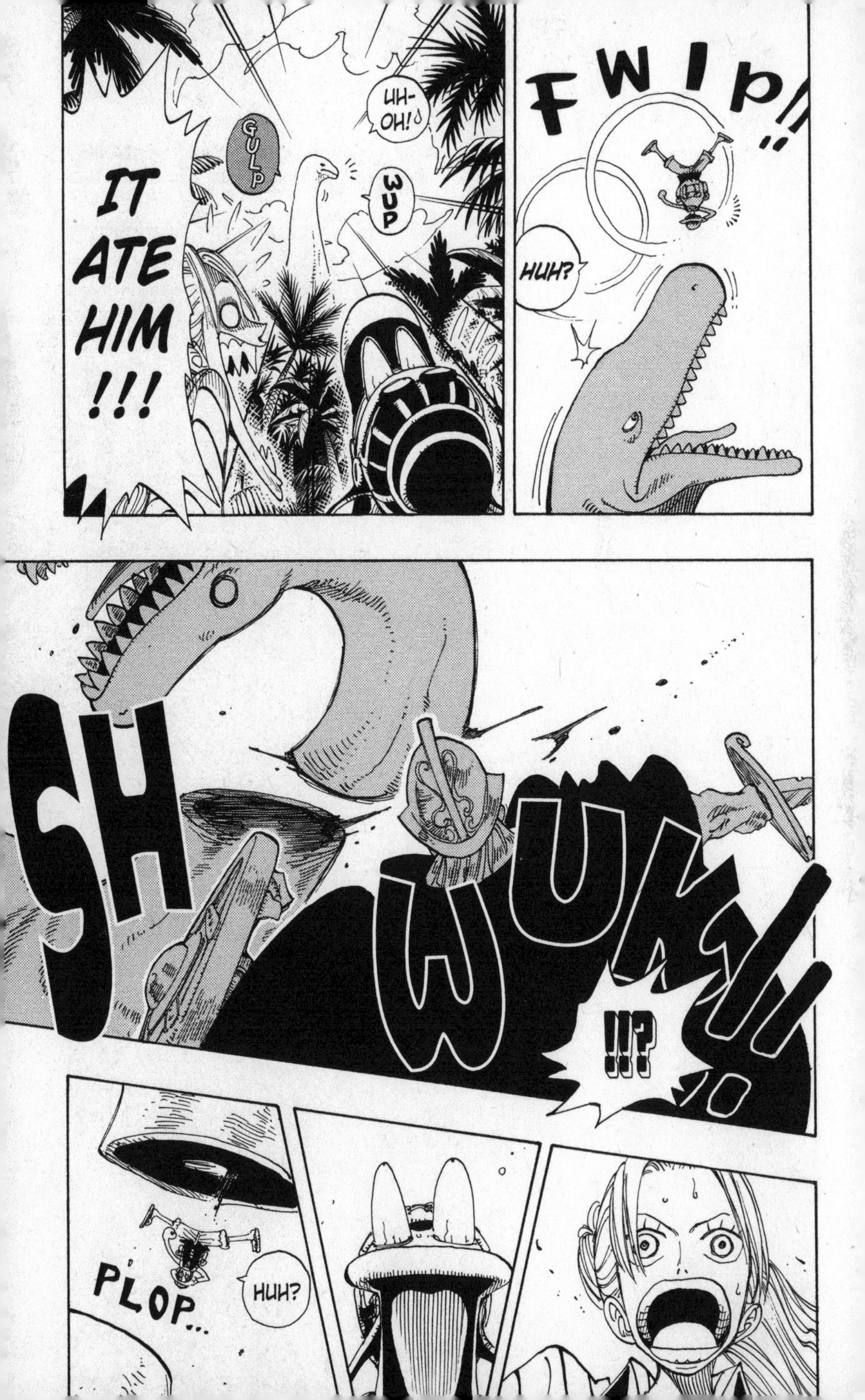
FWIP!!
HUH?
IT ATE HIM!!!
GULP
UH-OH!
WUP
SHWUNG!!
!!?
HUH?
PLOP...

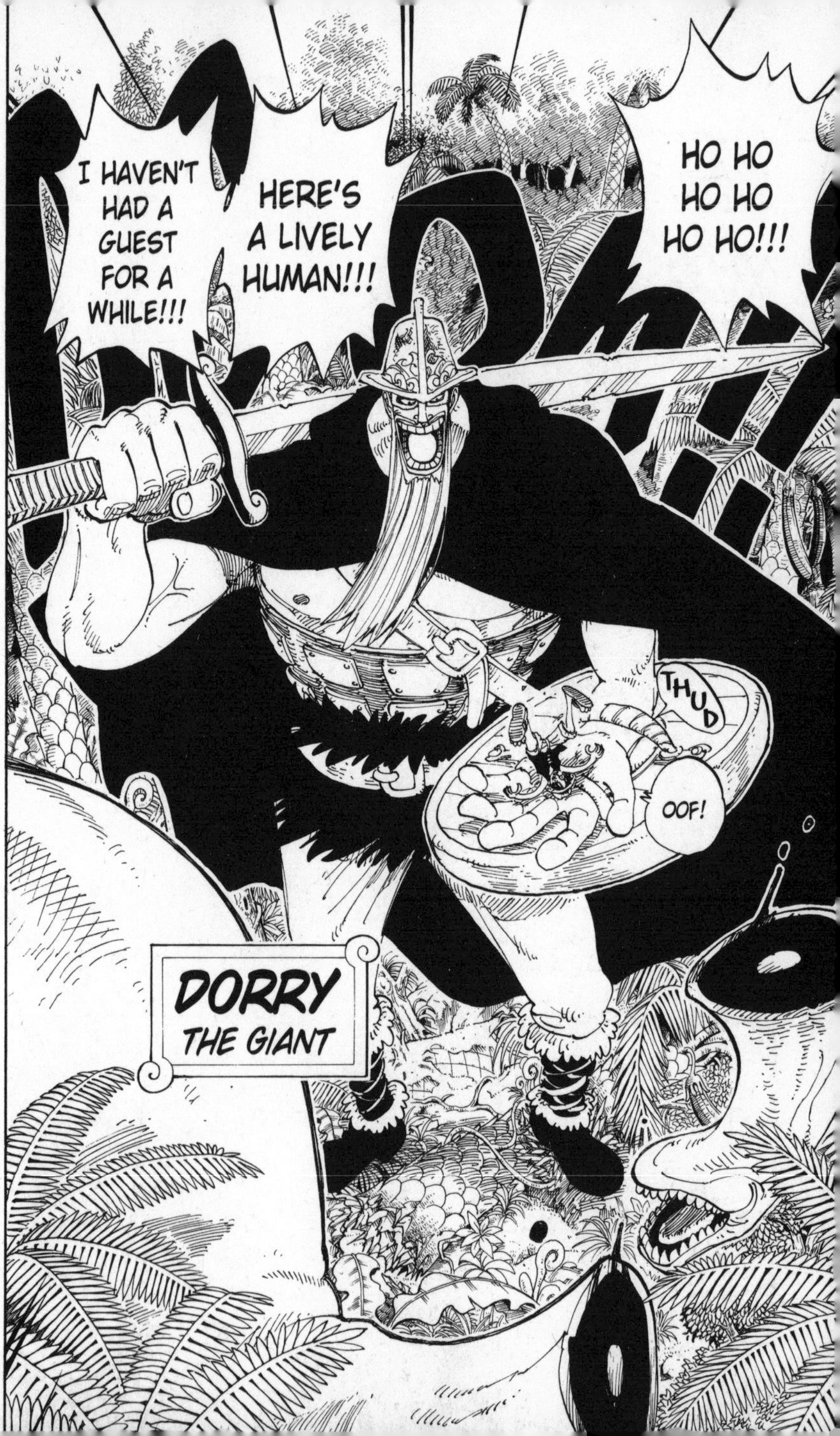
HO HO HO HO HO HO!!!
HERE'S A LIVELY HUMAN!!!
I HAVEN'T HAD A GUEST FOR A WHILE!!!
THUD
OOF!
DORRY THE GIANT

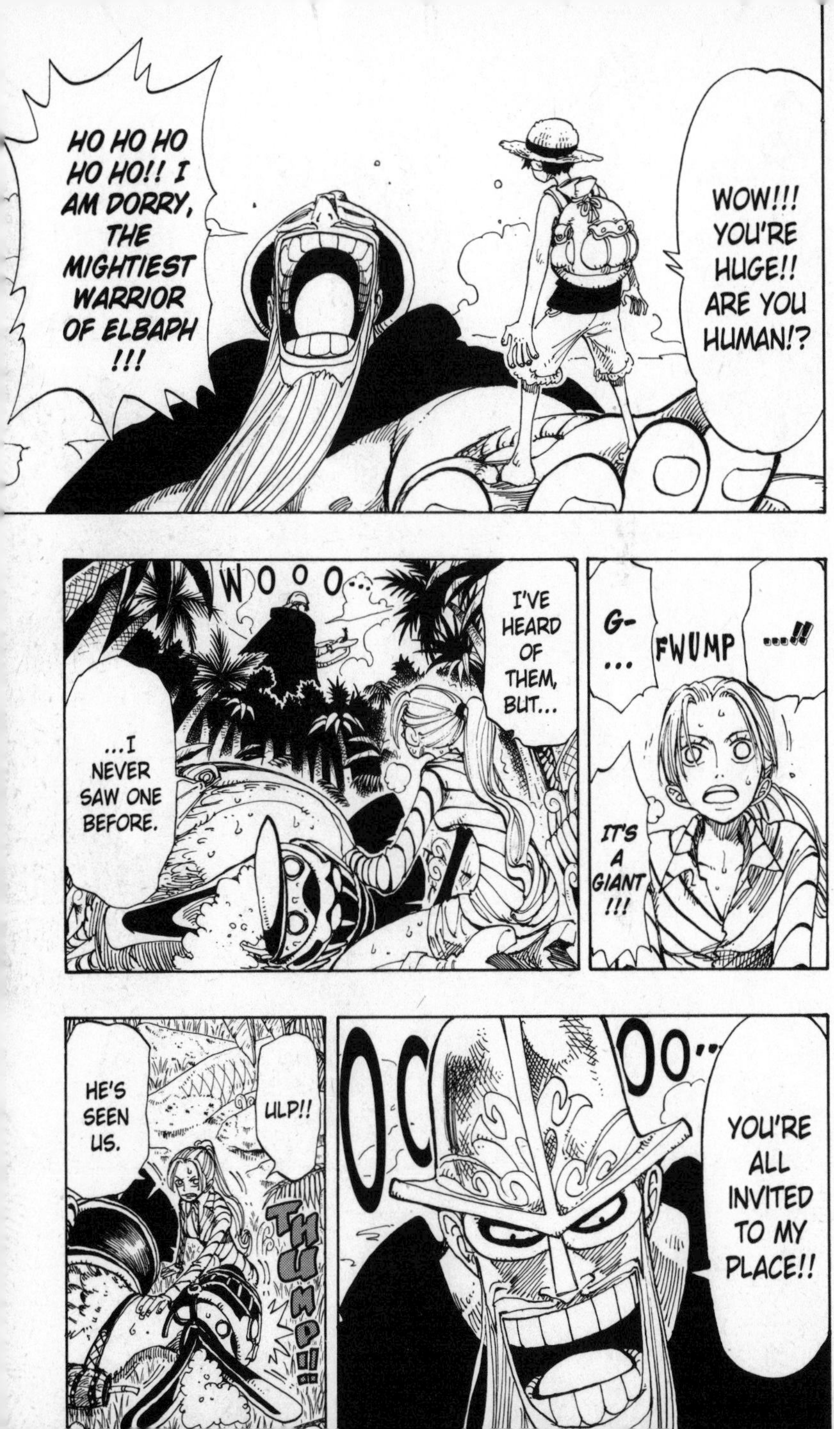
WOW!!! YOU'RE HUGE!! ARE YOU HUMAN!?
HO HO HO HO HO!! I AM DORRY, THE MIGHTIEST WARRIOR OF ELBAPH !!!
...!!
FWUMP
G-...
IT'S A GIANT !!!
WOOO...
I'VE HEARD OF THEM, BUT...
...I NEVER SAW ONE BEFORE.
OOOO...
YOU'RE ALL INVITED TO MY PLACE!!
ULP!!
HE'S SEEN US.
THUMP!!

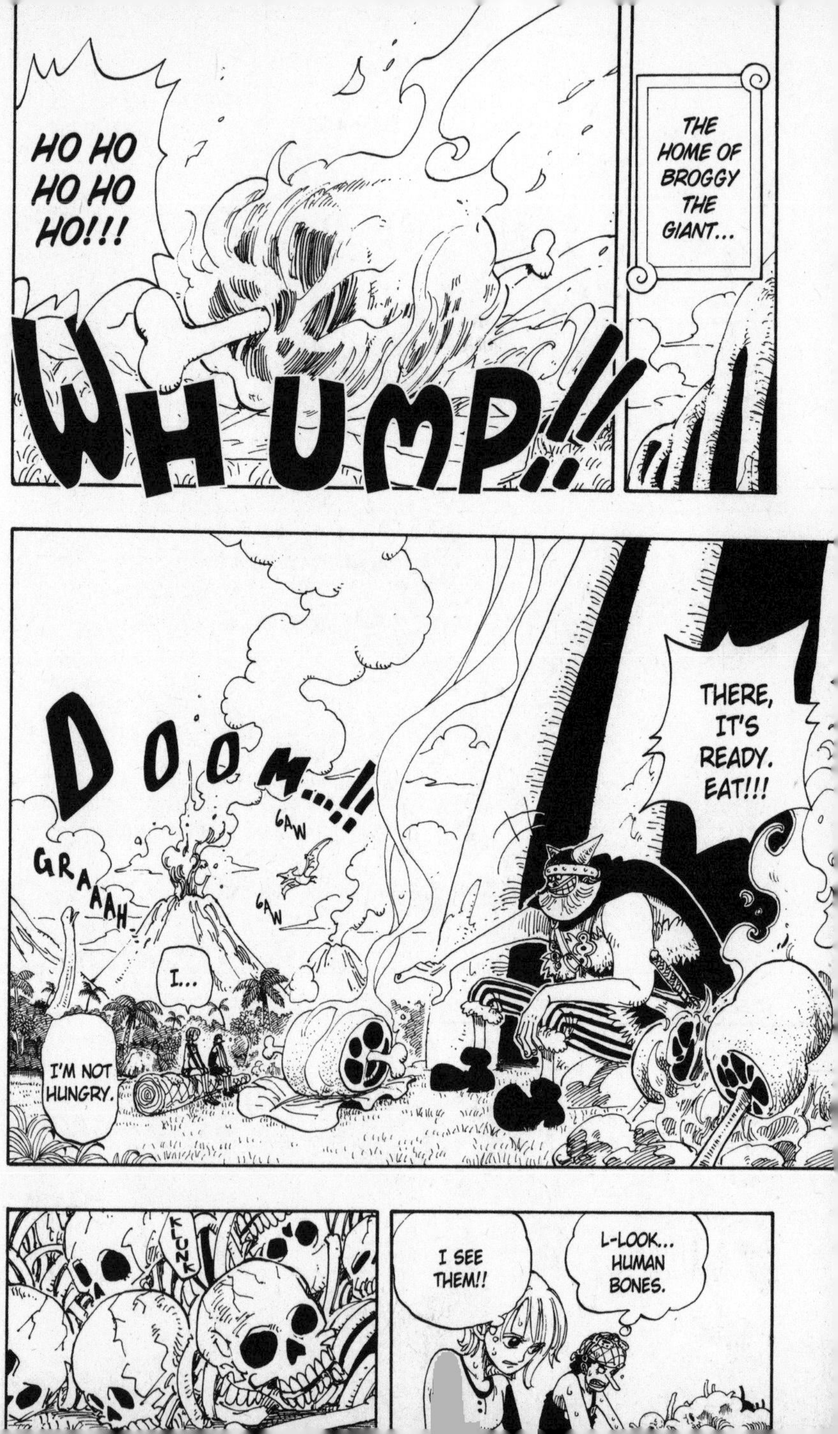
THE HOME OF BROGGY THE GIANT...
HO HO HO HO HO!!!
WHUMP!!
THERE, IT'S READY. EAT!!!
DOOM...!!
GAW
GAW
GRAAAAH
I...
I'M NOT HUNGRY.
L-LOOK... HUMAN BONES.
I SEE THEM!!
KLUNK

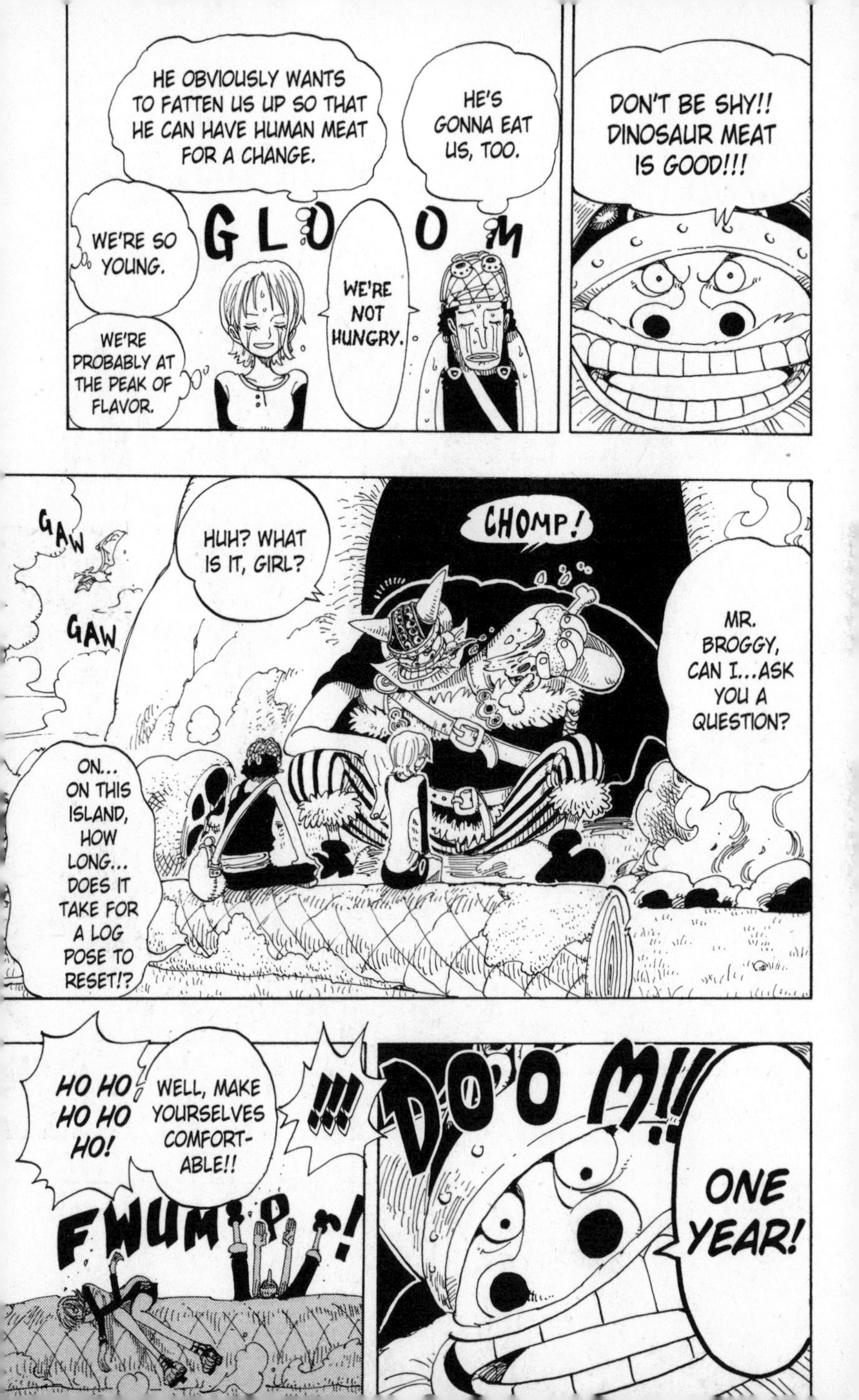
DON'T BE SHY!! DINOSAUR MEAT IS GOOD!!!
HE'S GONNA EAT US, TOO.
HE OBVIOUSLY WANTS TO FATTEN US UP SO THAT HE CAN HAVE HUMAN MEAT FOR A CHANGE.
GLOOM
WE'RE NOT HUNGRY.
WE'RE SO YOUNG.
WE'RE PROBABLY AT THE PEAK OF FLAVOR.
MR. BROGGY, CAN I...ASK YOU A QUESTION?
CHOMP!
HUH? WHAT IS IT, GIRL?
GAW
GAW
ON... ON THIS ISLAND, HOW LONG... DOES IT TAKE FOR A LOG POSE TO RESET!?
ONE YEAR!
DOOM!!
!!!
WELL, MAKE YOURSELVES COMFORT-ABLE!!
HO HO HO HO HO!
FWUMP!

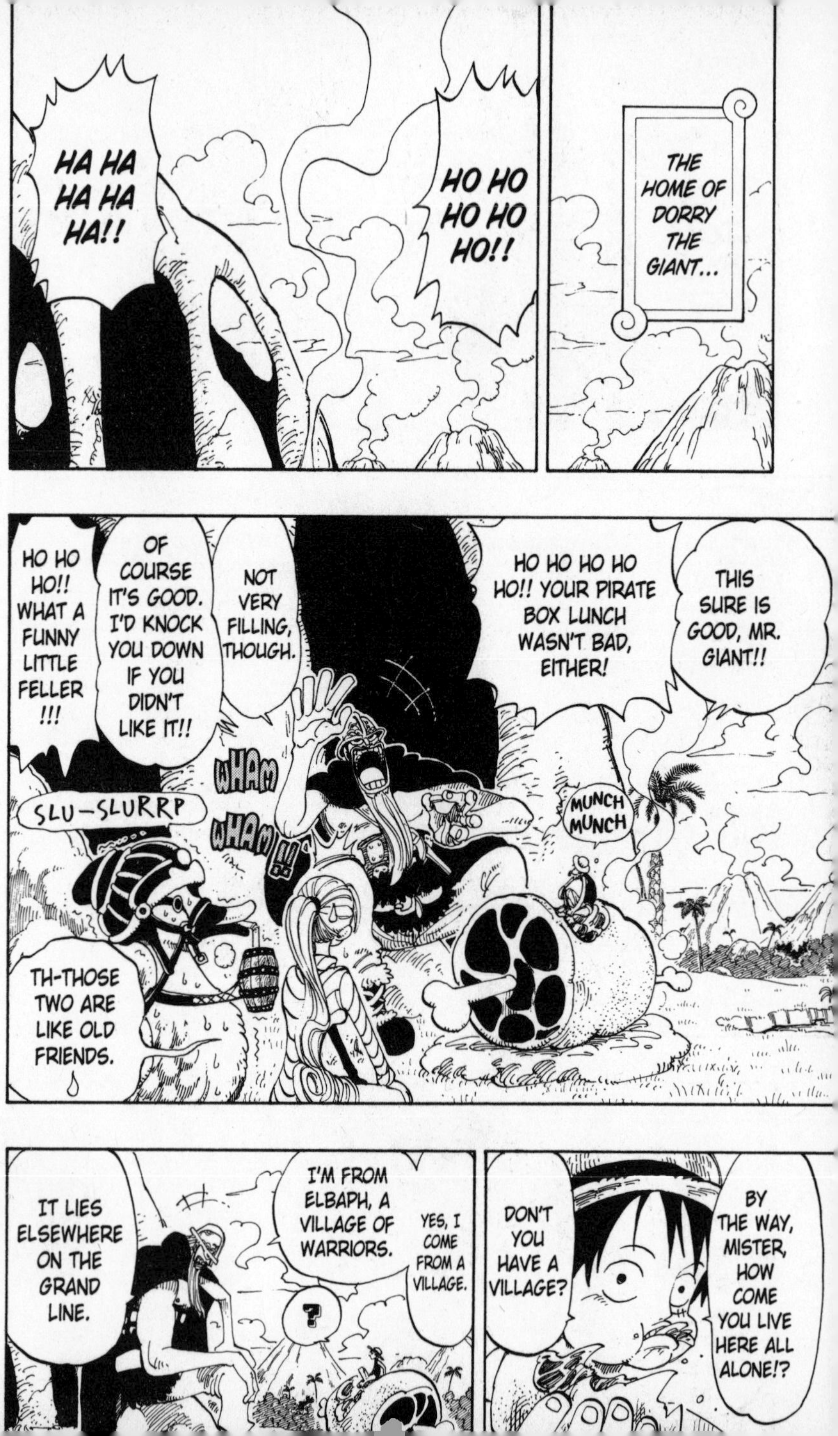
THE HOME OF DORRY THE GIANT...
HO HO HO HO HO!!
HA HA HA HA HA!!
THIS SURE IS GOOD, MR. GIANT!!
MUNCH MUNCH
HO HO HO HO HO!! YOUR PIRATE BOX LUNCH WASN'T BAD, EITHER!
NOT VERY FILLING, THOUGH.
WHAM WHAM!!
OF COURSE IT'S GOOD. I'D KNOCK YOU DOWN IF YOU DIDN'T LIKE IT!!
HO HO HO!! WHAT A FUNNY LITTLE FELLER!!!
SLU-SLURRP
TH-THOSE TWO ARE LIKE OLD FRIENDS.
BY THE WAY, MISTER, HOW COME YOU LIVE HERE ALL ALONE!?
DON'T YOU HAVE A VILLAGE?
YES, I COME FROM A VILLAGE.
I'M FROM ELBAPH, A VILLAGE OF WARRIORS.
?
IT LIES ELSEWHERE ON THE GRAND LINE.

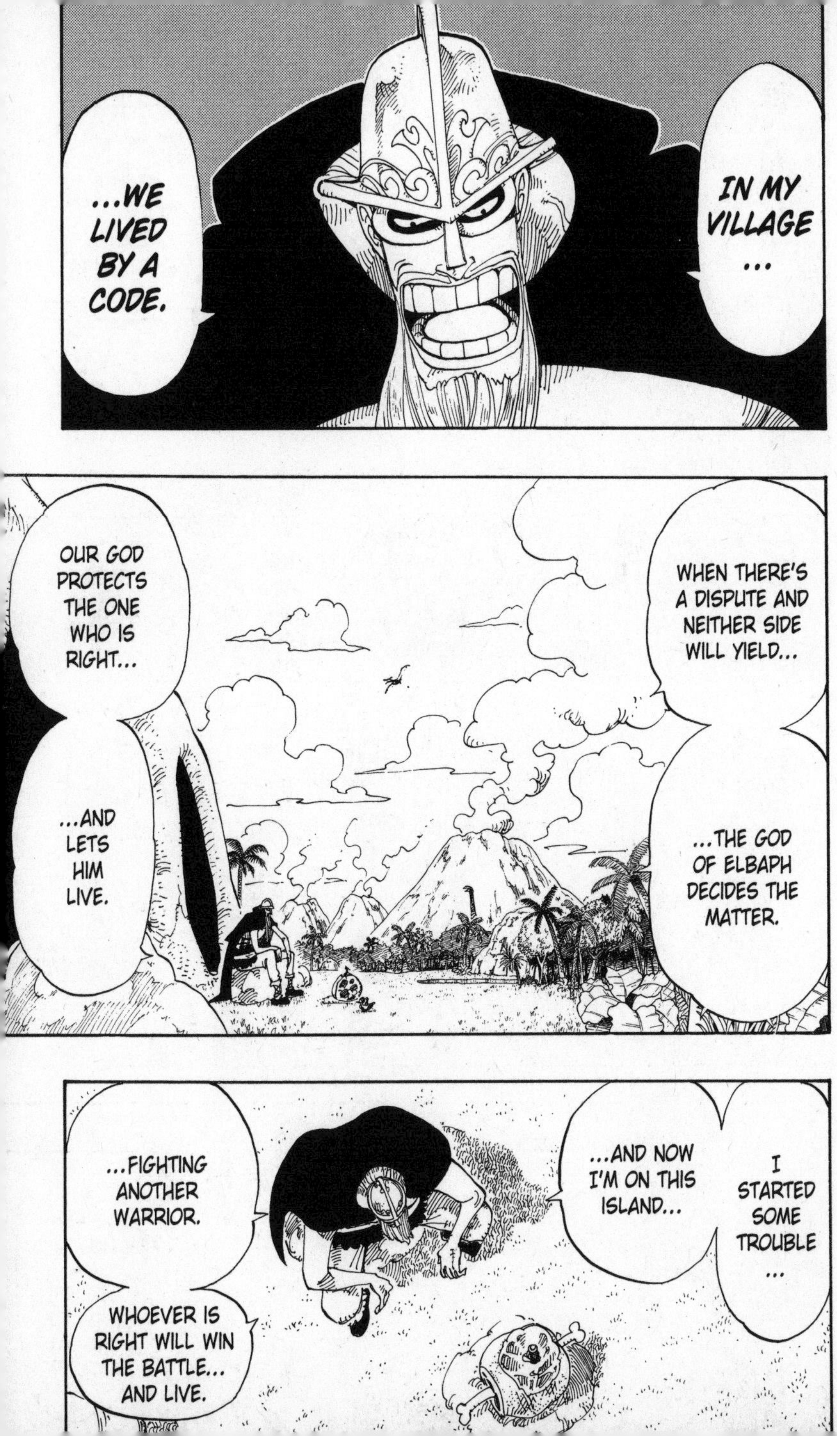
IN MY VILLAGE ...
...WE LIVED BY A CODE.
WHEN THERE'S A DISPUTE AND NEITHER SIDE WILL YIELD...
...THE GOD OF ELBAPH DECIDES THE MATTER.
OUR GOD PROTECTS THE ONE WHO IS RIGHT...
...AND LETS HIM LIVE.
I STARTED SOME TROUBLE ...
...AND NOW I'M ON THIS ISLAND...
...FIGHTING ANOTHER WARRIOR.
WHOEVER IS RIGHT WILL WIN THE BATTLE... AND LIVE.

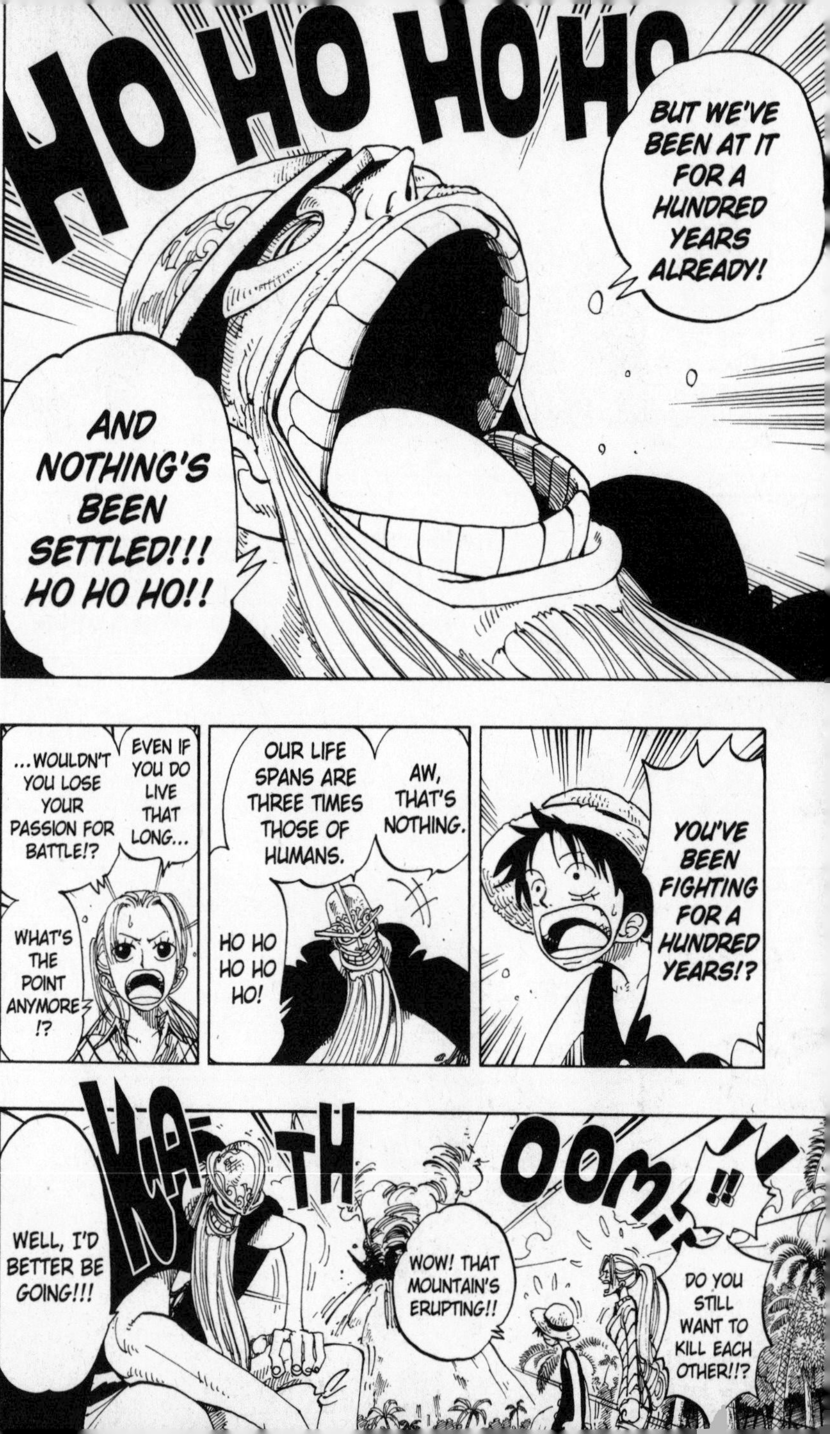
HO HO HO HO
BUT WE'VE BEEN AT IT FOR A HUNDRED YEARS ALREADY!
AND NOTHING'S BEEN SETTLED!!! HO HO HO!!
YOU'VE BEEN FIGHTING FOR A HUNDRED YEARS!?
AW, THAT'S NOTHING.
OUR LIFE SPANS ARE THREE TIMES THOSE OF HUMANS.
HO HO HO HO HO!
EVEN IF YOU DO LIVE THAT LONG...
...WOULDN'T YOU LOSE YOUR PASSION FOR BATTLE!?
WHAT'S THE POINT ANYMORE!?
KA- TH OOM!!
DO YOU STILL WANT TO KILL EACH OTHER!!?
WOW! THAT MOUNTAIN'S ERUPTING!!
WELL, I'D BETTER BE GOING!!!

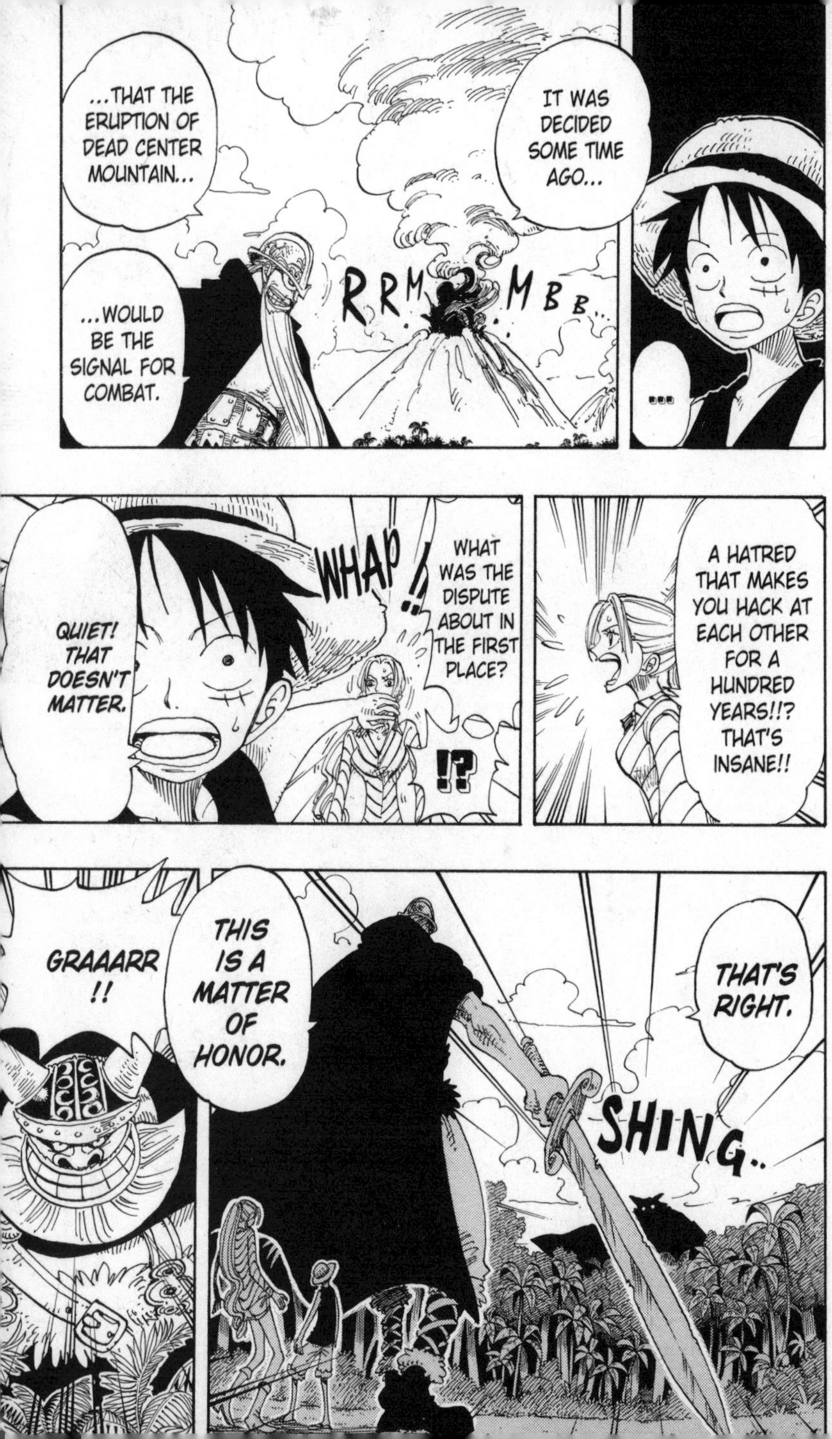
IT WAS DECIDED SOME TIME AGO...
...THAT THE ERUPTION OF DEAD CENTER MOUNTAIN...
RRMMBB...
...WOULD BE THE SIGNAL FOR COMBAT.
...
A HATRED THAT MAKES YOU HACK AT EACH OTHER FOR A HUNDRED YEARS!!? THAT'S INSANE!!
WHAT WAS THE DISPUTE ABOUT IN THE FIRST PLACE?
WHAP!!
!?
QUIET! THAT DOESN'T MATTER.
THAT'S RIGHT.
SHING..
THIS IS A MATTER OF HONOR.
GRAAARR!!

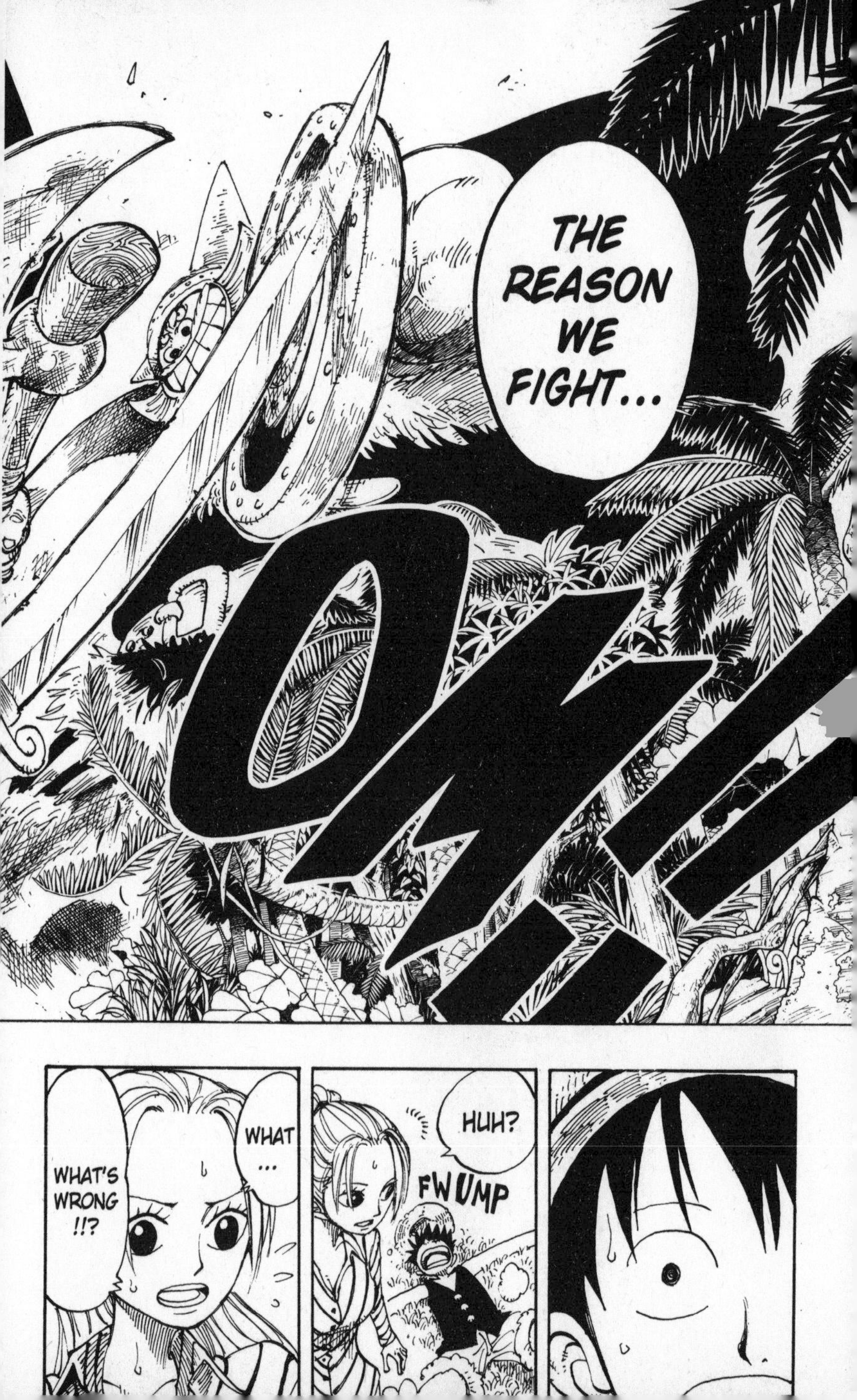
THE REASON WE FIGHT...
HUH?
FWUMP
WHAT ...
WHAT'S WRONG !!?

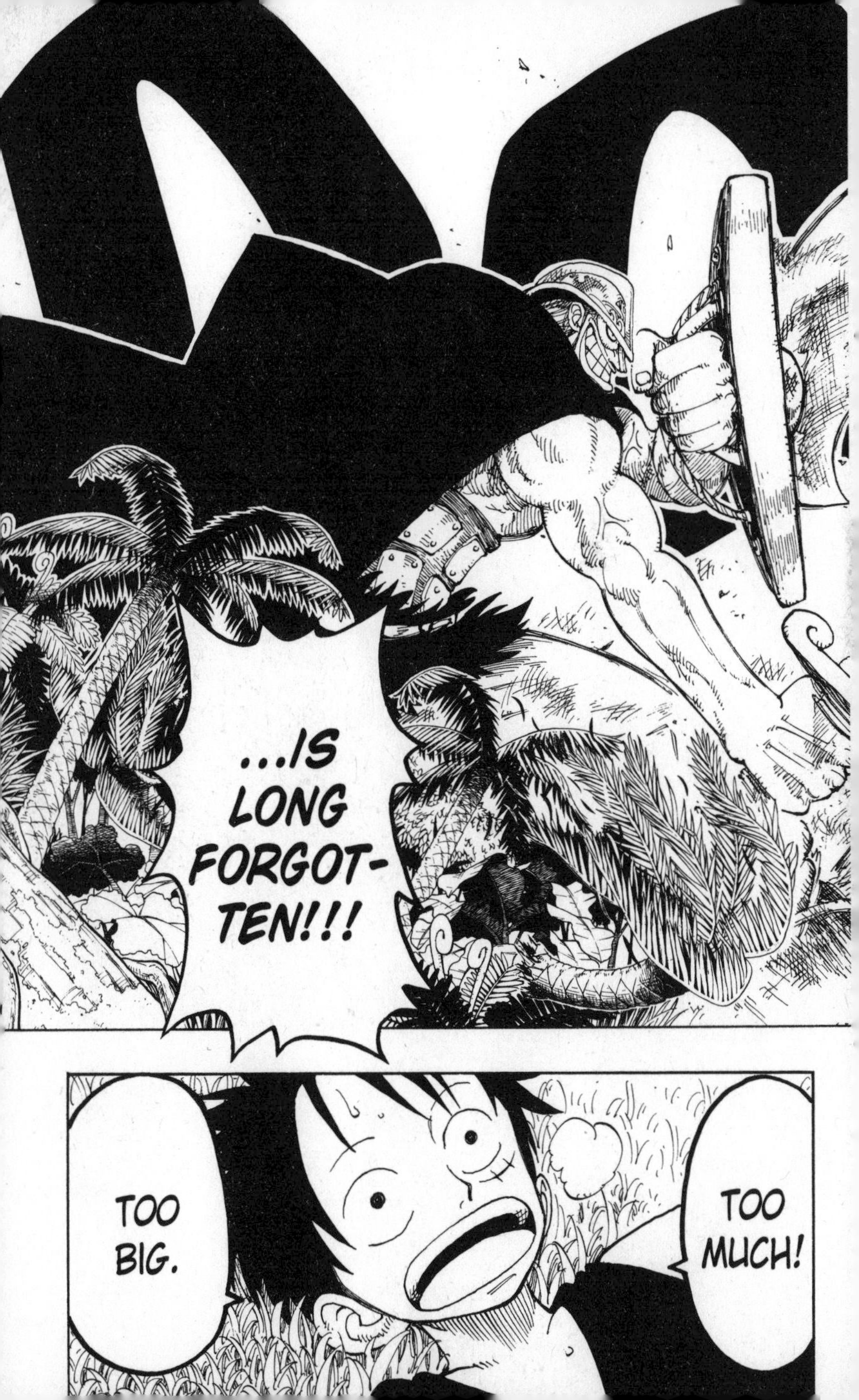
...IS LONG FORGOTTEN!!!
TOO MUCH!
TOO BIG.

DORRY AND BROGGY

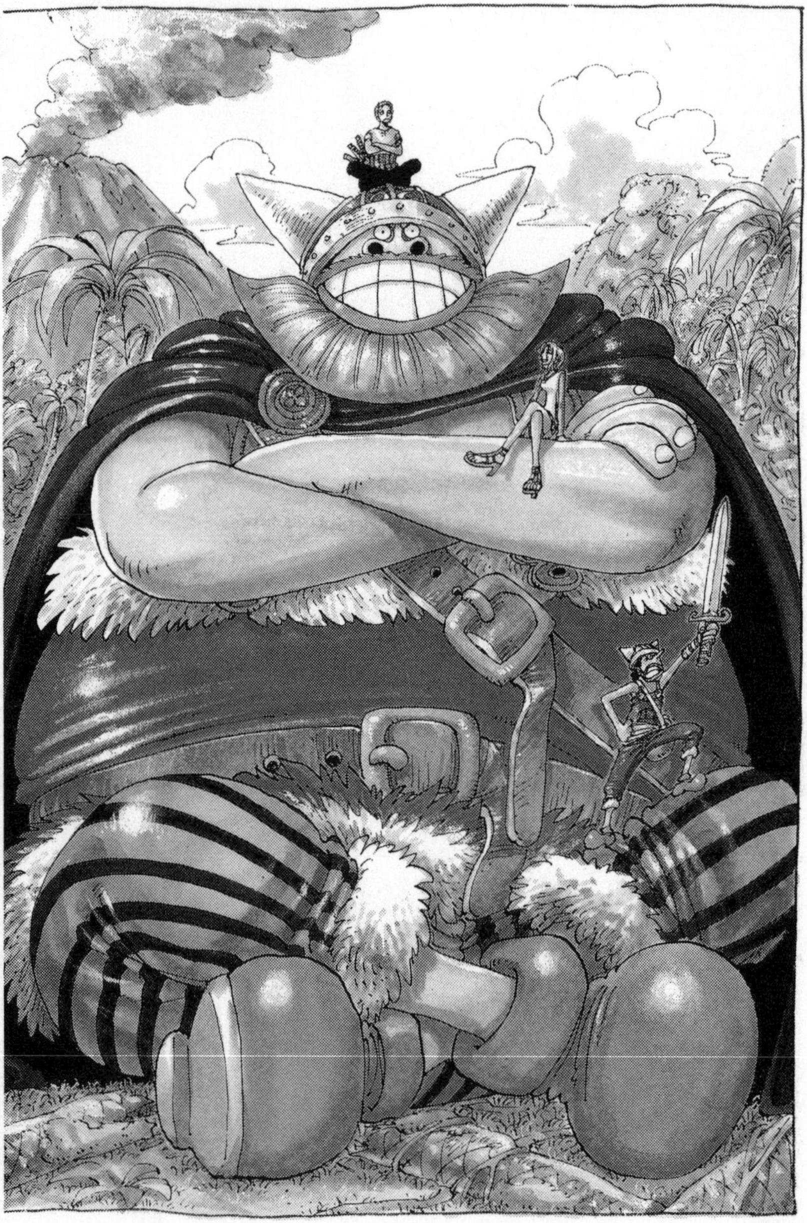

Chapter 117:

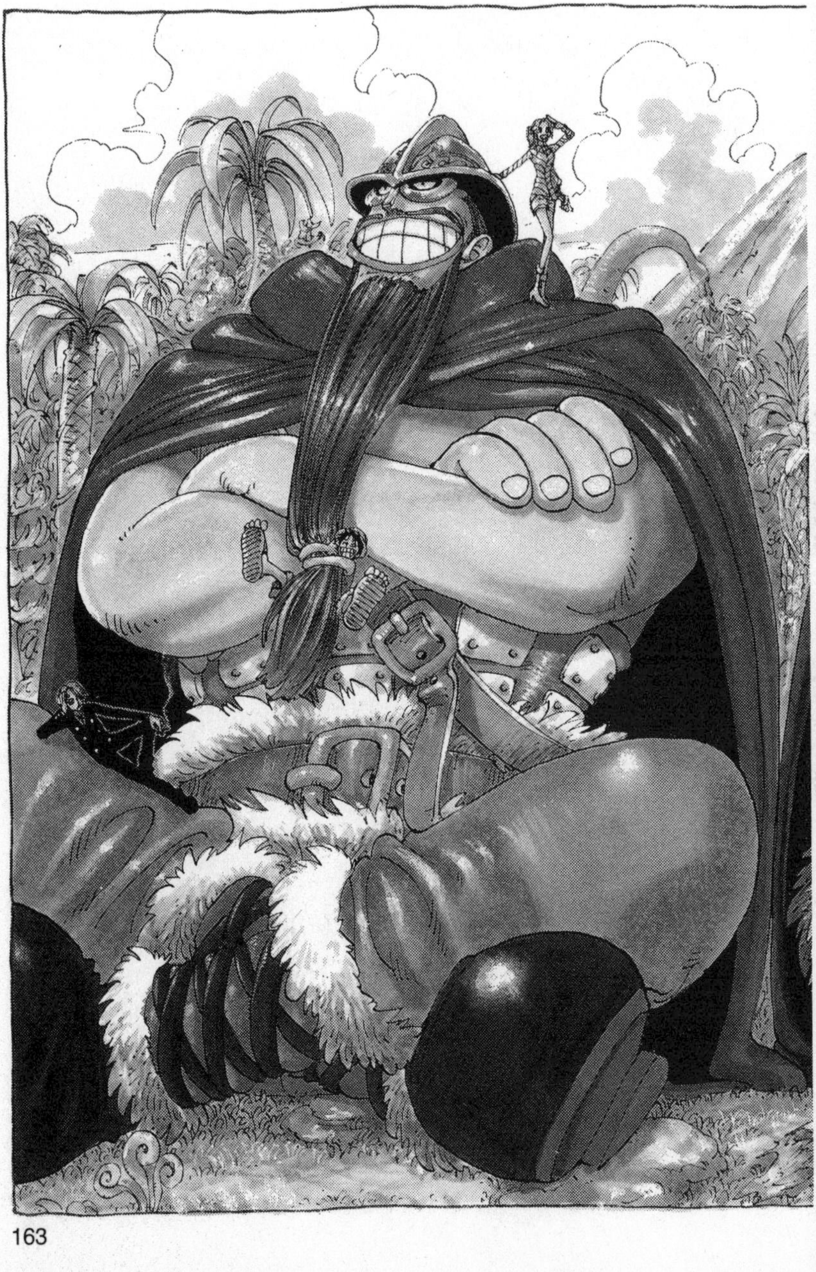

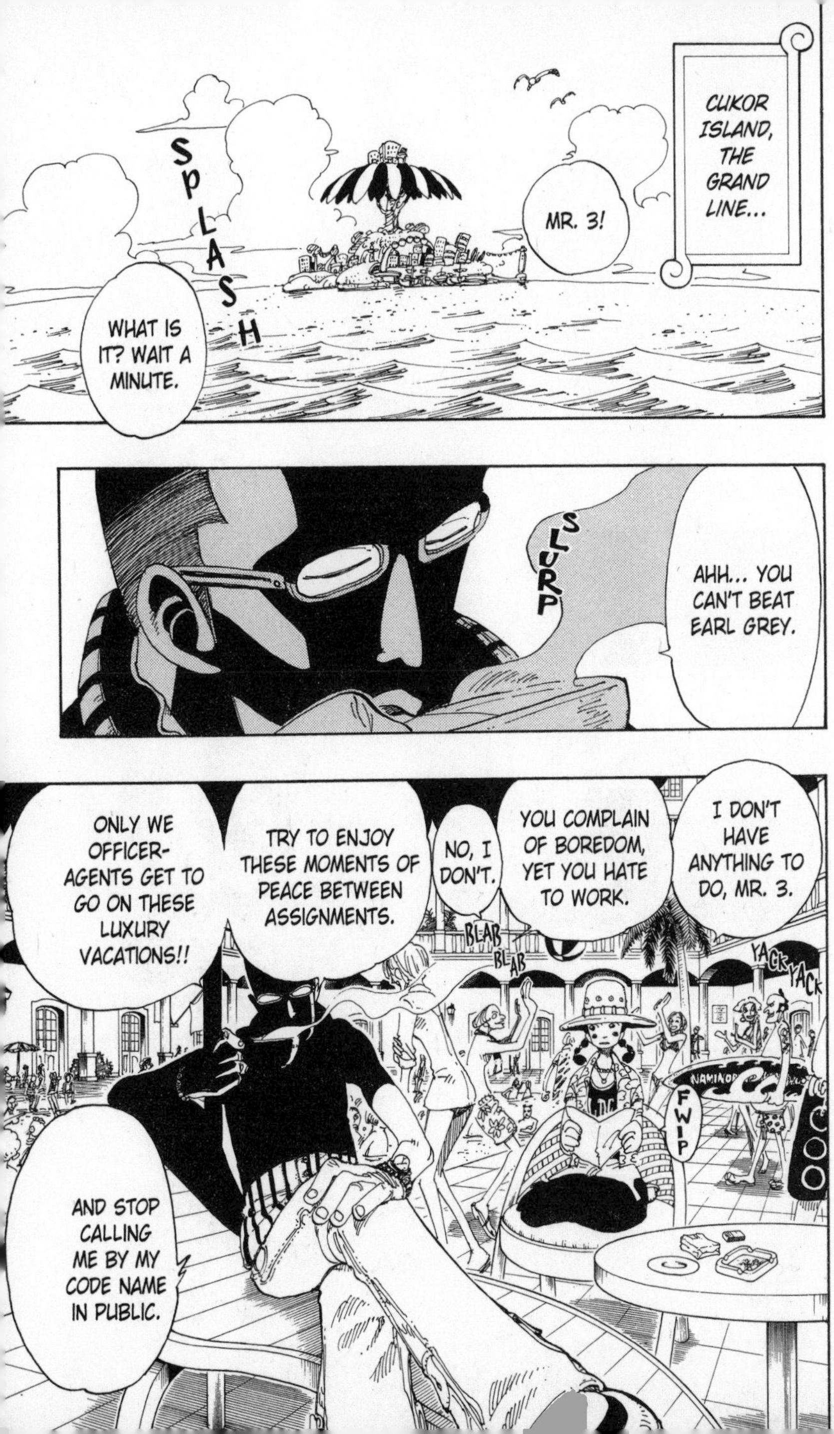
CUKOR ISLAND, THE GRAND LINE...
MR. 3!
SPLASH
WHAT IS IT? WAIT A MINUTE.
AHH... YOU CAN'T BEAT EARL GREY.
SLURP
I DON'T HAVE ANYTHING TO DO, MR. 3.
YOU COMPLAIN OF BOREDOM, YET YOU HATE TO WORK.
NO, I DON'T.
TRY TO ENJOY THESE MOMENTS OF PEACE BETWEEN ASSIGNMENTS.
ONLY WE OFFICER-AGENTS GET TO GO ON THESE LUXURY VACATIONS!!
YACK YACK
BLAB BLAB
FWIP
AND STOP CALLING ME BY MY CODE NAME IN PUBLIC.

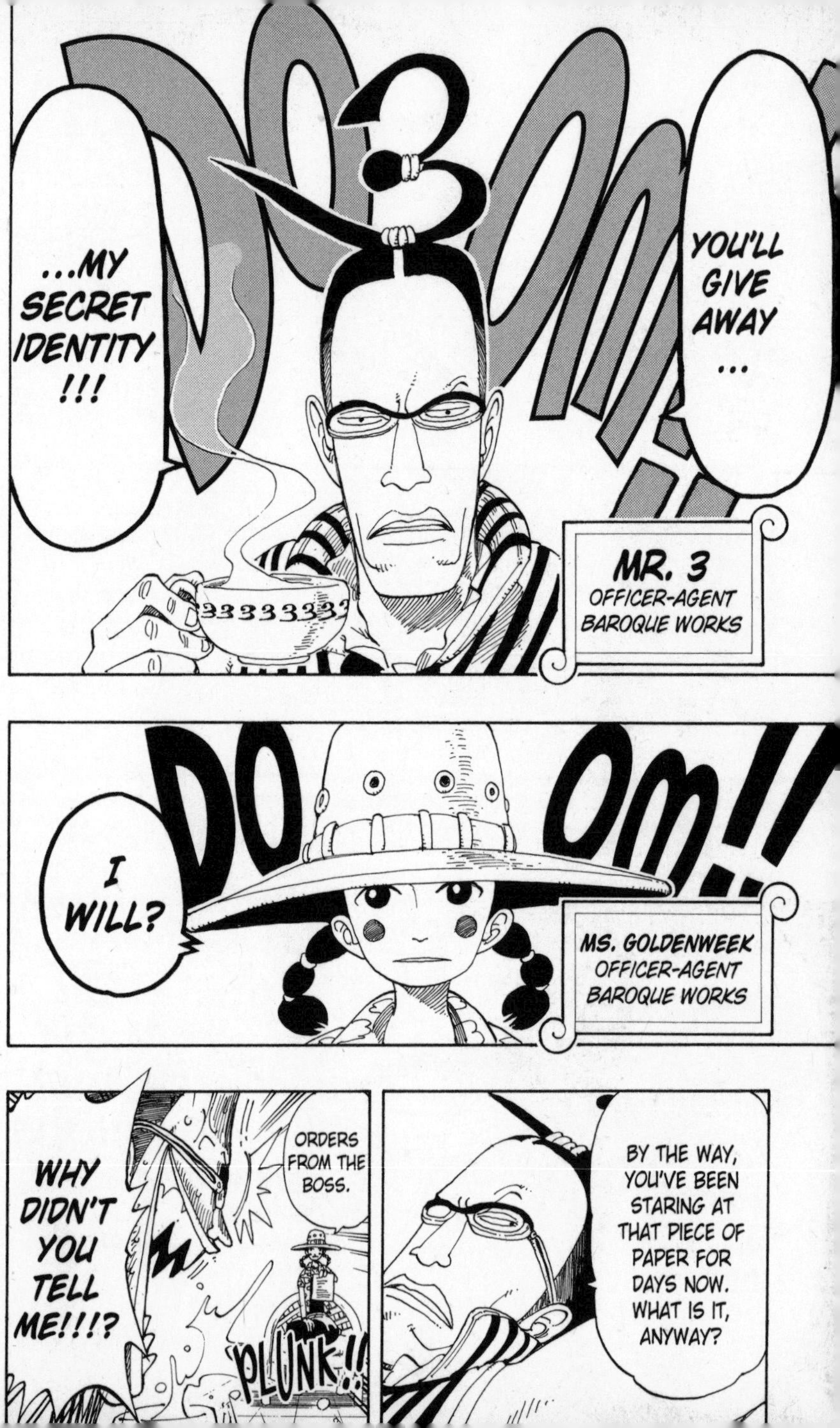
YOU'LL GIVE AWAY ...
...MY SECRET IDENTITY !!!
MR. 3 OFFICER-AGENT BAROQUE WORKS
DO OM!!
MS. GOLDENWEEK OFFICER-AGENT BAROQUE WORKS
I WILL?
BY THE WAY, YOU'VE BEEN STARING AT THAT PIECE OF PAPER FOR DAYS NOW. WHAT IS IT, ANYWAY?
ORDERS FROM THE BOSS.
WHY DIDN'T YOU TELL ME!!!?
PLUNK!!

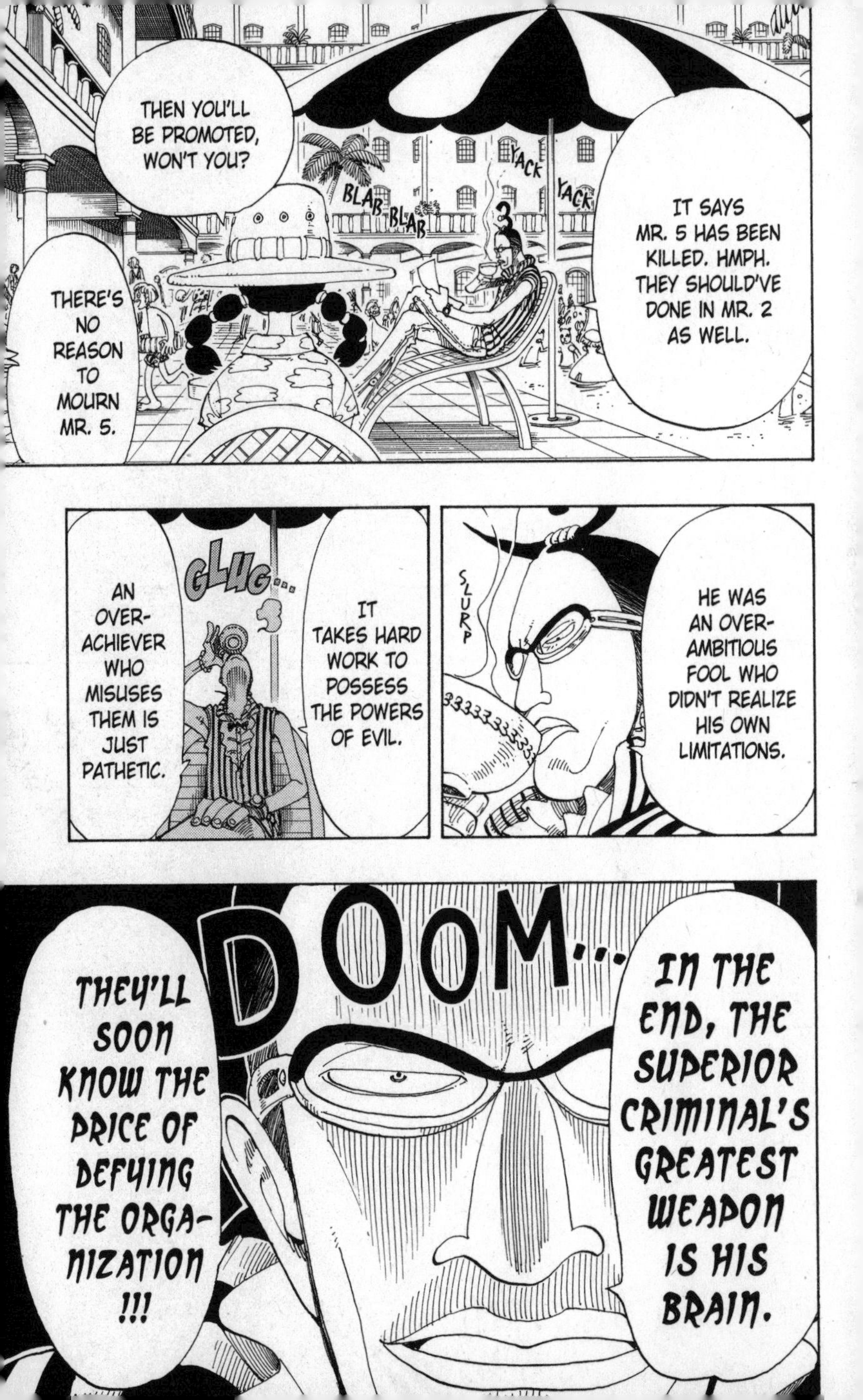
IT SAYS MR. 5 HAS BEEN KILLED. HMPH. THEY SHOULD'VE DONE IN MR. 2 AS WELL.
YACK YACK
BLAB BLAB
THEN YOU'LL BE PROMOTED, WON'T YOU?
THERE'S NO REASON TO MOURN MR. 5.
SLURP
HE WAS AN OVER-AMBITIOUS FOOL WHO DIDN'T REALIZE HIS OWN LIMITATIONS.
IT TAKES HARD WORK TO POSSESS THE POWERS OF EVIL.
GLUG...
AN OVER-ACHIEVER WHO MISUSES THEM IS JUST PATHETIC.
IN THE END, THE SUPERIOR CRIMINAL'S GREATEST WEAPON IS HIS BRAIN.
DOOM...
THEY'LL SOON KNOW THE PRICE OF DEFYING THE ORGA-NIZATION!!!

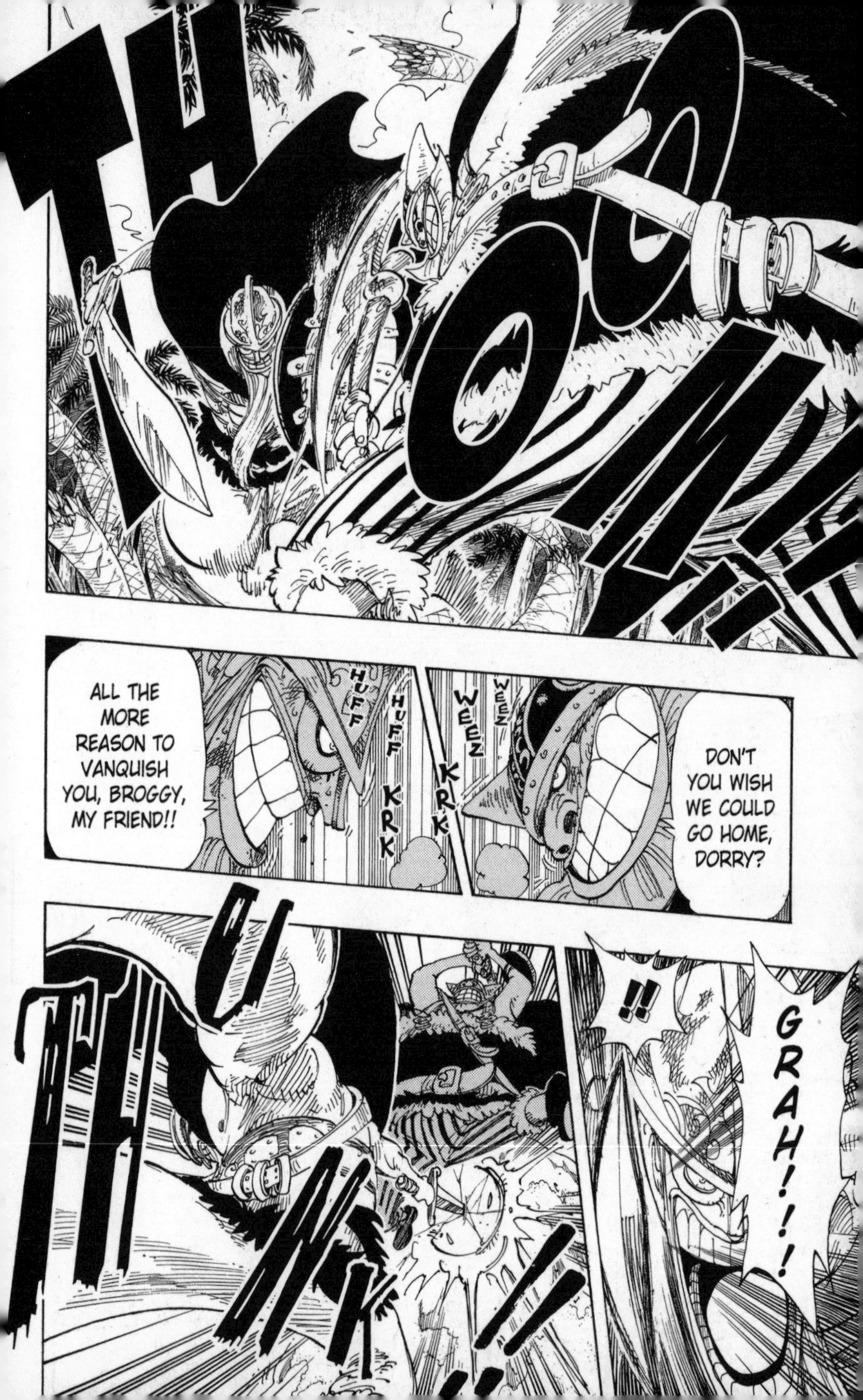
THOOOM!!
WEEZ WEEZ
KRK KRK
DON'T YOU WISH WE COULD GO HOME, DORRY?
HUFF HUFF
KRK
ALL THE MORE REASON TO VANQUISH YOU, BROGGY, MY FRIEND!!
!!
GRAH!!!
THWAK!!

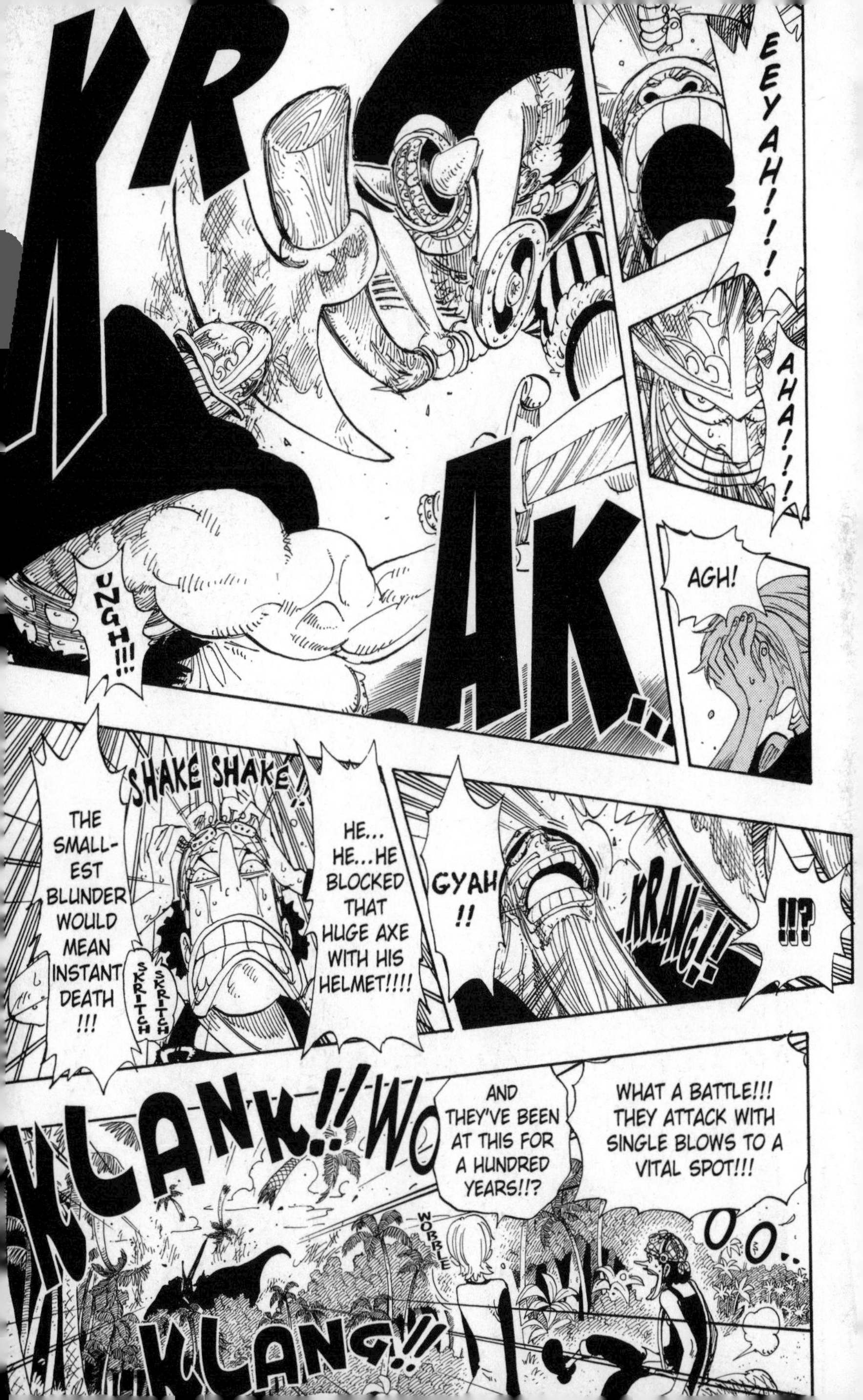
EEYAH!!!!
AHA!!!
AGH!
K'R
AK...
UNGH!!!
!!?
KRANG!!
GYAH!!
HE... HE...HE BLOCKED THAT HUGE AXE WITH HIS HELMET!!!!!
SHAKE SHAKE!!
THE SMALL-EST BLUNDER WOULD MEAN INSTANT DEATH!!!
SKRITCH SKRITCH
WHAT A BATTLE!!! THEY ATTACK WITH SINGLE BLOWS TO A VITAL SPOT!!!
AND THEY'VE BEEN AT THIS FOR A HUNDRED YEARS!!?
OO..
WOBBLE
WO
KLANK!!
KLANG!!!

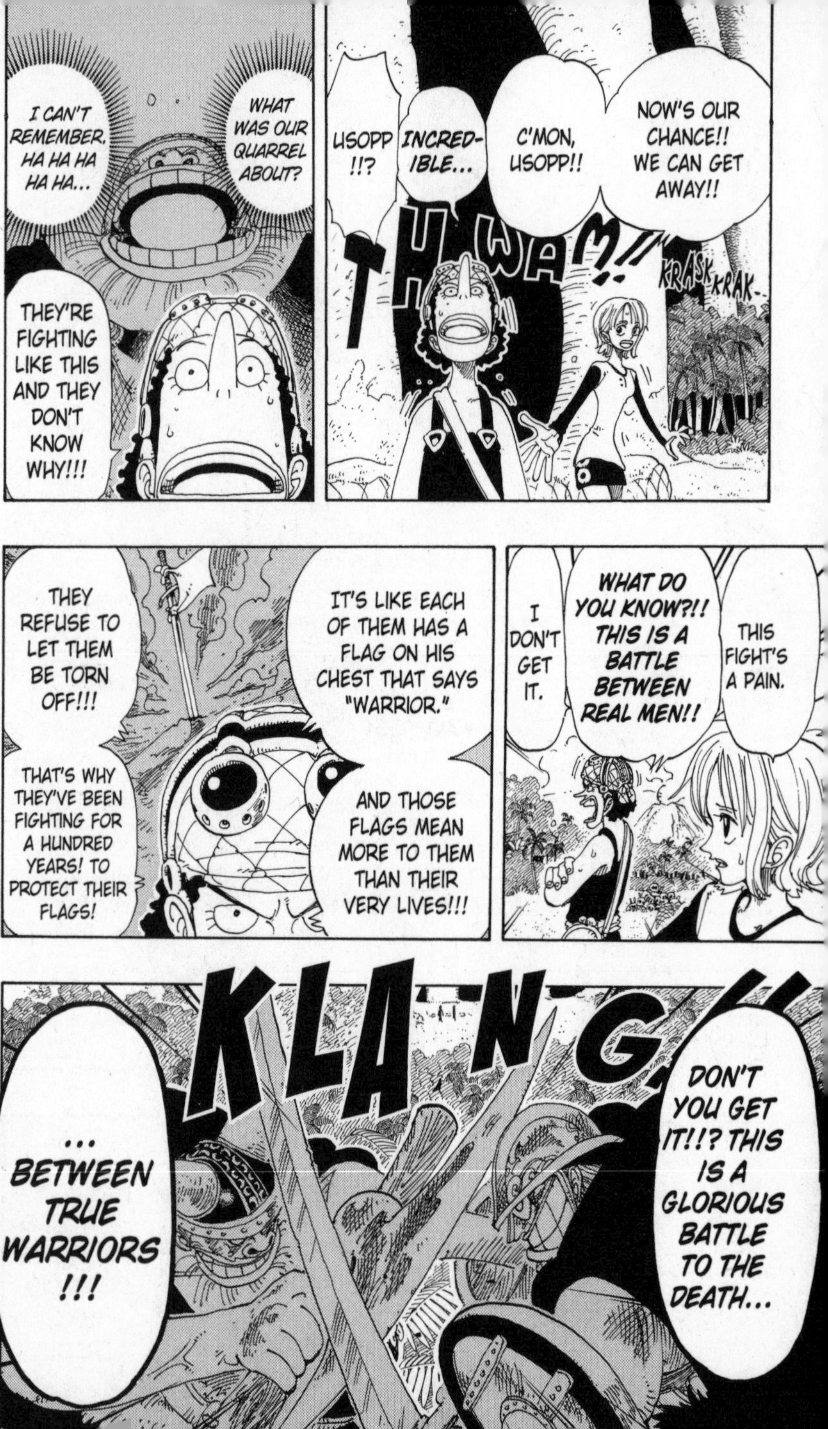
NOW'S OUR CHANCE!! WE CAN GET AWAY!!
C'MON, USOPP!!
INCREDIBLE...
USOPP!!?
THWAM!!
KRASK KRAK
WHAT WAS OUR QUARREL ABOUT?
I CAN'T REMEMBER. HA HA HA HA HA...
THEY'RE FIGHTING LIKE THIS AND THEY DON'T KNOW WHY!!!
THIS FIGHT'S A PAIN.
WHAT DO YOU KNOW?!! THIS IS A BATTLE BETWEEN REAL MEN!!
I DON'T GET IT.
IT'S LIKE EACH OF THEM HAS A FLAG ON HIS CHEST THAT SAYS "WARRIOR."
THEY REFUSE TO LET THEM BE TORN OFF!!!
AND THOSE FLAGS MEAN MORE TO THEM THAN THEIR VERY LIVES!!!
THAT'S WHY THEY'VE BEEN FIGHTING FOR A HUNDRED YEARS! TO PROTECT THEIR FLAGS!
KLANG!!
DON'T YOU GET IT!!? THIS IS A GLORIOUS BATTLE TO THE DEATH...
...BETWEEN TRUE WARRIORS!!!

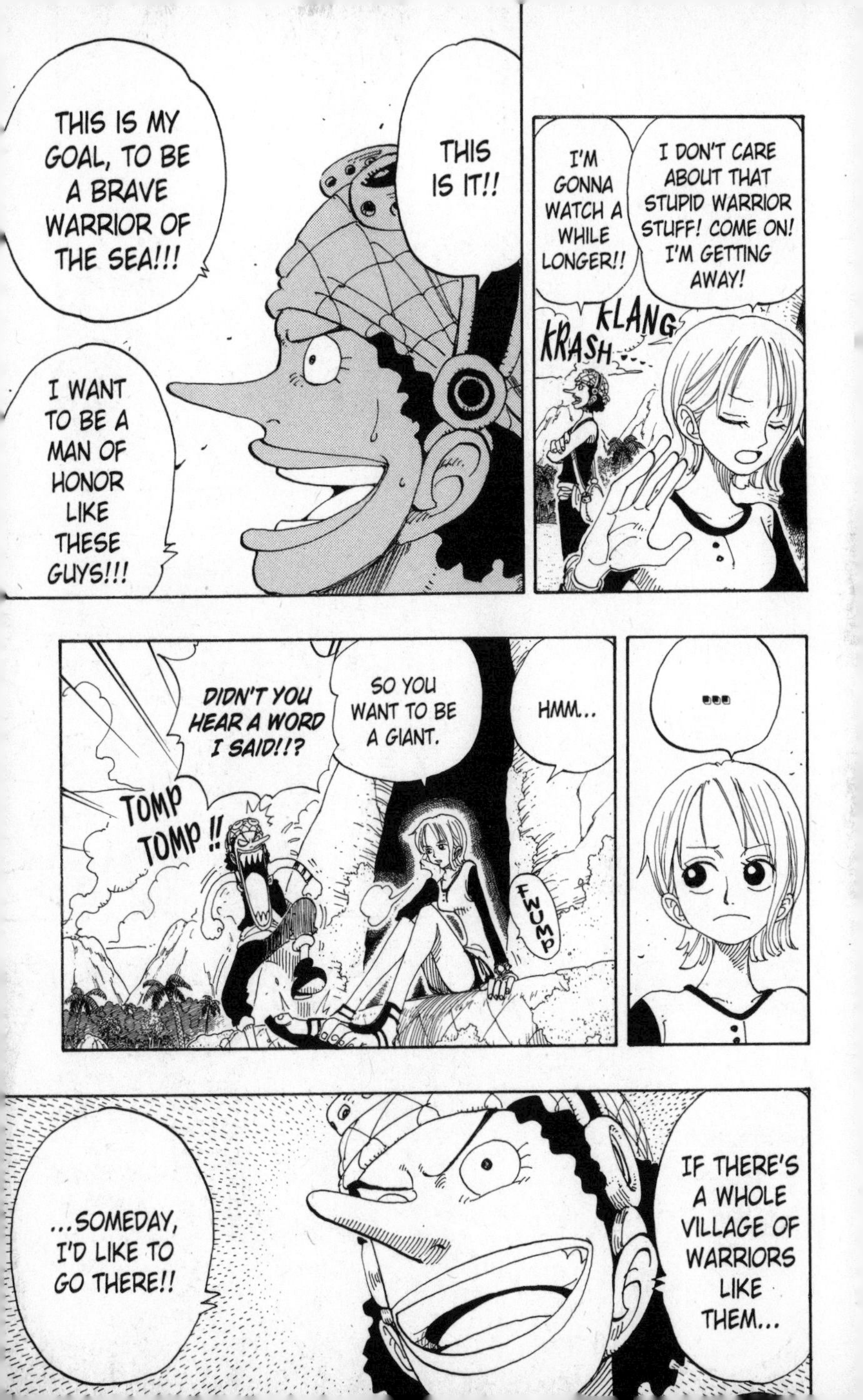
I DON'T CARE ABOUT THAT STUPID WARRIOR STUFF! COME ON! I'M GETTING AWAY!
I'M GONNA WATCH A WHILE LONGER!!
KLANG
KRASH
THIS IS IT!!
THIS IS MY GOAL, TO BE A BRAVE WARRIOR OF THE SEA!!!
I WANT TO BE A MAN OF HONOR LIKE THESE GUYS!!!
...
HMM...
SO YOU WANT TO BE A GIANT.
DIDN'T YOU HEAR A WORD I SAID!!?
TOMP TOMP!!
FWUMP
IF THERE'S A WHOLE VILLAGE OF WARRIORS LIKE THEM...
...SOMEDAY, I'D LIKE TO GO THERE!!

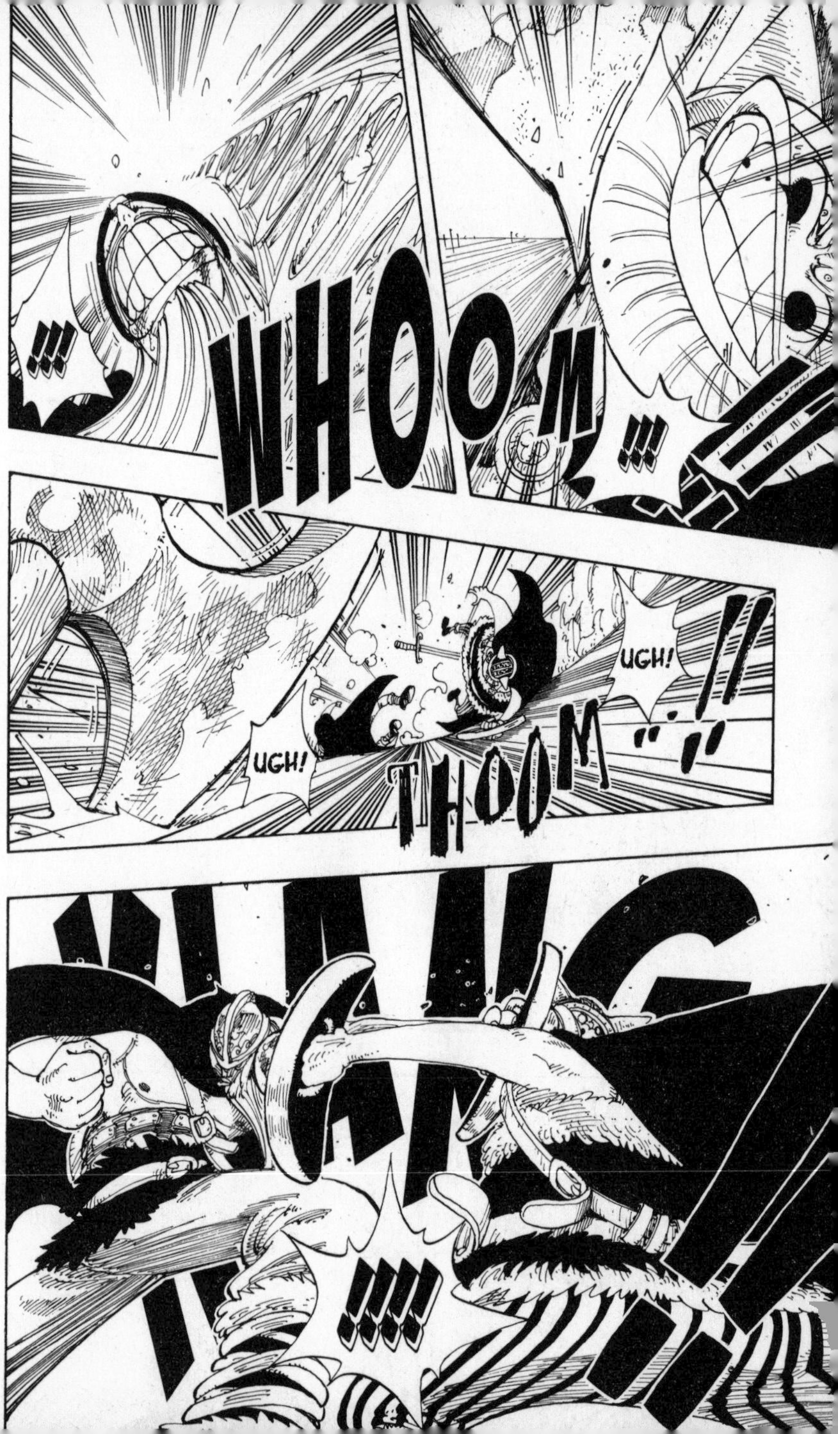
WHOOM!!!
!!!
UGH!
THOOM!!
UGH!

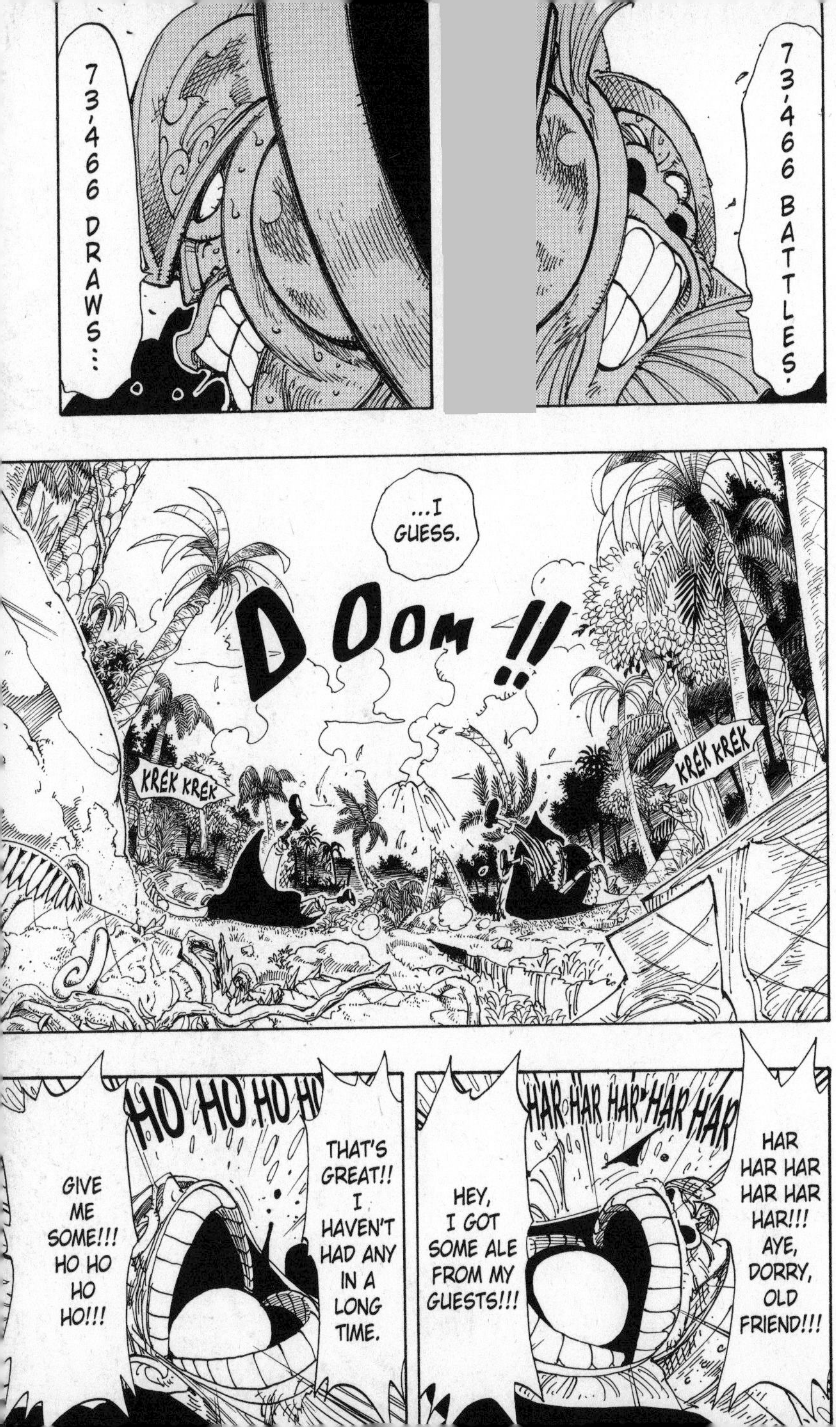
73,466 BATTLES.
73,466 DRAWS...
...I GUESS.
DOOM!!
KREK KREK
KREK KREK
HAR HAR HAR HAR HAR
HAR HAR HAR HAR HAR HAR!!! AYE, DORRY, OLD FRIEND!!!
HEY, I GOT SOME ALE FROM MY GUESTS!!!
HO HO HO HO
THAT'S GREAT!! I HAVEN'T HAD ANY IN A LONG TIME.
GIVE ME SOME!!! HO HO HO HO!!!

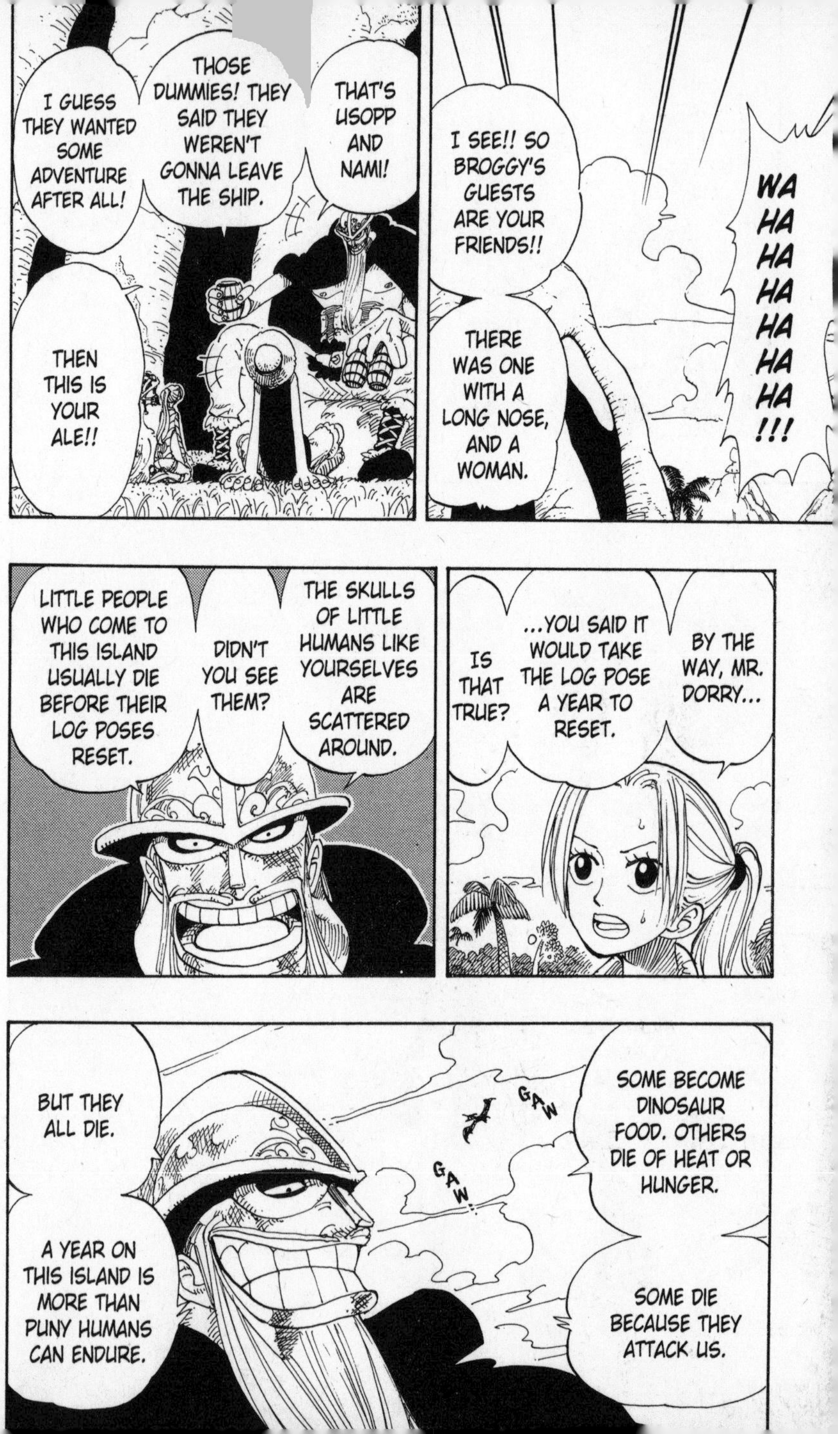
WA HA HA HA HA HA HA!!!
I SEE!! SO BROGGY'S GUESTS ARE YOUR FRIENDS!!
THERE WAS ONE WITH A LONG NOSE, AND A WOMAN.
THAT'S USOPP AND NAMI!
THOSE DUMMIES! THEY SAID THEY WEREN'T GONNA LEAVE THE SHIP.
I GUESS THEY WANTED SOME ADVENTURE AFTER ALL!
THEN THIS IS YOUR ALE!!
BY THE WAY, MR. DORRY...
...YOU SAID IT WOULD TAKE THE LOG POSE A YEAR TO RESET.
IS THAT TRUE?
THE SKULLS OF LITTLE HUMANS LIKE YOURSELVES ARE SCATTERED AROUND.
DIDN'T YOU SEE THEM?
LITTLE PEOPLE WHO COME TO THIS ISLAND USUALLY DIE BEFORE THEIR LOG POSES RESET.
SOME BECOME DINOSAUR FOOD. OTHERS DIE OF HEAT OR HUNGER.
GAW
GAW!!
SOME DIE BECAUSE THEY ATTACK US.
BUT THEY ALL DIE.
A YEAR ON THIS ISLAND IS MORE THAN PUNY HUMANS CAN ENDURE.

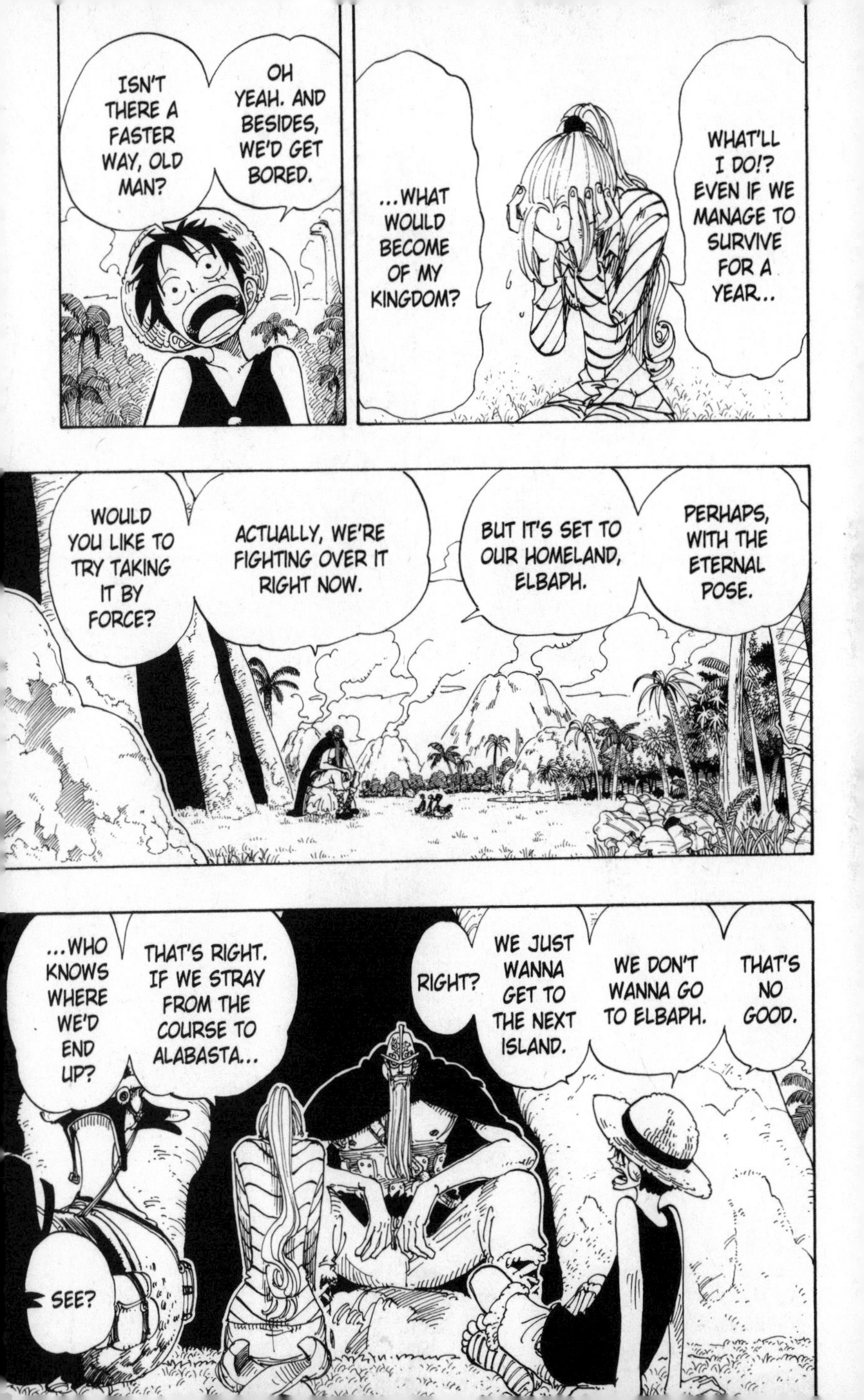
WHAT'LL I DO!? EVEN IF WE MANAGE TO SURVIVE FOR A YEAR...
...WHAT WOULD BECOME OF MY KINGDOM?
OH YEAH. AND BESIDES, WE'D GET BORED.
ISN'T THERE A FASTER WAY, OLD MAN?
PERHAPS, WITH THE ETERNAL POSE.
BUT IT'S SET TO OUR HOMELAND, ELBAPH.
ACTUALLY, WE'RE FIGHTING OVER IT RIGHT NOW.
WOULD YOU LIKE TO TRY TAKING IT BY FORCE?
THAT'S NO GOOD.
WE DON'T WANNA GO TO ELBAPH.
WE JUST WANNA GET TO THE NEXT ISLAND.
RIGHT?
THAT'S RIGHT. IF WE STRAY FROM THE COURSE TO ALABASTA...
...WHO KNOWS WHERE WE'D END UP?
SEE?

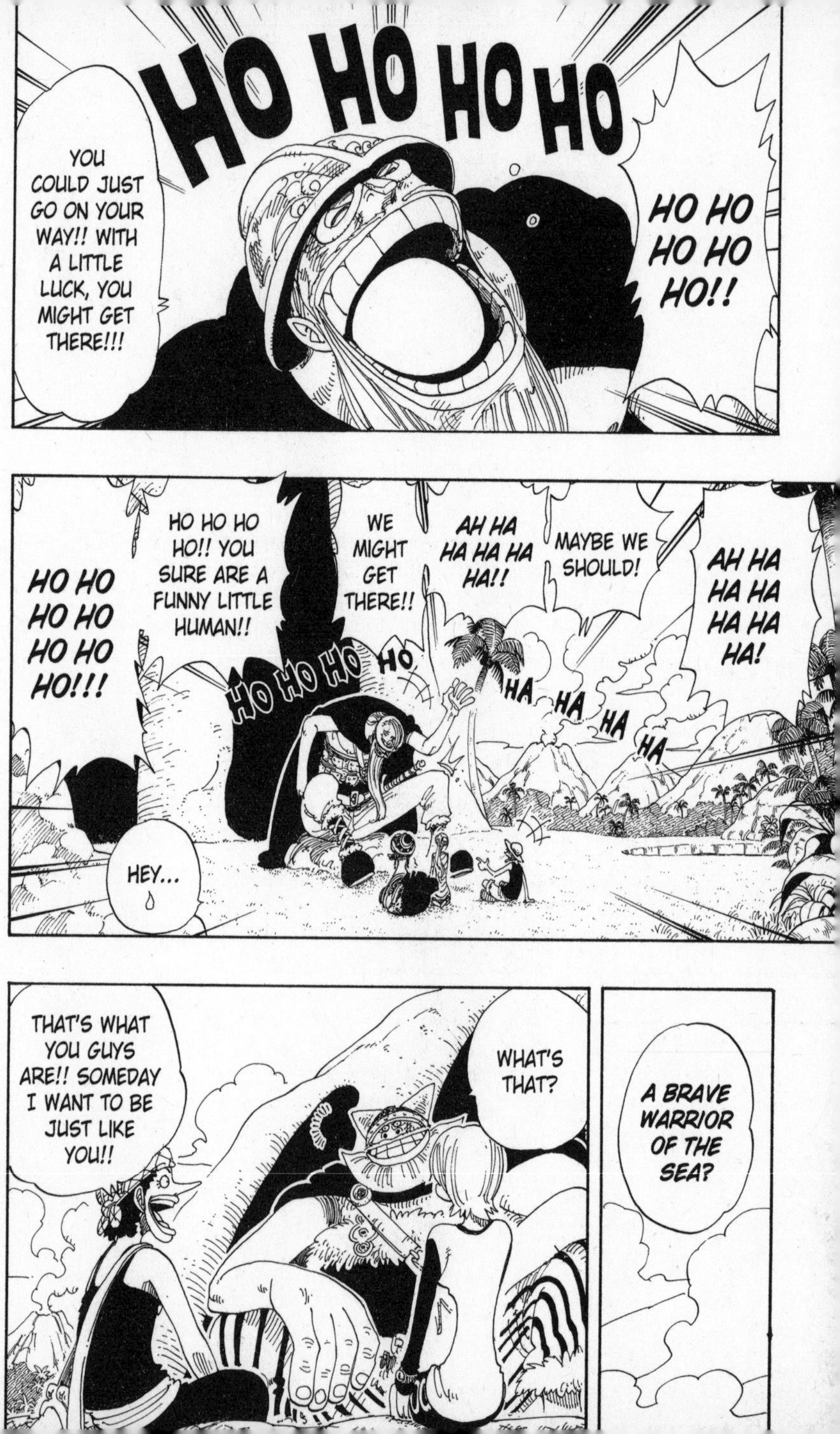
HO HO HO HO HO
HO HO HO HO HO!!
YOU COULD JUST GO ON YOUR WAY!! WITH A LITTLE LUCK, YOU MIGHT GET THERE!!!
AH HA HA HA HA HA HA HA HA!
MAYBE WE SHOULD!
AH HA HA HA HA HA!!
WE MIGHT GET THERE!!
HO HO HO HO!! YOU SURE ARE A FUNNY LITTLE HUMAN!!
HO HO HO HO HO HO HO!!!
HA HA HA HA
HO HO HO HO
HEY...
A BRAVE WARRIOR OF THE SEA?
WHAT'S THAT?
THAT'S WHAT YOU GUYS ARE!! SOMEDAY I WANT TO BE JUST LIKE YOU!!

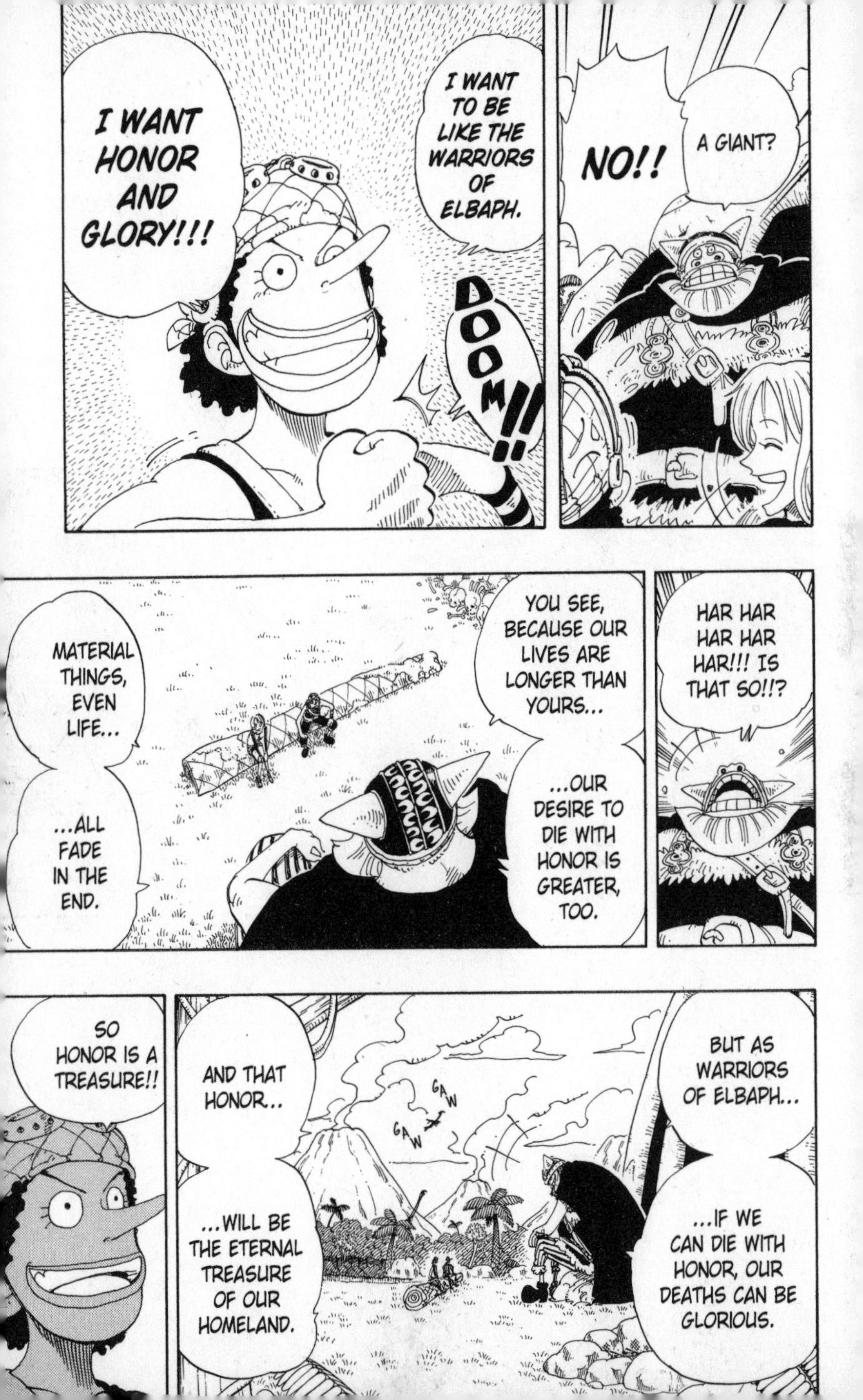
A GIANT?
NO!!
I WANT TO BE LIKE THE WARRIORS OF ELBAPH.
DOOM!!
I WANT HONOR AND GLORY!!!
HAR HAR HAR HAR HAR!!! IS THAT SO!!?
YOU SEE, BECAUSE OUR LIVES ARE LONGER THAN YOURS...
...OUR DESIRE TO DIE WITH HONOR IS GREATER, TOO.
MATERIAL THINGS, EVEN LIFE...
...ALL FADE IN THE END.
BUT AS WARRIORS OF ELBAPH...
...IF WE CAN DIE WITH HONOR, OUR DEATHS CAN BE GLORIOUS.
GAW
GAW
AND THAT HONOR...
...WILL BE THE ETERNAL TREASURE OF OUR HOMELAND.
SO HONOR IS A TREASURE!!

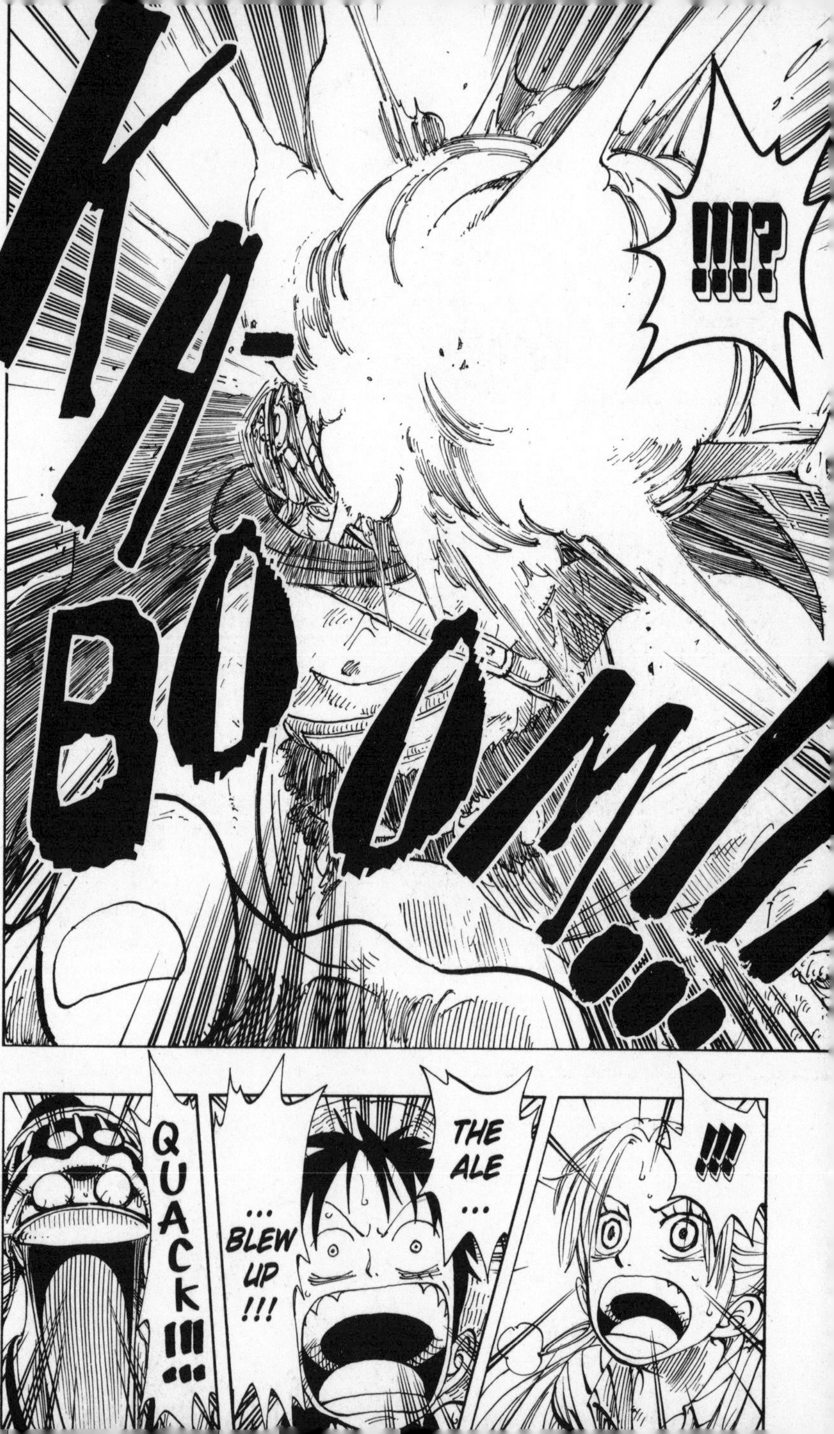
!!!?
KA-BOOM!!!
!!!
THE ALE ...
... BLEW UP !!!
QUACK!!!

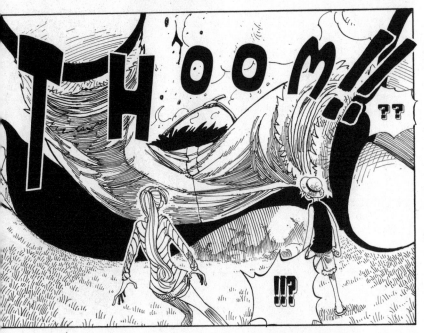

THOOM!!

??

!!!

MR. DORRY !!

MR. GIANT !!!

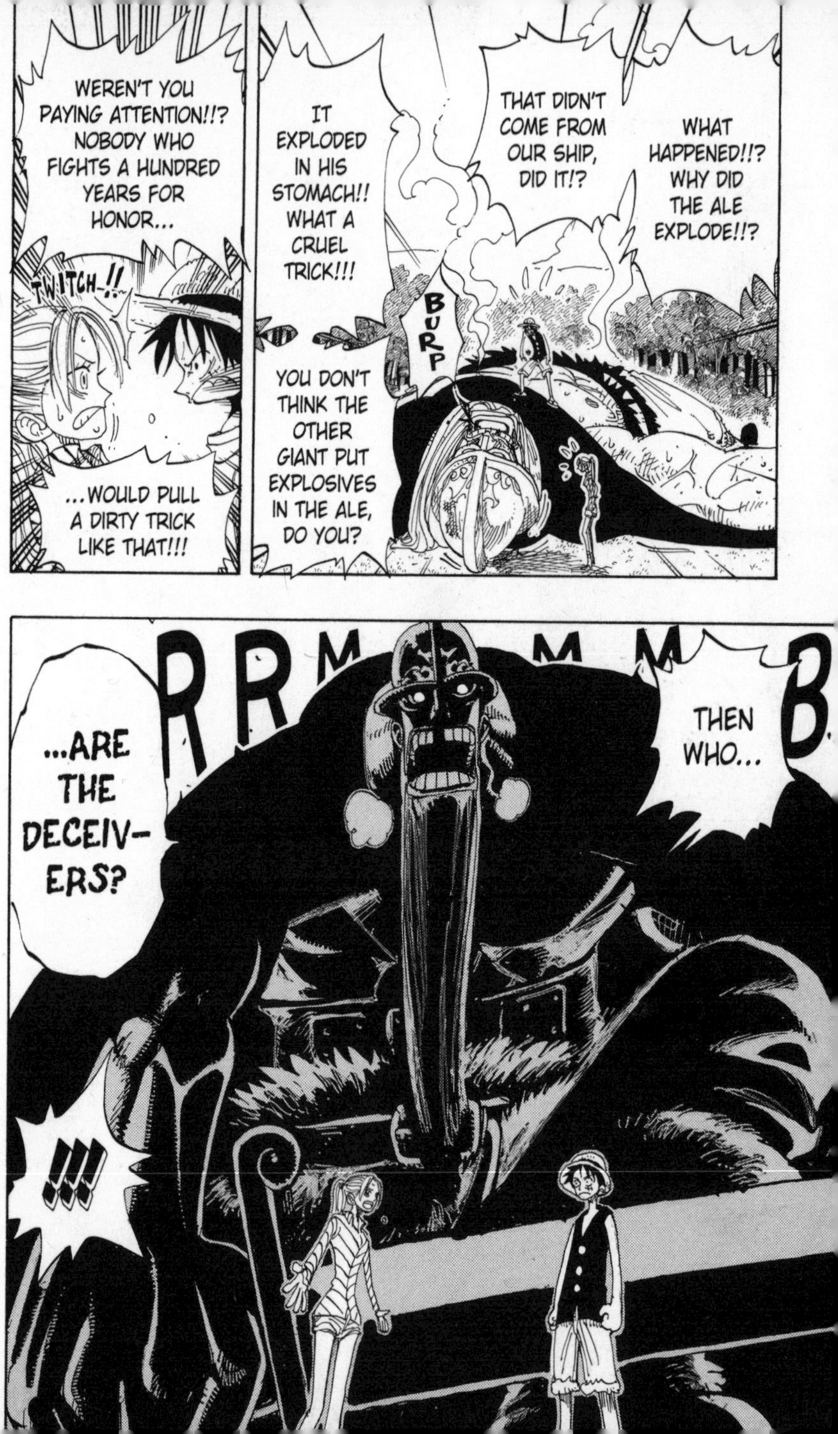
WHAT HAPPENED!!? WHY DID THE ALE EXPLODE!!?
THAT DIDN'T COME FROM OUR SHIP, DID IT!?
BURP
IT EXPLODED IN HIS STOMACH!! WHAT A CRUEL TRICK!!!
YOU DON'T THINK THE OTHER GIANT PUT EXPLOSIVES IN THE ALE, DO YOU?
WEREN'T YOU PAYING ATTENTION!!? NOBODY WHO FIGHTS A HUNDRED YEARS FOR HONOR...
TWITCH !!
...WOULD PULL A DIRTY TRICK LIKE THAT!!!
RRMMMMB
THEN WHO...
...ARE THE DECEIVERS?
!!!

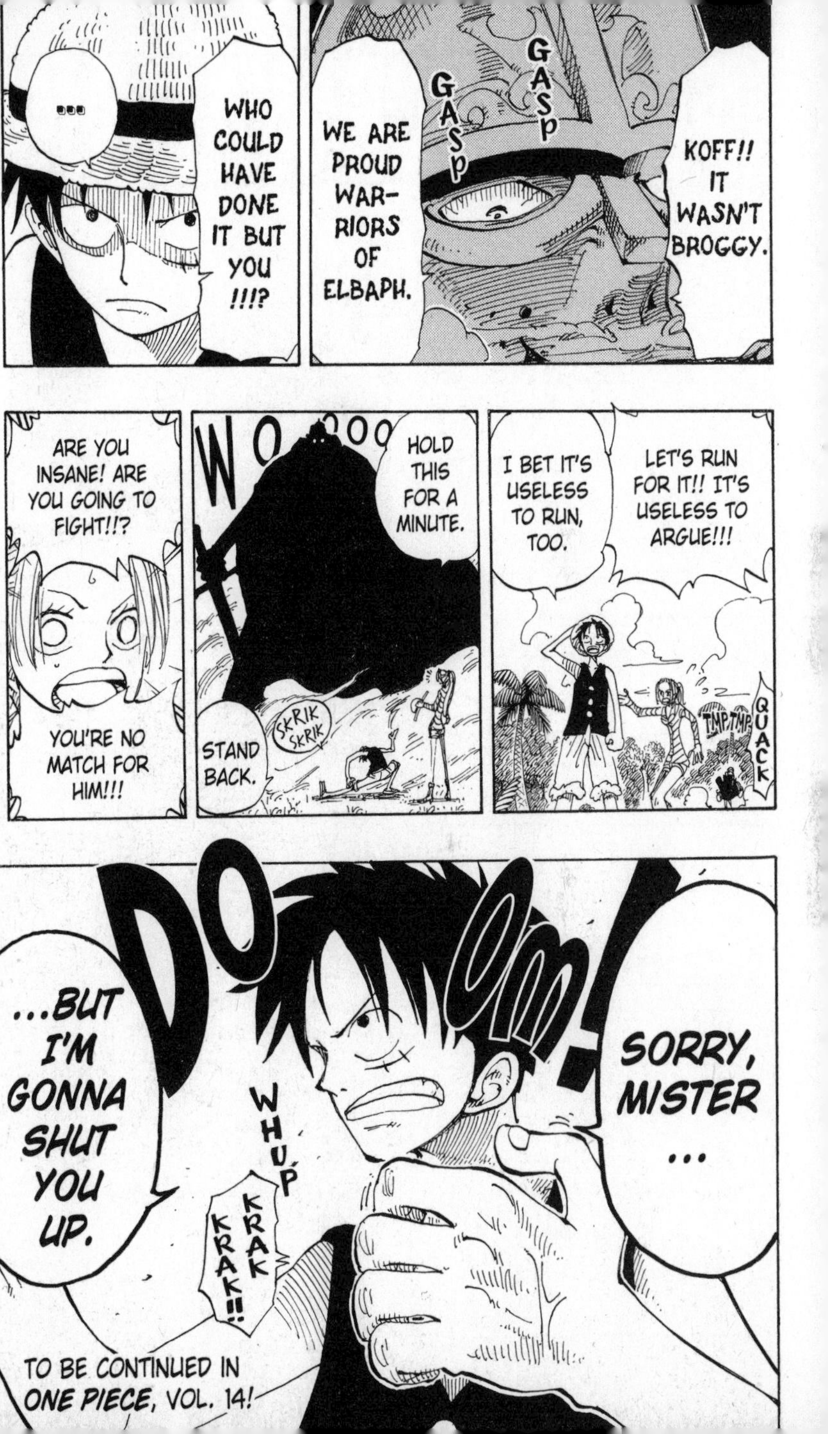
KOFF!! IT WASN'T BROGGY.
GASp GASp
WE ARE PROUD WAR-RIORS OF ELBAPH.
WHO COULD HAVE DONE IT BUT YOU !!!?
...
LET'S RUN FOR IT!! IT'S USELESS TO ARGUE!!!
I BET IT'S USELESS TO RUN, TOO.
TMP TMP
QUACK
WOOOO
HOLD THIS FOR A MINUTE.
SKRIK SKRIK
STAND BACK.
ARE YOU INSANE! ARE YOU GOING TO FIGHT!!?
YOU'RE NO MATCH FOR HIM!!!
SORRY, MISTER ...
DOOM!
WHUP
KRAK KRAK KRAK!!
...BUT I'M GONNA SHUT YOU UP.
TO BE CONTINUED IN ONE PIECE, VOL. 14!

⊗ONE PIECE WARS!!

◎ The other day I remembered a game that I
  invented in grade school and decided to revise it.
  So sometime when you're thinking, "Man, I'm so
  bored," play this game with your friends. It's easy.

◎ What you'll need to prepare: 
  ● A Tactics card
  ● A six-sided pencil

  ● Unshakeable Pirate Spirit (A little shaky is okay.)
  ● A Battlefield card (see p. 185) and an eraser

◎ What you won't need to prepare:
  ● Coffee (Please don't bother making any. I won't
    be staying long.)

◎ The Tactics Card

⊗ONE PIECE WARS
TACTICS CARD

NAME
Monkey D. Luffy

1	Gum-Gum Pistol	5
2	Gum-Gum Balloon	0
3	Fart	40
4	Gum-Gum Bullet	15
5	Gum-Gum Rocket	10
6	Gum-Gum Gatling Gun	30

POINTS

1. Write the name of a *One
   Piece* character you like
   under "name." (Anybody is
   fine.)
2. Draw the character next
   to the name. It doesn't
   have to be perfect.
3. Write down six techniques
   in the spaces below. You
   can make up your own, if
   you want.
   (Example: Ms. Makino's
   Smile Attack, etc.)
4. Assign points to each
   technique in multiples of 5,
   so that they add up to 100.
   (0 is also possible.)

◎ The six-sided pencil

Shave the paint off the tip and number each face from 1 to 6, turning the pencil into a die.

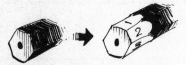

★ Prepare for Battle!

- This game is for two or more people.
- Find someone with a Tactics card. (If the person doesn't own this book, be a good sport and let him or her copy yours. Sharing good times is part of true pirate spirit.)
- When you find an opponent, take out your Battlefield card. Each player should draw a black dot on one of the 20 spaces on his or her opponent's card.

HYAA!
GRAH!

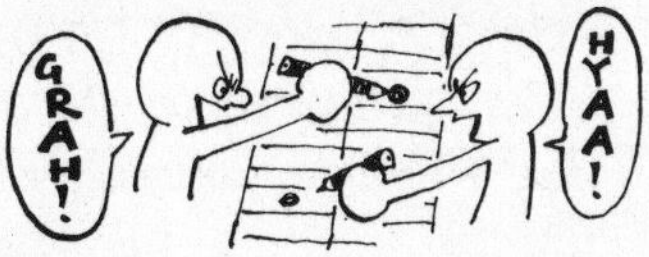

★ Attack!!

- Take out your cards and attack!!
- Do rock-paper-scissors. The winner rolls the pencil die to get the opponent's technique number and then blackens in the space on the opponent's Battlefield card that shows the corresponding number of points!!

YOW!
SKRIK
SKRIK

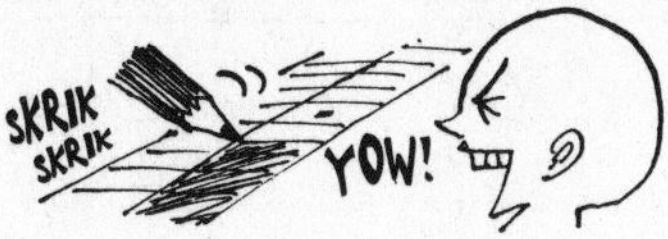

★ Bonus Buggy Dot

- If you land on the dot you drew, as you're blackening in a space, you get a Bonus Buggy Chance. Your attack accelerates. You get to attack again.
- The first one to reach 100 points wins!!

May you be victorious in battle.

ONE PIECE WARS
TACTICS CARD

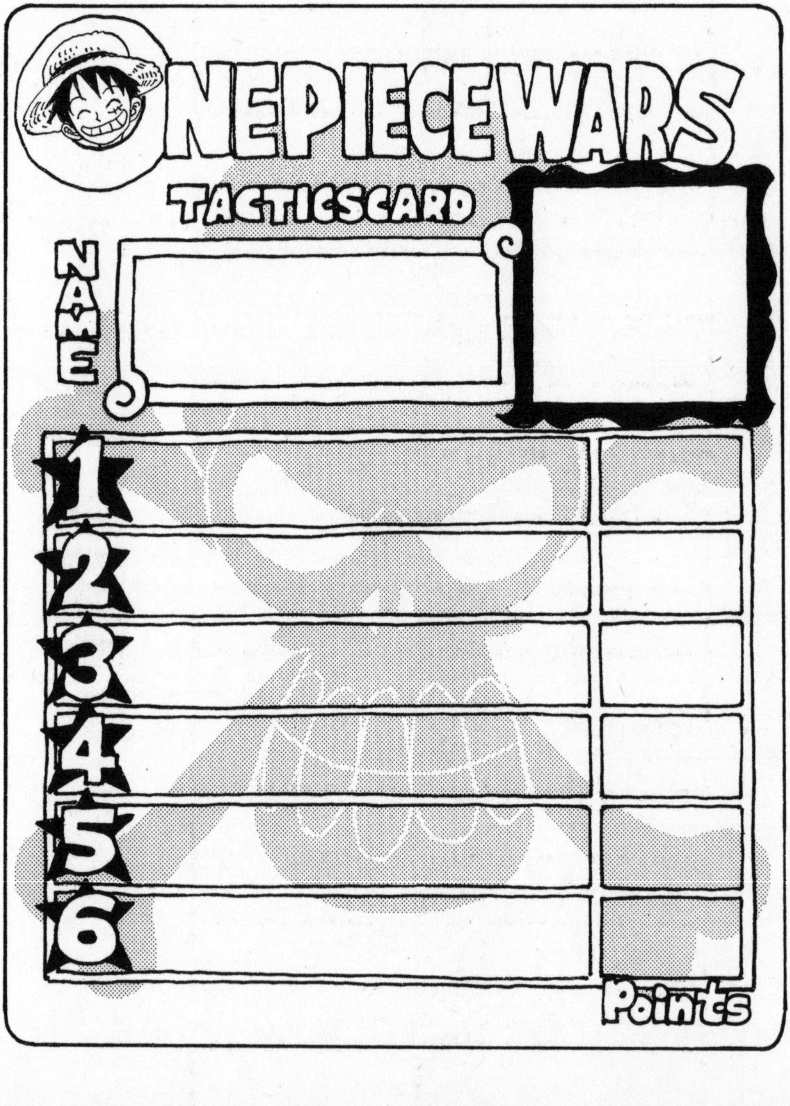
ONEPIECEWARS
TACTICSCARD
NAME
1
2
3
4
5
6
Points

BATTLEFIELD

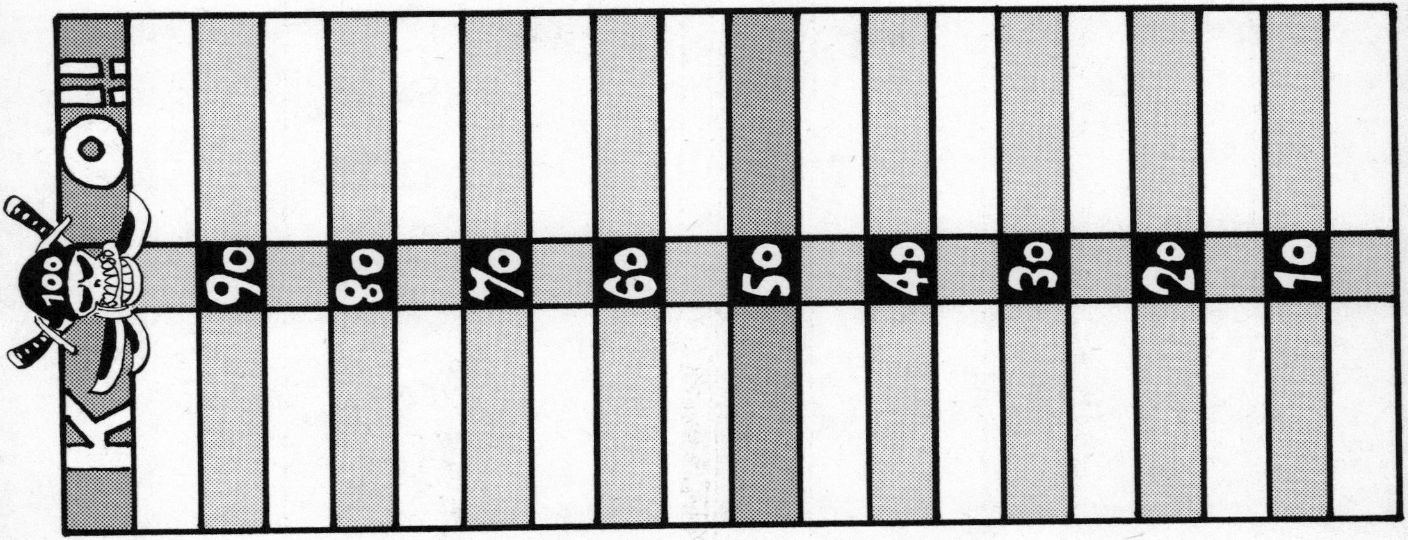

COMING NEXT VOLUME:

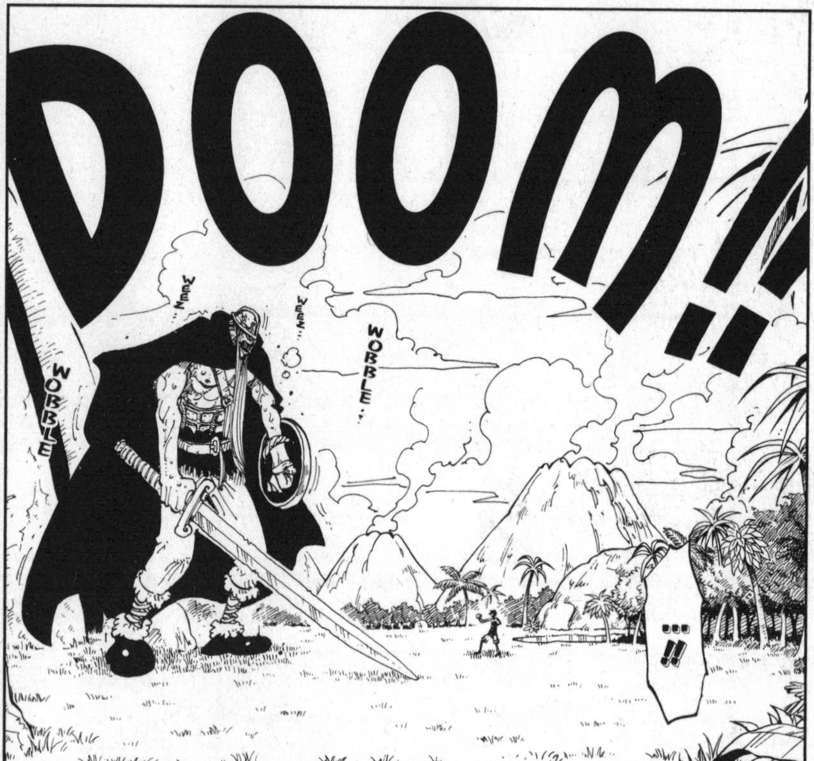
DOOM!!
WEEZ...
WEEZ...
WOBBLE
WOBBLE...
...!!

The battle of the giants continues as Luffy and crew try to figure out who gave Dorry the exploding ale! Luffy attempts to keep the giant from obeying the call to fight, but you can't stop a hard-headed warrior's pride, and Dorry goes anyway. How can he hope to win the 100-year battle in his wounded condition? And while this is going on, what are the sinister members of the Baroque Works up to? Find out for yourself in volume 14!

ON SALE NOW!

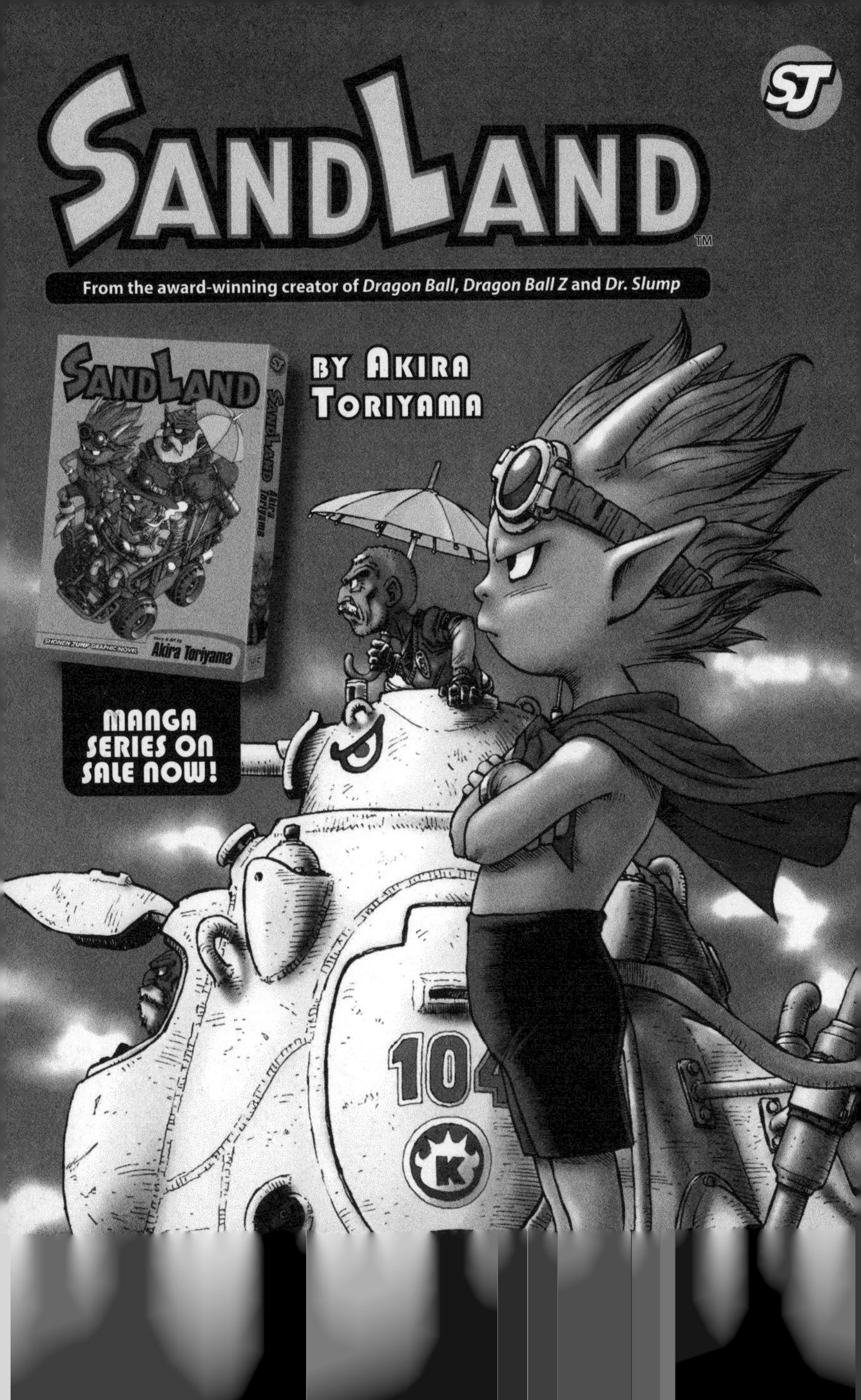
SJ
SANDLAND™
From the award-winning creator of *Dragon Ball*, *Dragon Ball Z* and *Dr. Slump*
BY AKIRA TORIYAMA
SANDLAND
SHONEN JUMP GRAPHIC NOVEL
Akira Toriyama
MANGA SERIES ON SALE NOW!
104

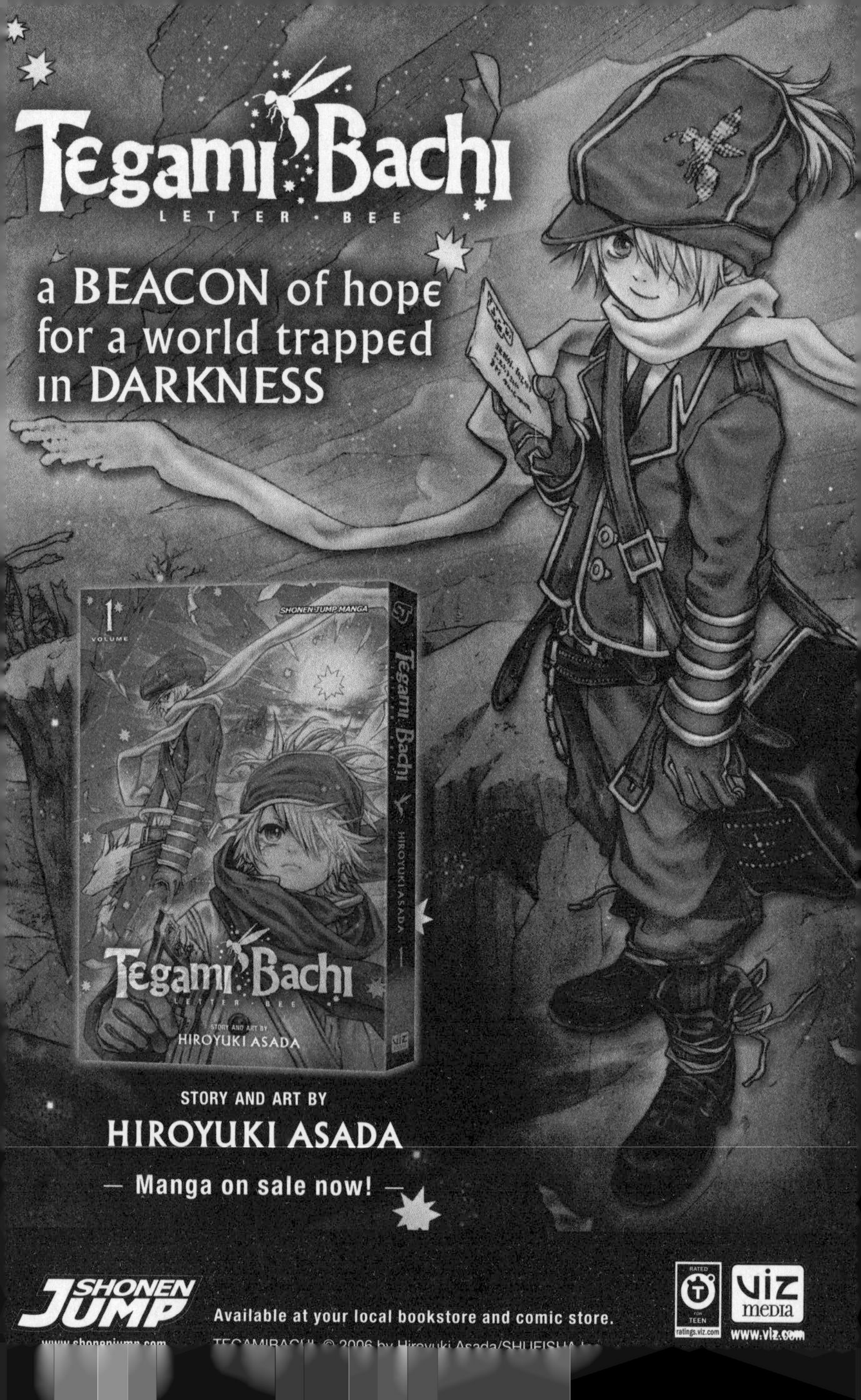
Tegami Bachi
LETTER · BEE
a BEACON of hope
for a world trapped
in DARKNESS
SHONEN JUMP MANGA
1
VOLUME
Tegami Bachi
LETTER BEE
STORY AND ART BY
HIROYUKI ASADA
STORY AND ART BY
HIROYUKI ASADA
— Manga on sale now! —
SHONEN JUMP
Available at your local bookstore and comic store.
RATED T FOR TEEN
ratings.viz.com
VIZ media
www.viz.com

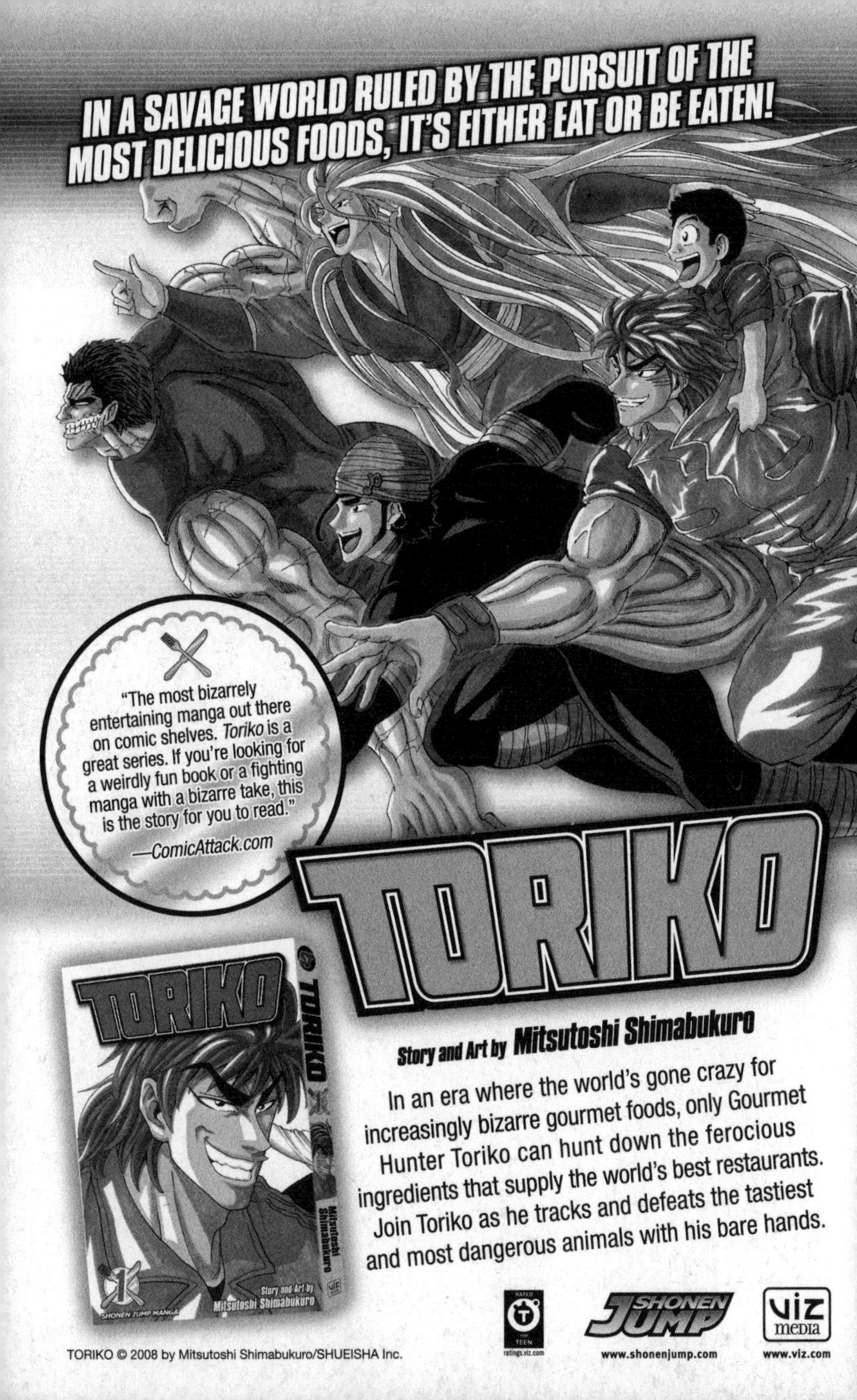
IN A SAVAGE WORLD RULED BY THE PURSUIT OF THE MOST DELICIOUS FOODS, IT'S EITHER EAT OR BE EATEN!
"The most bizarrely entertaining manga out there on comic shelves. Toriko is a great series. If you're looking for a weirdly fun book or a fighting manga with a bizarre take, this is the story for you to read."
—ComicAttack.com
TORIKO
TORIKO
1
SHONEN JUMP MANGA
Story and Art by Mitsutoshi Shimabukuro
Story and Art by Mitsutoshi Shimabukuro
In an era where the world's gone crazy for increasingly bizarre gourmet foods, only Gourmet Hunter Toriko can hunt down the ferocious ingredients that supply the world's best restaurants. Join Toriko as he tracks and defeats the tastiest and most dangerous animals with his bare hands.
RATED T FOR TEEN
ratings.viz.com
SHONEN JUMP
viz media
TORIKO © 2008 by Mitsutoshi Shimabukuro/SHUEISHA Inc.
www.shonenjump.com
www.viz.com

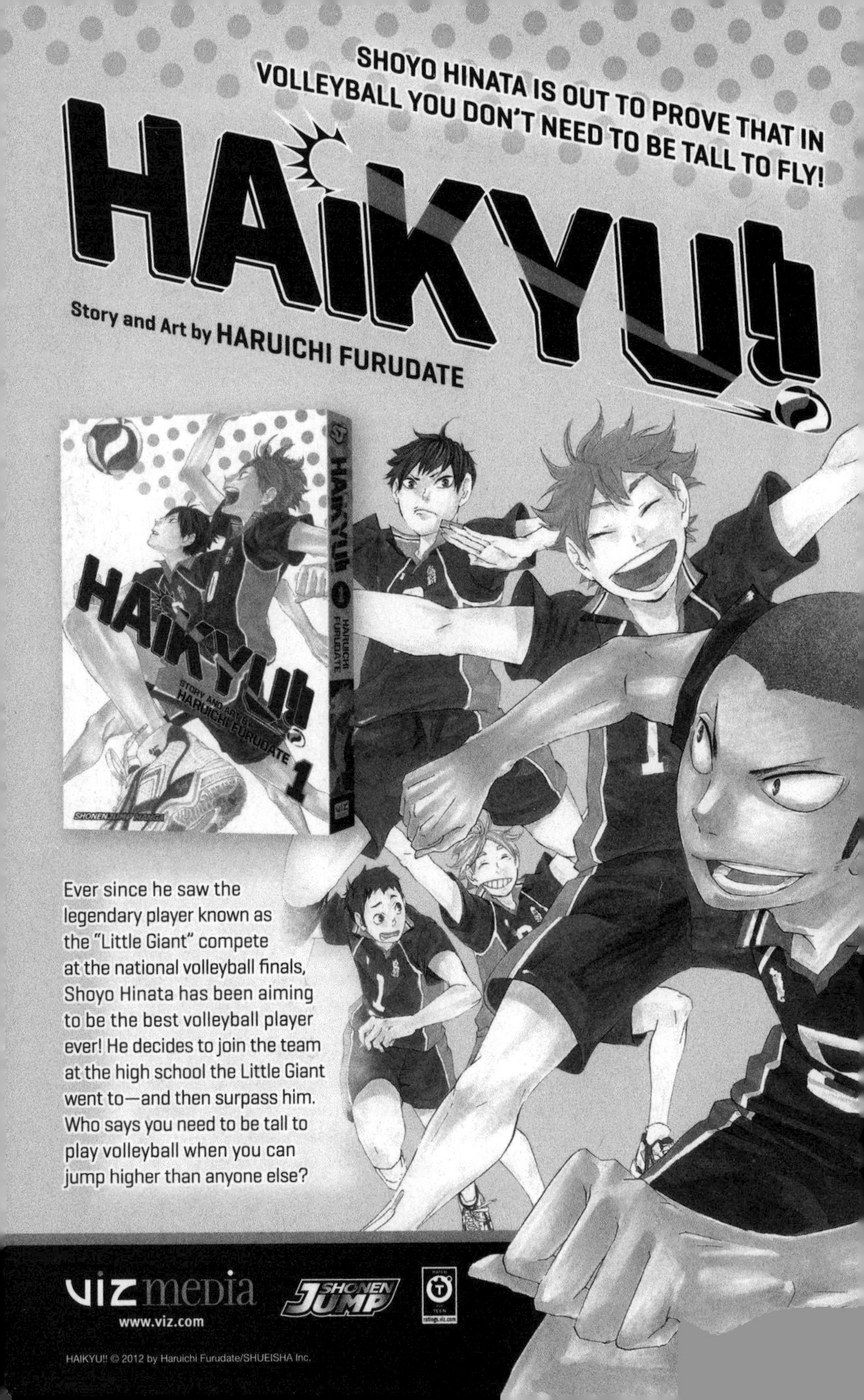
SHOYO HINATA IS OUT TO PROVE THAT IN VOLLEYBALL YOU DON'T NEED TO BE TALL TO FLY!
HAIKYU!!
Story and Art by HARUICHI FURUDATE
Ever since he saw the legendary player known as the "Little Giant" compete at the national volleyball finals, Shoyo Hinata has been aiming to be the best volleyball player ever! He decides to join the team at the high school the Little Giant went to—and then surpass him. Who says you need to be tall to play volleyball when you can jump higher than anyone else?
viz media
www.viz.com
SHONEN JUMP
HAIKYU!! © 2012 by Haruichi Furudate/SHUEISHA Inc.

You're Reading in the Wrong Direction!!

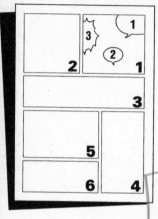

Whoops! Guess what? You're starting at the wrong end of the comic!

...It's true! In keeping with the original Japanese format, **One Piece** is meant to be read from right to left, starting in the upper-right corner.

Unlike English, which is read from left to right, Japanese is read from right to left, meaning that action, sound effects and word-balloon order are completely reversed... something which can make readers unfamiliar with Japanese feel pretty backwards themselves. For this reason, manga or Japanese comics published in the U.S. in English have sometimes been published "flopped" – that is, printed in exact reverse order, as though seen from the other side of a mirror.

By flopping pages, U.S. publishers can avoid confusing readers, but the compromise is not without its downside. For one thing, a character in a flopped manga series who once wore in the original Japanese version a T-shirt emblazoned with "M A Y" (as in "the merry month of") now wears one which reads "Y A M"! Additionally, many manga creators in Japan are themselves unhappy with the process, as some feel the mirror-imaging of their art skews their original intentions.

We are proud to bring you Eiichiro Oda's **One Piece** in the original unflopped format. For now, though, turn to the other side of the book and let the journey begin...!

—Editor